1 9 3 9

Michael Jabara Carley

1939

THE ALLIANCE
THAT NEVER WAS
AND THE COMING OF
WORLD WAR II

CHICAGO

Ivan R. Dee

The paperback edition of this book carries the following ISBN: 978-1-56663-785-5

Library of Congress Cataloging-in-Publication Data:
Carley, Michael Jabara, 1945–
    1939 : the alliance that never was and the coming of World War II / Michael Jabara Carley.
        p. cm.
    Includes bibliographical references and index.
    ISBN 1-56663-252-8 (alk. paper)
    1. World War, 1939–1945—Diplomatic history. 2. World War, 1939—Causes. I.
Title.   II. Title: Alliance that never was and the coming of World War II.

D748.B37   1999
940.53'112—dc21   99-24873

For Irusia, Mom, Big, Steve, Linde,

Grisha, Eddie, Jack, and Vo

I am wounded,

but I am not slain!

I'll but lie me down

and bleed a while.

And then I'll rise

and fight again!

—Percy's *Reliques* (1765)

Contents

Acknowledgments

IN 1997 my good friend Geoffrey Roberts asked me casually why I did not write a book about 1939. "You're the person to do it," he said, "now that so many Soviet documents have been published." At first I wondered whether there was a need for another book on appeasement, collective security, and the beginnings of the Second World War. There is, after all, A. J. P. Taylor's work, which is still provoking, Sidney Aster's study based on the British Foreign Office documents, and Donald Cameron Watt's later thick tome on the last year of peace—or rather, relative peace.[1] And I had already written a series of articles on Anglo-Franco-Soviet relations during the 1930s and the lead-up to war.[2] Nevertheless, the more I thought about it, the more I was drawn to Geoffrey's idea. As I pondered whether to embark upon this project, Lloyd Gardner introduced to me to Ivan R. Dee, who liked the proposal for a book on 1939 and encouraged me to proceed.

I have made two research trips to Moscow working on the 1920s, but the archivists at the Russian foreign ministry (AVPRF) could not arrange in sufficient time for me during my last stay to read files on 1938–1939. The Russian archives are in any event only "sort of" open, but the published papers for 1938–1941 give a good sense of Soviet foreign policy positions and objectives. Most of the new material for this period was published between 1990 and 1998, and thus far it has been little used. These documents provide a Soviet perspective on events that we have heretofore seen largely through Western eyes. More than that, the melding together of the four sets of documentary sources—British, French, Soviet, and German—creates a greater depth of field into still-controversial topics.

I undertook the research for this study in increments over a period of more than ten years, thanks to the financial support of the Social Sciences and Humanities Research Council of Canada. Without the Council's support, this work could not have been accomplished. Nor could my research have proceeded so well without the goodwill and helpfulness of many archivists in Paris, London, and Moscow. I extend my thanks to them all.

My intellectual world view began to develop in the 1960s but was disciplined under the guidance of the late John M. Sherwood, who died too young. Good friends and colleagues—among others, Joel Blatt, John C. Cairns, Richard K. Debo, William D. Irvine, William R. Keylor, Sally Marks, Geoffrey Roberts, Stephen A. Schuker, and Robert J. Young—have helped form my ideas, challenging and sometimes disagreeing with me, or I with them. Their friendship and collegiality are gratefully acknowledged. They know that I wrote this manuscript during an autumn-time of adversity. It was no easy task. But the old saw holds that good will issue from evil, *un bien pour un mal.* I hope this book proves out the traditional adage, and I raise my arms in celebration, feet dancing. *Nunc est bibendum.*

M. J. C.

Ottawa
April 1999

Preface

THIS BOOK is about the beginnings of the Second World War. I do not pretend that it is a comprehensive study of the events of 1939; rather, it focuses on relations among France, Britain, the Soviet Union, and Nazi Germany. I should warn readers at the outset that this is not postmodern history; it has nothing to do with semiotics, "realms of memory," or new literary criticism. It is a study of international relations at a crucial point in the twentieth century, based on published and unpublished government documents and the work of many historians, both my contemporaries and those who came before me.

This is not a pretty story. It is about appeasement and the failures of collective security in Europe against Nazi aggression. It is about moral depravity and blindness, about villains and cowards, and about heroes who stood against the intellectual and popular tides of their time. Some died for their beliefs, others labored in obscurity and have been nearly forgotten. We all know the villains and some of the heroes, but many of the latter—French, British, Soviet—are less familiar except to specialists in the field. In 1939 they sought to make the alliance that never was among France, Britain, and the Soviet Union. This is the story of their efforts: it is the background to the grand alliance created in 1941 without France but with the United States in order to defeat a demonic enemy.

Historians nowadays tend to take a more understanding view of appeasement than the first postwar generation of scholars who condemned the "Guilty Men" of the 1930s for having failed to provide for the national defense against fascism. There were violent attacks on "the men of Munich"—Neville Chamberlain, Sir Samuel Hoare, Sir John Simon, Lord Halifax, Georges Bonnet, Édouard Daladier, among others. "Low, dishonest decade," W. H. Auden's poetic image, seemed an entirely appropriate description of the wretched and murderous 1930s. Sir Lewis Namier was perhaps best known of these early historians who assailed the appeasers and their policies of concession to Nazi Germany.[1] There is also a strong cohort of Canadian, British, and American historians who saw appeasement as an expression of pro-fascist and anti-communist ideology, and who emphasized British government culpability in failing to pursue a vigorous anti-Nazi policy.[2] The contrary position holds that British foreign policy in the 1930s was misrepresented. It was not "a morality play," pitting anti-Hitler, pro-Soviet, anti-appeasers against pro-Hitler, anti-Soviet appeasers.[3] In fact, as this argument goes, the British Conservative government developed a calculated, realistic response to the rise of Nazi Germany in which the Soviet Union was not an important factor or a desirable ally.[4]

What has become orthodox interpretation holds that Britain had few policy options. It was compelled by economic and strategic constraints to limit rearmament in the 1930s and to think also of the defense of the British Empire. Japan was a potential adversary, and British resources were spread too thin to provide adequate security in both Europe and Asia. Likewise, the British economy could not afford across-the-board rearmament on a scale recommended, for example, by Winston S. Churchill or Sir Robert Vansittart, the permanent under-secretary, then chief diplomatic adviser in the Foreign Office. The air force would receive priority, the navy less so, and the army would be held to a few divisions and virtually no role in a European conflict.[5] If war came, the French army would have to bear the high cost in blood of fighting on land, and it was just this calculation that so embittered French generals and politicians.

The British Conservative government hoped to avoid war, not so much by deterrence as by appeasement. Of course, appeasement did not have, by certain British lights anyway, the craven, negative connotations we now associate with the word; it meant a reasonable effort to meet Adolf Hitler's "legitimate" grievances for revision of the Versailles treaty, which had settled the First World War. The Tory prime minister Neville Chamberlain, for example, thought Hitler could be brought 'round. Nazi Germany should be allowed to real-

ize its objectives in eastern and central Europe as long as it agreed to
limits and did not disturb security in the West. Hitler might then become more reasonable and more cooperative. And some Conservatives were not too concerned about limits if Hitler wished to sate
himself at the expense of the Soviet Union. As one Tory member of
Parliament put it so well, "Let gallant little Germany glut her fill
of . . . reds in the East. . . ."[6] In the end British Tories hoped to avoid
war even if the cost to others in eastern Europe might be high.
The prospect of war against Nazi Germany demanded cooperation
with the Soviet Union because otherwise the Anglo-French could not
win. A Soviet alliance would guarantee victory—yet it would also
lead to the spread of communist revolution and Soviet influence in
Europe. The "war-revolution nexus," as William Irvine called it,
came into play; a haunting prospect indeed as the 1930s drew to a
close.[7]

A similar evolution of interpretation has developed regarding
French appeasement and defense policy in the 1930s. Marc Bloch,
who wrote *Strange Defeat* just after the French collapse and died at
the hands of Nazi executioners in 1944, held that France was complacent, unprepared, badly organized, and incompetently led when
war began in 1939. Its generals quit the fight too soon. The French
equivalent of "Guilty Men" were the "Gravediggers," those French
leaders held responsible by the conservative French journalist Pertinax for the defeat of France in 1940. Jean-Baptiste Duroselle and
Eugen Weber argued that France was a "decadent," morally bank-
rupt society in the 1930s, riven with political animosities, plagued
with unstable governments that fell like ninepins, betrayed by leaders without courage or imagination, and subverted by fascist or
protofascist leagues bent on destroying the Third Republic.[8] René
Girault has written of a divided France rent by ideological divisions
between right and left that paralyzed the French government.[9] This
view of French politics and society is supported by many contemporary witnesses, including, incidentally, the three Soviet ambassadors
in Paris during the 1930s.

Like more recent assessments of British policy, we now have
work by Stephen Schuker, Martin Alexander, Elisabeth du Réau,
William Irvine, and Robert Young, among others, who hold that
French leaders were not as craven and incompetent as they might
have first appeared. French society was not so decadent: it was com-

ing around in 1939 and 1940, and the French collapse in May–June
1940 was a military defeat—calamitous to be sure, but nothing
more. In fact, given the economic, political, and military constraints
under which French leaders had to operate, they coped about as well
as might be expected. Schuker is at the forefront of these historians,
and his work on the Rhineland crisis in 1936 exemplifies the revisionist position. Irvine concludes simply that "it was not decadence
that led to 1940; it is 1940 that has led us to view the late Third Republic as decadent." "Two cheers for appeasement," as Schuker has
recently put it.[10]

However eminent the historians who take this view—or varia-
tions of it—it seems to me to be overdetermined, too mechanical,
and too clean. It holds that policymakers had no escape from their
dilemmas, though contemporary critics said they did. Even Weber,
who declared that French society faced an "inexorable march to
war," observed that the French were not helpless to influence their
fate.

> For men (and women, when they got the chance, which in those
> days was seldom) are not *objects* of history—playthings of tides,
> currents, laws that they can't inflect. They are responsible *sub-
> jects*: actors who write and rewrite their script while moving
> from one decision to the next or, failing to decide, resign the
> script to others. Each choice, each failure to make a choice com-
> mits them to a course and sets the limits of their further choices.
> Decisions and events are not the work of fate, and we are not its
> baubles unless we choose to be. Not individually, but taken as a
> whole, the French of the 1930s would not, could not decide.
> They allowed others to forge their destiny and had to pay for
> this abdication.[11]

The overdetermined explanation of the path to war in 1939 also
takes Anglo-French decision-making out of its social and political
context. Its main emphasis is on inadequate gold reserves, deflation-
ist monetary policy, inefficient bureaucratic or industrial structures,
and a necessarily slow process of rearmament. But the broader European social and political environment was tumultuous and
volatile: there were competing claims to the legitimacy of fascism
and communism, dashed aspirations and ideals, wrenching hatred,
fear of war and revolution, and the increasing willingness of states

to resort to violence. This turbulent environment also had an important impact on decision-making.

More recent work by R. A. C. Parker, for example, and my own, suggest a "counterrevisionist" position that takes up Weber's argument and in my case returns to earlier interpretations of the coming of the war. It points out that when policymakers said they had no options, opposition politicians challenged them. Other choices would have led elsewhere than to appeasement and the failure to form a broad European coalition against Nazi Germany.[12] But these other options must have led perforce to an alliance with the Soviet Union and quite possibly to war. And it was precisely this result that the politically dominant, anti-communist conservatives of France and Britain wished at almost any cost to avoid. In Duroselle's and Weber's view of decadence, anti-communism did not play an important role, but in my view, it did.

Historians have often focused on the failure of Anglo-Franco-Soviet negotiations and on the Nazi-Soviet nonaggression pact, which was a pivotal event in 1939. Stalin, the red tsar, was perfidious and had deceived the French and British while secretly negotiating with the Germans. "Glutinous knavery . . . surrounded the German-Soviet Non-Aggression Pact," wrote the Earl of Birkenhead.[13] On the other hand, Soviet historians such as V. Ia. Sipols, or earlier Western historians such as Namier, have asserted that the French and British did not intend to negotiate seriously and were just stringing along the Soviet government.[14] Donald Cameron Watt writes that such an interpretation ignores the earnestness of Anglo-French policymakers. The Soviet Union "destroyed British hopes of an Eastern Front" against Nazi Germany.[15] The French especially, reasserting their policy independence after several years under the British thumb, sought a Soviet alliance and pressed the British to do likewise.[16]

Geoffrey Roberts argues—as does Cameron Watt—that "the perception that British and French leaders were mainly motivated by anti-Bolshevism was completely off-beam." This is not a new idea: Keith Feiling wrote after the war that British prime minister Neville Chamberlain had no ideological prejudice.[17] The ideologues, say Cameron Watt and Roberts, were on the Soviet side.[18] The contrary view is not new either: anti-appeasement Conservatives accused Chamberlain and his circle of confusing their class interests for those of their country.[19] A. J. P. Taylor, in his *Origins of the Second World War*, aptly noted that Western reproaches with regard to the Nazi-Soviet nonaggression pact "came ill from the statesmen who went to Munich. . . . The Russians, in fact, did only what the Western statesmen had hoped to do; and Western bitterness was the bitterness of disappointment, mixed with anger that professions of Communism were no more sincere than their own professions of democracy."[20] When Taylor put forward this and other points about Western-Soviet relations, contemporaries did not accept them, thinking he was being deliberately outrageous. Nor were the archives open to buttress his arguments or to allow revision of them in light of what he would have found. The point is that now we have a substantial part of the archival record, and it bears out many of Taylor's suppositions.

Taylor, like the Russian historian Roy Medvedev and the political commentator Dimitri Volkogonov, concluded that the West left the Soviet government little choice but to conclude the nonaggression pact with Hitler.[21] But "few historians," writes Gabriel Gorodetsky, "take seriously the invariable Soviet claim . . . that the Soviet Union signed the pact under duress, regarding it as the lesser of two evils."[22] Some historians argue that Stalin preferred a Soviet-German agreement and was bent on it all along, but Roberts and Sipols counter that the Soviet movement toward a nonaggression pact was the result of uncertainty and drift. Soviet policy was poorly thought out, a fear-driven reversal occurring during a fortnight in August 1939.[23] Implicit in their arguments is that the Nazi-Soviet nonaggression pact was the result of the failure of Anglo-Franco-Soviet negotiations rather than the reverse.

In this and previous work I return to earlier explanations of the failure of Anglo-Franco-Soviet negotiations: in effect, that ideological anti-communism impeded Anglo-French efforts to conclude a war-fighting alliance with the Soviet Union against Nazi Germany. The Anglo-French rejection of numerous Soviet initiatives to improve relations during the interwar years, or to create an anti-Nazi coalition, especially during the period 1935–1938, greatly increased Soviet mistrust and cynicism. Western historians seldom consider the Nazi-Soviet nonaggression pact in this, its proper context. They look at it only within the short time frame of March–August 1939. From this narrow point of view, the nonaggression pact was a singular event demonstrating unmitigated Soviet perfidy. The Soviet government saw the matter differently: it was only "one double-cross deserves another," preceded by years of Anglo-French deception and bad faith, reaching a nadir in September 1938 at the Munich conference where Czechoslovakia was dismembered. From the Soviet point of view, Munich was an abdication and a betrayal. The Nazi-Soviet nonaggression pact, the Soviet tit-for-tat, was poor statesmanship, as many Russian historians now concede, but then, in the extreme tension of the last weeks of peace, it seemed like the only way to assure at least the short-term security of the Soviet Union.[24] The Soviet government, having long condemned France and Britain for appeasement, now took up the very same policy, and for the same reasons. If, after all, the "revisionists" can raise two cheers for Anglo-French appeasement, should they not also do the same for the Soviet equivalent?

In the end one is led back to the contemporary critics of Anglo-French appeasement to understand its dynamics and the alternatives. These critics were the Cassandras, dismissed as German-hating naysayers and gloom-seekers or purveyors of communist revolution because they said that Nazi Germany was bent on war and that the only way to restrain or defeat it was by forming a broad-based anti-Nazi alliance. Robert Vansittart, Churchill, Laurence Collier, one of Vansittart's subordinates, Maksim Maksimovich Litvinov, the Soviet commissar for foreign affairs, the French journalist Geneviève Tabouis, and French politicians Édouard Herriot and Georges Mandel were on the Cassandra list. They were a motley, imperfect group of heroes. Historians often look for villains; let us also identify these heroes, who stood nearly alone but held to their positions in adversity and were proved right in the end. With the exception of Churchill, none of these men and women were recognized in their lifetimes, and Mandel was murdered in 1944 by French fascists. We ought to be grateful that they saw Nazi Germany for the dark force it was, when many others regarded Nazism as merely a disagreeable but effective antidote to communism and popular unrest.

Leading Participants in the Drama

CHARLES ALPHAND, French ambassador in Moscow, 1933–1936.

FRANK ASHTON-GWATKIN, British Foreign Office economist, 1938–1939.

GEORGI A. ASTAKHOV, Soviet chargé d'affaires in Berlin, 1938–1939.

STANLEY BALDWIN, British prime minister, 1935–1937.

LOUIS BARTHOU, French minister of foreign affairs, 1934.

JÓZEF BECK, Polish minister of foreign affairs, 1932–1939.

EDWARD BENEŠ, president of Czechoslovakia, 1935–1938.

LÉON BLUM, député, 1919–1940; leader of the French Socialist party, French premier, 1936–1937, 1938.

GEORGES BONNET, French minister of foreign affairs, 1938–1939.

R. A. BUTLER, parliamentary under secretary of state at the British Foreign Office, 1938–1940.

SIR ALEXANDER CADOGAN, permanent under secretary of state in the British Foreign Office, 1938–1945.

NEVILLE CHAMBERLAIN, chancellor of the exchequer, 1931–1937; British prime minister, 1937–1940.

SIR HENRY CHANNON, member of parliament, 1935–1958; parliamentary private secretary to the under secretary of state for foreign affairs (R. A. Butler), 1938–1941.

SIR ALFRED ERNLE CHATFIELD, British minister for coordination of defence, 1939–1940.

CAMILLE CHAUTEMPS, many times a French cabinet minister; premier, 1937–1938.

ARETAS AKERS-DOUGLAS LORD CHILSTON, British ambassador in Moscow, 1933–1938.

WINSTON S. CHURCHILL, member of Parliament; British first lord of the admiralty, 1938–1940; prime minister, 1940–1945.

GEORGES CLEMENCEAU, French premier, 1917–1920.

LAURENCE COLLIER, head, Northern department, British Foreign Office, 1935–1942.

NICOLAE PETRESCU-COMNEN, Romanian minister of foreign affairs, 1938.

CHARLES CORBIN, French ambassador in London, 1933–1940.

ROBERT COULONDRE, French ambassador in Moscow, 1936–1938; in Berlin, 1938–1939.

SIR STAFFORD CRIPPS, British ambassador in Moscow, 1940–1942.

ÉDOUARD DALADIER, French premier, 1938–1940; minister of war and defense, 1936–1940; minister of foreign affairs, 1939–1940.

YVON DELBOS, French minister of foreign affairs, 1936–1938.

GENERAL JOSEPH DOUMENC, head of the French military mission to Moscow, 1939.

ADMIRAL SIR REGINALD PLUNKET ERNLE ERLE DRAX, head of the British military mission to Moscow, 1939.

ANTHONY EDEN, British secretary of state for foreign affairs, 1935–1938, 1940–1945; dominions secretary, 1939–1940.

WALTER ELLIOT, British minister of health, 1938–1940.

GENERAL MAURICE GAMELIN, chief of the French general staff, 1938–1939; commander-in-chief of the French army, 1939–1940.

EDWARD FREDERICK LORD HALIFAX, British lord president of the Council, 1937–1938; secretary of state for foreign affairs, 1938–1940.

OLIVER CHARLES HARVEY, principal private secretary to the British secretary of state for foreign affairs, 1936–1939; minister in the British embassy in Paris, 1940.

SIR NEVILE HENDERSON, British ambassador in Berlin, 1937–1939.

ÉDOUARD HERRIOT, député, 1919–1940; leader of the French Radical party, 1919–1936; cabinet minister, 1926–1936; premier, 1932; president of the Chamber of Deputies, 1936–1940.

ADOLF HITLER, fuehrer and chancellor of Germany, 1933–1945.

SIR SAMUEL HOARE, British secretary of state for foreign affairs, 1935; first lord of the admiralty, 1936–1937; home secretary, 1937–1939; lord privy seal, 1939–1940.

ROBERT HUDSON, secretary, British Department of Overseas Trade, 1937–1940.

JULES JEANNENEY, president of the French Senate, 1932–1940.

SIR HOWARD WILLIAM KENNARD, British ambassador in Warsaw, 1935–1939.

KAMIL KROFTA, Czech minister of foreign affairs, 1938.

EIRIK LABONNE, French ambassador in Moscow, 1940–1941.

PIERRE LAVAL, French minister of foreign affairs, 1934–1936; premier, 1935–1936.

ALEXIS LÉGER, secretary general of the French foreign ministry, 1933–1940.

MAKSIM MAKSIMOVICH LITVINOV, commissar for foreign affairs, 1930–1939.

DAVID LLOYD GEORGE, British prime minister, 1916–1922; independent Liberal member of Parliament, 1931–1945.

JULIUSZ ŁUKASZIEWICZ, Polish ambassador in Paris, 1938–1939.

IVAN MIKHAILOVICH MAISKII, Soviet *polpred* or ambassador in London, 1932–1943.

GEORGES MANDEL, Clemenceau's chef de cabinet, 1917–1919; député, 1920–1940; French cabinet minister, 1934–1936, 1938–1940.

JAN MASARYK, Czech minister in London, 1938.

ALEXEI F. MEREKALOV, Soviet ambassador in Berlin, 1938–1939.

VIACHESLAV MIKHAILOVICH MOLOTOV, Stalin's No. 2; chair of the Council of People's Commissars, 1930–1941; commissar, then minister for foreign affairs, 1939–1949.

BENITO MUSSOLINI, head of the Italian government and prime minister, 1922–1943.

PAUL-ÉMILE NAGGIAR, French ambassador in Moscow, 1939–1940.

LÉON NOËL, French ambassador in Warsaw, 1935–1939.

STEFAN OSUSKY, Czech minister in Paris, 1938–1939.

COLONEL AUGUSTE-ANTOINE PALASSE, French military attaché in Moscow, 1938–1939

JOSEPH PAUL-BONCOUR, French premier, 1932–1933; minister of foreign affairs, 1932–1934, 1938; many times a cabinet minister.

JEAN PAYART, French chargé d'affaires in Moscow, 1931–1940.

SIR ERIC PHIPPS, British ambassador in Berlin, 1933–1937; in Paris, 1937–1939.

VLADIMIR P. POTEMKIN, Soviet ambassador in Paris, 1935–1937; deputy commissar for foreign affairs, 1937–1940.

PAUL REYNAUD, French minister of justice, 1938; of finance, 1938–1940; premier, 1940.

JOACHIM VON RIBBENTROP, German minister of foreign affairs, 1938–1945.

SIR ORME GARTON SARGENT, assistant under secretary of state in the British Foreign Office, 1933–1939; deputy under secretary, 1939–1946.

KARL SCHNURRE, head of the economic policy department in the German Ministry of Foreign Affairs, 1938–1945.

FRIEDRICH WERNER VON DER SCHULENBERG, German ambassador in Moscow, 1934–1941.

GENERAL VICTOR-HENRI SCHWEISGUTH, French deputy chief of staff, 1935–1937.

SIR WILLIAM SEEDS, British ambassador in Moscow, 1939.

SIR JOHN SIMON, British home secretary, 1935–1937; chancellor of the exchequer, 1937–1940.

IOSIF V. STALIN, general secretary of the Communist Party of the Soviet Union, 1922–1953.

OLIVER STANLEY, president of the British Board of Trade, 1937–1940.

WILLIAM STRANG, head of the Central department in the British Foreign Office, 1938–1939; special mission to Moscow, 1939; assistant under secretary of state, 1939–1943.

IAKOV Z. SURITS, Soviet ambassador in Paris, 1937–1940.

GENEVIÈVE TABOUIS, French journalist.

SIR ROBERT GILBERT VANSITTART, permanent under secretary for foreign affairs, 1930–1937; chief diplomatic adviser to the foreign secretary, 1938–1941.

MARSHAL KLIMENT E. VOROSHILOV, Soviet commissar for defense, 1925–1940.

GENERAL JOSEPH VUILLEMIN, French chief of air staff, 1938.

ERNST VON WEIZSÄCKER, secretary of state in the German Ministry of Foreign Affairs, 1938–1943.

SIR HORACE WILSON, British Prime Minister Chamberlain's most important adviser, 1937–1940.

1 9 3 9

CHAPTER ONE

"A Long List of Disappointments"

A T THE END OF 1937, when the penultimate crises of the prewar period were about to break over Europe, the Soviet commissar for foreign affairs, Maksim Litvinov, met the French ambassador in Moscow, Robert Coulondre, to discuss the European situation. Both men saw grave dangers ahead, and both complained about the unhappy state of relations between their countries. There had been many failures in Western-Soviet cooperation against Nazi Germany. It was "a long list of disappointments," Litvinov remarked: the Soviet government had hoped for better.[1] A few months later the French embassy in Moscow could not have put it more eloquently than Litvinov himself.

> The Soviet government maintains the principles which it has not ceased to defend during these last years, of the need for the powers wanting to preserve peace to form a bloc, and to organize themselves to bar the way to the aggressors. The Muscovite Cassandra continues to preach the urgency of action for which there is not an hour to lose, but seeing that no one is listening and feeling that she is mistrusted, her voice little by little becomes more faint, and her tone more bitter.[2]

Nazi Germany threatened both France and the Soviet Union. They could either stand together, with Britain, or fall separately. Litvinov and Coulondre were critics of appeasement and advocates of collective security against Nazi Germany. The calamity and conundrum of the 1930s was that they, and others like them, could see the danger that threatened Europe, and yet they could not avert the catastrophe. This was Cassandra's curse.

II

It led to 1939. The year began better than it was to end. In January, only four months after the signature of the Munich accord, the French and British governments were slowly coming to the conclusion that Nazi Germany could not be appeased by concessions and that only military strength would hold it in check. This process of awakening was made easier by the German occupation of rump Czechoslovakia in March. In the spring of 1939 Anglo-Franco-Soviet negotiations began in order to create an anti-German alliance. It was the last chance to halt German expansion. Incredibly, the French and British governments hesitated to conclude. Negotiations were unsuccessful, and in August the Soviet Union signed a nonaggression pact with Nazi Germany. It was a stunning reversal: the two archenemies, who for years had heaped opprobrium on each other, suddenly composed their differences. The Anglo-French accused the Russians of a double-cross while the Soviet government rejoined that France and Britain had no lessons in duplicity to teach the Soviet Union.

For the British and French governments, the collapse of the Soviet negotiations was an immense policy failure. In 1939, and indeed since the Nazi rise to power in 1933, the Soviet Union had been the key to European peace and security. "It is well to remember," Sir Robert Vansittart, then chief diplomatic adviser in the Foreign Office, noted in early 1939, "that we had both Russia & Italy with us in the last war, & that we only just scrambled through. . . . France could have had no chance of survival *whatever* in 1914, if there had not been an Eastern Front. She only just survived as it was" (emphasis in the original).[3] The Red Army was large and well supplied, and the Soviet Union had immense natural resources. With Russia on their side, the Anglo-French would surely defeat Nazi Germany. Without it, they faced the gravest dangers. How could the French and British governments let slip from their hands this last chance to avert catastrophe?

On September 1 Nazi Germany invaded Poland; two days later Britain and France declared war. The British dominions soon followed London's lead. The fragile restraints that held back the European powers from the resort to war suddenly collapsed. "Clever hopes expire[d]", said W. H. Auden: air-raid sirens wailed and blackout curtains were drawn on the tenebrous, intermittent half-peace of the 1930s. A European war had come again only twenty years after the end of the last war with Germany. How could it be? "The unmentionable odour of death offends the September night," went Auden's verse. But 1939 was only the beginning of a cataclysm where tens of millions of people died cruelly and helplessly. Humanity, culture, mercy were forsaken. This war became an epic struggle where good opposed absolute evil. "Here's to the dead already," went the Royal Air Force tavern salute, "and here's to the next to die."

Rarely were the lines of conflict so clearly drawn, though for a time some people did not see the stakes in such unambiguous terms. War in Europe was the phony war after Poland was crushed. The Bore War, others called it, and it did not contribute clarity to a crusading purpose. Of course, when you shoot at the enemy, the enemy shoots back. But France and Britain were not ready for real hostilities and did not wish to provoke them. At the end of November 1939 fighting erupted at the periphery when the Soviet Union attacked Finland in what proved to be a short but bloody Winter War. Conservatives in France and Britain were anxious to help Finland, and some were anxious to make war on the Soviet Union. The Red Army was easy pickings, so it seemed, and a target infinitely more appealing than the formidable Nazi Wehrmacht. The prospect of fighting communists roused Anglo-French conservatives; fighting Nazi Germany filled many of them with doubt, gloom, and fear.

III

For many British Tories and French conservatives, cooperation with the Soviet Union had never been an acceptable alternative. Until 1939 fascism or Nazism was not an unmitigated evil, though it might be a disreputable form of government. On the contrary, fascism was an effective weapon against communism and socialism and a barrier to the expansion of bolshevism beyond the borders of the Soviet Union. The Russian Revolution of 1917 had for a time shaken the foundations of European capitalism. In 1919 the Bolsheviks announced the formation of the Communist International, the Comintern, and declared their intention to make a world socialist revolution. Contemporary Western images and discourse said it all: swarthy Bolshevik assassins appeared on right-wing election posters or on newspaper front pages, clenching knives between broken, blood-drenched teeth, ready for class mayhem and murder. The Bolsheviks threatened European civilization, murdered the innocent, raped and enslaved women, trampled everything in the way of their senseless, brutal pursuit of communism. Individualism, property, wealth, freedom—all would disappear under the Bolshevik's knife. In 1918 the Soviet nationalization of private investments and the denunciation of tsarist foreign debts, worth billions, struck at the heart of capitalism.

The threat was so grave that the Allied powers blockaded Soviet Russia, conspired with its internal enemies, and sent troops to stop the Bolshevik menace. The Allies did not have the power to overturn the revolution, but they were never reconciled to it and held on to their rancor and their fear long after the Bolsheviks had triumphed. The French and British refused until 1924 to extend de jure diplomatic recognition to the Soviet government, refused early on to trade with it, or then to extend credit for trade. The position was reasonable by their lights, for the Bolsheviks had not honored Russian public debts. Why should we lend new money to the Bolsheviks, said Western financiers, when they won't pay Russia's old debts? Because it's profitable, replied Soviet traders, and they tried to make it so. It may surprise but Bolsheviks made good businessmen, and Soviet-Western trade slowly increased. In spite of obstacles, Soviet diplomats attempted to build normal or at least correct political relations based on these commercial foundations. The Bolshevik leader, Vladimir Ilich Lenin, called such policy "peaceful coexistence." It was not easily pursued, because while Soviet diplomats labored for trade and correct relations in the West, the Comintern continued to trumpet the call for world revolution. The Comintern's activities were ineffectual and amateurish, but they vexed and frightened Western governments—vexed Soviet diplomats also because the Comintern disrupted their pragmatic approaches to the West.

Soviet diplomatic initiatives were thus largely unsuccessful, though trade continued to grow. Anglo-Soviet relations were ruptured in 1927, and Franco-Soviet relations nearly so a short time after. Some improvement later occurred, and the British resumed diplomatic relations in 1929. But the old animosities remained, and fears of socialism festered and burned. The red scare was periodically brought out and exploited by conservatives to fight national elections in 1924 in Britain and in 1919, 1928, and 1936 in France. In the United States, too, the red scare served the right. But the U.S. government withdrew from European politics in 1919 and refused until 1933 to recognize the Soviet Union. Between the wars, France and Britain were the Soviet Union's main antagonists in the West.

Readers may wonder what this has to do with 1939 and the beginning of the Second World War. Most historians associate the cold war with the period *after* 1945 and with the great struggle for hegemony between the United States and the Soviet Union. Red scare and reds, containment, peaceful coexistence, anti-communist electoral campaigns and fear mongering were all part of the post-1945 cold war. Yet these conspicuous signs of the cold war were nothing new. They were popular and commonplace during the interwar years, and they influenced the conduct of European foreign policy in fundamental ways. Interwar anti-communism became a serious impediment to the achievement of Anglo-French and European security, especially in the 1930s. Who was "Enemy No. 1," who was the paramount threat to European peace: Germany or the Soviet Union?

Politicians and statesmen asked this question regularly during the years between the wars. The French, who strategically were the most exposed, not having the English Channel to protect them, had the most to lose in another war with Germany. Geography forced France to face the fundamental question early on. Even at the beginning of the 1920s the center Radical party, and especially one of its leaders, Édouard Herriot, stood for closer relations with the Soviet Union to recreate a balance of power in Europe and restrain a resurgent Germany. At first glance one might think Herriot an implausible proponent of a Franco-Soviet rapprochement. He stood in the center of French politics: bourgeois, good-natured, bulky epicurean, mayor of Lyon, and leader of the Radical party in the Chamber of Deputies. Hardly the tough, stern-faced stereotype to risk his comfortable *joie de vivre* and political reputation, advocating bygones-be-bygones with Bolsheviks and ultimately a close Franco-Soviet relationship. But from his point of view, it was essential to restore good relations with Russia. France had been allied with tsarist Russia before 1914, and this alliance had been vital to French success in holding back the German armies during the early phases of the First World War. According to Herriot, the reestablishment of good Franco-Soviet relations was critical to French security. A red tsar or a white tsar must make no difference to France. Herriot was not alone in promoting these views, nor was it a position limited to the political center or left. Some conservatives also held to this line.

IV

At first, the rise to power of Hitler in January 1933 cleared up some of the questions about who was the greater threat to European peace and security. In 1933 the Soviet Union, which had maintained businesslike if not cordial relations with the post-Versailles Weimar German government, reassessed its foreign policy. Under Litvinov the Soviet government renewed its efforts to improve relations with the West. Litvinov was deputy commissar in the 1920s and in 1930 became commissar. He was an old Bolshevik who escaped tsarist imprisonment, published illegal newspapers, ran guns, and laundered illegal Bolshevik money. He spent a decade in exile in England, took a British wife, knew the West, and spoke several European languages. Unlike the Western caricature of the hardened, thuglike Bolshevik, Litvinov was a chubby, even dumpy-looking man who had an infectious smile and a well-developed sense of humor. To his comrades he was known by the affectionate name *Papasha*. In the business of state he was a tough, candid negotiator with a sharp mind and a sharper tongue, but he was supple and willing to bargain and compromise if it served the interests of his country. He abhorred Soviet domestic politics, which—along with luck—probably spared him from the Stalinist purges, and he hated the Comintern, which interfered with his businesslike relations with the West. His agenda was simple: peace and security for the Soviet Union and trade and cheap credit in the West to rebuild and develop the Soviet economy. Western diplomats sometimes were infuriated by Litvinov's direct language, but they almost all respected him and some even liked his openness and affability. "Look at him closely," the French foreign minister Louis Barthou said in 1934, "Does he look like a bandit? No. He does not look like a bandit. He looks like an honest man."[4]

Over the years, but especially at the beginning when the Soviet state fought for survival, Litvinov was subjected to "innumerable annoyances & indignities," according to R. A. Leeper, a British Foreign Office official and early go-between to the Soviet Union; but "I . . . found him, apart from occasional explosions, good-tempered & reasonable. He was in fact as frank & natural as the circumstances permitted."[5] Litvinov suffered many disappointments and policy setbacks, but none was greater than his attempt to build an anti-Nazi coalition. In his relations with Western diplomats he was quick to resort to cynicism or to express doubts and discouragement, but he was just as quick to pick up and persevere. His clarity of vision concerning the Nazi danger was as acute as Churchill's, if not more so, though readers of these lines will no doubt be less familiar with him. Like all the anti-appeasers, Litvinov had guts. His courage was immense, not only because he advocated an unpopular cause, that of resistance to Nazism—and it was unpopular until 1939 and even in 1940—but because he had to fear arrest and death from the very government he served. It is said that he slept with a revolver under his pillow to welcome Stalin's police. He never had to use it, but to do his job and serve his country in the oppressive, dangerous environment of Stalin's purges was terribly difficult, as he admitted to the French ambassador in Moscow in February 1939.[6] Litvinov is such an important participant in the events leading up to war in 1939 that he merits the reader's attention and respect.

Litvinov became the most prominent Soviet advocate of a new policy called collective security. Peace, he said, was indivisible. If peace were threatened in one part of Europe, it would be threatened in all of Europe. Nazi Germany, he argued, was the paramount enemy; it was rearming at breakneck speed, and Hitler glorified and was bent upon war. Litvinov stated repeatedly that the only way to assure European security was for France, Britain, and the Soviet Union to lead a coalition of states determined to deter Nazi aggression, or to defeat it in war should deterrence fail. As long as Germany was controlled by the Nazis, said Litvinov in 1934, so long would Germany be a "mad dog that can't be trusted, with whom no agreements can be made, and whose ambition can only be checked by a ring of determined neighbors." War, he said, was inevitable if Nazi Germany was not reined in.[7]

Litvinov gained a ready ear among some British and French officials and politicians who saw the danger. Vansittart, the permanent under secretary of the Foreign Office until the end of 1937, called proponents of a Soviet alliance "realists" who recognized the paramount danger of Nazi Germany. In the latter half of the 1930s the best-known British proponent of better relations with the Soviet Union was Churchill, who had earlier been an anti-communist "diehard," determined to "down the Bolshies." He had not gone soft on communism, but he argued that it was less of a threat to Britain than Nazism. Other realists also rang the tocsin. "There is a mad dog abroad once again," warned A. C. Temperley, a British delegate at the Geneva disarmament talks in the spring of 1933. "We must resolutely combine either to ensure its destruction or at least its confinement until the disease has run its course."[8] It would be ironic if Litvinov's image of the Nazi "mad dog" came from a British source.

Vansittart, or "Van" as he was called by people who knew him well enough, was the strongest and most courageous of the small band of British officials who fought unsuccessfully to alert the British government to the Nazi peril. He was a career diplomat who worked his way to the top of the Foreign Office. Confident, debonair, and exemplary ruling-class British, he had houses and servants, was a member of the modestly posh St. James Club, and enjoyed playing cards. Indeed, clubs and cards turned up as images in his minutes and memoranda. On the side he was also a respectable writer and playwright. This shows sometimes in his epigrams and turns of phrase, written in a large, flourishing hand. Vansittart was confident of his policies and worldview, to the point where he irritated his ministers, for no matter how great his influence and his power, the foreign secretary was still his boss. One of them, Anthony Eden, who did not like such a strong and willful permanent under secretary, said he was "in mentality" more a secretary of state than a permanent official.[9] Eden therefore wanted to get rid of him.

Vansittart practiced realpolitik, having neither permanent friends nor permanent enemies, only the interests of Britain to his mind. He did not like the Bolsheviks but learned to tolerate them and to advocate getting along with them when Nazi Germany threatened Europe. He was suspicious of the Germans and hated the Nazis, increasingly as the 1930s unfolded. Years of submission to Hitler's demands made Britain look like an enfeebled second-rate power, as he sometimes put it. He believed that power generated international respect and loyal allies, while the lack of it led to abuse of British interests and to isolation. He showed great impatience in the mid-1930s when the British government was too slow in rearming and refused to take the Nazi danger as seriously as he thought they should. And this impatience got him into trouble with his Tory superiors.

Vansittart developed a loyal following among some of his subordinates—his "boys," as they were sometimes known—in the Foreign Office. Among them were Ralph Wigram and Laurence Collier. Wigram died prematurely in late 1936, and Collier became Vansittart's main foil in promoting a British rapprochement with the Soviet Union and in opposing endless concessions and capitulations to Nazi Germany. This hurt Van's career and also Collier's. They thought certainly—if they thought about it at all—that their country's security was more important than their careers.

With regard to the Nazi danger, Vansittart was plainspoken, a quality not often appreciated by politicians. "The present regime in Germany," he said, "will, on past and present form, loose off another European war just so soon as it feels strong enough."[10] Few people in the British government listened to him, and when they did, they criticized him for alarmism, arrogance, and exaggerated animosity to Nazi Germany. His minutes in the Foreign Office files, initialed with a familiar, flamboyant "R," still tremble with frustration and anxiety for his country.

"I did what was possible," Vansittart wrote in his memoirs, "and that was not much."[11] He underestimated his effort. He did as much as any civil servant could have done to warn of his country's peril. "With every month that passes," he wrote in early 1935, "I obtain more evidence that confirms my suspicions & convictions as to Germany's ultimate policies & intentions. I think they will soon become evident to all but the biassed and the blind."[12] Or, in 1936: ". . . the facts of today are very hard and very black, whatever precarious hopes we may try to nurse along for tomorrow. . . . The Germany of today has no intention of remaining within her present boundaries . . . no matter what papers she may sign. . . ." Herr

Hitler promised "friendship & warm desire, but no deeds . . . follow," commented Vansittart: "It is always 'jam tomorrow' [but] 'Tomorrow never comes.' . . ."[13]

Vansittart sought to recreate the alliances of the First World War with Italy and Russia. That Italy was fascist and Russia communist did not matter if they would stand with Britain against Nazi Germany. Herriot and Litvinov had similar ideas. What was important was to establish a powerful anti-Nazi coalition of states. In 1934 Vansittart began to promote the idea of a rapprochement with the Soviet Union. For a while he received a hearing in the Conservative government. We need to keep the Soviet "friendly," Vansittart said in 1935, and we should not be led astray in pursuit of the "jack o' lantern" of placating Hitler. Only "timely realism" should guide us now.[14]

In pursuit of his policy, Vansittart began to see on a regular basis the Soviet ambassador in London, Ivan Mikhailovich Maiskii. Maiskii played an important role in the improvement of Anglo-Soviet relations. The ambassador was a former Menshevik who had come to London as Soviet counselor in 1926–1927 and then as Soviet ambassador in late 1932. ". . . Many avoided him," wrote Vansittart in his memoirs: "I was sorry, since his hold at home was precarious. . . . I thought that he might be killed if he were not a success." Maiskii was one of the *Litvinovtsy*, one of Litvinov's men and a partisan of collective security. Like Litvinov, he had spent time in exile in London before the Russian Revolution and knew English well. He was short with a round friendly face, Tartar mustache, and slight goatee, and a warm smile. Vansittart and Maiskii took a liking to each other; their wives, according to Maiskii, had eased matters by getting along first. "Helping lame dogs over stiles is no duty," wrote Vansittart, "when theirs is to bite, but my wife and I did our best to provide him and his with connections, and had them to meals *à quatre* or in company. . . ." With help like this, Maiskii cultivated a wide network of relationships with intellectuals, journalists, politicians, and ministers in London. These contacts, he believed, were important in explaining his government's positions and policies, so often distorted by the Foreign Office or in the anti-communist British press. Maiskii was good at his job, irrepressible in fact, so much so that many Foreign Office clerks were quick to anger at his successes and easy access to the British elite. During the war he became popular in London, and Stalin, just before his death in 1953, rewarded Maiskii's service to his country, like that of so many others, by having him arrested.[15] Luckily Stalin died a few weeks later, and Maiskii was eventually freed by Nikita Khrushchev to write his memoirs and to live to an old age.

Dining at the Vansittarts was not only convivial, it was also useful. Company sometimes included "Winston," and discussion focused on the nascent Anglo-Soviet rapprochement and its root cause—a rapidly rearming Nazi Germany. It was about this time that Churchill started to promote closer Anglo-Soviet relations. He had good working and personal relations with Vansittart, and Van arranged the dinner in June 1935 where Churchill first met the Soviet ambassador. They met *en famille,* according to Maiskii, and Churchill "had sought the possibility of chatting with me." The two men got along well and began to see one another regularly. Churchill, who shared Vansittart's view of the need to establish better Western-Soviet relations, became Maiskii's adviser, and not a bad one either. He declared that Soviet policy should be careful and patient. Die-hard Tories did not want cooperation with the Soviet Union, he warned: they thought Western security could be achieved through agreement with Nazi Germany, in exchange for German freedom of action in the east. This is rubbish! spat Churchill. Hitlerite Germany is "a huge, scientifically organized war machine, led by commonplace American gangsters." Litvinov is right, European peace *is* indivisible: if Hitler moves east, he will eventually turn back to the west and be all the more difficult to stop. Anglo-French partisans of an alliance with the Soviet Union would eventually prevail, Churchill thought, but victory would not come at once, there will be "zig-zags" (ups and downs) in British policy. The Soviet government must remain "patient and restrained." But the Red Army should arm to the teeth, because the "common enemy is at the gates." Die-hard enmity meant that direct Soviet participation in a grand anti-Nazi alliance could not be achieved at once. The die-hards would come around, said Churchill—but the trouble was, they did not.[16]

In 1936 Vansittart lost much of the influence he exerted over British foreign policy. His decline began after Italy invaded Abyssinia, or Ethiopia, in the autumn of 1935, wanting to expand its North African colonies. In December the ensuing crisis blew up. The foreign secretary, Sir Samuel Hoare, only six months in his post,

was forced to resign when Anglo-French plans for a generous territorial settlement with Italy leaked into the press. Vansittart received
some of the blame, and Italy, one of his anticipated allies against
Nazi Germany, was scratched from the coalition. He soon had to
scratch the Soviet Union too because the new foreign secretary, Anthony Eden, put a stop to the Soviet rapprochement. "I don't trust
[the Soviet]," Eden said, "& am sure there is hatred in his heart for
all we stand for."[17] It was the usual reasons: the Comintern, communist propaganda, Soviet hostility toward the British Empire, and
meddling in British domestic affairs. I do not want "exceptionally
intimate relations with the Soviets," remarked Eden, " 'Correct' is all
that they should be."[18] Most Tories—and the Tories counted most
because they controlled the British government—were ideologues
who accepted the Leninist concept that war bred socialism and that
another war would spread communism into the heart of Europe. An
alliance with the Soviet Union against Nazi Germany was therefore
undesirable.

V

The same policy debate took place in France along the same lines,
though it began earlier. Among the realists during the 1930s were
Herriot, Joseph Paul-Boncour, a socialist, and Louis Barthou, an
anti-communist conservative. Herriot and Paul-Boncour, who were
ministers of foreign affairs in 1932–1934, started a promising movement toward a Franco-Soviet rapprochement. In 1932 the French
government signed a nonaggression pact with the Soviet Union; in
1933 it sent a military attaché to Moscow; and in early 1934 it
signed a provisional trade agreement. Paul-Boncour's role in the
Franco-Soviet rapprochement is little recognized by historians, but
in 1933 he pushed for a Franco-Soviet trade agreement and began to
talk to Litvinov and the Soviet ambassador in Paris about collective
security against Nazi Germany. Paul-Boncour was a diminutive but
handsome man, with flowing locks of white hair. Some regarded
him as an intellectual lightweight, others saw him as a committed
anti-appeaser. One contemporary historian says he treated his work
as foreign minister as "a part-time job."[19] Not when it came to the
Franco-Soviet rapprochement. He pressed his officials hard to ob-

tain a trade agreement as a step toward better political relations.[20] In the spring of 1938, when Paul-Boncour briefly returned to the Quai d'Orsay as foreign minister, the British ambassador in Paris, Sir Eric Phipps, conspired to oust him from office for fear he might stiffen French policy against Nazi Germany.[21]

The growing Franco-Soviet rapprochement was a considerable achievement given the unstable political situation in France, where governments changed every few months. By the beginning of 1934 French public confidence in Parliament and indeed in parliamentary democracy was low. The depression had struck France late but hard: bankruptcies and unemployment were up, and salaries had declined by a third. Riots and street demonstrations in Paris were almost nightly events. Parliament was held in contempt: Paris bistros carried signs "No Deputies Served Here." French governmental instability worried the Narkomindel, the Soviet commissariat for foreign affairs.[22] In Moscow the French ambassador, Charles Alphand, was abashed to explain it away. Parliament, he told the Soviet official B. S. Stomoniakov in July 1933, was a "dirty business"; and the press belonged to the highest bidder.[23] Alphand perhaps did not know that even the Soviet Union bid for the favors of the French press.[24]

To Soviet officials, Alphand's comments must have seemed prophetic. In January 1934 the Stavisky scandal erupted when the French police caught up with the notorious confidence man Serge Alexandre, alias Sasha Stavisky, who had for years paid off government officials and even deputies to run his frauds and keep him out of jail. This was the "Republic of Pals," where "rigorously honest men were on good terms with fairly honest men who were on good terms with shady men who were on good terms with despicable crooks." The Republic nearly collapsed on February 6 when bloody right-wing riots erupted on the Place de la Concorde in Paris.[25]

These developments worried Soviet officials. Just before the riots, V. S. Dovgalevskii, the Soviet ambassador in Paris, warned Litvinov that French government and society were split between pro-Soviet and pro-German camps. Alphand tried to be reassuring: he did not think that French policy toward the Soviet Union would change. But he also acknowledged that some in the government bureaucracy and in outside influential circles opposed the Soviet rapprochement. "Our capitalists," he said, "are frightened by you."

Win over the government bureaucracy, Alphand urged, and relations would be better.[26] Communications from the Soviet embassy in Paris were more encouraging: Barthou, the new foreign minister, assured Dovgalevskii of his commitment to improved relations, and he undertook negotiations for the conclusion of a Franco-Soviet Pact of Mutual Assistance.[27]

Barthou adopted the Herriot/Paul-Boncour policy as his own, but he was killed the following October by Croatian fascists who assassinated the Yugoslav king Alexander in Marseilles. His successor, Pierre Laval, was a slippery, come-lately conservative with few fixed opinions. Soviet officials worried: would French policy continue as before? Laval gave assurances, but it was well known that he preferred a rapprochement with Nazi Germany. Litvinov did not believe Laval's assurances: France would only string along the Soviet Union in order to win big concessions from Germany.[28] In fact, Laval was unenthusiastic about close Soviet ties. He was a strong anti-communist, one of the only principles to which he stuck fast, and he had opposed the Franco-Soviet rapprochement in cabinet during Barthou's tenure at the Quai d'Orsay. Better relations with the Soviet Union, he said, would bring to France "the International and the red flag." And if there were a European war, it would lead to an "invasion" of bolshevism.[29]

Was the Communist International such a threat? In 1933 Alphand observed that it was an instrument of Soviet foreign policy as much as the Red Army, and that it was dangerous only to states hostile to the Soviet Union. "Give us credit," Marshal K. E. Voroshilov, the commissar for defense, would later say, "for not being so stupid as to get mixed up . . . in matters [French domestic politics] which do not concern us."[30] In a dispatch in 1935 the French chargé d'affaires in Moscow, Jean Payart, argued that the Soviet government was not in the least interested in world revolution and that the Comintern was dying.[31] These were the realists' arguments. Nazi Germany was the greater danger; the Comintern was an irritant, not a threat to European security.

Laval was no realist. A settlement with Germany was his *grande idée,* according to the Polish ambassador in Paris. Laval admitted as much to V. P. Potemkin, the Soviet ambassador in Paris succeeding Dovgalevskii: "My Germanophilia," he said, ". . . is the pacifism of the French people; without an improvement of relations between

France and Germany, peace would be impossible."[32] Laval had some support in London, especially among Foreign Office officials who did not like close Franco-Soviet relations. It is a "fatal policy," said Foreign Office assistant under secretary Orme Sargent, "which can . . . only lead to one ultimate result, namely a European war in which the Soviet Government, in their capacity of agents of the Third International, would probably be the only beneficiaries."[33] As in Britain, so in France, the war-revolution nexus was central to conservative opposition to closer Franco-Soviet relations.

Potemkin accused Laval of double-talk and playing hard to get, as though France were making a sacrifice in concluding an agreement with the Soviet Union.[34] Certainly Laval was stalling. In March 1935 the Soviet government issued what amounted to an ultimatum to complete negotiations on the mutual assistance pact. Litvinov put forward fresh proposals in April, which the French "blackballed."[35] Laval eventually concluded the pact because an intransigent Hitler left him little choice. On March 9 the Nazi government announced the existence of the Luftwaffe, the German air force, and a week later Hitler announced the reintroduction of conscription and a German army strength of 500,000 men. These actions were further incentive for better Franco-Soviet relations, but two powerful Quai d'Orsay officials, secretary general Alexis Léger and political director Paul Bargeton, were against them. They gutted the proposed pact of any force, ladening it with qualifications and hedges.[36] Laval was a good politician, however, and, anti-communist or not, French communists had votes in the Paris suburb of Aubervilliers where he sought reelection as mayor. So he went to Moscow in May 1935 to sign the mutual assistance pact in great pomp and circumstance. Shortly thereafter the Soviet Union also signed a mirror accord with Czechoslovakia, thus reinforcing the Franco-Soviet agreement and the 1925 Franco-Czech mutual assistance pact. Soviet commitments were contingent on French support for the Czechs, to make sure that France would not leave the Soviet Union in the lurch.

After promising speedy ratification of the mutual assistance pact and suggesting military staff talks to Stalin, Laval delayed ratification for the rest of the year and let the French general staff evade military conversations. The general staff blamed the delay on Laval, but the generals themselves were in no hurry to parley. Litvinov reckoned that if Laval remained in power, he would refuse to ratify the pact or would turn it into a "scrap of paper."[37] Often discouraged by French stalling, Litvinov sometimes fell into cynical despair over the duplicity of French policy.[38] In February–March 1936 the French Parliament finally ratified the Franco-Soviet pact, but by then it was already too late to make more of the pact than the paper it was written on.

However skeptical Litvinov might have been, the Soviet government between 1935 and 1937 pressed the French for staff talks and for access to war materiel from the French defense industry. The French government promised the goods but never delivered. And the French general staff turned away repeated Soviet requests for staff talks, even though in 1935 it had positive assessments of a major buildup of Soviet armed forces. The French calculated that staff talks might precipitate the Nazi reoccupation of the demilitarized Rhineland, or provoke British Tories, who were for the most part hostile to the Soviet Union and opposed closer Franco-Soviet relations. Poland, with whom France had concluded a military alliance in 1921, also created difficulties: it feared the Soviet Union more than it did Nazi Germany. There was no doubt in Warsaw about who was "Enemy No. 1." Such calculations had led the Polish government in January 1934 to conclude a nonaggression pact with Nazi Germany.[39] What made matters worse was the increasing polarization of French politics which occurred after the right-wing riots of February 1934. The center and left united in the Popular Front during 1935 to prepare for national elections the following year. The growing strength of the left frightened French conservatives and heightened their fears of closer relations with the Soviet Union.

When Laval fell from power in early 1936, the Soviet government must have thought good riddance. A palpably relieved Alphand cabled Paris that perhaps now the damage of recent months could be undone.[40] In February 1936 Litvinov met the new French premier, Pierre-Étienne Flandin, in Paris. We have our own "isolationists," Litvinov warned, but the Soviet government wanted clarity in its relations with France and not the uncertainty of the preceding eight months under Laval.[41] But Litvinov would never get the clarity he wanted. In March the Rhineland crisis erupted while the French Parliament was debating ratification of the Franco-Soviet pact. The Soviet embassy in Paris was discouraged by the weakness of the

Anglo-French response to the German military occupation of the de-militarized zone along the left bank of the Rhine. Hitler's action violated a crucial provision of the treaty of Versailles, and henceforth France could not go easily to the aid of its eastern allies. In spite of the high stakes, the French and British governments did nothing to counter the Nazi move. According to Potemkin, it was not hard to understand why. The French government was overdependent on British support and feared losing it by pursuing too aggressive a policy against Nazi Germany. There was also little confidence in Soviet military support in the event of war. We are far away, said Potemkin: we do not have a common frontier with Germany, and the Red Army is not ready for an offensive war. Georges Mandel, French cabinet minister and partisan of a Franco-Soviet alliance, began to meet with the Soviet ambassador. In the spring of 1936 Mandel told Potemkin that "no one [would] stand in the elections [in May] as a proponent of war and an advocate of a policy of firmness. . . . The elections will take place under the ill-omen of pacifism." In these circumstances Mandel thought the French government would have no choice but to wait and see, play for time, and hope for the maturing of public opinion under the influence of further Nazi aggression.[42]

Mandel's name will return many times in the pages of this book. A journalist in Paris at the turn of the century, he began to work for Georges Clemenceau, French premier during the last year of the First World War. Clemenceau, known variously as "the tiger" and later as *Père la victoire,* ruthlessly pursued the war against Germany, and Mandel became his right arm on the home front. "Defeatist" politicians were jailed; spies were shot; and no relent in the war against the *Boches* was permitted. Mandel gained a reputation as the premier's *exécuteur de basses oeuvres,* his hatchet man, a role for which he earned both fear and respect.

Mandel was a conservative but also a Jew, which did not fit well on the political right where anti-Semitism was common. He entered the government for the first time in 1934 as minister of posts. In 1936 he advocated the formation of a National Union government, and he pressed relentlessly for a Franco-Soviet military alliance. France had either to abdicate its security interests in eastern Europe or to collaborate with all those countries threatened by Nazi Germany. Mandel established ties with Potemkin and his successor, Ia.

Z. Surits, and their reports sometimes record conversations with him. One of the last Clemencists, he was convinced that war with Nazi Germany was inevitable, and he preferred to get on with it sooner rather than later.[43]

Time did not serve France and Britain as well as it did Nazi Germany. During the "red spring" of 1936 the Popular Front won national elections, and the Socialist Léon Blum became premier of France. Strikes and plant occupations soon broke out. To British Tories it seemed that France had sunk into a socialist morass. To French conservatives it looked like communism hid behind the Popular Front façade. British dispatches from Paris made dismal reading in the Foreign Office. In August 1936 Eden noted on one report: "To read this despatch is to feel France growing more 'red.' . . ." In September the British embassy in Paris submitted a report on "Sovietisation in France."[44]

Red spring was followed by red summer: civil war broke out in Spain. If the Popular Front unsettled the Tories, the outbreak of the Spanish Civil War unhinged them. Fascist Italy and Nazi Germany went to the assistance of the insurgents; the Soviet Union sent aid and advisers to the Republican government. France and Britain declared for nonintervention, which only helped the Spanish fascists, led by the rebel General Francisco Franco. "The Spanish situation is hell," Harold Nicolson recorded in his journal: it reinforced Tory pro-German and anti-Russian "tendencies." The British prime minister Stanley Baldwin was "much affected by the Spanish troubles," according to a source close to him. "I told Eden . . . ," said Baldwin, "that on no account, French or other, must he bring us in to fight on the side of the Russians." "On no account must we do anything to bolster up Communism in Spain," said another minister of the crown. Foreign intervention in Spain could lead to the formation of ideological blocs, warned one Foreign Office official, which was just what the British wished to avoid.[45] Vansittart passed on the message: if France went further to the left or closer to "the Soviet"—this was a common Foreign Office usage—British opinion would take it badly amiss. "The British Government was upheld by a very large Conservative majority," said Vansittart, "who were never prepared, and now probably less than ever, to make much sacrifice for red eyes." And the Spanish Civil War made the "red eyes" seem to burn all the more fiercely. It said a great deal that Vansittart delivered this message.[46]

In September 1936 Potemkin warned the French foreign minister, Yvon Delbos, that a "policy of capitulation" to fascist aggression would lead France to the loss of its allies and to isolation. Delbos protested that the government sought to avoid war, and that there was a growing fear of revolution in France. The British ambassador in Paris meddled in French domestic affairs, telling his French counterparts that more strikes in France would be considered undesirable in London. Potemkin was astonished: "Why does France permit the interference of a foreign government in its internal affairs?" Delbos replied that French "friendship" with Britain allowed to it certain liberties.[47] The juxtaposition between French complacency toward certain friendly British "liberties" and French sensitivity toward unfriendly Soviet "interference" could not have gone unnoticed by Potemkin.

In any event, Potemkin's warning had no effect whatsoever. In October Léger, the French Vansittart without the courage or vision, advised the Soviet chargé d'affaires that Franco-Soviet relations would suffer if the Soviet Union did not pursue a less aggressive policy in Spain. Léger was smug about Franco's advance toward Madrid, which, if successful, would mark the beginning of the ebb tide of bolshevism.[48] The negative strategic consequences for France of having another fascist state established on its borders, along with Germany and Italy, did not seem to matter. As Collier, Vansittart's stalwart amanuensis, noted in 1937: "People . . . seem to lose all consideration for the interests of their country, as opposed to those of their church or of their class, when they deal with affairs in Spain. . . ."[49]

Events inside the Soviet Union were also troubling. The Stalinist purges of old Bolsheviks began to spill buckets of blood in the summer of 1936, and they did not improve Anglo-Franco-Soviet relations. They were grist to the mill of the anti-Soviet right in Britain and France. But the blood purges—along with the Popular Front victory and the Spanish Civil War—occurred *after* the French and British governments had moved away from a rapprochement with the Soviet Union—at a time, by the way, when British and French military estimates of the Red Army were relatively positive.[50] And even when French estimates in the autumn of 1936 soured, they were not entirely hostile, not even deputy chief of staff General Victor-Henri Schweisguth's negative report on Red Army maneuvers in the autumn of 1936.[51] French generals observed that the Red Army could not maintain a sustained offensive, but the French army never contemplated offensive operations from behind the elaborate Maginot line of frontier fortifications. And the British, with their *two* not so ready divisions, were incapable of any offensive operations in Europe.[52] It was the Anglo-French pot calling the Soviet kettle black. The Red Army, however, could be counted on to be formidable in defense of Russian territory, and its ability to provide war materiel and supplies to Poland and Romania would be crucial in the long, grinding war that the Anglo-French envisaged against Nazi Germany. Even the anti-red General Schweisguth conceded it. By the logic of Anglo-French military strategy, Soviet assets should have been valuable and worth negotiating for.

One need only read what Laval or Eden, and many of their colleagues, had to say in 1934–1936 to explain why they did not embrace Anglo-Franco-Soviet cooperation.[53] These explanations were in the main grounded in fear of socialist revolution and the spread of Soviet influence in Europe. Fear of war was equaled by fear of revolution—and fear of victory. An Anglo-Franco-Soviet alliance would certainly triumph, but at what cost? War meant ruin, the decline and collapse of the old European order; victory risked the spread of communism on the crest of the advance of the Red Army into Europe. Hence the Stalinist purges merely hardened opponents and inhibited partisans of better relations.

Late in 1936 Robert Coulondre arrived in Moscow as the new French ambassador, succeeding Alphand. In his first meeting with Litvinov on November 10, Coulondre complained about communist propaganda in France. The position of the Radicals was critical to good Franco-Soviet relations, and they were running scared of communism. Litvinov gave assurances and in fact did not care a jot about French Communists. He observed to Coulondre that France and the Soviet Union had a common interest in safeguarding the peace against Nazi Germany. Hitler sought to disrupt this unity of purpose by whipping up fears of communism. Would France play into Nazi hands?[54] Coulondre did not report his reply, but Litvinov's plea would have fallen on deaf ears in any case. The irony here is that the French Communist party before the spring elections had *supported* the Radicals, counting on them to pursue in government an anti-fascist policy and a close alliance with the Soviet Union. French Communist and Socialist electoral gains, combined with Radical losses, upset the French Communist strategy and undermined their relationship with the Radical party. Now domestic ideological fears of the *French* Communist party spilled over into foreign policy and destabilized fragile Franco-Soviet ties. The strength of the French Communists, combined with the outbreak of the Spanish Civil War, frightened the *grande bourgeoisie* and the general staff. General A. J. Georges, deputy chief of staff, thought the mutual assistance pact should be abandoned altogether. He feared the progress of communism in France and the possibility of a general strike. Georges's colleagues, Generals P.-H. Gérodias and M.-E. Debeney, considered the Soviet pact a dupe's game for which the dead Barthou was responsible.[55] By the end of 1936 Litvinov's policy of collective security had suffered serious setbacks. Herriot in Paris reckoned that Franco-Soviet relations had been "poisoned."[56] In Britain the situation was similar.

Litvinov ridiculed the British and French governments, ". . . who believe that preparations to resist openly-planned aggression can only be made with the consent and participation of the instigators of that aggression. . . ." Litvinov challenged the West to choose between collective security "and falling in meekly with the wishes of these aggressors." The latter course, he warned, could only be "a rapprochement of the lobster with the shark."[57]

While the Soviet government doubted French commitment to the mutual assistance pact, it continued to press for military staff talks. At the end of June 1936 Litvinov had raised the issue with the foreign minister, Delbos, as did E. V. Girshfel'd, the Soviet chargé d'affaires in Paris, with the deputy chief of staff, General Schweisguth. Girshfel'd conceded that the lack of a common Soviet-German border impeded Franco-Soviet military cooperation, but unless the French and Soviet staffs met to discuss common defense issues, there could be no serious cooperation between them. The French government feared provoking Germany: would staff talks have to wait until Hitler was ready to attack?[58] The unfortunate answer to this question became only too apparent in 1939.

When Schweisguth traveled to the Soviet Union to observe Red

Army maneuvers in September 1936, the deputy commissar for war, M. N. Tukhachevskii, asked the unwelcome question again.[59] So did Litvinov with Blum the following month. With remarkable candor, Blum suggested that talks were being "sabotaged" by the general staff and by the war minister, Édouard Daladier. Soviet orders for war materiel were also being blocked by the military bureaucracy. Potemkin commented that the Soviet government was beginning to doubt French sincerity in furthering the buildup of Soviet arms.[60] "Repeated" Soviet initiatives for staff talks put the French government ill at ease, but Daladier was afraid "to alarm certain friendly powers and to provide Germany with the easy pretext of an attempt at encirclement." The French war ministry blocked the sale of modern military, especially naval, materiel, likewise because of anticipated British objections. It did not mind, however, selling obsolete equipment to the Soviet Union.[61]

Not all members of the Blum government were hostile to staff talks. Blum himself was open-minded, and his air minister, Pierre Cot, was prepared to start staff talks without cabinet approval on the narrower basis of air force cooperation. Daladier resisted, but Cot pressed on, ready to drag the government along after him.[62] On November 6, 1936, he seemed to win the point as the cabinet agreed to start staff talks initially with the Soviet military attaché. The breakthrough was deceptive: Daladier and the chief of staff, General Maurice Gamelin, went along to take the initiative out of Cot's hands and to reassert control. "It would be difficult," noted Schweisguth, "to delay any longer without the risk that the air ministry would take control of the movement. . . ."[63] On November 9 Blum advised Potemkin that Cot's initiative was to be broadened and that Gamelin was coming around. "In comparison with the previous situation," he said, "it was a step forward." The Soviet government appeared to take Blum at his word but feared the negative consequences if the talks failed.[64]

Matters worsened in 1937. In January cabinet minister Camille Chautemps told Potemkin that staff talks might provoke a German-Italian "preventative war," and that the British opposed them. The Soviet government had no intention of forcing itself upon the French, replied Potemkin, but it was a mistake for France to be constantly looking over its shoulder at Germany in expectation of its next outburst and to be subordinating its foreign policy to direction from London.[65]

Delay and duplicity became the main tactics to scuttle the staff talks. Gamelin told Schweisguth, "We need to drag things out." When a Soviet response to French queries arrived, Schweisguth noted Gamelin's order: "we should not hurry, but avoid giving to the Russians the impression that we were playing them along, which could lead them into a political volte-face [i.e., a rapprochement with Germany]."[66] Gamelin and Daladier headed the movement; Léger took charge at the Quai d'Orsay, the French foreign ministry.

Schweisguth met the new Soviet military attaché several times, but it was all a charade. "The situation is still the same," noted Schweisguth—"gain time, without rebuffing the Russians and without proceeding to staff talks. . . ." Daladier calculated that France could do without Soviet support, but not without the British. The British government had trouble "swallowing" the mutual assistance pact; it would choke on a military agreement.[67] Léger assured Blum that the war and foreign ministry bureaucracies would loyally respect the government's policy on staff talks, but this was dust in the eyes; not even Daladier intended to respect government policy.[68] For Daladier and Gamelin, it was a case of taking one step forward in order to take two steps back.

In February 1937 the Soviet military attaché, A. S. Semenov, met with Schweisguth and his superior, General Louis-Antoine Colson. Semenov said that if Poland and Romania would permit passage across their territory, the Red Army would assist France with all its forces in the case of a German attack. If not, Soviet assistance would necessarily be more limited, but the Soviet government was prepared to send troops to France and to provide air support—no doubt a chilling prospect to the red-obsessed French general staff. In return, the Soviet government wanted to know what assistance France could offer in case of German aggression against the USSR.[69]

Blum saw Potemkin on February 17 after Semenov had met Colson, thanking him for the "direct and comprehensive" Soviet proposals. Blum wondered if Romania might be persuaded to accept Red Army passage on the assumption that Poland would remain neutral. Potemkin replied that he had "before hand resigned himself to the refusal of Poland to fulfil its obligations as an ally."[70] A few days later Blum met Daladier, Léger, and Gamelin. Daladier's marginal notes blame Schweisguth for delays in the talks, but this is untrue; Daladier and Gamelin were calling the shots, Schweisguth was simply a faithful executor of their policy.[71] According to Schweisguth's notes, Stalin himself had written a "very cordial" letter in favor of a Franco-Soviet military alliance. Potemkin had read it to Blum, who was impressed. But Daladier remained "skeptical."[72] Schweisguth met Semenov on March 19, asking more questions about Soviet military capabilities. As for Franco-Soviet cooperation on the ground, Schweisguth indicated that it would be "extremely difficult" and would depend on "political factors" with respect to Poland, the Baltic, and elsewhere.[73] The Soviet commissar for defense, Marshal Voroshilov, reacting angrily to the additional questions posed by Schweisguth, refused further discussions. The Soviet general staff had indicated what it was prepared to do in the event of German aggression against France and had asked in return what the French would do in the case of a German attack on the Soviet Union. Instead of an answer, the French had put more questions. Negotiations were deadlocked.[74] And the British Foreign Office intervened heavily in April and May 1937 to make certain that the deadlock remained. Eden and Vansittart applied the pressure. But as late as the end of May, Blum and Cot still sought to advance the talks.[75] Aware of French dissension, Potemkin from Moscow advised the new Soviet ambassador in Paris, Surits, not to press the issue. Open discussion in the French government could only make matters worse.[76]

The Soviet government did not help itself in these negotiations. The Stalinist purges continued and in mid-1937 decimated the Red Army high command. Senior commanders, such as Marshal Tukhachevskii, were accused of treason before drumhead courts and summarily executed. While there was little concern in France over the elimination of old Bolshevik revolutionaries who had been thorns in the side of the West, the disappearance of many respected Soviet commanders seemed to weaken the military capabilities of the Red Army. Either the Soviet Union was riddled with traitors or it was governed by madmen who had turned on their best generals.[77] Whichever the case, the purges of the Red Army gave the French general staff an ideal pretext for dropping further discussion of military cooperation.

The Soviet estimate of French reliability also declined. Ambassador Surits in Paris, another *Litvinovets*, wrote a devastating situation report, sufficient to bolster Duroselle's or Weber's interpretations of "decadent" France. The fear of tomorrow, wrote Surits in November 1937, grew stronger every day; the French saw danger on all sides and had lost their nerve. Britain was France's main ally, and the French government would maintain its ties with London at any cost, even though the British took little account of French interests. The "Red danger" and "hatred of socialist revolution" dominated the political agenda. Soviet interests and those of France were diverging on almost every point of the compass. For the French government, the mutual assistance pact was merely an insurance policy against a Soviet-German rapprochement.

French policy seemed incomprehensible to Surits because of the government's betrayal of its own national interests, especially in Spain. The only way he could explain it was in the domination of class over national interests, and in French submission to British power, perceived to be the only real protection against Nazi Germany. For France and especially for Britain, it was evident that the Soviet Union would play the decisive role in the struggle against fascism and that the defeat of fascism would lead to the growth of Soviet influence in Europe. At this cost, victory over fascism was undesirable. The French, said Surits, were headed toward "complete capitulation to Hitler and [Benito] Mussolini."[78]

At the end of 1937 the Soviet government was deeply worried about the European situation and about the weakening Franco-Soviet relationship. Ambassador Coulondre warned Paris against the dangers of a Soviet withdrawal from Europe because of the failures of collective security. It was a "long list of disappointments," Litvinov said, and it raised doubts in Moscow about relations with France. Just as important, Coulondre advised that the negative consequences of the purges on the Red Army would correct themselves quickly. Soviet military strength was far from negligible; rearmament was the highest priority, and the Soviet industrial plant was one of the strongest in Europe. The Soviet Union could play an important supporting role (*d'adossement*): its offensive power would be limited by logistical problems but would be important nevertheless to France and Britain. France did not have to like the Stalinist regime, said Coulondre; the entente with the Bolsheviks was not the result of sentimentality, any more than was the French alliance with the tsars. Don't forget, he advised, why in the first place we wanted better relations with the Soviet Union. When we negotiate with people like the Nazis, who habitually brandish a pistol in our faces, it's best not to give the impression that we are denying to ourselves the support of one of our strongest allies. The more so, since if we forfeit Soviet support, Moscow could look to reestablish better ties with Nazi Germany to avoid political isolation.[79]

Coulondre was a French realist. He was a career diplomat who in the 1920s had been a delegate at the failed Franco-Soviet conference of 1926–1927 to settle economic and political differences. In 1926 he became the *sous directeur, Relations commerciales,* the economic and trade section of the Quai d'Orsay. He was closely involved in the trade negotiations under Paul-Boncour which led to the January 1934 Franco-Soviet trade agreement. He then worked to implement a plan for trade credits or a loan to the Soviet Union to solidify political relations. This project was sabotaged by the Banque de France, among others, in January 1936, about the same time a similar project was scuttled in London by Eden.[80] When Alphand asked to be transferred from Moscow, Coulondre was the ideal person to replace him. One of Coulondre's greatest preoccupations was the danger of Soviet policy reversal and a Nazi-Soviet rapprochement.

When Litvinov granted an interview to the French correspondent in Moscow of the influential Paris daily *Le Temps,* he did not need to be as reserved as he might have been with Coulondre, and he was not. He gave a lecture on Hitler's methods, and no one can deny now that he was right. Thus, according to Litvinov, when Hitler declared that he wanted to undo the territorial clauses of the Versailles treaty, he said to the French, all the clauses except Alsace-Lorraine (which was French territory); to the Poles he said, except Danzig and the Polish corridor; and so on. How much confidence could you have in such statements? The Nazis "have renounced nothing, neither Alsace-Lorraine nor any other territories stripped away at Versailles." The French and British governments would perhaps learn. "As for us, we can wait. We are not directly threatened. Germany will not absorb central Europe in a day. We have the time to see what is coming." When the journalist asked Litvinov what he meant, the commissar suggested that "other combinations were possible."

"With Germany?" asked the journalist.

"Why not?" replied Litvinov.

"But . . . is it possible?"

"Perfectly."

Commenting on this interview, Coulondre did not need to add much more than he had already conveyed to Paris: ". . . if the Soviet Union is not with us, it will be against us."[81] This was scarcely the first time that Litvinov had let drop this grenade, or the first time the Anglo-French disregarded it. His line's a "bluff," observed Orme Sargent in 1935; it was the "argument which Litvinov has used all along in order to bring the French Government up to the scratch. . . ."[82] The French had "let themselves be bluffed and dazed by Russian threats and promises."

> If Russia is allowed to dictate to France—and ourselves—the conditions on which we are to carry on its [sic] affairs of Western Europe—and that is what it is rapidly coming to—we may say goodbye to any European settlement. We shall have all our time cut out in pulling the chestnuts out of the fire for M. Litvinoff![83]

VI

The British did not want to pull *French* chestnuts out of the fire either. Anglo-French relations were nearly as strained as relations with the Soviet Union. After the end of the First World War, diverging interests began to separate the two allies. France wanted security against a resurgent Germany and wanted British support to maintain it. Britain had the comfort of the English Channel to provide security against invasion, and sheltered behind the French army. The British government did not wish to see France dominate Europe and therefore welcomed the resurgence of German economic and political strength. The French were insecure and doubted whether they had the force to resist a new German onslaught, let alone dominate Europe. Between 1932 and 1934 when Herriot, Paul-Boncour, and

Barthou headed the French foreign ministry, France pursued a more resolute course for security against Nazi Germany while the British government thought in terms of disarmament and accommodation. The British considered the French to be insensitive and belligerent, but the French thought Britain was shirking, hiding behind the English Channel, and willing to let France carry the main responsibility and risk for security in western Europe. For France, Britain was its main ally; for Britain, France was a sometimes quarrelsome, sometimes timorous associate, to be tolerated because the French army, after all, defended British security interests in Belgium and Holland.

The French high command recognized that the British could not make a serious contribution on the ground, and they wondered how the French army could hold off Nazi Germany on its own.[84] In London, Vansittart warned his superiors repeatedly that the French expected a substantial British army on the continent. "No Frenchman or Belgian," said Vansittart, "would ever accept the proposition that they could do the land fighting and we would, for our own convenience, limit ourselves to air and sea."[85] Lord Stanhope, the under secretary of state for foreign affairs, was unsympathetic: "They want a promise of land forces & this is just what we shall be most unwilling to give."[86] Vansittart warned that England could find itself isolated if Anglo-French relations grew cold.[87] Such warnings had no effect. Neville Chamberlain, who succeeded Baldwin as prime minister in May 1937, opposed the dispatch of large ground forces to France and held back financial resources to expand the British army before 1939.[88]

Implicit in Chamberlain's defense policy was letting someone else do the fighting in Europe, presumably the French, or better, the Russians. In 1936 the British government could send two divisions to France; in 1937 it did not plan to send more than five. "Two, and two more later," Stalin would later facetiously remark.[89] This was a long way from the approximately sixty British divisions on the western front during the First World War. In 1935 Marshal Philippe Pétain reckoned that the British army was for the "parade ground" only, not for fighting in Europe. Gamelin tried to coax the British, but most British generals were disinclined to increase their commitment of ground forces to France. In 1937 the chief of the imperial general staff recognized that the French army could perhaps not fight Germany alone, that it was "apprehensive of the future" and lacked confidence to fight the next war with materiel from the last.[90] Occasional flashes of insight changed nothing: British offers of immediate ground support to France remained limited to two divisions.

French policy was not less "egotistical" and dishonest than the British. Behind its frontier fortifications, the Maginot line, the French army did not plan to take the offensive against Germany for its putative allies, the Soviet Union, Poland, and Czechoslovakia, or to defend Austria.[91] French commanders would only have been embarrassed to be asked by eastern allies about offensive plans, since they had none worthy of the name. According to Gamelin, the army was incapable of taking the offensive. But the French general staff sometimes exaggerated German strength in order to justify doing nothing.[92] "Count every foeman twice, and shirk the fight" puts the position more epigrammatically. The French general staff had no influential innovators to break down hidebound, inflexible thinking. There were few improvisers in the French high command who could think fast on their feet. Everything had to be just so and by the book, though war is full of the unexpected and almost never allows generals to arrange for everything to be just so.[93] Hence, when someone like Mandel said, use the tools you have to fight the Germans, the general staff was incapable of responding. The French government and high command nevertheless expected their allies to fight while France did not.[94] The offensive was a burden for others to bear. "War somewhere else," said the French. The difficulty was that France's eastern allies had no offensive intentions either. Czechoslovakia planned to remain on the defensive in a Franco-German war.[95] Poland's principal defenses faced east, not west, except in 1938 when it threatened hostilities against Czechoslovakia for the Polish share of territorial provender parceled out during the Munich crisis.[96]

Fight to the last Frenchman, the British seemed to say; nothing doing, not us, came the French reply, let the burden fall on the Czechs, Poles, and Russians. Who then would fight against Nazi Germany? Everyone planned that it should be someone else. There was far too much of each-for-himself in France and Britain, but this mentality suited Hitler's plans of dividing his enemies so that he could defeat them one by one.

Anglo-French tensions were exacerbated in the spring and summer of 1936 by the Rhineland crisis, the Popular Front electoral victory, and the outbreak of the Spanish Civil War. Soviet support for the Spanish Republicans created fears among conservatives that Spain could go communist. Hitler constantly played upon these fears not only to aid the Spanish fascists but to cause dissension among his adversaries. The British government was determined to discourage French support for Republican Spain or closer Franco-Soviet cooperation. Nor would the British scruple at interference in internal French politics to prevent a resumption of a strong French policy against Nazi Germany. "We . . . have means of influencing the French Government," Sargent observed, "and British support and approval is still of great value to France."[97] Sargent's willingness to intervene in France became stronger after the outbreak of the Spanish Civil War. "We ought to be able to strengthen the French Government in its efforts—or indeed bring pressure to bear to force it—to free itself from Communist domination, both domestic and Muscovite. Even though this might involve at a certain stage something very like interference in the internal affairs of France. . . ." "By hook or by crook" France had to be kept from " 'going Bolshevik' under the influence of the Spanish civil war. . . ."[98]

The Soviet Union was thus an additional source of Anglo-French friction. Even in the 1920s the French government did not wish to alienate British Tories by becoming too friendly with "the Soviet." And here was an ironic twist and a source of bitterness for some French politicians: while the British did not want France to improve its security through closer relations with the Soviet Union, the British would not give France the military and political support it needed in lieu of closer Franco-Soviet relations.

VII

One way out of these contradictory interests and expectations for both France and Britain was to permit Nazi Germany to expand eastward and/or southeastward. Indeed, on this point there was wide agreement. Sargent put the main argument in 1935: "If . . . we closed to Germany all means of expansion in the east, where she is less likely to come into conflict with British, or indeed any other, interests than elsewhere, we must be prepared for German pressure down the Danube to be increased proportionately." The British ambassador in Berlin, Sir Eric Phipps, warned against putting up too much "barbed wire" in the east or south, lest the Nazi "beast" head west. Sargent agreed: "I have never quite been able to accept the truth of M. Litvinov's dictum about the 'indivisibility of peace.' . . ."[99] In the late 1930s British and French intelligence services assumed that Nazi Germany would first move east. And this prospect did not overly disturb the French and British governments. Baldwin, then Chamberlain, for example, looked with relative equanimity upon the prospect of a Soviet-German conflict. Baldwin told Conservative colleagues in 1936:

> We all know the German desire, and he has come out with it in his book [i.e., Hitler's *Mein Kampf*], to move east, and if he should move East I should not break my heart. . . . There is one danger, of course, which has probably been in all your minds— supposing the Russians and Germans got fighting and the French went in as the allies of Russia owing to that appalling pact they made, you would not feel you were obliged to go and help France, would you? If there is any fighting in Europe to be done, I should like to see the Bolshies and the Nazis doing it."[100]

And there was no change in attitude when Chamberlain became prime minister. He said in cabinet in November 1938: ". . . our attitude would be governed largely by the fact that we did not wish to see France drawn into a war with Germany on account of some quarrel between Russia and Germany, with the result that we should be drawn into war in France's wake."[101] The British Secret Intelligence Service considered the Soviet Union to be the real enemy, and so of course did the French general staff.[102] This anti-Soviet animus led to intelligence estimates that dismissed reports of Soviet military strength. No one wanted to hear about the merits of an unwanted and dangerous Soviet ally. Technical arguments about Red Army shortcomings cloaked the ideologues' anti-communist animosity.[103] It was facile, self-deluded thinking, for once Hitler had glutted himself in the east, he could turn back west with far greater strength, as Churchill, for one, had observed. In view of these Anglo-French prejudices and malevolent ideas—about which Litvinov and his ambassadors were well informed—it might appear remarkable that the Soviet government stuck with collective security for as long as it did. It may be presumed that only Hitler's animosity kept the Soviet Union from considering alternatives to Litvinov's policy. But as the British ambassador, Chilston, pointed out, the Soviet government knew of no better policy and so was left with collective security, however ineffective it might be.[104]

CHAPTER TWO

"Thou Art Weighed in the Balance and Found Wanting"

ON OCTOBER 5, 1938, Winston Churchill, the Tory gadfly and backbencher, rose to speak in the House of Commons debate concerning the government's foreign policy after the Munich conference had dismembered Czechoslovakia. Churchill had for several years opposed the British government's too leisurely rearmament policies and its appeasement of Nazi Germany. He was an extraordinary man: soldier, journalist, historian, politician, and minister of the crown. He also possessed great physical and intellectual courage, and was not afraid to speak out against prevalent opinion. Indeed, the keepers of political orthodoxy had reason to fear him in debate in the House or in the pages of the British press. Churchill was a master of the English language and an eloquent speaker who despised Nazism and Adolf Hitler and condemned the British government for failing to see the obvious danger threatening Europe. He often formulated his metaphors and epigrams in terms of light and darkness, good and absolute evil. His speeches made the prime ministers Stanley Baldwin and Neville Chamberlain and their colleagues on the government front benches cringe in anger or jeer derisively as Churchill's bolts hit their marks. "For five years I have talked to the House on these matters, not with very great success," Churchill said in March 1938 after Hitler's *Anschluss,* the annexation of Austria. "I have watched this famous island descending incontinently, fecklessly, the stairway which leads to a dark gulf. It is a fine broad stairway at the beginning, but after a bit the carpet ends. A little farther on there are only flagstones, and a little farther on still these break beneath your feet. . . ."[1]

When Churchill rose again in the House on October 5, 1938, he was in some ways the avenger of what he saw as Britain's soiled honor. He had suffered from months of helpless observation as events led toward the Czech war crisis in September. Churchill had tried, by virtue of his important network of informants, to warn of Hitler's real intent and to stiffen the government's back to stop Nazi aggression in Czechoslovakia. But Chamberlain considered "Winston" to be no more than a renegade against whom the parliamentary whips had to be on their guard. After opening his speech with some polite comments, Churchill warned the House of his intent: "I will . . . begin by saying the most unpopular and most unwelcome thing . . . what everybody would like to ignore or forget but which must nevertheless be stated, namely, that we have sustained a total and unmitigated defeat. . . ." After running through the main events of the crisis, Churchill lamented: "All is over. Silent, mournful, abandoned, broken Czechoslovakia recedes into the darkness. . . ."

Then came his clear admonition to the government and to the House:

> Our loyal, brave people . . . should know that there has been gross neglect and deficiency in our defences; they should know that we have sustained a defeat without a war, the consequences of which will travel far with us along our road . . . when the whole equilibrium of Europe has been deranged, and [they should know] that the terrible words have for the time being been pronounced against the Western Democracies: 'Thou art weighed in the balance and found wanting.'

Finally there was his penultimate warning: "And do not suppose that this is the end. This is only the beginning of the reckoning. This is only the first sip, the first foretaste of a bitter cup which will be proffered to us year by year unless, by a supreme recovery of moral health and martial vigour, we arise again and take our stand for freedom as in the olden time."[2]

II

In early 1938, on the eve of the great crises of the prewar period, the situation in Europe could not have been worse. The three major powers in a position to deter or stop Nazi Germany were divided by ideological prejudices and by wrongly perceived differences of interest. In France deep internal divisions paralyzed the French government: the line of least resistance was to follow a British lead, *la ligne anglaise,* and appeasement of Nazi Germany. It was not hard to see where this would lead, because Austria and Czechoslovakia appeared to be the German government's immediate targets. French officials gave assurances to the Soviet Union that Franco-Soviet relations were unchanged, but Litvinov and his ambassador in Paris knew better. Delbos, still the French foreign minister, even complained to the Soviet ambassador in February that France was isolated, but Surits could barely refrain from pointing out that the French government had only itself to blame. Who knew what French policy would be tomorrow, Litvinov observed to Coulondre.[3] In the aftermath of *Anschluss,* which the French and British governments could not or would not stop, Potemkin reported that the new French premier—Blum again, though his government would last less than a month—was in a state of panic. And Vansittart in London did not hide from Maiskii his "irritation," but really his anger, toward Chamberlain's appeasement of Nazi Germany.[4]

There was no doubt that Czechoslovakia would be threatened next. With Austria in German hands, Czechoslovakia was surrounded to its waist by German territory, and only the northern frontier was well fortified. The situation looked bad but might still be saved if France and the Soviet Union would cooperate and hold firm. In the days after *Anschluss,* they reaffirmed publicly their commitments of support for Czechoslovakia. Litvinov proposed a multilateral conference to discuss security measures to preserve the peace. But the Soviet government was skeptical of France's determination to honor its treaty obligations. So were the Czechs: France would not move without Britain, observed Stefan Osusky, the Czech minister in Paris, and Britain would not move at all in central and eastern Europe.[5]

On March 14 Churchill in the House of Commons renewed his call for the formation of a "grand alliance" of Britain and France and the states of eastern Europe. If Churchill did not mention the Soviet Union in his speech in the House, it was not far from his mind. He revealed his position to Maiskii a few days later, but first he upbraided him for the horrors of the purges.

"Explain to me, please," he asked Maiskii, "what is going on in your country?" What could Maiskii say? That the revolution had gone mad, devouring its leaders, or that the Soviet Union was filled with traitors? Instead Maiskii offered a rant on Leon Trotskii, Stalin's exiled nemesis and Churchill's "evil genius of Russia." Churchill seemed happy enough to accept the ambassador's explanations, having crossed swords with Trotskii during the Russian civil war, and broken his when Trotskii was commissar for war and drove the British out of Soviet Russia. It is an irony worth noting that Trotskii also advocated a "united front" against Hitler. The former adversaries were much alike in other ways. Both were brave men, unafraid in war and politics; both were renegades and defiant in defeat. Winston would never admit it, but he and Trotskii would have made formidable allies against Nazism.

Churchill was not long off his main preoccupation: "I hate Nazi Germany and I work constantly for the creation of a 'grand alliance.'" For this "we need very badly a powerful Russia . . . but because of recent events, Russia had ceased to be a serious factor in international politics." Then Churchill gushed about Stalin's buildup of Soviet armaments in lines which he would not have used in the House of Commons, though Maiskii may have embellished the saying of them.[6] In any event, Churchill recovered quickly from his discouragement with the purges. He had to, because, as he told Maiskii, without the Soviet Union a grand alliance would not work. He also continued to advise prudence to the Soviet government. If Soviet policy were too aggressive, it would provoke "an explosion of anti-communist feeling" and cause greater difficulties in creating an alliance.[7]

Chamberlain wanted nothing to do with Churchill's grand alliance, and the Foreign Office quickly rejected Litvinov's call for an international conference. Czech suspicions about Chamberlain's indifference toward German eastward expansion were warranted. "You have only to look at the map," Chamberlain wrote to his sister Ida, "to see that nothing that France or we could do could possibly save Czecho-Slovakia from being over-run by the Germans if they wanted to do it." And though Churchill did not mention the Soviet Union, Chamberlain knew it was in the back of the renegade's mind. "Russia is 100 miles away," with no common frontier with Germany or Czechoslovakia. And the Russians were "stealthily and cunningly pulling all the strings behind the scenes to get us involved in war with Germany. . . ."[8] Chamberlain's attitude toward "the Russians" was widespread among conservatives in Britain and France, which meant that the Soviet government had to walk a fine line, though it would never be fine enough for the Anglo-French right. If the Soviet Union was too aggressive, the ideologues would shout that it was a "warmonger," trying to drag Europe into war and communist revolution; if it was too aloof, they would claim that "the Soviet" was bluffing and unreliable. It was not for nothing that Churchill counseled the Soviet government to be prudent.

Unlike Churchill, who believed the Soviet Union was crucial to an anti-Nazi coalition, Chamberlain thought otherwise. Sir Horace Wilson, Chamberlain's main adviser, even told Maiskii that while the prime minister was less "anti-Soviet" than Baldwin, he did not think that Anglo-Soviet relations were either "pressing or practically important." He was therefore little interested in them and quite content to let them drift. According to Wilson, Chamberlain had set his main task as the "appeasement of Europe" through agreements with Italy and Germany. The prime minister fully anticipated German expansion in central and southeastern Europe, even possible German "absorption (in one form or another)" of the small central European and Balkan states. "But he thinks that this is a lesser evil than war with Germany. . . ."[9]

Chamberlain is a central figure in this story, and his name remains entangled in the Anglo-French appeasement of Nazi Germany. Gaunt in appearance and in his late sixties as the Munich crisis began, he looked a little puritanical, dressed in an old-fashioned collar and morning suit. He became British prime minister in 1937 after having been many times a cabinet minister, most recently as chancellor of the exchequer since 1931. He was intelligent, hardworking, and tough. The prime minister would not shirk a fight in the House of Commons when the opposition was looking for blood. One colleague called Neville "an autocrat with the courage of his convictions." No poltroon, Chamberlain pursued the appeasement of Hitler with just such convictions.

The prime minister was intolerant of criticism and carried grudges. He was "a good hater," according to A. J. P. Taylor. Chamberlain despised David Lloyd George, the former Liberal prime minister, and disliked Churchill only a little less. They were both "pirates": "LlG," as Chamberlain wrote in his letters to his sisters, was that "unscrupulous little blackguard," and Winston "the worst of the lot."[10] The prime minister was heavy-handed and obstinate but also good at bureaucratic finesse, going around opposition to his policies. He did this often during the Munich crisis to get what he wanted.

Obstinacy, overconfidence, and a weakness for flattery were shortcomings. Chamberlain was sure that *he* could reason with "Herr Hitler," that he could obtain agreement with him, and that Nazi Germany could be brought around even if other states had to pay the price for it. He dismissed those who warned of catastrophe and wanted to arm to the teeth. He got rid of Vansittart as permanent under secretary at the end of 1937 and relished the victory. "I suspect that in Rome & Berlin the rejoicings will be loud & deep," the implication being that this was all to the good.[11] In the debates over rearmament he held a tight hand over the budget, so that when war came Britain was ill-prepared for it and could send only a handful of divisions to fight in France. When Hitler tried flattery during the Munich crisis, Chamberlain fell for it like a stone. And while Chamberlain was prepared to deal with Hitler, he would not countenance an alliance with Stalin.[12] When it became clear even to the "biassed and blind," as Vansittart put it, that Hitler was out for war and that the Soviet Union was essential to an anti-Nazi coalition, Chamberlain used every maneuver and finesse he knew to prevent the conclusion in 1939 of a war-fighting alliance with the Soviet government. Chamberlain's policies were an inadvertent death wish, which was only barely averted.

III

In the spring of 1938 the Nazi threat to Czechoslovakia raised important logistical questions. Passage of Red Army troops and supplies across Poland and Romania was one such question, because the Soviet Union did not have a common frontier with Czechoslovakia. This "passage" issue was not new; it had been discussed since 1934 without resolution, though from the Polish point of view it had long since been resolved. The Polish government would under no circumstances allow the Red Army across Poland to assist Czechoslovakia against a German invasion. The Romanian position was less categorical and subject to flexibility if France would show firmness in supporting the Czechs. The Romanian king Carol had even said privately to Paul-Boncour and Gamelin in 1936 and 1937 that he would find some way to allow Red Army forces across northern Romania. Edvard Beneš, the Czech president, believed that if France pressed the Romanians to agree to passage rights, it would be decisive in assuring effective assistance to Czechoslovakia and thus in deterring German aggression. But this was just the problem. How can we believe that France will come to our rescue, asked King Carol, when France would not protect its own vital interests against the German occupation of the Rhineland? In April 1938 Soviet confidence in French resolve was also low. As Potemkin assessed the situation, French policy remained "cowardly and passive," and this only made the Czech situation all the more grave.[13]

Litvinov raised the passage issue in May when he met Georges Bonnet, the new French foreign minister in Daladier's cabinet. In what would become a familiar refrain for Bonnet, he asked how the Soviet Union intended to help Czechoslovakia. Litvinov replied that the Soviet government did not have sufficient influence on Poland and Romania to obtain passage of its troops. France would have to intervene. Military staff talks, he added, should be organized to discuss concrete measures to help the Czechs. Bonnet said that the Polish and Romanian governments were adamantly opposed to Red Army passage. As for staff talks, discussions could be conducted by the French military attaché in Moscow. There were no French or Czech general staff officers in Moscow, Litvinov replied.[14]

Georges Bonnet was a major figure in the events leading to Munich and to the outbreak of war in 1939. He was the French Chamberlain in some ways, not as powerful, not as respected, but his name is most closely associated in France with the opprobrious noun *appeasement*. He was of moderate height, a somewhat strange-looking man, twenty years younger than Chamberlain, gangly, with a large nose—to rival Cyrano's, one joker said—and it seemed to throw his head out of balance. He was a Radical but leaned to the right in his party. He won a seat in the Chamber of Deputies in 1924 and was several times a cabinet minister before a brief stint as French ambassador in Washington. After the Blum government fell in April 1938, Bonnet became foreign minister. Incoming premier Daladier chose Bonnet over the incumbent Paul-Boncour because the latter stood for a firm policy against Nazi Germany and confirmation of French treaty obligations to Czechoslovakia, among other items. This aroused opposition in the Chamber of Deputies and in London. The Foreign Office thought Paul-Boncour was dangerous, and Phipps, the British ambassador, now in Paris, lobbied to get rid of him. Bonnet was the right man for the job: he said that France could not support Czechoslovakia without British support. Just so, Chamberlain must have thought.

This was also a relatively popular position in France, if put in the right way. Put in the wrong way, it called into question France's treaty obligations to other countries and French honor, an important commodity in foreign relations if one needed allies, as the French certainly did. Bonnet was the ideal person for this particular job because he was evasive and secretive. He was also talented, up to a point—until his counterparts caught on—at talking out of both sides of his mouth and at working in the shadows. In short, he was an intriguer: his lack of candor made Bonnet an ideal foreign minister for the times, but it also made him the target of great enmity. A lack of courage at critical moments added to the rancor. Bonnet was Mandel's *bête noire*: he considered him a funk and a traitor. "His long nose," said Mandel, "sniffs danger and responsibility from afar. He will hide under any flat stone to avoid it."[15]

Bonnet gathered thorns of opprobrium the way others gather flowers of praise. Churchill said after the war that he was "the quintessence of defeatism, and all his clever verbal manoeuvres had the aim of 'peace at any price.'" Vansittart, in a classic comment in early 1940, noted that "M. Bonnet . . . had better trust to time and oblivion rather than coloured self-defence. He did a lot of really dirty work in 1938. . . . One must always expect a certain amount of sharp practice when great issues are at stake. But if I ever had to play cards with M. Bonnet again I would always run through the pack quickly first, just to make sure that the joker had been removed."[16]

Soviet officials, in particular Litvinov, simply did not believe anything Bonnet said, especially when he talked about French commitments to Czechoslovakia or to the Soviet Union. Bonnet shared the ideological prejudices of the center-right and the right concerning the spread of communism into Europe in the event of war. "Bonnet is absolutely convinced," Phipps reported in September 1939, "that Stalin's aim is still to bring about world revolution. . . ."[17] If France really wanted close ties with the Soviet Union, the first step would have been to dismiss Bonnet.

The meeting in Geneva between Bonnet and Litvinov by no means closed the discussion on two of the major issues of the Czech crisis: passage rights and staff talks. Sergei S. Aleksandrovskii, the Soviet ambassador in Prague, was recalled to Moscow in April for discussions with Stalin, Litvinov, and other members of the Politburo, a measure of the importance which the Soviet government gave to the Czech situation. In a report from Moscow of these discussions, Coulondre emphasized the importance of staff talks, essential if real military assistance was to be offered to Czechoslovakia.[18] The Soviet government, Coulondre advised, had given numerous signs of its willingness to discuss concrete measures of support for Czechoslovakia, and it was their opinion that with France, means would be found to overcome geographical barriers.[19] The key question was, what would France do? Staff talks were a test of French intentions. The Soviet Union was willing to start them; would France agree? No, came the reply. Léger told the Czech minister in Paris, Osusky, that the French government did not wish to proceed further with military conversations because they were a powerful source of conflict between right and left in France.[20] Léger might have added that the French general staff and the Tory government in London adamantly opposed them.

News in the West of the continuing Stalinist purges impeded the defense of Czechoslovakia. Litvinov tried to conduct Soviet foreign policy without noticing them, but in the West the purge trials were most certainly noticed. "There is something rotten—very rotten—in the State of Russia," noted Sir Lancelot Oliphant, assistant permanent under secretary in the Foreign Office: it's "a weak reed to lean on." This was a prevalent view.[21] On the other hand, Coulondre and Colonel Auguste-Antoine Palasse, the French military attaché in Moscow, provided information on the strength of Soviet armed forces, which identified shortcomings in offensive capabilities but generally bespoke of an ally worth having, with a formidable *poten-tiel de guerre*. For providing such information to Paris, Palasse was assailed by his superiors.[22] It proves the old saw that there are none so blind as those who will not see.

On May 19, 1938, a brief war scare developed, and Czechoslo-vakia called up a class of reservists based on what turned out to be erroneous reports of a German military buildup. Czech "defiance" angered Hitler, and soon thereafter he ordered his generals to pre-pare war plans against Czechoslovakia, to be ready for execution at the end of September. "It is my unshakable will," said Hitler, "that Czechoslovakia shall be wiped off the map."[23] This was not immedi-ately known to the French and British governments, though it would scarcely have been startling news. The false alarm frightened them nevertheless, signaling the all too real, imminent possibility of war.

IV

The war scare prompted the French government to sound out Poland about its support, though the Poles had already offered nu-merous indications of their intent. On May 22 Bonnet called in the Polish ambassador in Paris, Juliusz Łukasiewicz, to ask what the Polish policy would be. "We'll not move," replied Łukasiewicz. The Franco-Polish defense treaty included no obligation in the event of war over Czechoslovakia. If France attacked Germany to support the Czech government, then France would be the aggressor. Not ap-parently overreacting to this extraordinary statement, Bonnet then inquired about the Polish attitude toward the Soviet Union, stressing the importance of Soviet support, given Polish "passiveness." Łukasiewicz was equally categorical: "the Poles considered the Rus-sians to be enemies . . . [we] will oppose by force, if necessary, any Russian entry onto [our] territory including overflights by Russian aircraft." Czechoslovakia, Łukasiewicz added, was unworthy of French support.[24]

If Bonnet had any doubts that the Polish ambassador was not ac-curately representing his government's views, these were quickly put to rest by Field Marshal Edward Śmigły-Rydz. He told the French ambassador in Warsaw, Léon Noël, that the Poles considered Russia, no matter who governed it, to be "Enemy No. 1." "If the German remains an adversary, he is not less a European and a man of order; for Poles, the Russian is a barbarian, an Asiatic, a corrupt and poisonous element, with which any contact is perilous and any compromise, lethal." According to the Polish government, aggressive action by France, or the movement of Soviet troops, say even across Romania, could prompt the Poles to side with Nazi Germany. This would suit many Poles, reported Noël: they "dream of conquests at the expense of the USSR, exaggerating its difficulties and counting on its collapse." France had better not force Poland to choose between Russia and Germany, because their choice, according to Noël, could easily be guessed.[25] As Daladier put it to the Soviet ambassador, "Not only can we not count on Polish support, but we have no faith that Poland will not strike [us] in the back." Polish loyalty was in doubt even in the event of direct German aggression against France.[26]

Although French officials often pointed out to the Poles that they had an interest in supporting Czechoslovakia and in resisting German aggression against it, the Poles saw matters otherwise. Their attitude toward the Czechs was hostile and covetous: Czechoslovakia was an unviable state and a nesting ground for communists. It held the district of Teschen, which the Poles claimed as irredenta. The likely German offensive against Czechoslovakia seemed an opportune time to settle old scores and to seize Teschen.[27] In April the French ambassador in Berlin, André François-Poncet, told the Soviet chargé d'affaires that Poland was "clearly helping Germany" in its anti-Czech activities. The ambassador threw up his hands in a gesture of helplessness—but was the French government really so helpless?[28]

At the end of May the Poles let it be known that there was no possibility of saving Czechoslovakia and that they would not tie their hands regarding Teschen.[29] Litvinov instructed Surits to warn the French government of Polish intentions. "We would want to know in advance if France, in the event our decision to prevent the intervention of Poland, considers itself bound to Poland by virtue of the Franco-Polish treaty of alliance."[30] The Soviet chargé d'affaires, Girshfel'd, met Bonnet on June 7 to carry out Litvinov's instructions: "The Soviet government," he said, "expects a clear answer." After avoiding one, Bonnet said he would get back to him. The issue had to be "studied." Bonnet was pessimistic, having read Noël's report

of his meeting with Śmigły-Rydz.[31] Girshfel'd saw Bonnet a week
later, and this time received an answer to Litvinov's question: the
French government would consider itself released from its obligations under the Franco-Polish alliance if Poland attacked Czechoslovakia.[32]

French mistrust of Poland was long-standing, and French officials sometimes said they would take a hard line if necessary. "If
Poland does not want to follow France into a military alliance with
the Soviets . . . *eh bien,* we will do without [Poland]," said General
Maxime Weygand in 1933. "We will count on Russia, and not
bother any more about Poland," rejoined foreign minister Barthou
in 1934. *Tant pis pour la Pologne*—tough luck for Poland, said
Chief of Staff Gamelin in 1938, if the Polish government sided with
the Nazis in a war against Czechoslovakia.[33] When the crisis came,
the French government could not follow such sound opinion. It did
not do so because, as Ambassador Noël warned, if France insisted
on Soviet passage rights, or if it denounced the Franco-Polish alliance, Poland would move into Hitler's camp. Coulondre noted that
the Anglo-Franco-Soviet alliance would win a war against Nazi Germany, but Poland would be crushed by the Red Army and Soviet influence would extend into central Europe, perhaps into Germany or
even into France itself.[34] Fear of victory paralyzed the French as
much as fear of defeat. And of course the Poles played upon French
fears. This is why in May Bonnet avoided giving a direct answer
when Litvinov asked for French intervention to secure Red Army
passage rights across Poland and Romania.

V

These consultations between the French and their putative allies may
have been little more than theatre. On April 28–29 Daladier and
Bonnet had met in London with Chamberlain and other members of
the British government. After putting up a strong argument against
Chamberlain's position, Daladier concluded by accepting it. There
would be no Anglo-French military defense of Czechoslovakia; the
Czech government would have to secure what terms it could from
Germany, with the help of the British.[35] The British government pursued this policy throughout the summer with French acquiescence,

sending a mission to Prague under former cabinet minister Edward Lord Runciman at the beginning of August to mediate a settlement between the German population in the Sudetenland and the Czech government.

Daladier's name has already appeared several times in this story. He was premier during the Munich crisis and throughout 1939, and he played a major role in the formation of French foreign policy in this critical period. He was less conniving than Bonnet and better respected, and to people who knew him only slightly or through the press he had a reputation for decisiveness which events proved to be undeserved. He was short, stocky, bullnecked, and not an unpleasant-looking man. He had physical courage, having fought in the First World War, winning a field commission and citations.

Daladier rose quickly through the ranks of the Radical party in the 1920s, leaning left with Radical Young Turks and willing to work with the Socialists. In the 1930s he moved to the center-right, and some people believed he could fill the shoes of Georges Clemenceau to lead the nation against Germany. He held many cabinet posts, including minister of defense, and had already been premier twice in 1933–1934 before taking the job again in April 1938. Daladier was known affectionately as "Dala," also as the "Bull of the Vaucluse," the electoral district he represented. According to Chamberlain, he was a "bull with a snail's horns." Someone else said he was not a bull but a hesitating cow. He often appeared strong at the outset, only to give way later as he had done in London in April when he met Chamberlain and the British. Daladier was not to be counted on in a fight over "high politics," though few French politicians of this period were of stronger mettle. For lower forms of politics, Daladier was better suited: he was obsessed, some said, with *combinarderies politiciennes,* or backroom dealing.[36]

Daladier inclined toward conciliation of Nazi Germany, though he sometimes talked tough. He considered Britain to be France's main ally, and he shared the ideological prejudices of the French center and right against the Soviet Union. He opposed the strengthening of the Franco-Soviet mutual assistance pact, opposed staff talks with the Soviet high command, and opposed Red Army passage rights across Poland or Romania to strike at the enemy. In September 1938 Daladier pleaded with the German chargé d'affaires in Paris, of all people, that war would ruin France and Germany alike. After the fighting, "revolution, irrespective of victors or vanquished, was as certain in France as in Germany and Italy. Soviet Russia would not let the opportunity pass of bringing world revolution to our lands. . . ." Cossacks, Daladier later lamented to the American ambassador in Paris, "Cossacks will rule Europe."[37] Some historians calculate that the French premier strongly favored a Soviet alliance in 1939, though the evidence does not support this position, as readers shall see. Neither Bonnet nor Daladier was the right man to strengthen ties with the Soviet Union as the Nazi peril grew.

The weak Anglo-French position on Czechoslovakia did not go unnoticed. Maiskii reported a conversation with his Czech counterpart, Jan Masaryk, on August 6, in which the latter complained bitterly of heavy British pressure on the Czech government to make "the maximum number of concessions to the Sudeten Germans." Almost every week the foreign secretary, Lord Halifax, called in Masaryk to demand new concessions, greater speed in negotiations, and the rapid conclusion of an agreement. Nearly every fortnight Masaryk was obliged to fly to Prague to deliver new British demands for concessions.[38] In a meeting two days later, on August 8, with Oliphant, the assistant permanent under secretary, Maiskii observed that "all the actions of British diplomacy in Czechoslovakia were directed not at bridling aggression, but at bridling the victims of aggression." Oliphant tried to defend the position but without great conviction, admitting that Maiskii's analysis of British policy was widely shared in Europe.[39] A week later Maiskii conveyed the same message to Halifax. The Soviet Union was greatly alarmed, he said, by Anglo-French policy that was "weak and nearsighted" and would only encourage further aggression. Responsibility for a new world war would lie squarely with the Western powers. The Anglo-French spoke loudly in Prague about the need for concessions and softly in Berlin where Hitler "ignored all their démarches." To Maiskii's surprise, so he said, Halifax made no attempt to defend British policy.[40]

Similarly the Czech minister in Paris, Stefan Osusky, warned that the settlement of the Sudeten problem could become the object of trade-offs between France, Britain, and Germany at the expense of Czechoslovakia. "The British and French, in as much as they are supporting and defending us, will arrogate to themselves the right to recommend to us how we in Czechoslovakia must decide the [Sudeten] question. This is why we should expect British and French pressure on Czechoslovakia to become even greater . . . , the more Germany conditions a return to political negotiations with France and England on a settlement of the Sudeten question."[41]

The French fared no better than the British in the eyes of Czech and Soviet diplomats. Indeed, Surits saw Munich coming. The French and British were not disposed, he said in July 1938, to defend Czechoslovakia. The British wanted to obtain by negotiations from the Czechs what Hitler wanted to take by force. The French government recognized that if it could not stop the seizure of the Sudeten borderlands, Nazi Germany would take the strategic advantage in any future war and a hegemonic position in central Europe. In France there was no disagreement on this point—disagreement came in what to do about it. A large majority of the French did not think they had sufficient military and economic strength to act on their own to stop Hitler in Czechoslovakia. Hence the French needed allies, and here, according to Surits, began all the great divisions within the French government and French opinion.

"Simple logic" would suggest the Soviet Union as a natural ally, and this view was held by a range of opinion from the French Communists to cabinet minister Paul Reynaud on the right. The Soviet Union, according to Reynaud, had what Britain did not have, and which was essential in any war with Nazi Germany: powerful land and air forces. And yet in the calculation of its Czech policy, the French government counted least on the Soviet Union. It had not once consulted the Soviet Union before important decisions and only reported them after the fact, and then not always. In spite of its mutual assistance pacts with the USSR and with Czechoslovakia, the French government had never requested joint discussions of defense issues. Surits explained the French position as a result of British influence. While not attacking the Franco-Soviet pact directly, the British held that it should not be overplayed because it could complicate peace initiatives. Even though Daladier himself, according to all of Surits's informants, had a sound appreciation of Soviet military strength, in the last analysis he would not alienate the British for the sake of the Soviet Union.

Mandel and Reynaud, who stood for a stronger French policy, went to see Surits and encouraged the ambassador to threaten Daladier with a withdrawal of Soviet support in order to smarten him up. But Surits did not think such tactics would work since Daladier counted only on the British as a real ally. The Soviet ambassador was discouraged:

> When you look carefully here at the press . . . when you observe this panicky fear mixed with awe of German force and German "power" [*Macht*], when day in and day out you are witness to an endless showing of heels, to concessions, to the gradual loss of independence in foreign policy, when, finally, you see, with each new day, how the voice of fascism rises and becomes more impudent, one cannot help but feel a terrible foreboding.

To all this, said Surits, he must add the daily course of joyless relations with the French. With regard to the acquisition of war supplies, Daladier promised deliveries and his *apparat* sabotaged and delayed. And the French fear of anything carrying a Soviet seal on it had grown to such an extent that the Bibliothèque nationale, the national library in Paris, had even refused an exhibit of Soviet books.[42]

The Czech foreign minister, Kamil Krofta, also was none too charitable toward the French or the British in discussions with the Soviet ambassador Aleksandrovskii. He did not like British pressure for concessions to Germany. But what do you want? he asked: "little Czechoslovakia" cannot risk a rupture with Britain. "And what will Czechoslovakia do, if France also betrays it?" According to Aleksandrovskii, Krofta singled out Bonnet for special contempt.

> Bonnet is a frightful coward, a narrow French petty bourgeois. He all the time declares formally that France will fulfil its obligations and will go to the aid of Czechoslovakia in case of an attack on it. But this same Bonnet takes fright at the least incident and constantly reiterates that the responsibility for a military clash must fall on Czechoslovakia and that therefore it must do everything possible to avoid even the shadow of such a responsibility. If it were only Bonnet who said that the French would support Czechoslovakia, then Krofta quite simply would not believe it. Fortunately, this [affirmation] had been confirmed by others in France.[43]

Unfortunately it would soon become evident that these other assurances were as worthless as those of Bonnet.

And yet Litvinov still tried to organize resistance to Nazi aggression. In June he was optimistic that France would consider itself released from its treaty obligations if Poland attacked Czechoslovakia. This was a position that Coulondre had confirmed—though he did not yet have instructions to do so—in a three-way conversation with Litvinov and Zdeněk Fierlinger, the Czech ambassador, at a diplomatic reception in Moscow on June 9. Litvinov thought that Poland should be given a warning "not to play with fire." According to Fierlinger, their conversation was noticed especially by journalists and German diplomats.[44]

But Litvinov was easily worried by French irresolution. Only a few weeks later (on July 12), he called in Coulondre to ask again about the French position in case of a Polish attack on Czechoslovakia. Coulondre was surprised by the question, and Litvinov replied that his query was related to the hypothesis that France would not consider itself obligated to assist Czechoslovakia. As Coulondre had noted before, this question was related to another hypothesis, that the Soviet Union was contemplating intervention to aid Czechoslovakia, even if France should stand aside. Coulondre thought this an unlikely possibility, but he also noted that Litvinov did not ask idle questions. "This is a man who is direct . . . and comes to the point." If he's asking, it's because the Soviet government is also asking, which could explain, added Coulondre, Red Army troop concentrations in the western Ukraine.[45]

Coulondre respected Litvinov: earlier that spring he had recorded how impressed he was by the commissar's "realism" and by "the moderation of his tone." "One has the impression that here the situation is viewed with seriousness and *sang-froid* and that party considerations are subordinated to reasons of state." Later in the summer Coulondre went out to Litvinov's dacha to discuss foreign policy issues, and in particular Soviet-Romanian relations, since Romanian consent for Red Army passage was vital to the defense of Czechoslovakia. Litvinov agreed with Coulondre that the Soviet government should make a greater effort to improve relations with Romania, but it worked both ways. Actions speak louder than words, said Litvinov: Romania had put itself in the train of the Polish government, which was serving as a procurer for Nazi Germany.[46]

Coulondre's reports had no influence on French policy, though when Bonnet received alarming intelligence about Nazi military intentions, he was quick to ask what the Soviet Union intended to do. In one such case at the end of July, Coulondre replied that the Soviet government made no secret of its analysis of the situation. The aggressor states were "carnivores" who would attack other weaker states. "We should recognize," said Coulondre, "that if they [the Soviet government] are maladroit, exasperating . . . sometimes . . . , the Soviets are realists, they look at things directly, they see states the way they are and not the way they would want them to be." As for the latest alarming intelligence report, Litvinov shrugged, saying he had been giving such warnings for a long time.

Draw the bayonet, said Litvinov, as the Czechs had done in May, and the situation might take another direction. Hitler was bluffing and preparing a vast theatre production of threats and military demonstrations to induce France and Britain to surrender.

But calling Hitler's bluff might lead to war, said Coulondre.

It's possible, replied Litvinov, but we need to face the crisis with a united front and brave hearts.[47]

This conversation took place a few days before a serious military confrontation between Soviet and Japanese armed forces on the Manchurian frontier. The Red Army had the better of the fighting. Had the French and British governments been looking for evidence of Soviet resolve and military capability, here it was.[48]

VI

Unfortunately the French and British were not looking for such evidence; they were looking for a way to avoid war with Nazi Germany at the price of Czechoslovakia. Maiskii met Sir Horace Wilson in early September and found him in a discouraged and pessimistic mood. He was not as confident, Maiskii noticed, as he had been in the spring about achieving quick agreements with Hitler and Mussolini. "These dictators," Wilson remarked, "are very difficult people." So much so that Wilson was "very nearly in a panic," not knowing what "trouble" to expect next from Hitler. "And from this derived Wilson's readiness to pay off Germany at any price." Maiskii pointed to the danger of a Nazi *Mittel Europa* if Czechoslovakia fell, a greater danger for France and Britain, he observed, than for the Soviet Union. Wilson avoided saying it, but Chamberlain did not believe this hypothesis to be true. He thought the Soviet Union had the most to fear from Nazi eastward expansion, and this prospect did not trouble the prime minister. In any event, Wilson doubted whether Britain should challenge Hitler now because of an uncertain hypothetical danger a few years into the future. The prospects looked "frightening" to Wilson, and he went on about them at some length.[49] This could not have been encouraging news in Moscow, though it was certainly no surprise.

Nor was the news much better from the French. Perhaps it was theatre, perhaps it was nervousness or funk, but Bonnet kept pressing about what the Soviet Union intended to do to support Czechoslovakia. Bonnet's pressing set off an important series of meetings in late August and early September which remains to this day a source of controversy. It started at the end of August as the Czech crisis headed toward its dénouement. The German ambassador in Moscow, Friedrich Werner von der Schulenberg, went to see Litvinov on a visit of protocol but really for important business. Schulenberg raised the issue of the Czech crisis and asked about British, French, and Soviet intentions. "I replied firmly to him," Litvinov recorded, "that the Czech people, to the last man, will fight for their independence, that France in the event of a German attack on Czechoslovakia would march against Germany, that England, whether Chamberlain liked it or not, could not leave France without support, and we also will fulfill our obligations to Czechoslovakia."[50] Krofta reported Litvinov's statement to his ambassadors in London and Paris, whence Bonnet heard about it. He then directed Payart, the French chargé d'affaires in Moscow, because Coulondre was on leave, to ask for clarification from Litvinov.[51]

Payart saw Potemkin for this purpose on August 29. The deputy commissar replied that Litvinov "considered it expedient" to offer his view on the likely consequences of a German attack on Czechoslovakia. Potemkin discreetly avoided reference to Litvinov's remark concerning British support whether Chamberlain liked it or not. As Payart put it, Litvinov merely confirmed his long-standing position. When Payart expressed the hope that Hitler would not provoke a war over Czechoslovakia, Potemkin responded that Hitler's position would be based on a calculation of the likely opposition to his plans. This too had long been Litvinov's view.[52]

Bonnet received still more indications of the increasing gravity of the Czech situation, and again, following the now-familiar pattern, instructed Payart to see Litvinov to ask what the Soviet Union proposed to do. Bonnet advised that the French ambassador in Berlin had informed the German government that if it attacked Czechoslovakia, France would honor its commitments. Increased German military preparations suggested an attack sometime in September. What could the Soviet government do in view of the fact that the Polish and Romanian governments would not grant passage rights to the Red Army? "In spite of all his efforts," Bonnet had not succeeded in obtaining positive replies, while the Polish government was categorical that it would stop any attempt at passage. On September 1 Payart put all this to Potemkin, who made no comment except to say that he would forward the information to higher authority.[53]

The following day, September 2, Payart saw Litvinov to make Bonnet's official inquiry. According to Litvinov's record of the meeting, he replied that France was obligated to assist the Czechs independent of any Soviet action. Since Soviet support was conditional on that of France, the Soviet government had more of a right to ask what France intended to do. Litvinov said that if France backed Czechoslovakia, the Soviet Union would fulfill its obligations with the utmost determination, using every possible avenue of support. In the event that Poland and Romania raised difficulties, Romania at least might alter its position if the League of Nations pronounced a judgment against German aggression. Since the process might be slow, the League should be alerted at once, so that if aggression occurred, the question would be addressed quickly. Even if there were no unanimous decision, the moral effect of a majority decision could be considerable, especially if Romania voted with the majority. As for concrete military assistance to Czechoslovakia, the issues should be addressed by a meeting of the general staffs of the Soviet Union, France, and Czechoslovakia. We are ready to participate in such talks, said Litvinov.

It was necessary, Litvinov added, to do everything possible to prevent a military conflict. After *Anschluss*, Litvinov reminded Payart, the Soviet Union had proposed a conference of interested powers. It considered that such a conference now, including Britain, France, and the Soviet Union, might gain the moral support of the

American president Franklin Roosevelt and would have the best chance of discouraging Hitler from further adventures. But the parties must act quickly before Hitler committed himself.[54]

Payart's account of the meeting largely corresponded with Litvinov's but added an interesting detail. Romanian foreign minister Nicolae Petrescu-Comnen had recently informed his Czech counterpart Krofta that while the Romanian government would object to the passage of Soviet ground forces, "it would close its eyes to overflights of its territory." Comnen later confirmed this position. And while Payart's first cable to Paris did not mention Litvinov's proposal for staff talks, a following cable (published only as a footnote in the *Documents diplomatiques français*), inexplicably dated two days later, added this crucial point. Had Payart simply forgotten to include it in his first record of conversation? Litvinov worried that Payart might not convey the message accurately, and he therefore asked Surits to report its contents directly to Bonnet. Indeed, he feared that Payart was looking for an evasive or negative reply in order to lay any responsibility for failure on the Soviet government.[55] Bonnet undoubtedly was, but not Payart.

Surits informed the Narkomindel that he had learned "from a very solid source" that any time staff talks were discussed in the French cabinet, British opposition was always raised as an obstacle. One minister, whose name Surits did not know but suspected was Camille Chautemps, indicated that British officials had given him the definite impression that the British government "most of all" feared Soviet intervention in European affairs because the success of Soviet arms "could pave the way to communism in central Europe." Nevertheless, at the last meeting of the French cabinet, Surits reported, a group of ministers had insisted "that contact be established with us, and that as a result of their pressure came Payart's démarche." "I fully acknowledge that having made this démarche under pressure, Bonnet secretly calculated that we would give a negative reply, or in any case an answer useful for arming him with reasons against contact. This is why I really welcome Litvinov's reply, and I ask authorization to notify some other members of Cabinet of it."[56]

It should be no surprise that Soviet diplomats did not trust Bonnet; many people in France did not trust him either, and this included cabinet ministers Mandel and Reynaud. From London,

Maiskii reported having seen the French ambassador Charles Corbin, who knew nothing about Litvinov's meeting with Payart. Strange, thought Maiskii, in view of normal French loquaciousness. There was nothing in the British press either, which led Maiskii to suspect that the French government wished to keep the meeting quiet to minimize its political effect.

On September 3 Corbin complained to Maiskii that the lack of clarity and firmness in British declarations regarding Czechoslovakia only increased the possibility of war. In Berlin they were convinced, said Corbin, that Britain and France would not stand in the way of a German military operation. But Corbin repeated that France would fulfill its obligations in the event of war.[57]

It is not clear whether Maiskii acted on instructions, but within twenty-four hours of receiving the record of the Litvinov-Payart meeting, he passed news of it to Churchill. In fact, Churchill published in *The Gathering Storm* a copy of his letter to Halifax describing the meeting, "from an absolutely sure source," which accurately noted Litvinov's main points to Payart. "I considered the declarations of M. Litvinov so important," wrote Churchill, that he wanted to be certain that Halifax was informed.[58] Litvinov's declarations were important, but they did not circulate easily. Labour leader Hugh Dalton described this affair in his memoirs. He noted that Halifax demurred in response to Churchill's letter. And he concluded that "It was a very grave matter that Bonnet should have lied to British Ministers about Russian intentions"—and, Dalton might have added, to his own people as well.[59] But this is getting a little ahead of the story.

Payart must have wanted to confirm Litvinov's statements of September 2 because he went back to see Potemkin three days later, the commissar having left for Geneva. Payart went through Litvinov's various proposals, and Potemkin confirmed each one with respect to League action and its purpose, a multilateral conference, and staff talks. In addition, Payart asked what the Soviet government would do in the event of a Polish attack on Czechoslovakia. We have no treaty obligation to the Czech government in this eventuality, said Potemkin, but "we would not thereby deny ourselves the right to take this or that decision at our discretion if Poland attacks Czechoslovakia."[60]

Payart does not appear to have reported this further conversation with Potemkin, though he did send a dispatch giving Litvinov's more complete statement to Schulenberg concerning the likely result of a German attack on Czechoslovakia. "It's not for love of the Czechs that [France, Britain, and the Soviet Union] will fight," said Litvinov, "but for reasons of . . . influence and balance of power. In regard to the Soviet Union, it had no role in the creation of the Czech state, but it must now oppose any growth in strength of Hitlerite Germany which is driven by motives of aggression and a readiness to resort to use of force." Payart concluded that Czechoslovakia was one of the "external bastions of the Soviet Union." "The Soviet interest in defending it appears to be the best guarantee of the sincerity of its intentions."[61]

This dispatch was not received by the *Direction politique,* the political directorate of the Quai d'Orsay, until September 20. Although it is doubtful whether Payart's report would have made any difference, the *Direction politique* on September 6 circulated a note concluding that Litvinov had been "evasive" with Payart, hiding behind "procedural arguments." It made a "bad impression," said the Quai d'Orsay note. These are puzzling conclusions based on Payart's cables. In any event, the *Direction politique* concluded that more information was needed, and it acknowledged that the Soviet embassy in Paris had received information from "certain Parisian milieux" and from foreign diplomatic sources that "France was not resolved to go to war with Germany in defense of Czechoslovakia." Because of the French government's refusal to enter into staff conversations with the Red Army high command, "the Soviets have . . . towards us a certain mistrust which can explain, if not justify, a reserve which is no longer appropriate in the present circumstances." Here was an understatement worthy of the finest traditions in French diplomacy.[62]

The French were not in a strong position to persuade the Soviet government of their commitment to the Czechs. The Czech president, Beneš, advised Aleksandrovskii that the French and British were applying "frantic pressure [for further concessions] with direct threats of leaving Czechoslovakia to the mercy of Hitler." And Chilston told Potemkin that the French, in his opinion, were "not at all disposed to fight."[63] Here was British effrontery at its worst, since *Chamberlain* was "not at all disposed to fight."

But discussions continued. Coulondre, back in Moscow after

leave, saw Potemkin on September 11; the same day Bonnet met Litvinov in Geneva. He recognized that the Soviet government was unhappy with the lack of French independence from the British, and that it doubted French loyalty to its treaty obligations. So the ambassador sought to clear the air. He would not deny the importance of French relations with Britain, but this did not mean that France would sacrifice Czechoslovakia and the Soviet Union for the sake of its relations with Britain. Unfortunately Payart's cable concerning his meeting with Litvinov put the emphasis on diplomatic measures, and this created some concern in Paris. Coulondre affirmed that French determination to support Czechoslovakia was unshakable and that such support might be necessary in the coming days. In these circumstances it was essential that there be no misunderstandings between France and the Soviet Union.

Potemkin reiterated the three points of Litvinov's meeting with Payart, to wit: League action with a view to obtaining at least tacit Romanian support for Red Army passage rights; an Anglo-Franco-Soviet conference and joint declaration warning Germany against an attack on Czechoslovakia; and general staff conversations. To this Potemkin added that there should be no doubt about Soviet determination "to fulfil, together with France, all its obligations according to the Soviet-Czech pact 'with the use of all means available to us for this purpose.' "

Only a careless interpretation of Litvinov's statement, said Potemkin, could lead anyone to think that it was evasive or unclear. Coulondre admitted that his first impression had been mistaken, and he hoped a meeting between Bonnet and Litvinov in Geneva would further clarify the situation. According to Potemkin, Coulondre stated that France was fully prepared for staff talks.[64]

Coulondre's account of this meeting contains some differences. Litvinov's three-point plan is clearly laid out. But Potemkin's fourth point concerning Soviet determination to fulfill its obligations, along with France, is not repeated. Coulondre attributed strained Franco-Soviet relations to the Comintern, and no doubt Potemkin had heard this refrain so many times that he did not bother to record it. Coulondre's statement, according to Potemkin's account, that France was ready for staff talks does not appear in Coulondre's report. Coulondre came away with a favorable impression of the meeting; Potemkin was friendly and encouraging, though the acting commissar did not record his personal view. Coulondre urged Bonnet to move quickly to work out with the Soviet government the details of collaboration, not just in the present crisis but in the longer term to check the eastward expansion of Nazi Germany.[65]

While Bonnet had a tin ear to Coulondre's advice, it was deaf when he saw Litvinov in Geneva. According to Litvinov, Bonnet declared that the British had rejected Litvinov's call for a trilateral conference, and that he did not know what the British were doing in Berlin to avert war. When Bonnet advised that Halifax had informed the French government that Britain had no obligations toward Czechoslovakia, he threw up his hands: "He says it's impossible to do anything." Litvinov reported that Bonnet made no proposals, ". . . and I also was reserved."

Bonnet did tell Litvinov about Comnen's reiteration—which in the circumstances was good news—that while the Romanian government would not permit the passage of the Red Army, the overflight of Soviet aircraft was another matter. "If Soviet aircraft fly high over Romania, then they will not be seen." Romania was checked on this question only by Polish objections. "When Bonnet said to the Polish envoy [Łukasiewicz] that if Poland does not want . . . to help Czechoslovakia, then at least do not hinder Romania; the ambassador gave me to understand, that Poland on this point will not agree, and that Romania without its consent can make no decision." Bonnet thought Poland might change its position, said Litvinov, "but this song we have heard for a long time." And Litvinov reported another French song: "Bonnet confirms that France has not put nor will put any pressure on Czechoslovakia."[66] This was untrue.

Bonnet's account of the meeting reflects Litvinov's reserve, though the commissar repeated the Soviet position described in his meeting with Payart. When Bonnet asked about the importance of Soviet air and ground support, Litvinov replied that this should be discussed in staff talks. Bonnet concluded that the Soviet Union would subordinate its action to League approval and the consent of Romania, and that this would provide the Soviet Union with an escape clause at the moment when France had committed itself. Bonnet's conclusions are surprising, first because Litvinov did not lock himself into the League framework; he saw League action as a strategy, among others, to bring Romania on side, which Comnen suggested was possible.[67] Second, Bonnet had not the slightest intention of committing France to support the Czechs, so there was no chance of the Soviet Union running out since France and Britain had already done so. Moreover, in Bonnet's account of his meeting with Comnen, the latter confirmed that Romania would take a few badly aimed potshots at Soviet planes, and that would be that. But Comnen reiterated that Romania was hindered in what it could do by Poland, which held the keys to support in the east for Czechoslovakia.[68] One other point is worth making: Litvinov was far more reserved with Bonnet than Potemkin and Coulondre had been with each other. And this divergence no doubt can be explained by Coulondre's greater interest in Franco-Soviet cooperation. As for Potemkin, it is inconceivable that he would have been so positive *according to his own record* without the approval of higher authority.

The atmosphere in Geneva was giddy with the prospects of war. "The League is now really only an anti-dictator club," recorded the well-connected Tory M.P. Henry Channon. "The bar and lobbies of the League's building are full of Russians and Jews who intrigue with and dominate the press, and spend their time spreading rumours of approaching war, but I don't believe them, not with Neville at the helm. He will wriggle out somehow." Channon spoke of lavish parties, as though they would be the last before war broke out, much like the grand ball before the Battle of Waterloo. The League was a "racket" and Litvinov "the dread intriguer," though not "so evil as Maisky." Better hope for world war, Litvinov was overheard to tell the Spanish Republican premier, otherwise, "you're fucked."[69]

Coulondre soon learned of the failure of the Bonnet-Litvinov meeting and confidentially informed Fierlinger, his Czech counterpart. It must be a misunderstanding, thought Coulondre, in view of Potemkin's statement of the same day to him. Fierlinger then went to see Potemkin, who thought there was no misunderstanding but rather a deliberate "game" by Bonnet. Fierlinger asked Potemkin to repeat the Soviet government's earlier commitment, and he did so.[70] Coulondre cabled Paris that, according to Litvinov, Bonnet had rejected the Soviet proposals, and that, according to Potemkin's statement to Fierlinger, France did not want Soviet collaboration. But Coulondre believed Bonnet's account of the meeting rather than the Soviet's, and asked that Prague be warned. The question of staff talks must be addressed "without delay," Coulondre advised, in order to dissipate any ambiguity.[71] Apparently the French ambassador did not understand, or did not say, that Bonnet's reserve had prompted Litvinov's mistrust and thus the commissar's own reticence. No doubt Litvinov's reserve played into Bonnet's hands. Had he gone further, however, Litvinov would have played into the hands of the French appeasement press, always ready to accuse the Soviet Union of wanting war to promote ruin and revolution. Soviet diplomats could not win: either they were shirkers or warmongers. Potemkin concluded that "the French continue to play the fool."[72]

No doubt Bonnet played the fool of a sort, but not Coulondre or Payart, who did what they could to improve the situation. In the aftermath of the Munich conference, Maiskii reported to Moscow that he had learned from Swedish sources that Payart had immediately reported his conversation with Litvinov and expected instructions from Paris. But Payart never received the instructions, nor even an acknowledgment of his report. Payart was beside himself and told the Swedish minister in Moscow that Bonnet "was clearly trying to hide the contents of the conversation from members of the French government." Not only from them, added Maiskii, but also from French diplomats abroad: "I was astonished to learn" that Corbin, for example, was unaware of the Payart-Litvinov meeting five days after it had occurred.[73]

Czech diplomats had a better sense of the respective positions of Bonnet and Litvinov. "From a competent source," Masaryk reported that Bonnet had apparently told the British ambassador in Paris that it was "necessary to preserve the peace even if Czechoslovakia had to be sacrificed." "France is neither ready nor willing to fight." Masaryk's report was accurate: Bonnet made this statement to the British ambassador on September 13. Phipps said Bonnet "seems completely to have lost his nerve." The Czech minister in Berlin drew a similar conclusion: "Peace will be saved, but Czechoslovakia will be sold." Fierlinger, on the other hand, noted that Soviet policy was based on the position that concessions to aggressor states only created the impression of weakness and whetted the aggressors' appetite for more.[74]

Litvinov drew his own conclusions. On September 14 in Geneva he saw Herriot and Paul-Boncour, the architects of the Franco-Soviet rapprochement. Litvinov repeated his statement to Payart about which his colleagues were "apparently insufficiently briefed." Herriot was extremely pessimistic, according to Litvinov: "he spoke confidentially about the weakness of France ... and even about the difficulty for it to play the role of a great power." The conclusion was unavoidable: "There is no doubt that Czechoslovakia will be sold out, the only question is whether Czechoslovakia will be reconciled to it."[75] Fierlinger heard from Potemkin about this meeting: "Herriot and Paul-Boncour were surprised by the positive and firm position of the USSR. ... Bonnet has hidden everything. ..."[76]

VII

Early on September 15, 1938, Chamberlain and Horace Wilson flew to Berchtesgaden to negotiate with Hitler about the fate of Czechoslovakia. Chamberlain had discussed his mission with neither the French nor the Czechs, but he agreed to the principle of the cession of Czech territory to Nazi Germany. Soviet alarm at this development made its way into the Moscow rumor mill and then into the newspapers. Coulondre reported that the Soviet government feared a four-power pact (Britain, France, Germany, Italy) directed against it. Rumors were being put about in Moscow, Coulondre advised, that if such an accord were concluded, the Soviet Union would reexamine its foreign policy and denounce its pact with France. Coulondre warned, again, that among Soviet policy options would be a rapprochement with Germany. To avoid this danger, France should do everything possible not to alienate the Soviet government.[77]

Soviet consternation also appeared in Geneva, where Litvinov condemned Chamberlain's talks with Hitler: the Czechs, like the Ethiopians, should trust no British promises. Chamberlain was mistaken, said Litvinov, if he thought a new capitulation would save the peace. The cession of the Sudetenland to Nazi Germany would only lead to the disappearance of Czechoslovakia. The Anglo-French capitulation would mean a further loss of prestige and influence. And Hitler would not stop there; he would make fresh demands, and war would inevitably break out in conditions even more unfavorable to France and Britain.[78] Tories, such as Channon, took a different view of Chamberlain's journey to Berchtesgaden. Channon was at a British diplomatic dinner in Geneva when news arrived of the prime minister's initiative. "The company rose to their feet electrified, as all the world must be, and drank his health. History must be ransacked to find a parallel."[79]

On September 18, two days after Chamberlain returned from Berchtesgaden, the chief of the French air staff, General Joseph Vuillemin, sent a very negative, pessimistic estimate of French air power to Daladier. He had visited Germany in August, where his counterparts put on an impressive show of force which had produced the desired intimidating effect.[80] With this pessimism ringing in their ears, Daladier and Bonnet went to London to meet the British. Daladier performed his usual act of objecting to, then accepting the cession of Czech territory. The British and French agreed to a proposal to the Czech government calling for the cession of territory where more than half the population was German. News traveled fast. Fierlinger reported from Moscow:

> French policy is characterized here as open betrayal. This is the opinion of the overwhelming majority of the diplomatic corps. Potemkin advises that in London the biggest coward proved to be Bonnet who talked about inadequate French aviation and unwillingness of the Soviet Union to help us. Potemkin's personal opinion comes to this, that the Franco-Soviet pact is now useless. Evidently tomorrow the Soviets will denounce Bonnet's deceit.

The pact with France is "not worth twopence," Maiskii trenchantly observed.[81]

Litvinov revealed "Bonnet's deceit" on September 21 in a speech at the League of Nations, where he described the statements made to Payart and Coulondre in Moscow.[82] Two days later he reiterated the Soviet position in a meeting in Geneva with Wilson and Edward Lord De La Warr, the lord privy seal. According to Litvinov's account, the British asked the usual questions about what the Soviet Union intended to do. Litvinov, exasperated, repeated what he had said in his speech two days earlier. It took a great deal of temerity, Litvinov said in so many words, for French and British officials to be asking the Soviet Union what it might do when their governments ignored the USSR and did not keep it informed at a moment when the fate of Europe was at stake. Litvinov wanted to know what France and Britain were going to do. When De La Warr persisted in asking what military actions the Soviet government contemplated, Litvinov replied that these were matters for general staffs to discuss, but that the Soviet Union was not about to move before France, "especially after what has occurred in the last few days." De La Warr informed Litvinov privately of a split in the British cabinet and said that Daladier and Bonnet had become somewhat more resolute. Litvinov was skeptical: "These [two], but especially Bonnet, in London held even more capitulationist positions than Chamberlain." And yet Litvinov was still willing to encourage a stronger Anglo-French policy.[83] And also a stronger Soviet position, because in a separate cable on the same day Litvinov recommended a partial Soviet mobilization, perhaps simultaneously with France, where the position appeared to be stiffening. Matters had gone too far to scare off Hitler with mere joint declarations; stronger action was needed, and quickly.[84]

None of Litvinov's efforts could stop the juggernaut of capitulation, though its very speed almost threw it off the rails. On September 21 the Czech government yielded to heavy Anglo-French pressure and agreed to the cession of territory to Germany. The French and British had threatened to abandon Czechoslovakia if it did not give way. Mandel and Reynaud worked surreptiously to encourage Beneš to resist, but to no avail. On September 22 Chamberlain rushed back to Godesberg to give Hitler the good news, only to discover that the Fuehrer had upped his demands and threatened war before the end of September if Czechoslovakia did not at once agree to the German occupation of the Sudetenland, lock, stock, and barrel.

In Paris three cabinet ministers, Mandel, Reynaud, and Jean Champetier de Ribes, contemplated resignation to protest against French policy. But on September 24 the Czechs mobilized, and the French began to call up reservists. Mandel explained to Surits that the announcement of his resignation had been put off. Bonnet was the chief culprit of French "capitulation," said Mandel: he had "intentionally distorted the position of the USSR, and in particular hidden [Litvinov's] proposal calling for a meeting of general staffs." Nor could Daladier be counted on; he was "weak and indecisive." According to Surits, the "Mandel-Reynaud group" had prepared a sweeping indictment against Bonnet's defeatism. The situation was thus a little improved.[85]

Phipps still lobbied French politicians for the British position. He told Herriot that the purges had weakened the Red Army, though the British ambassador had apparently not heard of the success of Soviet forces on the Manchurian frontier against Japan. Herriot replied: "In the days of the French revolution, we shot a lot of generals and the result was good. I think the French Armies would have done even better if more generals had been shot."[86] Herriot was saying in effect that whether the purges had hurt or not hurt the Red Army, it made no difference. France needed the Soviet alliance against Nazi Germany. This had been Herriot's main line, his *idée fixe,* since the early 1920s.

In London, Halifax told Masaryk on September 24 that the prime minister thought Hitler was someone with whom one could negotiate, and that once he had obtained the Czech Sudetenland, he would leave Europe in peace. Masaryk could not believe his ears, so Halifax repeated what he had said. The Czech minister gave a more detailed account to the Soviet chargé d'affaires, who passed it on to Moscow. It's the "Hitler-Chamberlain auction sale," Masaryk told Churchill.[87] The next day Voroshilov informed the Soviet military attaché in Paris of a partial Soviet mobilization on the Polish frontier and directed him to pass on the information to Gamelin. By the end of September the Soviet mobilization was massive, including sixty infantry divisions, sixteen cavalry divisions, three tank corps, twenty-two tank brigades, and seventeen air brigades spread out along the Polish and Romanian frontiers.[88] Whether these forces would have marched and in what circumstances are open questions. The Soviet effort nevertheless compared favorably with that of the British, who were capable of sending only two partially equipped divisions to France—and these were not even mobilized.

When Chamberlain returned to London he met a balky cabinet which did not like to give in to Hitler's ultimatum. Daladier and Bonnet made another "pilgrimage" to London for an indecisive meeting where the French premier was as balky as Chamberlain's cabinet. On September 26 the Foreign Office published a communiqué warning that if Hitler attacked Czechoslovakia, France was bound to go to its aid and that Britain and the Soviet Union would stand by France. In Paris one might have thought that the British communiqué would have been welcomed, which is why Bonnet did not like it. He attempted to prevent its publication in the French press and put out a rumor that the communiqué was a Vansittart forgery. The appeasement press duly picked up the refrain. Mandel openly accused Bonnet of weakness and treason. Bonnet thought Mandel, Reynaud, and others of a like mind were "crazy." He appealed to deputies in the Chamber: "You . . . must stop this war; we are heading for a disaster. This war would be a crime." Bonnet had good connections with the press and encouraged them to oppose a hard line against Germany.[89]

Chamberlain also disliked the Foreign Office communiqué and kept trying to finesse around those of his colleagues who were reluctant to capitulate. Wilson went back to Berlin on September 26 with a new letter from Chamberlain to see an irate Hitler, who again threatened war by the end of the month if Czechoslovakia did not capitulate. In Paris, Quai d'Orsay political director René Massigli, not a Bonnet supporter, heard about this latest initiative, informing Osusky and characterizing it as just another proposal at the expense of Czechoslovakia.[90] On the same day, September 26, Vuillemin submitted a report to the air minister, saying that the French air force stood no chance against the Luftwaffe. Of course, France would not have faced Germany alone, "Colossus Germany," as the Tory Channon called it. Again, the French were counting every foeman twice, and the Czech and Soviet armed forces not at all. There was sometimes a direct correlation between unwillingness to fight and unwillingness to fight alongside the Red Army. In October, after the Munich crisis was over, Vuillemin recommended that France "break with the Soviets."[91]

On September 27 Surits advised Moscow that Bonnet was still searching for some "new compromise" adding more Czech territory to that already offered to Hitler. And Surits added: "From circles close to Mandel, we know that Bonnet again said at today's cabinet meeting that France was not ready, that it would be subject to attack on three fronts, and so on; even Daladier was exasperated, but with Mandel there was an open row."[92] There was also abuse in the streets of Paris. Flandin, the former premier, had a poster pasted to the walls of the capital: "You are being deceived! People of France . . . A cunning trap has been set . . . by occult elements to make war inevitable. . . ." The appeal came close to counseling resistance against mobilization, and the police were ordered to tear down the poster, though this did not stop Bonnet from receiving Flandin at the Quai d'Orsay.[93]

VIII

A new complication developed on September 22 when the French government noted German troop movements away from the Polish frontier and corresponding Polish troop concentrations on Czech borders. To the French this suggested Nazi-Polish cooperation, or at least collusion: Nazi Germany was counting on Polish neutrality, and Poland on the seizure of the Teschen district as German troops moved into the Sudetenland. On the same day Krofta informed Aleksandrovskii of the Polish troop concentrations and asked the Soviet government to warn off Poland by threatening the denunciation of the 1932 Soviet-Polish nonaggression pact.[94]

The Soviet government must already have had confirming intelligence on these Polish troop movements, for early the next day Potemkin called in the Polish chargé d'affaires to deliver the warning requested by Krofta.[95] Potemkin also advised the French ambassador of the Soviet démarche. In the ensuing conversation, Coulondre expressed cautious optimism in a turnabout of Anglo-French policy. He hoped that France and Britain would not make further concessions to Hitler, and he told Potemkin that he considered the French and Soviet pacts with Czechoslovakia to be fully operational. According to Potemkin, "Coulondre thinks that we must dispel the atmosphere of mutual distrust existing between the USSR and France." The ambassador said that if French policy turned around, as he hoped it would, the two countries could then work closely together. Not surprisingly, Coulondre did not share these hopes with Bonnet.[96]

The Soviet warning failed to douse the Polish craving for Teschen. The Poles calculated that the Anglo-French would abandon Czechoslovakia and that therefore the Soviet Union would do nothing. But the French and British were disturbed by the Polish position, especially since it could spin the crisis out of control, leading to war, with Poland in the Nazi camp. The Soviet press also gave the Poles a lesson in "what's good for the goose is good for the gander."

Not only were there minorities in Czechoslovakia, *Izvestiia* pointed out, there was also a Ukrainian minority in Poland. What would Colonel Beck say if these Ukrainians demanded a plebiscite to determine their future?[97]

Colonel Józef Beck was the Polish foreign minister and a key subordinate of Marshal Józef Piłsudski, the Polish nationalist leader who had died in 1935. Beck began his career as a soldier during the First World War, but after the war he was increasingly chosen for diplomatic work and in 1932 he became foreign minister. Like Piłsudski, Beck was a Polish nationalist who hoped to reestablish Poland as a great power, as it had been in the sixteenth and seventeenth centuries. Their efforts were unsuccessful, and this failure left Polish nationalists sour and quick to take offense. Yet they tended to carry on the business of state as though Poland *was* a great power— dangerous conduct in the 1930s as Nazi Germany grew stronger and more predatory. Beck leaned toward Germany in the late 1930s, which brought Poland into conflict with the Soviet Union. Essentially the Polish government tried to ride the tiger's back, and ultimately could not do so. If Poland then fell out with its other great neighbor, Russia, it would be in grave danger.

Beck was the *bête noire* of just about everyone in Europe. The French and British mistrusted him, though the feeling was mutual. In his personal life he was an arrogant dandy with a taste for drinking and beautiful women. Litvinov regarded him as a Nazi pimp. Nevertheless, as long as the Soviet Union pursued a policy of collective security and close relations with France, it sought periodically to improve relations with the Poles. For the Soviet government knew that Poland was one of the keys to French misgivings about the Franco-Soviet mutual assistance pact. Beck was unresponsive to Soviet overtures. Polish opposition to collective security and Polish collusion with Nazi Germany immensely irritated Soviet and French diplomats and led ultimately in September 1939 to Poland's disappearance.

In a meeting with the British ambassador on September 24, Beck said that Poland would not "tie its hands" regarding Teschen; "it did not have belligerent intentions but it could not agree that German demands being satisfied, Poland should receive nothing." Put another way, Beck said he did not intend to leave to Germany the exclusive benefits of a dismemberment of Czechoslovakia. Anyway, added Beck, there was nothing to worry about because the Czech government had indicated verbally to the Polish minister in Prague that it agreed in principle to the cession of territory to Poland. The Poles had other ways of sending their message to Paris: when the French military attaché asked for information on German troop movements, his counterpart could say little in view of the French position on Teschen. If Germany entered Czechoslovakia, this Polish officer added, Poland would take advantage of the situation to act in its own interests.

The French ambassador in Warsaw, Léon Noël, reported that the Polish government was split between moderates and hard-liners on the Teschen question. The moderates held the upper hand for the moment, Noël said; to prevent the hard-liners from regaining control, France should encourage the Czechs to accept Polish demands. The Czechs might be hoping for Polish action to prompt Soviet intervention, throwing Poland into the German camp and leading to an "ideological war," with Italy coming in on the German side. Coulondre challenged Noël's reasoning: if Poland attacked Czechoslovakia, it would already have cast its lot with Nazi Germany, and Soviet intervention would be only a riposte. As for Italy, Soviet action was more likely to discourage it from joining the war rather than the opposite. In spite of Coulondre's advice, Bonnet was willing to act as an intermediary to persuade the Czechs to hand over Teschen if Poland would "change camps."[98]

IX

While this tawdry spectacle unfolded, Coulondre recommended to Paris on September 24 that staff talks begin immediately with the Soviet Union, a recommendation he repeated three days later. Although Quai d'Orsay officials supported Coulondre's recommendation, the French deputy chief of staff, General Colson, did not like to see the Red Army building up its forces on the Polish frontier, since Poland still hesitated on which side to join. But at the height of the crisis, on September 28, Bonnet sent a brush-off to Coulondre: an information exchange might take place between the Soviet military attaché in Paris and the French general staff—not what Coulondre, or Litvinov, had in mind.[99]

As Bonnet declined staff talks, the Czech government rejected Hitler's Godesberg ultimatum, which was too much to swallow in Prague. On September 28 the London morning papers announced the mobilization of the fleet; and the Red Army continued to concentrate forces on the frontier with Poland. It looked like war. In the nick of time, however, Chamberlain saved the peace by asking for yet another meeting with Hitler and asking Mussolini for help in getting it. In the afternoon of September 28, Chamberlain was relieved to learn that Hitler had agreed to a meeting at Munich. "In the air," reported Maiskii, "it feels like Chamberlain is preparing for a new capitulation. . . ." Tories took it better, as Channon noted: after the news was reported in the House of Commons, it "rose and in a scene of riotous delight, cheered, bellowed their approval. We stood on our benches, waved our order papers, shouted—until we were hoarse. . . ." Neville alone was fighting off "the dogs of war," said Channon: "he seemed the incarnation of St. George." Good Ol' Brolly! Halifax told Maiskii on September 29 that Chamberlain had agreed to go to Munich without consulting the French. The British government did not contemplate Soviet participation, knowing that Hitler would not accept it and that the "last chances" to prevent war would then be lost.[100]

The results of the Munich conference are well known. Apart from minor concessions, Hitler got what he demanded. Chamberlain thought it was a great triumph for reason and for Anglo-German understanding.[101] There was just one loose end to tie up: the Polish desire for Teschen. On September 30 the Polish government issued an ultimatum. Bonnet did not like it, especially after he had assured the Polish ambassador in Paris, Łukasiewicz, that the French government would do everything possible to obtain "an amicable settlement." Bonnet swallowed his irritation and pressed the Czech government to agree. Not known for his foresight, Bonnet observed that the Poles might come to regret their action when one day they were subjected to the same methods.[102] In Moscow, Coulondre knew nothing and telephoned Potemkin for news. "It's another surrender," said Potemkin. The Czechs had capitulated, and the Poles were already moving into the Teschen district. Potemkin implied, said Coulondre, that the Czech capitulation had eliminated any basis for Soviet intervention.[103] How quickly time would pass: the Polish victim of 1939 was only months following the Polish aggressor. "Grovelling in villainy," said Churchill, the Polish vulture picked at left-over Nazi carrion.[104]

X

It was finished. Czechoslovakia was surrendered, and then Prague capitulated. "The German dictator," Churchill said, "instead of snatching his victuals from the table, has been content to have them served to him course by course." There remained only to calculate the gains and losses. Chamberlain was well satisfied with his work, though "pleasantly tired" after his exertions. It's "peace with honour," "peace for our time," he told London crowds. "Good old Neville!" they cheered. "For he's a jolly good fellow . . . ," they sang.[105] In the House of Commons in early October, Chamberlain claimed victory and the beginning of an Anglo-German understanding. Alfred Duff Cooper, first lord of the admiralty, who resigned in protest, Churchill, and others condemned the Munich settlement as an unmitigated, catastrophic defeat. Churchill was the most eloquent: "It is the most grievous consequence which we have yet experienced of what we have done and of what we have left undone in the last five years—five years of futile good intention, five years of eager search for the line of least resistance, five years of uninterrupted retreat of British power. . . . Do not let us blind ourselves to that." Later he flung at Chamberlain: "The Government had to choose between war and shame. They chose shame, and they will get war, too." Churchill was right, but the House voted 366 to 144 in favor of the government's policy. Neville's "the Man of our Age," M.P. Channon said. Churchill, Duff Cooper, and the others were only "that little group of 'Glamour Boys' . . . attempting to torpedo the Prime Minister. . . ."[106]

The situation in France was similar: there was immense public relief that war had been avoided. A somber and shamed Daladier came back to Le Bourget airport thinking he would receive rotten eggs from the crowd gathered to wait for him. Instead they cheered. "What asses!" Daladier was heard to mutter. The right swore vengeance against Mandel and Reynaud for having led France so close to war. If there were war, went one epigram, "Then our first bullets will be for Mandel, Blum, and Reynaud." One supposes

Blum was thrown in for good measure because he was the Popular Front premier and a Jew. On October 4 the vote in the Chamber of Deputies in favor of Munich was 535 to 75. Roll of dishonor and of honor: the latter included Henri de Kérillis on the right, Jean Bouhey, a Socialist, and the seventy-three Communist deputies. Even Blum jubilated that peace had been saved. The Communists were condemned as warmongers with Moscow at their lead. Frenchmen, do not despair, said the right-wing press: only the warmongers in Moscow have suffered a defeat. Communism is war, war means communism.[107] After hearing all this story again, can we really say "two cheers for appeasement"?

Maiskii summed up the situation: "The League of Nations and collective security are dead." A period would now begin where brute force and the mailed fist were celebrated and would govern Europe.[108] Litvinov in Paris, on his way home from Geneva, had an unavoidable meeting with Bonnet, who sought to justify Munich by the need to buy time for rearmament. I doubt, replied Litvinov, that time for rearmament will compensate for the loss of the one-and-a-half-million men of the Czech army and its strategic position in Europe.[109] Litvinov's comment—an inadvertent reply to Vuillemin— was mere prelude to the harsh Soviet analysis that followed. In a line resembling one of Churchill's, *Izvestiia* noted that the Anglo-French capitulation, while appearing to have avoided war, had only made it inevitable. And France and Britain would have to wage this war in far more adverse conditions. In the semi-official French-language *Journal de Moscou* there was worse to come: "After the Munich capitulation, who will believe in the word of France, who will remain its ally?" The French had condemned themselves to isolation. But the Soviet Union itself feared isolation, as Coulondre reported to Paris, and this situation was dangerous for France.[110]

With the "neutralization" of Czechoslovakia, Coulondre observed, the way to the southeast was open to Nazi Germany. Who would or could stop the Germans now? Would Hitler turn his sights on the Ukraine? Certainly the Soviet government was contemplating these questions. It reckoned that France and Britain would not oppose German expansion in central or eastern Europe. And it considered the joint declaration of peaceful intent signed by Chamberlain and Hitler on September 30—which Chamberlain had waved at London crowds—as a British offer of its good offices to facilitate

German eastern ambitions, conditional on leaving western Europe in peace. This "complicity," as it was perceived in Moscow, gave the Munich accord a sword's point directed at the Soviet Union.

Coulondre speculated on Soviet options. Moscow had lost all confidence in collective security but would not openly denounce it, at least for the moment. The only other option was a Soviet-German rapprochement at Polish expense. Such a policy would be a *pis-aller*, a last resort, but might divert Hitler away from the Soviet Union at least for a time. "I have reason to believe that this idea is already in the minds of Soviet officials," said Coulondre. "To several of my colleagues, M. Potemkin has recently repeated what he said to me: 'Poland is preparing its fourth partition.'" Echoing the Soviet view, Coulondre concluded that French prestige and morale had been badly damaged by the Munich crisis. France would be in "mortal peril" if it suffered another such defeat.[111]

From Paris, Surits did his own summing up of the extent of the French catastrophe. It was a "second Sedan," the devastating French defeat of the Franco-Prussian War of 1870. Germany, without firing a shot, had gained a population of more than three million, had acquired more than ten thousand square miles of territory with important factories and mines. France had deprived itself of its most faithful ally in central Europe, one and a half million Czech soldiers—on and on he went. The far left claimed that France had been betrayed by a conspiracy of the financial oligarchy aided by such cabinet ministers as Bonnet. But the real explanation was more complicated. There had been no popular support for Czechoslovakia, apart perhaps from a bothersome sense of unwanted obligation; no understanding that the fate of Czechoslovakia affected the vital interests of France. On the contrary, ". . . for days we were all witnesses to the most disgraceful scenes when cowardice was elevated to virtue by cheering, thoughtless crowds and when the capitulators were glorified as national heroes." Among the more passive sectors of the French population there was a sense of relief that they had "survived the ordeal" and been "spared in the end the nightmare of war." "The organizers of capitulation" had skillfully exploited the deeply rooted popular fear of war and unwillingness to fight. This was their "most powerful trump" against those who hoped to take a strong line against Hitler.

Surits was willing to leave to future historians the task of sorting out the various positions of all the parties to this tragedy, but he returned to the themes of his earlier reports to Moscow. Among the "Munichmen" were those who considered war with Germany through an "ideological" prism. They feared that the defeat of Germany would lead to a triumph of bolshevism while the Soviet Union was an ally of France. No sacrifice or concession was too high a price to pay to prevent this outcome.

> All the hypocritical and false information about the weakness and lack of preparedness of the USSR, all this anti-Soviet campaign of lies and slander, which recently has been so abundant and methodically plastered across the pages of the venal press, was intended not only to justify capitulation but also to hide the real fear of the right before the possible success of Soviet arms in war.

France had to save itself from this undesirable and burdensome ally. In fact, according to Surits, the French right hoped to provoke the Soviet Union into denouncing the mutual assistance pact. The ambassador was careful to say that the Daladier government did not entirely share the program of the right. Most of the cabinet had capitulated out of "fear and lack of faith in their strength" and out of fear of defeat. Surits concluded his report by noting that with the exception of Mandel, none of the present leaders of France felt capable of waging a modern war. "Not one of them has the will, the energy, the grip, or the élan of Clemenceau and even of [Raymond] Poincaré." Munich had created a completely new situation, said Surits, and there was no way to predict the future direction of French policy.[112]

Soviet diplomats were incensed by French and British allegations and insinuations that the Soviet Union was weak and halfhearted in its defense of Czechoslovakia. France and Britain were in no position to criticize, and when they did, the Soviet government considered it to be unmitigated gall and hypocrisy. So when Edward Lord Winterton, a British cabinet minister, made such a public statement in early October, Maiskii went straight to Halifax to protest.[113] The ambassador would have been angrier still if he had known that the Foreign Office at the height of the Munich crisis had forwarded to the Quai d'Orsay a report from their embassy in Moscow denigrating Soviet military strength because of the purges. The Quai d'Orsay, probably Bonnet himself, leaked the information verbatim to the anti-communist Paris daily *Le Matin,* greatly embarrassing the Foreign Office since the report could be traced to Chilston. It was awkward to be exposed like this, justifying Soviet allegations and suspicions. "I begin to think," noted Collier, "that there is no honest way out of this impasse!" It is traditional diplomatic practice to avoid telling the truth when necessary, and this is in effect what the Foreign Office instructed Chilston to do. Although the subterfuge did nothing to improve Anglo-Soviet relations, Winterton, on Halifax's urging, "invited Maiskii to a meal and buried the hatchet with him."[114]

The Soviet government's anger was not so easily appeased, and Coulondre heard more of it in Moscow. He paid a farewell call to Litvinov, having been named French ambassador in Berlin, and expressed regret at his failure to improve Franco-Soviet relations. Litvinov observed that the French government, having negotiated a mutual assistance pact with the Soviet Union, had then systematically evaded military talks to strengthen it, even when Czechoslovakia was threatened. "Now I have to conclude," he said, "that the French government never thought to actualize at any point the assistance envisioned by the pacts [including Czechoslovakia] and that there was thus no need to conduct further enabling negotiations." According to Litvinov's account, Coulondre replied that this statement was too categorical, noting that the British had discouraged the French government from concluding a military agreement. There was no need to say it; Litvinov was well informed.

When Coulondre asked what could be done now, Litvinov replied that the position lost in Czechoslovakia could not be retrieved or redressed. It was a catastrophic defeat. The Anglo-French could do one of two things: capitulate completely, conceding hegemony in Europe to Nazi Germany, or they could decide at last to resist. In the first case, Hitler would take a little time to digest his new conquests before turning perhaps on the British Empire. He would probably think it too dangerous to attack the Soviet Union. In the second case, France and Britain would have to turn to Moscow, and then "they will try to speak to us in a different language."[115]

Coulondre's account of this meeting is without the commissar's acerbic edge. He stressed Litvinov's main point that a general settlement with Nazi Germany was impossible and that, in other words, war was unavoidable. According to Coulondre, Litvinov emphasized the possibility of a Nazi-Soviet rapprochement in the event that Hitler decided to advance in the west, though Litvinov did not refer to it in his account of the meeting. Perhaps Coulondre wished to wake up Paris to this dangerous possibility. For it was Litvinov's second option of resistance to Nazi Germany that Coulondre wanted to pursue and that he thought the Soviet Union would prefer to follow. He reasoned that this option offered the only real security for the Soviet Union against Nazi aggression. But Coulondre warned—and it will be well for readers to remember it, when Anglo-Franco-Soviet negotiations began in 1939—that the Soviet government, having learned from past experience, would demand "precise guarantees of assistance" in any future agreement with France and Britain.

And in case the Quai d'Orsay might wish to avoid facing up to realities, Coulondre heavily stressed the danger of a possible Nazi-Soviet rapprochement, even foreseeing imminent unofficial Soviet approaches in Berlin. The price of such a rapprochement—the only one likely to appeal to Hitler—would be the partition of Poland. "Fear's a poor councillor," said Coulondre, and the Soviet Union might turn to Nazi Germany for want of allies. Coulondre set what should have been the Anglo-French agenda for the coming months in emphasizing the importance of getting Poland and the Soviet Union to cooperate against the real enemy of both, Nazi Germany. Anglo-French weakness had led the Poles and might lead "the Soviet" to compose with Hitler. It would be difficult to persuade the Polish government to contemplate "a more accurate evaluation of its vital interests," but France must try to encourage Soviet-Polish military cooperation in a broader alliance with France and Britain. It was the last chance to reestablish a European equilibrium, and it should not be neglected. Time's running out, he said in effect; we need to know whom we can count on and who can count on us.[116]

On October 18 Bonnet avowed to Surits that he hoped for stronger Franco-Soviet relations, but Litvinov replied with contempt. "Bonnet's most recent declaration . . . has as little meaning as the Anglo-French declaration that 'they do not intend to exclude us from the resolution of European questions.'" Hitler would decide these questions, and the Anglo-French would not contradict him. Chamberlain and Daladier would do anything to obtain agreement with Germany and Italy. "And of course for them it is not profitable to break with us now, for then they will deprive themselves of a trump in negotiations with Berlin." They would only turn to the USSR if Hitler made demands that were too big even for them to swallow.[117] Ironically, Litvinov's view of Western-Soviet relations as an Anglo-French trump with Germany mirrored Coulondre's view of the Franco-Soviet pact as possible payment for a Nazi-Soviet rapprochement. Litvinov instructed Surits not to be dragged into political discussions of unknown purpose with Bonnet, nor even to offer solely personal opinions.[118]

Coulondre's departure from Moscow should have been marked by cordial Franco-Soviet farewells, given the ambassador's commitment to better relations. But Soviet bitterness over the Munich agreement would not allow for it. On October 19 the *Journal de Moscou* published another article condemning the Munich capitulation: France had lost everything "without even being able to say 'except for honor.'" This passed the measure, said Coulondre, and he went to see Potemkin, then Litvinov about a retraction. Litvinov refused, noting the absence of any reciprocity in retractions for the far more offensive insults in the French press heaped upon the Soviet Union. And Litvinov cabled Surits, "I would have laughed" if there had been any retractions in Paris. He eventually begrudged his personal regret to Coulondre but refused to publish it.[119]

The French and British governments appear to have failed to understand the depth of Soviet distrust and animosity after Munich, though individuals like Coulondre and Vansittart had some sense of it. More representative were Anglo-French views that ranged from strong contempt to mild condescension, and such attitudes did not help when in 1939 the magnitude of the Nazi threat finally penetrated even the thickest heads among the Munichmen.

The British government view of the Munich aftermath reflected of course the prime minister's position. Chilston's October 18 report from Moscow, dated the same day as Coulondre's, did not apprehend the urgency or danger of a situation which he judged to be unremarkable. The Soviet government would probably not denounce the Franco-Soviet pact and would not intentionally withdraw from European affairs. There was no warning of a possible Nazi-Soviet rapprochement. Chilston commented on the Winterton affair as though it was just the Soviet playing up "now that the danger is over." Chilston did remark on gossip in the Moscow diplomatic community about Litvinov's future in view of the failure of collective security. Litvinov "has scarcely been visible since his arrival [from Geneva] and has spent very little time at his office; and I understand from a well-informed source that he has daily spent many hours in consultation with Stalin and Molotov at the Kremlin." Chilston's curiosity was sufficient for him to wonder what Stalin might think of the post-Munich situation, "now that Litvinov's year-long and untiring efforts to realise his policy of collective security against Germany would appear, for the present at least, to have fallen into the water." The ambassador did not foresee Litvinov's disappearance: "Not only does any radical change of orientation or of policy seem to be most improbable for the present, but in any case Litvinov would appear to be irreplaceable; and he is likely to conform to whatever new line the Kremlin may decide to pursue.[120] These were quite different conclusions from those of Coulondre.

Not all British officials, cabinet ministers, and politicians were as complacent as Chilston. Every informed British citizen knew what Churchill thought. Vansittart did his best inside the Foreign Office to warn of the danger, as he had been doing for years. The Munich settlement appalled him: "We are already being reduced to the rank of a second-class power—indeed we have reached that point already. . . . And, unless we emerge from that status with almost miraculous celerity, we shall soon be getting our marching-orders from Berlin. . . ."[121] Not a very different comment from Litvinov's. Vansittart also vented his spleen to Maiskii about French "intrigues" in London against the Soviet Union. And Maiskii reported finding him in a very "anti-Chamberlain" mood, but "ready, as before, to do battle for his line." Vansittart asked Maiskii about future Soviet policy and was relieved to hear that the Soviet government would not draw any hasty conclusions. Vansittart "urged us not to withdraw from Europe, since this would have catastrophic consequences for world affairs and for the struggle against the aggressors."[122]

Several cabinet ministers, Walter Elliott, Oliver Stanley, and De La Warr pressed Chamberlain to accelerate rearmament and improve relations with the Soviet Union. Chamberlain evaded direct answers to these appeals and rejected the grim prognostications of the Churchill-Vansittart group.[123] The Soviet government was well informed on Chamberlain's position from Maiskii's reports of meet-

ings with cabinet ministers and other "influentials." Lord Beaverbrook, financier, newspaper mogul, and future cabinet minister, told
Maiskii in October that "despite the Munich experience and the
criticism of the Munich agreement, Chamberlain remains convinced
that a European 'peace settlement' can be achieved through diplomatic negotiations with Hitler and Mussolini without recourse to
stronger measures." Chamberlain was willing to go a long way in
making concessions to achieve this end, and was contemplating no
resistance to German expansion in southeast Europe and Turkey. On
the contrary, he calculated that the creation of *Mittel Europa* would
bring Hitler into conflict with the Soviet Union. Chamberlain believed there was no immediate threat of a big war, nor therefore any
reason for all-out British rearmament, though some acceleration
would take place. Hence he would not hear of a ministry of supply
or wartime rearmament measures; no, for Chamberlain, said Beaverbrook, it was "business as usual."[124]

In late October, at breakfast with the secretary of state for war,
Leslie Hore-Belisha, Maiskii heard complaints about the inadequa-
cies of the Royal Air Force and the failure of British aircraft production to keep up with Germany. And like Beaverbrook, Hore-Belisha
noted that there was no plan for the creation of a ministry of supply
or the wartime mobilization of industry. Why the slow tempo of
rearmament? asked Maiskii, as if he did not know the answer.

> Hore-Belisha, shrugging his shoulders, replied somewhat sarcas-
> tically that the prime minister's apartments are now strewn with
> flowers, which he receives from all parts of the country from his
> many admirers; that the prime minister seriously believes that
> Munich was a victory and believes in the possibility of the paci-
> fication of Europe by means of delicate handling of Hitler and
> Mussolini.

Maiskii, who sometimes enjoyed the use of understatement, noted
that Hore-Belisha was "skeptical" about the prime minister's expectations.[125]

Samuel Hoare, then the home secretary, told Maiskii a few weeks
later that the government was well satisfied with the present situation in Europe: war had been avoided in Czechoslovakia, Spain was
no longer a danger, and Hitler's expansion toward the southeast was
a "natural process" and not alarming. "We can therefore count on

at least two years of peace," suggested Hoare. Rearmament could be brought up to a "suitable" level "by normal means."[126]

"The international situation is becoming ever more clear," Litvinov wrote to Surits in November. Chamberlain would go down the path he had marked—or rather that Hitler had marked for him—until the end. And France would be dragged along after him, willing or not.[127] Later that month Payart called on Litvinov to ask his views on the international situation. Litvinov was a little irritated by this opening.

We should be asking Britain and France what *they* think, replied Litvinov.

I ask only for myself, Payart said, not for my government. I believe in collective security, he continued, and I wonder what you see as the possibilities of it now.

The French and British governments would go on making concessions to Hitler, Litvinov said, but eventually public opinion would force them to stop. And then they would return to "the old path of collective security" because there was no other way to protect the peace. "Of course England and France will come out of this period [of appeasement] greatly weakened, but nevertheless even then the potential powers of peace will exceed the potential powers of aggression."

The question of Comintern activities in France inevitably came up. Payart complained about a Comintern manifesto calling for the overthrow of the French and British governments, handing it to Litvinov. The commissar looked at the paper and offered a correction: the manifesto called for the overthrow of "governments of betrayal and treason." "I remarked to Payart," Litvinov wrote, "that if the governments of Chamberlain and Daladier want to identify themselves with those named in the manifesto, then they should have a grievance. . . . We of course do not answer for the Comintern. . . ."[128] This black humor revealed the depth of Litvinov's bitterness over Munich.

Payart also made a record of this conversation, and it does not refer to the exchange over the Comintern. It does have other interesting nuances: "Litvinov confirmed my impression" that if Soviet isolation or a Soviet rapprochement with Germany could not be excluded, for now these options were off the table. Payart further reported: "Litvinov indicated to me that the USSR had not abandoned the idea of collective resistance to the aggressor and continued to make it the basis of its foreign policy." In Litvinov's record of conversation he makes no such direct declaration, though it may perhaps be inferred.[129] Was Payart making more of Litvinov's statements than was warranted in order to promote collective security in Paris? Or did Litvinov prefer not to record such direct statements in his notes of the conversation? The available evidence does not permit an answer, though it may be assumed that Payart did not wish to irritate the Quai d'Orsay with Litvinov's cynicism, and that Litvinov did not want the British and French to take anything for granted about Soviet policy. What can be said with certainty in the aftermath of the Munich crisis is that there were two worldviews of the European situation and two alternative policies for dealing with it. Time would tell which worldview and which policy would prevail.

"1939 Will Be the Decisive Year"

O N T H E E V E of the new year, in London, Paris, and Moscow, there was uncertainty about where Hitler would next turn his sights, east or west, and what should or could be done about it. The British and French were complacent about further Nazi expansion in the east. It was normal that Germany should dominate central Europe, otherwise there would be war every fifteen or twenty years, according to Halifax. And why should Britain risk war to save the Soviet Union?[1] The French had the added worry of what Italy might do in the Mediterranean. The Italian government sensed weakness after Munich, and at the end of November 1938 fascists in the Italian legislature shouted demands for "Nice, Corsica, Tunis." Unlike Germany, Italy was a potential adversary that the French reckoned they could handle, but strained Franco-Italian relations added another factor of instability to an already precarious international situation.[2]

To Chamberlain's mind, the French should try to conciliate Italy and most certainly not be dragged into war on account of the Soviet Union. The British government worried that France could be drawn into such a war because of French commitments under the Franco-Soviet mutual assistance pact. Some in the Foreign Office suggested telling the French to drop the Soviet pact, but in the end Halifax thought they should sit tight to see how Franco-German relations developed.[3] As Surits reported from Paris after Munich, there was open talk in the French right-wing press that France should abandon its commitments, such as they were, to Poland and the Soviet Union. But not everyone was so categorical. Ambassador Phipps thought that to denounce the Soviet pact "as a unilateral concession to Germany in the hope of securing goodwill would be gratuitously naive."[4] At the end of November, at an Anglo-French meeting in Paris, Bonnet assured Chamberlain that the Franco-Soviet pact was so hedged with League unanimity and consultations that Chamberlain's worries about France being dragged into a war by Russia were groundless.[5]

Rumors circulated that the Nazis were looking to the Ukraine to satisfy their growing territorial appetite. For Bonnet this was both a relief and a concern, and all the more reason to unburden France of dangerous commitments. Soviet ambassadors, of course, reported these and other speculations to Moscow. On December 6 Lloyd George invited Maiskii to a meal to discuss what was then a popular guessing game: where would Hitler strike next? Lloyd George thought that Hitler would go east and that Poland would be his next target. The Soviet Ukraine might be a long-term Nazi ambition, but it was a more dangerous objective. Two days later Maiskii saw Vansittart, again over the dining table, and again for the same guessing game. But Van salted this discussion with bitterness over Chamberlain's foreign policy. Hitler would not rest on his laurels long before turning on other prey, said Vansittart: there would be some new campaign in the coming months. But where? It was popular in government circles to think that the Ukraine would be Hitler's next target. Vansittart was not so sure. In any event, he thought a reappraisal of British policy was needed.[6]

Mandel and Surits met on the same day in Paris to speculate on the same subjects. Mandel had information that the Ukraine was Hitler's next target, but that in the meantime Poland and Romania might suffer the same fate as Czechoslovakia. If this happened, Mandel said, "it would mean the end of France." Mandel told Surits that Bonnet was contemplating the repeal of the military clauses of the 1921 Franco-Polish alliance, but he did not think Daladier would go so far.[7]

These rumors were fed by the arrival in Paris on December 6 of Joachim von Ribbentrop, the Nazi foreign minister, who came to Paris to sign an understanding with Bonnet to maintain "peaceful and good neighborly relations." The agreement touched off speculation that Bonnet had agreed to a "free hand" for Hitler in the east in exchange for peace in the west. According to anti-appeasement journalist Geneviève Tabouis's account of the Ribbentrop-Bonnet discussions, Ribbentrop asked for the free hand but Bonnet "managed to murmur: '. . . not . . . just now.'"[8] Litvinov, always suspicious of Bonnet, could not figure out what the French quid pro quo might be for the Nazi agreement, and he instructed Surits to find out.[9] Apparently it did not occur to Litvinov that this French "understanding" was not worth more than the paper signed by Hitler and Chamberlain, which the latter had brought home from Munich with so much hubris.

Bonnet might have liked to give the Nazis a free hand in the east, but other French cabinet ministers, calculating that war was inevitable, wanted to protect the Franco-Soviet pact, and they were not reluctant to say so to Surits.[10] This support was only enough to keep the anti-Soviet opposition at bay; there was still too much resistance to close relations with the Soviet Union for the pact to be anything more than a paper agreement. Deputy chief of staff Colson summed up the army position after Munich: "Russia has demonstrated, in spite of the bluff of Litvinov's speech [on September 21] in Geneva, both its military incapacity and its desire to stay out of a conflict which could risk exposing its domestic regime to the hard blows of the German army. The USSR, fundamentally an Asiatic power, will probably intervene in a European conflict only when it sees the possibility to advance its [communist] ideology on the ruins of a civilization weakened by war."[11] Based on such assumptions, the French general staff in its planning and speculations about Hitler's next moves scarcely envisaged a role for the Soviet Union, even when the military attaché Palasse, like Coulondre, warned of a possible Nazi-Soviet rapprochement.[12]

This ideological view of the Soviet Union permeated far and wide in Anglo-French governing circles. Less than a month later Oliver Harvey, Halifax's private secretary, who could scarcely be accused of communist ideas, recorded in his diary: ". . . the real opposition to re-arming comes from the rich classes in the [Conservative] Party who fear taxation and believe Nazis on the whole are more conservative than Communists and Socialists: any war, whether we win or not, would destroy the rich idle classes and so they are for peace at any price. . . ."[13] "Since war would mean the triumph of the

forces of Bolshevism on the Continent," Phipps told William C. Bullitt, the United States ambassador in Paris, "any sacrifice necessary
to avoid war must be made." Bullitt shared such views.[14]

None of this was anything new to the Soviet government. In January 1939 French journalist Tabouis met Litvinov in Geneva. She
was well informed about the French government's position on the
pact with the Soviet Union, and had heard Bonnet testify before the
Chamber's foreign affairs commission. "I have made a thorough
study of the Franco-Russian pact," Bonnet said. "And I discover
that we are not tied by it. We do not have to repudiate it, because
we are not committed by it to automatically join Russia." Tabouis
did not want to tell Litvinov about Bonnet's statement, but he knew
already: "Moscow now realizes perfectly well that there is little it
can count on from the British and French, unless it is the policy expressed by the French Press." At this point Litvinov handed Tabouis
a copy of *Matin,* the anti-communist daily. It featured a front-page
article advising: "Direct German expansion towards the East . . . and
we will rest easy in the West."[15]

II

The Anglo-French became less complacent and more interested in
the Soviet Union when in January 1939 other rumors circulated that
Holland and western Europe were the targets of Nazi ambition.
Suddenly it seemed less desirable to break commitments to the So-
viet Union. And Anglo-French anti-appeasers, largely silenced after
Munich, began to speak up again.

In Britain, reappraisal took place within the Foreign Office.
Foreign Secretary Halifax was not as sanguine as Chamberlain
about the prospects of an accommodation with Nazi Germany, and
everyone knew what Vansittart thought. Maiskii sent an interesting
appraisal of the British mood in early January. He thought Chamberlain's optimism about a general settlement had dimmed. Although the prime minister continued to believe in an agreement with
Germany and Italy, many of his colleagues did not, or had increasing
doubts. Hitler and Mussolini, said Maiskii, were largely responsible
for the "sobering" of British opinion.[16]

This "sobering" showed up in discussions in the Foreign Office.

At about the same time Maiskii submitted his report to Litvinov, a seemingly academic paper by a Foreign Office clerk and future permanent under secretary, Harold Caccia, reviewing John Wheeler-Bennett's book on the Soviet-German treaty of Brest-Litovsk in 1918, touched off an important exchange of views on Anglo-Soviet relations.

Caccia's memo suggested a reexamination of British policy toward the Soviet Union in light of the perspective offered by Wheeler-Bennett's book. Recalling that Lenin had agreed to accept "the assistance of French imperialism against German brigands," he asked why the British government should not adopt the same policy, working on the principle that " 'Russian murderers' might in certain eventualities be a lesser danger than 'German brigands.' " This was Churchill's position. Caccia suggested that the new British ambassador in Moscow, Sir William Seeds, attempt to meet Stalin to "clarify" Anglo-Soviet relations, applying Lenin's first principle.

The memorandum soon had attached to it minutes from the lowest Foreign Office clerk to Halifax himself, reflecting the gamut of opinion toward the Soviet Union. Central (Europe) department official D. W. Lascelles asked, ". . . what is there to clarify?"

> Essentially . . . [Anglo-Soviet] relations are based on a mutual and inevitable antipathy and on the realisation that the other party, in attempting to cope with the German menace, will act empirically and solely with an eye to its own interests. The Russians know quite well that if they are attacked by Germany we shall neither assist them nor join in the attack. . . .

Lascelles conceded, however, that a little talk with the Soviet might "have a certain prophylactic effect on the Germans, and it might also . . . be of some use . . . against the English critics of His Majesty's Government." Other mid-level Foreign Office officials, such as Collier and William Strang, head of the Central department, picked up on this idea and pushed it forward, though resisted by Oliphant and by Sir Alexander Cadogan, Chamberlain's "sane, slow man" who succeeded Vansittart as permanent under secretary.[17]

Collier argued that it had been a mistake to keep the Soviet Union "at arms' length" because "it gratuitously advertised to Hitler and Mussolini and the Japanese that they can deal with each of us in isolation; and I think there is something to be said for giving Stalin at least a negative assurance that we will do nothing directly or indirectly to assist Hitler's eastern plans. . . ." A change in policy "would go some way to remove the general criticism that the present policy of H.M.G. is biased, for 'ideological reasons,' against collaboration with the Soviet Union and in favour of collaboration with Germany and Italy."

"Russia is no friend of ours, though in certain circumstances she might be an ally," commented Frank Ashton-Gwatkin, the Foreign Office economist. "Her various incursions into European politics have been most mischievous, eg, Franco-Soviet pact, Spanish intervention, false encouragement given to the Czechs. But she remains a very important makeweight in the uncertain balance of Europe. . . ."

Cadogan opposed an approach to Moscow since the British government had nothing to offer: "we should very soon have to disclose the emptiness of our cupboard." Stalin could ask bothersome questions about what Britain might or might not do in the event of a Soviet-German conflict. He might, for example, "ask whether 'no indirect assistance [to Germany]' means standing aside and giving Germany a free hand. And that is not an easy question to answer—at best I do not think we could give Stalin the answer he wants. . . ."

Cadogan's views would have confirmed Soviet suspicions about British complacency in eastern Europe, but they did not fully satisfy Halifax, who invited Vansittart to comment. "Anglo-Soviet relations," Vansittart wrote,

> are in a most unsatisfactory state. It is not only regrettable but dangerous that they should be in this state, and a continuance of it will become a great deal more dangerous very shortly. They are in a bad state because the Russians feel, and I think it is an incontestable fact (at any rate it is a very widely stated one), that we practically boycotted them during 1938. We never took them into our confidence or endeavoured to establish close contact with them, and this fact accounts for the gradual drift towards isolation that is going on in Russia. That fact and that tendency we ought to correct and correct soon.

Vansittart was not sure how to proceed. "What the Russians need is a gesture." He suggested sending a cabinet minister—either Robert Hudson or Oliver Stanley—to the Soviet Union under the cover of ongoing trade negotiations. Halifax asked Vansittart to see him about his idea.[18] This marked a certain progress—if one favored better relations with the Soviet Union—but it was not a dramatic change in policy. Chamberlain still hoped for a general settlement with Hitler. He would not let the Foreign Office go very far toward Moscow, and Cadogan was there to keep Halifax from straying off course.

Halifax was unlikely to stray too far. In the autumn of 1937, while lord president, he had met Hitler in a highly publicized visit to Germany. Halifax "told me" recorded Tory M.P. Channon, that "he liked all the Nazi leaders, even Goebbels, and he was much impressed, interested and amused by the visit. He thinks the régime absolutely fantastic, perhaps even too fantastic to be taken seriously. . . . I was rivetted by all he said. . . ."[19] Halifax succeeded Eden as foreign secretary in February 1938, much to Chamberlain's relief, for he considered Eden to be too difficult to manage. Before Munich, Halifax had supported Chamberlain's policy toward Germany, though he wavered during the crisis in September and then again in 1939. He was upper-class British, a member of the House of Lords, very Tory, and notably Anglican. Tall, lanky, balding, personable, he was self-effacing and hard to anger, preferring to avoid direct conflict. As foreign secretary, Halifax was influenced by Cadogan but listened to Vansittart and sometimes followed his advice, to Cadogan's chagrin. While Chamberlain adamantly opposed better relations with the Soviet Union, Halifax was more flexible, though not enthusiastic. He often saw Maiskii, who could try his patience, but being the archetypical English gentlemen, he almost never showed irritation. Halifax was not a hard-line appeaser, but he was disposed to keep open the door to a German change of position, even after the war began.

On the day Vansittart wrote to Halifax about a mission to Moscow, he also went to see Maiskii to complain—neither discreetly nor for the first time—about Chamberlain's policy. Vansittart was in "great anxiety," noted Maiskii; he was "highly dissatisfied with the state of affairs both in England and in France. . . . In his view, 1939 will be the decisive year." Vansittart argued that British, French, and Soviet interests were identical, and that if they were not careful Hitler would pick them off one after the other—"as an artichoke is eaten leaf after leaf." Having listened for a while, Maiskii answered that Vansittart was preaching to the converted; "the USSR had all along been upholding the principle of collective security, while London and Paris had been systematically undermining it." At the end of their conversation, Vansittart expressed "hope that in England the policy of 'appeasement' would soon come to a deservedly inglorious end."[20]

III

While Maiskii waited to see if Vansittart's hopes came to pass, diplomatic activity increased between Berlin and Moscow. On January 5 the former German ambassador in Moscow, Rudolf Nadolny, and the commercial counselor in Moscow, Gustav Hilger, approached Alexei F. Merekalov, the Soviet ambassador in Berlin, to ask if the Soviet government would be willing to resume negotiations for a 200-million-mark credit which had been suspended in March 1938. The Germans, reported Merekalov in his cable to Moscow, said they were prepared to negotiate and would be willing to make concessions on terms and length of credit and on lower prices. No references to political relations or negotiations were mentioned, and in the published excerpt of the cable Merekalov offered no comment on the German initiative. Anastas I. Mikoian, the commissar for external trade, replied three days later that the Soviet government was willing to renew credit negotiations based on the conditions proposed by the Germans. Mikoian suggested that negotiations take place in Moscow.[21]

Merekalov returned to see Emile Wiehl, the director of the economic section of the German foreign ministry, to inform him of Mikoian's reply. Wiehl was pleased to have this news and said he would do what he could to obtain a positive reply from his superiors. The next day Merekalov attended the annual New Year's diplomatic reception in Berlin. He reported meeting Hitler there: "Visiting with the ambassadors, Hitler greeted me, asked about living in Berlin, about family, about my [recent] trip to Moscow; he emphasized that he was familiar with my visit to Schulenberg in Moscow; he wished me success and said goodbye." Then Ribbentrop and other government officials approached, but they limited themselves to polite generalities. Merekalov drew no political signif-

icance from this encounter, nor did he link it to the proposed re-
newal of credit negotiations.[22]

Eight days later Merekalov went back to see Wiehl, who was
joined by Karl Schnurre, head of the German trade delegation, and
by Hilger. The Germans did not like the idea of negotiations in
Moscow, but agreed anyway. Schnurre would go after a three-day
stopover in Warsaw at the end of January; he would stay in Moscow
until the middle of February and would then return to Warsaw for
negotiations with the Poles. Merekalov asked if Schnurre had the
necessary plenipotentiary powers to negotiate orders and terms of
trade, and Schnurre said he did. Everything seemed set for the negotiations, including a visa for Schnurre's wife so she could see the
sights of Moscow.[23]

The French and British governments learned of the planned negotiations during the course of the fortnight before they were to
begin. Anglo-French reaction was almost indifferent, which may surprise readers in view of Coulondre's many warnings of the danger of
a Nazi-Soviet rapprochement. At the Foreign Office, Collier, who
was always on the alert for signs of improved Nazi-Soviet relations,
did not make much of the reports of imminent negotiations. From
Moscow, Payart reported news of Schnurre's expected arrival in
Moscow and speculated that the talks might go beyond purely economic issues.[24]

On January 27 journalist Vernon Bartlett published an article in
the London *News Chronicle* on the "danger" of a "German-Soviet
rapprochement." The following day Wiehl telephoned Merekalov to
say that negotiations were off. Schnurre was recalled to Berlin on
unforeseen, urgent business, and Wiehl could not say when the mission might be rescheduled. Merekalov speculated that the "clamor"
over foreign press reports about a Nazi-Soviet rapprochement had
led to the cancellation of Schnurre's trip to Moscow.[25]

Litvinov also speculated on the erasure of Schnurre's mission,
but his mistrust of the French and British was so profound that it
seemed to border at times on paranoia. He instructed Merekalov to
find out what had happened, offering the lead that while the Germans may have been worried by unwanted publicity, the French and
British might be even more concerned. Don't be in such a hurry to
settle with the Soviet Union, they might say to the Germans, wait for

new concessions from us. Rumors of a Bonnet return visit to Berlin seemed to reinforce these suspicions.[26]

Litvinov's speculations were off beam this time. The British scarcely noticed the Schnurre mission while Payart's warnings fell on deaf ears in Paris. The *News Chronicle* article was republished in the Moscow papers without comment, prompting Payart to observe that in earlier days such a piece would have provoked Soviet indignation. It appeared that the article might have been Soviet inspired, Maiskii having connections with Bartlett, and it signaled Soviet disappointment with collective security and the preparation of Soviet opinion, in case of need, for a radical change in foreign policy. Payart's warning was clear: the Bartlett article "can be considered as the beginning of a possible turning point, and as such it deserves the most serious attention."[27] Payart's warning should have been taken seriously, but the "turning point" had not come yet.

Having made this demonstration of the possibilities, if the French and British governments continued to yield to Nazi intimidation, Soviet officials gave more encouraging messages to the French and British embassies in Moscow. In a discussion with Ambassador Seeds, Litvinov expressed his repugnance at improved Soviet-German economic relations; so many German technicians, said Litvinov, meant so many German spies.[28] And Potemkin told Payart that while Soviet grievances, as represented in the Bartlett article, were justified, its conclusion, about a possible Nazi-Soviet rapprochement, was the author's alone, not that of the Soviet government.

Payart asked Potemkin if the Germans wanted to move from economic to political negotiations. "I expressed my doubts," said Potemkin, "but on the spot I coolly reminded Payart that we never refused to improve our relations with [other] governments and that in the protocol to the Franco-Soviet pact we, and the French also, recognized the desirability of political collaboration with Germany within the context of strengthening peace and collective security." It was ironic, was it not, continued Potemkin, that Nazi Germany was more willing than France to sell the Soviet Union war materiel? And here Potemkin touched upon a long-standing grievance dating back to 1936: French sabotage of Soviet orders for military supplies. Payart was anxious about Nazi-Soviet economic discussions—as

Potemkin noticed—though he reported that Soviet dispositions toward France and Britain had improved since the end of January. We should hasten to take advantage of this situation, Payart warned, or we run the risk of a Soviet volte-face toward Nazi Germany.[29]

But Nazi-Soviet relations then went quiet. Wiehl told Merekalov that Schnurre would not go to Moscow but that negotiations could be conducted by the German ambassador Schulenberg and the counsel Hilger in Moscow. The Germans wished to avoid a hubbub in the press, said Merekalov, by sending a mission direct from Berlin. And there were two meetings with Mikoian in February, though nothing conclusive emerged from them.[30]

IV

Incredibly, at the Quai d'Orsay there was no noticeable reaction to Payart's reports, though there were signs that Vansittart had succeeded in gaining a modest opening to the Soviet government. In Moscow, Seeds informed Litvinov on February 19 that the British government would send Robert Hudson, secretary for the Ministry of Overseas Trade, to Moscow. Hudson would discuss trade matters, but Seeds hinted that London hoped for a general improvement in relations. Litvinov picked up the hint but complained of endless Anglo-French capitulations: assurances to the contrary "nowadays . . . were freely given and as freely broken." Litvinov singled out Bonnet for particular scorn, referring to him as a "natural capitulator." Under the circumstances, Litvinov said, the Soviet Union would "keep aloof." Seeds insisted that a change of mood had occurred in England. All to the good, replied Litvinov, but what was needed was a change in *action*.[31]

At the same time a new French ambassador arrived in Moscow to replace Coulondre. He was Paul-Émile Naggiar, a career diplomat whose last posting had been in China. Like Alphand and Coulondre, Naggiar was a strong advocate of better Franco-Soviet relations, but his advice to Paris, like that of his predecessors, was insufficiently heeded. Naggiar met Litvinov for the first time on February 8 and Potemkin the following day. They gave him the usual message that the Soviet Union was ready for cooperation with France and Britain, but that this readiness had not been reciprocated in the past. If the

Anglo-French attitude changed, the Soviet government would welcome it. But if not, we can get along without you; "we are not going
to beg" for your support.

Potemkin was more forthcoming than Litvinov, but he chided the
French government for taking a passive role in eastern Europe, leaving Poland and Romania to their fates. The Polish alliance, the
Franco-Soviet pact, relations with the Little Entente (Yugoslavia,
Czechoslovakia, and Romania) appeared to be past stages of French
foreign policy. Naggiar protested that this conclusion was "premature," though he admitted that in France there was opposition to cooperation with the Soviet Union. Insofar as you endeavor to
strengthen French cooperation with us, said Potemkin, you can
count on our full support in Moscow. In Litvinov's brief account of
the meeting—though not in Naggiar's, naturally—was the observation that the ambassador "gave to understand" that he did not
entirely agree with the "capitulationist policy" of his government.[32]

Whatever Naggiar might say, reports from Paris were not encouraging. Surits submitted a lengthy account of conversations with
Blum and Mandel, among other French politicians and ministers.
The overall picture was grim, another piece of evidence to support
Duroselle's and Weber's views of "decadent" France. The French
government assumed complacently that its "former friends" would
all find their way back into the French camp at the right time, without the French having to do anything to assure their support. Only
when rumors circulated of Nazi flirtations with Poland or of a shift
in Nazi-Soviet relations was this complacency shaken. "Such 'signals,'" Surits observed, "are therefore not without usefulness."

As for French politicians, Blum was extremely pessimistic and
expected Daladier and Bonnet to lead France "to a new Sedan."
And this, said Surits, from the leader of the largest and most powerful party in the French parliament! Mandel, however, was "the
complete opposite" of Blum. He was "absolutely devoid of any sentimentality. This is in the purest sense a rationalist with a proclivity
to cynicism and a strong inclination to conspiracy and intrigue."
Mandel was working quietly to undermine Bonnet, wrote Surits.

> He picks up facts, rumors, materials, and bides his time. During
> the September days [in 1938] when he foresaw impending war
> and played for the first time the role of a second Clemenceau, he

had already soaped the [hangman's] rope for Bonnet. He is keeping quiet now, but his hatred for Bonnet has not weakened. If
you want to know anything about Bonnet, you have to go to
[Mandel].

Surits said he had obtained important information about Bonnet's
recent clandestine efforts to improve relations with Germany and
Italy before they became public. Bonnet was preparing a new initiative to persuade Hitler that France would not interfere with Nazi
Germany's eastward expansion. Mandel concluded that "rotten
compromises" and concessions would never satisfy the aggressors,
"and with each new crisis it will be ever more difficult to avoid war
and that finally war will be imposed on France in the worst possible
conditions."[33]

In mid-February Litvinov, more than his deputy Potemkin, was
pessimistic in his appraisals of Anglo-French policy. To Maiskii's as-
sertion that opposition to appeasement was growing, Litvinov
replied in effect that Chamberlain and Bonnet had deep pockets for
concessions to Hitler and Mussolini. "It is not true that the resources for concessions have supposedly run out or are running
out." The British and French had decided to avoid war "at any
price." "Of course, I do not claim absolute truth in my prognosis,
and any surprises are possible. . . ."[34]

When Litvinov saw Naggiar again on February 22, he had in
mind Surits's letter as he complained about the weakness of French
policy. But Litvinov was less cynical with Naggiar than with
Maiskii. He affirmed that the Soviet Union would continue to support the policy of collective security if the French government would
support it too, even though the post-Munich situation was less favorable. The British and French governments, however, could not go
on ducking out at critical moments. Naggiar, like Payart before him,
warned Bonnet categorically that if they did, the Soviet Union could
come to terms with Germany—whatever Litvinov's preferences.[35]

V

In London meanwhile, Maiskii kept probing for changes to the better in British policy. He reported in early March that Chamberlain

and a number of ministers had appeared at a reception at the Soviet embassy. Maiskii even had a chat with the prime minister, who suggested that the international political situation was improving and that Hitler and Mussolini had assured him they wished to achieve their objectives peacefully. The London press has made much of the embassy visit, said Maiskii, calling it a sign of improved relations. The ambassador would not go that far: Chamberlain's visit could be bait to lure Hitler into better dispositions, or a gesture to mute opposition critics attacking the government for its unwillingness to improve relations with the Soviet Union.[36]

Litvinov remained cynical. He agreed with Maiskii's speculations about the motives of Chamberlain's visit to the Soviet embassy, but he also thought the prime minister might have sneaking doubts about his ability to slake the aggressors' thirst for new conquests. If war threatened, Chamberlain might think it a good idea "to drop a hint" to the Soviet government about better relations. Litvinov saw nothing but ruse and maneuvering: Chamberlain wanted Hitler to go east, but if the Germans had thoughts of going in the opposite direction, the British would threaten them with an alliance with the eastern powers. "I will not be surprised," noted Litvinov, "if in reply Hitler makes the same kind of gestures to us." Still, Litvinov seemed open to the possibilities in London, after speculating a bit on the purposes of the Hudson mission to Moscow. ". . . While considering English gestures with a certain amount of skepticism and mistrust, I consider them far from useless especially in view of our worsening relations with Japan."[37]

Soviet-Japanese relations had been strained for some time. In 1938 border skirmishing had occurred along the Manchurian frontier, in which the Red Army had taken the upper hand. Stalin may have hoped this outcome would reestablish Soviet military prestige damaged by the purges. The Japanese were bogged down in fighting in China, and the Soviet government was supporting the Kuomintang of Chiang Kai-shek in the obvious interest of keeping Japanese attention away from its Siberian frontiers. But Japanese border infringements continued in early 1939 and preoccupied the Soviet government.[38] These concerns were an additional incentive to keep the way open to improved relations with Britain.

Maiskii continued his quest for signs of a turnabout in British policy. He met Hudson and R. A. Butler, the parliamentary under secretary of state, at the Foreign Office for lunch on March 8. As Maiskii was leaving, he told Hudson that he was "quite convinced that we, the British Empire, were unable to stand up against German aggression, even with the assistance of France, unless we had the collaboration and help of Russia." Hudson replied that he thought Britain and France were changing direction and would eventually triumph, with or without the Soviet Union. Hudson recorded this exchange, concluding that Maiskii, having gone "out of his way to raise these questions . . . may indicate a certain nervousness in the minds of the Russian government." Vansittart was exasperated when he saw the memorandum, leaving a note for Halifax.

> There is unfortunately a great deal of force in what M. Maisky says: for example the British and French air forces are *utterly* unequal to standing up to the *whole* German air force. It is quite essential that a portion should be immobilized on the German Eastern Front. I see little utility in denying these self-evident facts, or in not trying to bring the Russians out of their isolationist tendencies instead of pushing them back in that direction. . . .

"Surely," Vansittart concluded, "when a foreign ambassador talks like this there is a very obvious, and infinitely preferable gambit that sticks well out of the ground." On March 14 Halifax left a note for Vansittart indicating that he had spoken to Hudson, warning him "against taking a line that would encourage Russian 'withdrawal.'"[39]

Maiskii's account of this meeting indicates that Hudson was by no means encouraging Russian "withdrawal." Quite the contrary, according to Maiskii, Hudson made it clear that there had been in the last two or three months a shift in British policy. The Tory government had "firmly decided to maintain its empire and its position as a great power." To this end, apart from rearmament, Britain would need allies, among them the Soviet Union. "Here in London, however, many people assured him [Hudson] that the USSR now did not want collaboration with the Western democracies, that it is inclined more and more to a policy of isolation, and that therefore it was pointless to seek a common language with Moscow." The Hudson mission, according to Maiskii, far from being strictly limited to matters of trade, was intended to clarify "do we want or do we not want a rapprochement and collaboration with London." Opposition to closer relations with the Soviet Union had "almost been surmounted." Hudson was ready to discuss in Moscow any issue, economic or political, though he did not yet have firm instructions from the cabinet. "Hence Hudson's visit to Moscow could play a large role in the determination of the future orientation of British foreign policy. . . . Personally Hudson would desire very much that this orientation moved on the line London-Paris-Moscow." He is an ambitious politician, said Maiskii, "but I do not think Hudson could take the general line which he developed in today's discussion without the sanction of Chamberlain."[40]

It is rare that records of the same discussion diverge as much as do these by Hudson and Maiskii. If Maiskii's account is correct, Hudson made strong overtures for better relations. This would have pleased Vansittart but appalled Chamberlain, who would not have given such license to his minister. A good reason then why Hudson may have underplayed to his colleagues what he had said to the Soviet ambassador. Maiskii confided to Butler after talking to Hudson that what he had heard "was too good to be true," and that he deeply distrusted Chamberlain's policies.[41] But this skepticism does not appear in his report to Moscow, an indication that Maiskii was playing an honest role in trying to improve Anglo-Soviet relations.

On March 9, the day after his talk with Hudson, Maiskii reported further signs of the British shift in policy. According to the press mogul Beaverbrook, Chamberlain had admitted to Churchill that his policy toward Germany had failed. Of course he would continue his efforts to ease Anglo-German tensions, but he no longer believed in the possibility of "solid friendship with Berlin." This realization, said Beaverbrook, explained the British "shift" toward the Soviet Union, a shift well supported by public opinion. Butler confirmed the shift in another talk with Maiskii and stressed the importance of the Hudson mission as a sign of the change in British policy. And Maiskii also met *Times* correspondent Sir Basil Liddell Hart, and he too confirmed the shift in policy, noting that "the British government, it's true, a little late, has come to the conclusion that without the USSR neither strategically nor politically could it guarantee the integrity of the Empire."[42]

At this point Stalin intervened by firing a shot across Anglo-French bows. On March 10 he gave a much-noticed speech at the

18th Congress of the Communist Party of the Soviet Union. It was chiefly about domestic issues, but it included important passages on foreign affairs. Stalin enunciated the usual Soviet line about the failures of collective security and the capitulation of France and Britain to intimidation from the aggressor states. He also played the guessing game about which way, east or west, Hitler would turn next for prey. Nazi Germany might indeed be eyeing the Soviet Ukraine, as the Western democracies appeared to hope. But Stalin noted facetiously that Nazi Germany had disappointed these expectations by turning its sights westward. Then Stalin summed up Soviet policy: "We stand for peace and the strengthening of business relations with all countries." While the Soviet Union stood "for the support of nations which are the victims of aggression and are fighting for the independence of their country," Stalin warned that Soviet policy aimed "to be cautious and not allow our country to be drawn into conflicts of warmongers who are accustomed to have others pull the chestnuts out of the fire for them."[43] Contemporaries, Ribbentrop and Schulenberg, for example—and now often historians—made much of Stalin's comment on "pulling chestnuts out of the fire" as a signal to Nazi Germany of an interest in negotiations. But the speech as a whole was a restatement in more detail of the Litvinov policy; the "chestnuts" reference was based on the apprehension of being left in the lurch by France and Britain to face Germany alone.[44] This was the mirrored fear of the French and British to be left to fight a war against Germany, only to see the Soviet Union stand aside or come in at the last to spread communism into a devastated Europe.

Stalin's words were noticed in London. On March 14 Vansittart followed up with Maiskii, saying that Hudson had a mandate from the cabinet to discuss both economic and political issues. In view of the unstable European situation, it was important to make the most of Hudson's mission and give it maximum publicity. Vansittart reckoned that a German move into rump Czechoslovakia was imminent and would be "the last nail hammered into the coffin of Munich." The prospect was no surprise to Vansittart, who reckoned it would be "a hard blow to the prime minister and generally to all the advocates of 'appeasement.'" But Vansittart had his own worries, for he asked with some apprehension if in Moscow there was really an interest in talking to Hudson about political issues. Judging from some of Vansittart's remarks, Maiskii observed, Stalin's recent speech had

had the necessary effect. An interesting aside by Maiskii indicating that the speech was a "signal," as Surits called them, to warn against taking the Soviet Union for granted or trying to lead it down the garden path. Maiskii gave vague assurances that Litvinov would see Hudson to discuss appropriate issues. According to the ambassador, Vansittart more than ever wanted to establish "the closest possible contact between London and Moscow, and he argued with me at great length about how important it is that the Hudson mission be a success."[45]

The next day, March 15, the German army marched into Prague, disrupting the leisurely pace of change in British policy. "What a day of shattered hopes," Channon wrote in his journal. So much for Hitler's respect for self-determination, thought most diplomats in Berlin, and for his promises not to redraw any more European frontiers.[46] The jokes in Berlin at Chamberlain's expense were cruel but revealing. The Soviet chargé d'affaires, G. A. Astakhov, reported this one after Chamberlain's visit to Rome in January: ". . . Mussolini lists his demands [to France]: Djibouti, Tunis, Corsica, Nice, and so on. To all this, Chamberlain replies: 'Agreed.' . . . Mussolini adds: 'And also your umbrella.' Chamberlain: 'Pardon me, but surely that's mine.' "[47] Even Chamberlain and Cadogan, who lost no love for Vansittart, had to admit he had been right all along. It galled the prime minister to have to listen to Vansittart's "Ah! that's just what I expected. He's [Hitler] keeping you quiet with soft words while he prepares for his next spring."[48]

The news continued to be bad. On March 17 rumors circulated that Germany had issued an ultimatum to Romania to accept draconian political and economic demands, and that Hungary was also being threatened. The Foreign Office sent cables to neighboring states asking what their position would be in the event of German aggression against Romania. To Russia went a cable asking if the Soviet Union would assist the Romanian government. "Now we have begun to flirt with Russia," Channon noted. "We must be in very low water indeed to have to do that."[49] Chamberlain still hoped the situation might be saved, though he realized that the occupation of rump Czechoslovakia had delivered a serious blow to his policies.[50] The prime minister's somnolent awakening did not mean that he intended Van's "gestures" to Moscow to become a headlong rush to intimacy.

This is just what Vansittart had in mind, and he called in Maiskii to see him two days after the Nazi entry into Prague. Foreign Office officials—and historians—often denounced Maiskii for his round-about lobbying and conniving with opposition politicians, journalists, and ministers of the crown. But here is an example of where the tables were turned: it was Vansittart who lobbied Maiskii for a grand alliance against Nazi Germany.

> Vansittart invited me to come to see him and he immediately spoke about events in central Europe. He appeared very uneasy and at the same time almost triumphant. Having declared that he was speaking to me in a completely private capacity and only on his personal initiative, Vansittart began with [the comment] that the annexation of Czechoslovakia marked the final blow to the policy of Chamberlain. All the rats were abandoning the sinking ship.... There can be no doubt.... The policy of "appeasement" is dead, and a return to it is impossible.

"I expressed skepticism several times and in different forms," said Maiskii, "about the seriousness of the change which was taking place, referring to experience and to past precedents, but Vansittart strongly argued that I was not right and that the foreign policy of the prime minister had suffered a complete collapse." Now a new era would begin, said Vansittart, where his policy would be triumphant—that of creating a "powerful anti-German bloc." We must act quickly for Hitler, encouraged by his successes, will not wait long to strike again. But where? In what direction? The guessing game again. Vansittart thought Romania might be the next target. Whatever the direction of Hitler's next attack, the only way to stop him was to build an Anglo-Franco-Soviet bloc including the other threatened European states. And Vansittart mentioned again his hopes for the Hudson mission, which was to set out on the following day. It could have a greater importance than first envisioned.

Vansittart also admitted difficulties. Franco-Soviet relations were cold. Was there not something the Soviet government could do to signal an improvement? Maiskii was cautious, saying he could not speak for his government, but personally he doubted whether the initiative could come from Moscow. And what of Soviet relations with Poland and Romania? asked Vansittart. If Romania resisted

German aggression, would the Soviet Union lend military assistance? "I can't say," Maiskii replied: "your questions catch me off guard." All he could do was refer Van to Stalin's recent speech and the Soviet government's willingness to help the victims of aggression. I understand your answer, said Vansittart, but "the moment has come when Britain, France, and the Soviet Union must decide in advance what they are willing to do in any given eventuality."

> The misfortune of 1938 was that Hitler rained blows on a divided, unprepared Europe; if in 1939 we want to oppose German aggression, Europe must be united and prepared. The first step for this must be a rapprochement between London, Paris, and Moscow, and the preparation of a general plan of action before and not at the moment of crisis.

Maiskii pointed out once again that Vansittart was preaching to the converted; it was London and Paris that had "systematically sabotaged any collective resistance to the aggressor." "I completely agree," Van replied, but "there's different music playing now." Think it over, and let's talk again next week. Maiskii asked Moscow for instructions on how to respond.[51]

What an extraordinary meeting. Vansittart's triumphant enthusiasm and sense of vindication are well captured in Maiskii's report. The ambassador sounded almost overwhelmed by Vansittart's blunt speaking. Would that it had been so easy. Cold realities soon dampened Vansittart's enthusiasm, however clear his vision.

The following day, March 18, Halifax called in Maiskii to confirm Vansittart's emphasis on the importance of the Hudson mission. Although the cabinet had not given Hudson highly binding instructions, "he is ready to discuss in Moscow any question—not only economic, but also political." "Personally, [I am] counting on Hudson," said Halifax, "to be able to dispel the suspicions in Moscow concerning the intentions and foreign policy of the British government and thereby to prepare the ground for closer cooperation between our two countries...." And Halifax added that he hoped Hudson could upon his return home allay "doubts which exist in England concerning the USSR." Maiskii surmised that Halifax had been hearing a lot of "anti-Soviet fables about 'the weakness' of the Red Army, and he hopes that Hudson can bring from Moscow solid counter arguments." Halifax also broached the subject of Romanian aid, though of course Maiskii did not have instructions and could again only refer to Stalin's speech of March 10.[52]

Maiskii's accounts of meetings with Halifax, Vansittart, Hudson, and Butler show a British government more interested in improving relations with the Soviet Union than do the British records of the same meetings. A case in point is Vansittart's loss of temper over Hudson's report of his talk with Maiskii on March 8. These discrepancies in Soviet and British records may indicate that Maiskii's British counterparts were not reporting their enthusiasm for better relations because of Chamberlain's opposition. A suspicious reader might suggest another explanation, that Maiskii fabricated or exaggerated British enthusiasms. But Maiskii's communications are too numerous and too consistent in their message for fabrication and exaggeration.

Litvinov was skeptical of the turnaround in British policy. He replied cautiously to the British request for the Soviet position on assistance to Romania, but promised to consult his government, or rather Stalin. He did this and replied to Seeds by proposing a five-, eventually a six-power conference, including France, Britain, the Soviet Union, Poland, Romania, and Turkey. Nothing would come of one government asking others about their intentions; a joint consultation was needed. Litvinov suggested Bucharest as the venue, which might strengthen Romania's position.[53] The rumor of a Nazi ultimatum to Romania proved to be untrue; the Romanian foreign minister denied knowing anything about it. And Halifax scuttled Litvinov's proposal for the six-power conference: it was premature and risky since its success could not be guaranteed. Halifax added that no minister was available to go to a conference, but the British government would certainly have found one had it wanted to attend.[54] Bonnet told Surits that he agreed in principle with Litvinov's proposal, though he doubted whether Romania really wanted Soviet support. "Personally I do not exclude the possibility," Surits observed, "that Bonnet, who is far from enthusiastic about fighting for Romania and would have preferred a more evasive reply from us, is deliberately trying . . . to increase our mistrust of Romania." Then, as an afterthought, Surits added: "But it is of course possible that this time he is not lying."[55]

Events surrounding the Romanian false alarm were like a splash of cold water in the face. Litvinov saw them as a cautionary note against the information he was receiving from Maiskii about the shift in British policy. "As you know from Comrade Maiskii's numerous cables," Litvinov wrote to Stalin, "Hudson has instructions to raise not only economic but also political questions." "We need to decide beforehand what position we will take in negotiations with him." "It cannot be denied" that events in Czechoslovakia and elsewhere have aroused British public opinion and that the Liberal and Labour parties as well as some Conservatives disapprove of Chamberlain's policies and want collaboration with the USSR. "This does not mean, however, that Chamberlain and his circle and the most thick-headed part of the Conservative party are persuaded about the need for a radical change in foreign policy." Moreover, the annexation of Czechoslovakia and the threat to other countries in southeastern Europe fit into Chamberlain's conception of German eastward expansion. He could not say this openly and therefore was obliged to give ground to public opinion. A flirtation with Moscow could ease future British negotiations with Germany, making Hitler more pliant. Perhaps Chamberlain also had doubts about his ability to reach terms with Hitler and Mussolini.

I think, said Litvinov, that all these calculations led Chamberlain to visit our embassy in London and to send Hudson to us. None of this ties his hands, though it allows him to some degree "to stop the mouth of the opposition." "Chamberlain would be more than glad . . . if negotiations with Hudson do not produce any results and if the responsibility for this could be laid on the Soviet government." We should have no illusions about Chamberlain's motives, Litvinov said, but we ought not to give the impression of self-imposed isolation or a lack of interest in collaboration, so that he can find *post facto* justification for his Munich policy. "As far as we know, Hudson does not have plenipotentiary powers to make definite proposals to us." We should not make any definite proposals either: "It suffices for us to explain our position based on your speech of 10 March. . . ." Then Litvinov proposed the text of a statement in this sense, which Stalin approved, to be read to Hudson when he arrived in Moscow on March 23.[56]

In London Vansittart met the Soviet ambassador again on March 20. "He beamed all over," reported Maiskii, "and was in very high spirits."

"I asked you to come," said Vansittart, "in order to say that

things are going well, and that the goals for which I have fought
for so many years are beginning to come about." Vansittart repeated
the main points of his previous meeting with Maiskii. It was especially important to demonstrate that Britain and the Soviet Union
stood in the same camp and formed a front against Nazi Germany.
Appeasement was finished; there was no going back to it. We must
act quickly, Vansittart said: "Anti-German sentiment in Britain now
stands very high." But there were still elements within the government "ready to sabotage the cross-over to the new position."[57]

VI

Where were the French in all the events leading up to the Nazi entry
into Prague? The simple answer is nowhere. Cable traffic from Paris
to the embassy in Moscow was routine from the beginning of January until March 23, eight days after the Nazi entry into Czechoslovakia. After Naggiar's first reports of meetings with Litvinov and
Potemkin, Bonnet sent an audacious cable to Moscow denying that
France had abandoned collective security during the Munich crisis.
No government had done more than France to assist Czechoslovakia. Here was a statement sufficient to justify a caricature of the
lying, double-talking Bonnet. The French government, he also advised Naggiar, was doing everything possible to speed the conclusion
of Soviet orders for war materiel. No Soviet official would have
believed it, and Naggiar scribbled in the margin of the cable that
nothing was in fact done.[58]

On March 15, with German troops marching into Czechoslovakia, Surits reported that Bonnet had talked to him about the desirability of improving Franco-Soviet relations. Bonnet even offered to
send a trade mission to Moscow, copying the British idea. French
opinion increasingly thought Hitler intended to move west, Surits
reported; eastward expansion was merely preparation for a westward offensive. "In this respect Stalin's speech has made a very
strong impression."[59] Litvinov appeared contemptuous in forward-
ing Bonnet's inquiry to Stalin; he speculated that the proposed
French trade mission might be used for political purposes. "It seems
to me that we should permit France least of all to resort to such a
ruse."[60]

Six days later, on March 21, Bonnet went to London for consultations with Halifax. "The Russians needed watching," Bonnet said. "They liked to make public declarations for propaganda purposes which did not correspond with their real intentions. It was therefore necessary for each party to say exactly what it was prepared to do."[61]

Halifax and Bonnet also discussed what action should be taken to avert further Nazi aggression. While the British government did not like Litvinov's proposed Bucharest conference, it countered with a four-power declaration calling for consultations in the event of a threat to the political independence of any European state. The signatories of the declaration—Britain, France, Poland, and the Soviet Union—would "consult together as to what steps should be taken to offer a joint resistance" to any such threat. As Cadogan put it, London was only inviting "*consultation* in face of any threat. It will be in the course of further exchanges of view that we shall attempt to define what, in given circumstances, any of the committants might be prepared to *do*" (emphasis in the original).[62] The French agreed to the British proposal on March 22. In Moscow, Seeds put the question to Litvinov on March 21 and received a favorable reply the following day. But Litvinov expressed doubts as to whether Poland would go along.[63]

Daladier did too. He advised Surits that he had agreed to the four-power declaration but thought Poland might refuse to sign, and that the British would then withdraw their proposal. According to Surits, "[Daladier] himself considers cooperation between England, USSR, and France to be sufficient, and he is ready to move on an agreement concluded only between these three countries."[64]

For Litvinov this was a difficult time. By early 1939 the Stalinist purges had decimated the Narkomindel; many of his friends and close associates had disappeared. "How can I conduct foreign policy," he said to Naggiar in February, with the Lubianka prison across the way?[65] In March Payart found Litvinov to be tense because of criticism in Moscow of his policies. Common wisdom in the diplomatic community was that Litvinov's days were numbered. Voroshilov, for one, was said to favor a Soviet-German rapprochement; but Stalin opposed it.[66] Among Litvinov's few surviving colleagues were Potemkin, Surits, and Maiskii. Were they spared to keep open the option of Soviet-Western cooperation against

Nazism? Or was it simply a tyrant's whimsy? Soviet diplomats, like other Soviet officials, worked under a suspended death sentence, not knowing if or when it would be imposed.

Doubts about Poland's willingness to adhere to a four-power declaration proved to be justified. On March 24 the Polish foreign minister Beck rejected the British proposal, not wishing to provoke Hitler. At the same time there was other bad news. Germany annexed from Lithuania the German-speaking port city of Memel, and the Romanian government signed a preferential trade agreement with Germany. Events seemed to be spinning out of control, which did not steady the nerves of statesmen trying to protect themselves from German aggression. Maiskii attended a diplomatic reception in London for the French president Albert Lebrun. "Funk and depression," he reported, were everywhere. "Memel . . . is the camel-breaking straw," Channon noted, "and the Cabinet is now unanimous that 'something must be done.' . . ."[67]

The Polish refusal to sign a four-power declaration irritated the French. Secretary General Léger thought Beck was "entirely cynical and false" and just looking for an excuse "to tuck in closer to Germany," even at the expense of Romania. Beck's policy was "hand to mouth . . . and . . . in his country's and his own interest he only wanted to get off the difficulties of the moment even at the cost of being the vassal (perhaps the chief vassal) of the new Napoleon."[68] This assessment was not too far wrong: on March 25 Beck proposed a modest compromise to Hitler concerning Danzig, the German port city administered under a League of Nations commissioner, and the Polish corridor. Under the treaty of Versailles, Danzig had been set up as a "free city." Likewise the Polish corridor had been created to give Poland direct access to the Baltic Sea—but in so doing it had cut off East Prussia from the rest of Germany. This was a long-standing German grievance even before 1933, and Hitler was determined to put it right. Beck hoped that some compromise could be reached on Danzig, sweetened by assurances of a continued anti-Russian, anti-communist Polish policy.[69]

Noël, the French ambassador in Warsaw, reiterated in January 1939 that many Poles feared the Germans less than the Russians; forced to a choice, they would collaborate with Germany. Noël reported the comment of the Soviet military attaché, who observed that the Poles would let themselves be crushed rather than accept

Soviet aid. Counseling patience, Noël said the Poles would have to be coaxed along.[70]

It was the old question of whether the Polish government would permit the Red Army to cross its territory to meet the Nazi enemy. This was a crucial issue in 1938, though French and British diplomats had earlier reported the difficulty. Soviet troops, Payart had noted, once on Polish territory might not want to leave. The Polish government, having taken Soviet territory in 1919–1920, understandably feared that the Soviets might one day want to take it back. Little wonder, Sir Howard Kennard, the British ambassador in Warsaw, commented after Munich, that collective security had foundered on Polish opposition.[71]

The British were more disposed than the French to follow Ambassador Noël's counsels of patience. Although the British government took a dim view of the Polish seizure of Teschen, its attitude to the Poles in March 1939 was to let bygones be bygones. Léger was not so easy to convince, though one Foreign Office clerk remarked that the French were always a little hard on Colonel Beck.[72] Léger advised the British to use "very clear and firm language" with the Poles, and so did the French ambassador Corbin. "He thought the strongest pressure must be brought to bear upon Poland, even to the extent of threats, to secure her collaboration." Strong language had not been characteristic of the French in recent years, and it still was not. Léger complained of being "surrounded by reticence." Much of it was of his own making, though Léger was right in telling the British chargé d'affaires in Paris that France and Britain should not subordinate their attitude to those governments, those "corollaries," with whom they were consulting. "That would be to put the cart before the horse. These governments would decide their attitude in accordance with the intentions of France and Great Britain."[73]

It did not happen; the tail still wagged the dog. The reasons were the same as during the Munich crisis. Bonnet told the British that it would be ". . . an advantage if Soviet help could be accepted by both Poland and Roumania. The important thing, however was not to give Poland (or, indeed Roumania) a pretext for running out on account of Russia."[74] Chamberlain had similar thoughts: he really could not blame the Poles for refusing to associate with the Soviet Union. This would provoke German retaliation. And then what could Britain and France do? "It's like sending a man into the lion's

den and saying to him 'Never mind if the lion does gobble you up: I
intend to give him a good hiding afterwards.'" And Chamberlain
concluded:

> Was it worth while to go on with Russia in that case? I must
> confess to the most profound distrust of Russia. I have no belief
> whatever in her ability to maintain an effective offensive even if
> she wanted to. And I distrust her motives which seem to me to
> have little connection with ideas of liberty and to be concerned
> only with getting every one else by the ears. Moreover she is
> both hated and suspected by many of the smaller states notably
> by Poland[,] Rumania and Finland so that our close association
> with her might easily cost us the sympathies of those who would
> much more effectively help us if we can get them on our side.[75]

And thus Chamberlain concluded that a four-power declaration was
"dead," proving Daladier's misgivings to be correct. The Chamber-
lain-Bonnet view of the Soviet Union remained pervasive. The day
after Chamberlain wrote the above lines to his sister, the British military attaché in Paris reported a meeting with Colonel Maurice
Gauché, chief of the French army's office of intelligence assessment,
the 2ᵉ Bureau:

> ... he was convinced that the democracies could expect nothing
> in the way of military assistance from Russia. It was to Stalin's
> interest now as always that the democracies and totalitarian
> states should cut one another's throats, which would pave the
> way for bolshevism and effectively safeguard Russian territory;
> but he was no more interested in seeing the totalitarians van-
> quished by the democracies than *vice-versa*.[76]

VII

While these developments were unfolding in Paris and London,
Hudson arrived in Moscow on March 23. He met with Litvinov on
his first day to discuss high politics. Hudson repeated Vansittart's
lines to Maiskii in somewhat more muted fashion. Last September,
said Hudson, we could not fight, now we can. There had been a big
shift in British public opinion. No government could hold power if it

sought to return to appeasement. "There will not be a second Munich." According to Litvinov, Hudson said he had come to Moscow with an "open mind" and was ready to listen to Soviet ideas about future cooperation.

Litvinov responded by reading to Hudson the statement he had sent to Stalin for approval. Basically it said that for five years the Soviet Union had been making proposals for collective security, all of which had been ignored or rejected by the French and British governments. They had instead chosen appeasement, making surrender after surrender and achieving nothing more than to encourage the aggressors' appetites for more. In spite of it all, the Soviet government had not abandoned its willingness to cooperate with other countries wanting to resist aggression. But having made so many unsuccessful proposals in the past, the Soviet government felt that it now must wait for France and Britain to take the initiative. If they made proposals, the Soviet Union was prepared to "examine and discuss" them. Litvinov added that the Munich policy had destroyed "international confidence and . . . the authority of the great powers among the small states." It would not be restored if future Anglo-Franco-Soviet cooperation was limited to simple question-and-answer exercises.[77]

Some differences appear in the British and Soviet accounts of this meeting. According to Seeds's cable, Hudson declared that there was no use regretting the mistakes of the past, it was time to think about the present and future. Litvinov said the Soviet government "would be prepared to consult with H. M. Government and other governments regarding all suitable measures of resistance whether diplomatic or military or economic. He made it clear that he had in mind the possibility of resistance by force of arms."[78]

Seeds's later, more reflective dispatch contained a healthy dose of British sarcasm: "Litvinov's historical review was most comprehensive. . . . Developed with his usual mastery of the subject. It exhibited the constant retreat of the Western Democracies . . . culminating in the Munich capitulation and the cold-shouldering of the Soviet Union." Hudson defended the position with "the only argument which can appeal to an unsentimental realist like Litvinov," that "we had no option at the time"; we didn't have the guns.

Touching but lightly as he generally does in conversation with me on British weakness (in contradistinction to his habit when conversing with a French representative), he said that France was practically done for: she was, as he put it, full of German agents, disaffected and disunited, at the mercy of certain leading politicians whom he profoundly distrusted. He foresaw in the not far-distant future a Europe entirely German from the Bay of Biscay to the Soviet frontier and bounded, as it were, simply by Great Britain and the Soviet Union. Even that would not satisfy German ambitions but the attack, he said smiling happily, would not be directed to the East.[79]

Litvinov left out of the Soviet record his view of the French and the happy smile at the thought of Hitler's armies moving west. These were Litvinov's personal feelings, no doubt shared by many of his colleagues. But Litvinov often vented his spleen and then got down to business. And the official Soviet welcome to Hudson and his party was laid on thick with visits to the theatre and lavish victuals and receptions.[80]

Hudson, Seeds, and Litvinov next talked during an intermission at the theatre. Litvinov's record is long, and discussions must have gone on well into the second act. The British showed him the brief cable they had sent or were intending to send to London. Litvinov bristled that a one-hour meeting could be reduced to eight or ten lines. "Screening the correctness of the notes gave me the impression of a sounding of our readiness to go as far as a military alliance or mutual military support, although at the time of the first conversation Hudson expressed reservations that he had not by any means a military alliance in mind." Then a long conversation ensued concerning Poland, Romania, and various trade issues. On the last point Litvinov's temper flared when Hudson suggested that Britain could make do without Soviet trade. Talk like that might work with small countries, Litvinov remarked, but two great powers could do without each other's commerce. It was better to look for terms of agreement profitable to both parties. On the larger issues, Seeds and Hudson protested against the USSR's "lack of faith in Britain and our unwillingness to believe that the British government wanted to break with past policies and begin anew."

Litvinov concluded that Hudson came to Moscow only to feel

out the Soviet government on its willingness to collaborate and conclude a possible military alliance, perhaps looking for specific Soviet
proposals—though "of course this does not mean that England is
now striving for such an agreement. England wants only to have in
hand all the elements necessary to make a decision in the future
under the appropriate circumstances."[81]

Hudson also conducted lengthy negotiations with Mikoian concerning trade matters, and though no deals were struck, there were
no mishaps either. On political issues Hudson also talked to
Potemkin, and during this conversation Hudson hewed more closely
to the Vansittart line. Perhaps he had been frightened by Litvinov's
impatience with the lack of substance in their discussions. Hudson
told Potemkin that he thought war with Nazi Germany was inevitable, and that to face this war an Anglo-Franco-Soviet alliance
would be essential. Hudson said Britain could send nineteen divisions to France, which would have been news to the imperial general
staff, since only two divisions could be sent at once. The conversation went on with various sorts of generalities, as though it were an
after-dinner conversation. Potemkin later concluded trenchantly that
Hudson's mission, "begun without serious preparations," had been
a failure. Potemkin was reminded of Gogol's Khlestakov, the inspec-
tor, who presented himself as an important person but who in fact
was not.[82]

Litvinov advised Maiskii of the failure of the mission. The more
so, said Litvinov, because of the issuance of the Tass communiqué,
which "greatly spoiled the mood of the English, and yes, ours
also."[83] The communiqué included a passage indicating that discussions of the international situation had taken place. When Cadogan
heard about it in London, he immediately cabled back to Seeds that
the passage concerning political discussions was undesirable and
should be deleted, though by then Tass had already released the
communiqué.[84] Nothing could have been more calculated than
Cadogan's objection to arouse Soviet suspicion and irritation.

On Litvinov's instructions, Maiskii went to the Foreign Office
for an explanation. It was an unfortunate mistake, according to
Cadogan, and he was sorry if the Soviet government had got the
wrong impression. Maiskii speculated that Cadogan did not like to
see the secretary for overseas trade involved in political discussions,
the more so since trade, not politics, was supposed to be Hudson's

main brief. "What jumped up at the eyes," reported Maiskii, was "that Cadogan spoke about the . . . incident with some agitation, unusual for him, and he pronounced Hudson's name with clear irritation. Apparently Cadogan was annoyed that a man from the trade department, and even more, someone promoted by Vansittart (with whom he is not on very good terms), also wanted 'to meddle in politics.'" Put bluntly, Cadogan "did not mind putting a spoke in the wheel" of the mission. Maiskii told Cadogan that the incident had made a bad impression in Moscow, not because anyone was inclined to exaggerate its meaning but because people like Halifax, Vansittart, and Hudson himself had strongly underlined the political importance of the mission. Cadogan's intervention gave the impression of "some kind of dissonance."[85]

There *was* dissonance inside the British government. Chamberlain wanted nothing to do with the Soviet Union, insofar as that was possible, and neither did Cadogan. Signals to Maiskii from Vansittart, Hudson, and even Halifax were apparently for Soviet ears only; they were not recorded in Foreign Office minutes. And Maiskii underestimated by a long way the animosity between Cadogan and Vansittart. Van is a "prize ass," Cadogan recorded in his diary: "I have *not* pushed to get rid of him, but I think now I ought to" (emphasis in the original).[86] As Litvinov put it to Surits: "The Hudson mission had produced no results, though it is true we expected none, and the goal itself of the mission was not clear either to us, or apparently to the English themselves."[87] Vansittart had a clear idea of what was needed, and he must have been disappointed with the failure to achieve it. But he could not challenge Chamberlain, nor even Cadogan.

VIII

Because of Polish opposition to a four-power declaration, Chamberlain cast about for another solution, though the Foreign Office failed to inform Maiskii or Litvinov. In fact, Chamberlain wished to keep the Soviet Union at a long arm's length in order not to irritate Poland. But Halifax warned that it would be unwise to give the Soviet government "the idea that we were pushing her to one side." And a cabinet minority spoke in favor of getting on better with the

Russians, since they were the only strategic force capable of deterring Nazi Germany.[88]

On March 29, in a well-known story which therefore bears mention only in passing, Ian Colvin, a Berlin correspondent of the *News Chronicle*, reported information to the Foreign Office suggesting an imminent German attack on Poland. In the discussion of what to do, Cadogan suggested a British guarantee of Poland intended to discourage German aggression. Chamberlain and Halifax agreed, and on March 31 the guarantee was announced in the House of Commons.[89] Colvin's information proved to be erroneous, but the guarantee had nevertheless been made.

In these last developments in March, the British neglected to involve or inform the Soviet government. The British failure to do so, consistent with Chamberlain's desire to keep the Soviet at a distance, had the predictable result of irritating Litvinov, who was already highly vexed with the British. When Cadogan called in Maiskii on March 29, it was not only to discuss the Hudson mission communiqué. Cadogan advised that Poland was adamantly opposed to being associated with the Soviet Union in a four-power declaration, so the French and British governments were now discussing a four-power bloc composed of Britain, France, Poland, and Romania. "The USSR for awhile will remain to the side," said Cadogan, "but in the next stage it also will come in . . ." under conditions to be negotiated.

"I listened with great astonishment to Cadogan," reported Maiskii, "knowing of the English secular dislike of firm commitments in general and on the European continent in particular. . . ." And on and on he went, describing how he had put this question directly to Cadogan: "Let's say that tomorrow Germany attacks Poland, will England in this case declare war on Germany?"

"To my astonishment," said Maiskii, Cadogan replied in the affirmative, subject of course to cabinet approval. Maiskii continued to express skepticism, smiling at Cadogan's protestations.

"Why do you laugh?" asked Cadogan.

"Because your new plan, if it is generally realized, which I am far from believing, would represent something like a revolution in the traditional foreign policy of Great Britain, and here, as is well known, they do not like revolutions."

"Yes, of course it would be a revolution in our foreign policy because for so long we could not take a final decision." And Cadogan added that he did not yet know what the government would do, though he thought it would go ahead with the guarantee.[90]

Not surprisingly, the Soviet government was unpersuaded that a revolution had occurred. Chamberlain's announcement in the House of Commons mentioned only Poland, and the wording did not define a clear *casus belli*. According to Maiskii, the wording was hedged and vague; according to Litvinov, it offered the British an escape clause on the Polish corridor and Danzig. On April 1 Litvinov was visibly angry in a meeting with Seeds because the British government had not formally advised the Soviet Union of the failure of the four-power declaration. But his grievances did not stop there. The British government had rejected out of hand his proposal for a six-power conference, and then, with less than three hours' notice, Halifax had asked for approval of Chamberlain's parliamentary declaration before Litvinov had even seen it. The "Soviet Government ha[s] had enough," Litvinov told Seeds, "and would hence forward stand apart free of any commitments." Seeds protested the British government's goodwill, but Litvinov waved him off and walked out of the meeting.[91]

After the prime minister announced the Polish guarantee in the House of Commons, he called in Lloyd George for a chat about the international situation. This was an uncharacteristic gesture by Chamberlain, who was not generous to adversaries and to this one in particular. In the ensuing discussion Lloyd George asked the prime minister about the role of the Soviet Union in the formation of a bloc against Nazi aggression.

The Poles and Romanians don't like the idea, replied Chamberlain. Russian participation is therefore problematic.

Then why did you risk the British commitment to make war against Nazi Germany?

The danger is minimal, Chamberlain replied. Our information is that the Germans will not risk a two front war.

"And where is the 'second front' to be?" asked Lloyd George.

"Poland," replied Chamberlain.

To this reply Lloyd George roared with laughter and mocked the prime minister. Poland, you say? "It has no respectable air force, nor a sufficiently mechanized army. Polish armament was less than outstanding, and from an economic and internal political point of view,

Poland is weak. There can be no 'Eastern front' without the active support of the USSR." "Without a firm agreement with the USSR," said Lloyd George, "I consider your statement today to be an irresponsible, hazardous gamble which may end very badly."[92]

Lloyd George succinctly summed up the British and French dilemma. No agreement with the Soviet Union meant no second front in Europe. The British cabinet had recognized that Britain and France could not stop Poland and Romania from being overrun, yet the British prime minister used this very argument with his sister not to bring in the Soviet Union but to keep it away.[93] The Liberal leader Archibald Sinclair explained to Maiskii that it was sleight of hand. Given Polish and Romanian hostility, the Soviet entry "fee" into matters of European security would be the provision to Poland and Romania of arms and raw materials and a refusal to supply Nazi Germany. Halifax later confirmed Sinclair's information by asking if the Soviet government would agree to provide Poland with munitions.[94]

Chamberlain's mistaken assumption was that the Soviet government would agree to play this subordinate role in which Britain would determine when and how the Soviet Union would intervene to protect its own interests. Maiskii's correspondence shows that some British officials and ministers saw the need for immediate action "to get on" with Moscow. Unfortunately this British message to the Soviet government, through Maiskii, had to be camouflaged at home because of Chamberlain's opposition.

In the last fortnight of March the Bucharest conference proposal, the four-power declaration, and the Hudson mission all failed. These failures undermined Maiskii's numerous reports of a change in course in British policy. And yet in spite of these failures and the urgency of the situation, there remained a certain British arrogance toward the Soviet government and, worse, a mocking dismissal of Soviet mistrust of France and Britain. As for France, apart from a few conversations in late March among Surits and Bonnet and Daladier, the French government took a passive role in relations with the Soviet Union. Rumors abounded of Bonnet's duplicity and double-talking. No one, least of all in Moscow, trusted him or put much faith in the French government. In spite of these unfavorable circumstances, there arose one last chance to form an Anglo-Franco-Soviet bloc, and it began in early April.

"Russia Has
100 Divisions"

A T THE BEGINNING of 1939 the British government had been considering the resumption of trade negotiations with the Soviet Union to encourage or intimidate it into buying more British manufactured goods. The balance of trade was greatly to Soviet advantage and a constant source of irritation to British officials. Their quest for bargaining leverage led to contemplation of a trade embargo. It soon became clear that this was not a good option, as international political issues took primacy over international trade. "Russia has 100 Divisions," observed S. D. Waley of the Treasury department, "and in the event of trouble it might be a decisive factor to have Russia on our side."[1] Waley was not a general, but he did not need to be in order to recognize the strategic importance of the Soviet Union.

The Stalinist purges had done grievous harm to the officer corps of the Red Army, but the purges had not eliminated the Soviet Union as a military factor in eastern Europe. Damage had also been done by the Anglo-French right, which used the purges as a justification for not cooperating with the Soviet Union against Nazi aggression. Both French and British military sources considered the Red Army to be a formidable force, whatever its imperfections, and worth having as an ally. The French military attaché in Moscow, Palasse, for example, had reported in April 1938 that the Soviet high command was recovering from the purges and that the Red Army's war potential should be rated high. The general staff dismissed this report, but

Palasse stuck to his guns. The Red Army could put 250 divisions in the field one year after mobilization. It could defend its territory, and its offensive capabilities, though limited, could seriously wound an enemy.[2] British military reports drew similar conclusions. The British military attaché in Moscow, R. C. Firebrace, reported in early March 1939: "The Red Army is at present loyal to the régime and would fight, if ordered to, either in an offensive or a defensive war. . . . It has suffered severely from the 'purge,' but would still prove a serious obstacle to an attacker. . . ."[3]

In early 1939 the British government could immediately send to France two divisions to join approximately eighty-five French divisions facing Nazi Germany. By all accounts the Soviet Union could more than equal this strength at the outset of war. It should be remembered that Anglo-French military strategy was based on the *guerre de longue durée,* a long war, where a tight land and sea blockade coupled with a defensive strategy on land would eventually reduce Nazi Germany to defeat. Offensive operations were to be only the finishing stroke. It does not take a professor of military science to recognize that the Red Army would have been a valuable resource in pursuit of such a strategy. Even if the Red Army was only a formidable defensive force, the Soviet Union could deny to Germany its vast natural resources, and it could provide large stocks of armaments and supplies to eastern allies such as Poland and Romania, should their governments wish to have them. The main Anglo-French criticism of the Red Army was that it could not sustain strategic offensive operations, because of both the purges and inadequate communications networks. But the Anglo-French had no immediate intention of taking the offensive against the Wehrmacht. Chamberlain repeatedly referred to the military weakness of the Soviet Union in spite of evidence to the contrary. Not wanting to ally with the Soviet Union, Chamberlain made use of any argument to justify his position.

II

This was where matters stood until the end of March. But circumstances began to change, and Chamberlain's position became increasingly difficult to defend. Public opinion in both Britain and

France shifted against Nazi Germany after the Prague occupation. Chamberlain came under heavy attack at home from the opposition parties for not bringing in the Soviet Union. They accused him of being driven by "ideological" motives. Chamberlain denied it: the Poles also objected to the Soviets, and so did fascist Spain and Salazar's Portugal, among others, including Canada. Expediency, not ideology, dictated British policy.[4] But the tail still wagged the dog. Litvinov noted in a cable to Maiskii: ". . . it is up to Chamberlain and Daladier, not Beck, to have the last word. This is not the first time England is addressing to us proposals for co-operation and then taking them back, pointing to the real or possible objections of first Germany, then Japan, and now Poland."[5] Chamberlain's own letters to his sisters reveal his ideological animus toward the Soviet Union.

Beck came to London on April 3 to discuss a bilateral military agreement. The British wanted Poland to support Romania in case of a Nazi threat. There was nothing doing from Beck. He already had the British guarantee in his pocket, so he had no need to provide a quid pro quo. Poland wished to avoid provoking Hitler; Romania was on its own. Worse, Beck failed to advise the British—in fact he lied—about increasing Nazi pressure on Poland itself. For starters, Hitler wanted to annex Danzig and wanted an extraterritorial route across the Polish corridor to East Prussia. Chamberlain had claimed that Poland was the key to the situation. Now he began to realize his mistake.[6] Britain could not keep Poland from being overrun, and Chamberlain refused to conclude with the only power that could, the Soviet Union. *Nu, khorosho*, fine, then, as the Russians like to say. "We know very well," Litvinov wrote on April 4, "that to hold back and stop aggression in Europe without us is impossible and that the later they [the Anglo-French] appeal for our help, the higher our price will be."[7]

First Potemkin, then Litvinov called in the Polish ambassador, W. Grzybowski, in early April to grill him on the reasons for the Polish refusal to associate with the Soviet Union in the British four-power declaration. Were reports in the press true about Polish opposition? asked Potemkin. Grzybowski gave the stock answer that Poland wished to remain neutral between Germany and the Soviet Union. Potemkin replied that Poland's future position would depend on Hitler's mercy. If Germany threatened, Poland would be compelled to accept support from the other great powers if it wished to protect its independence.

With Litvinov, Grzybowski tried to slip away from hostile Polish statements against the Soviet Union, but the commissar would not let him do it.

Polish policy was dangerous given Hitler's avidity for conquest, Litvinov observed. As for Poland's "neutrality," he had not noticed it during the Munich crisis.

Poland would turn to the Soviet Union when necessary, Grzybowski replied.

Take care not to do it too late, Litvinov warned.[8] This was good advice. On April 11 Hitler approved new war plans, "Operation White," for the isolation of Poland and the destruction of its armed forces. Hitler had not yet decided on war, but if Poland declined to make the necessary concessions, he intended to crush it.

British publish opinion and opposition pressure for better relations with the Soviet Union were difficult to resist, but some British officials and the prime minister were not yet persuaded of the need. Halifax assured Maiskii of the British government's desire to create a broad coalition to protect the peace, and this coalition would not be formed without the Soviet Union. But the Foreign Office flatly rejected Maiskii's informal suggestion of a visit by Litvinov to London to prepare negotiations. Sargent and Cadogan, both as hostile as ever to the Soviet Union, thought this a dreadful idea. It would "arouse the deepest suspicion in every country where the Soviet connection is feared. . . . I hope we will not allow Maisky's fictitious grievances and Litvinov's assumed sulks to push us into action against our better judgement." Sargent suggested "calling the Soviet bluff by asking them point blank to make us a definite and detailed scheme showing the extent to which and the manner in which they are prepared to cooperate with other governments. . . ."

"I agree," Cadogan chimed in. "Personally, I regard association with the Soviet as more of a liability than an asset. But I should rather like to ask them what they propose, indicating that we don't want a lesson in 'moral issues,' but some practical indication of what they propose should be done." Halifax concurred, with qualifications: ". . . of course we want if we can—without making a disproportionate amount of mischief . . . —to keep them in with us. . . ."[9]

III

While the British rejected the idea of a Litvinov visit to London, diplomatic stirrings began in Paris. The French government finally snapped out of its languor toward the Soviet Union at the beginning of April. On April 2 Payart gave a warning heard many times from the French embassy in Moscow. If France ignored the Soviet Union, it would do so at its peril. He reported Litvinov's quip to Seeds that an isolationist policy might after all be best for the Soviet Union. Payart noted that such remarks were an effort to stimulate Anglo-French interest, as no doubt they were. But Payart warned that Litvinov's cynical comments "almost always indicated the alternate policy directions of other Soviet leaders." The Soviet government had the impression of being successively plied and then rebuffed and played with so as to be isolated and compromised with Nazi Germany. Litvinov was sick and tired of the Anglo-French cold shoulder and "fed up" with Polish and Romanian hostility. He did not intend the Soviet Union to be a lightning rod for Nazi aggression.[10]

Whether it was Payart's warning or the mounting European crisis, the French cabinet appears to have directed Bonnet to see Surits to discuss the possibilities of collaboration. On April 5 Bonnet inquired about the Soviet interest in supporting Poland and Romania against Nazi aggression, even referring to the passage in Stalin's speech of March 10 about Soviet support for the victims of aggression. Bonnet was vague about French intentions, said Surits, but one thing was clear: he wanted Moscow to take on obligations in the east and probably also the main blow from Nazi Germany. Bonnet advised that the French government would have proposals to make in a few days concerning security arrangements in eastern Europe. Surits discounted this meeting as merely a ruse by Bonnet to give the impression that he was consulting with the Soviet government. Naturally, Bonnet's account of the meeting was somewhat different, but it put heavy emphasis on what the Soviet government might do and little at all on what the French would do to support Poland and Romania.[11]

Bonnet called Surits back to the Quai d'Orsay on April 7—the same day Italian armies invaded Albania—and again stressed the need for Franco-Soviet cooperation to support Poland and Romania.

DANZIG, THE POLISH CORRIDOR, THE BALTIC STATES, AND FINLAND

Finnish territory ceded to Russia after the Winter War

SWEDEN

FINLAND

Gulf
of
Bothnia

Lake
Ladoga

Åland
Isles

Turku

Virolahti

Viipuri
(Vyborg)

Helsinki

Leningrad

Hango

Gulf of Finland

Krasnaya
Gorki

Stockholm

Dago

Reval (Tallinn)

ESTONIA

Lake
Peipus

Ösel
(Saarema)

Parnu

Parnu

Dorpat
(Tartu)

Gulf
of
Riga

Gotland

Walk (Valka)

Gauja

U.S.S.R.

Windau
(Ventspils)

Riga

LATVIA

Öland

Lipau (Liepaja)

Mitan
(Jelgava)

Dvina Daugava

Baltic
Sea

Dunaburg
(Daugavpils)

Memel
(Klaipeda)

Memel
District

LITHUANIA

Memel

Tilsit

Kaunas
(Kovno)

Vilna

GERMANY

Danzig

EAST
PRUSSIA

N

Polish
Corridor

Suwalki

POLAND

Vistula

Oder

Warsaw

0   25   50   75   100 MILES

Surits said little in reply except to note the difficulties in offering support to a country that did not want it. The ambassador nevertheless promised to report Bonnet's comments to Moscow. Surits also advised of an earlier meeting with Daladier, who had railed against Polish policy, which he thought could only lead to ruin. A number of French notables called on Surits in early April, including Gamelin, who also criticized Beck, regretted "mistakes of the past," and said it was time to rally all those forces willing to resist aggression. Other French military officers, including the former chief of staff, Maxime Weygand, said it was important to have "a firm agreement with Russia." "Communism should be fought on the internal plane, and I favor the suppression of the Communist Party in France," said Weygand. "On the external plane, ideology must not interfere with strategic needs." Of course, there was no consensus on this point. Virtually as Weygand spoke, Gamelin's chief of 2^e Bureau was dismissing Soviet cooperation as a means of spreading bolshevism in Europe.[12]

Litvinov duly reported Bonnet's message to Stalin along with a devastating assessment of French policy:

> Bonnet is the most determined and uncompromising advocate of the so-called Munich policy. I think he is still ready to continue the earlier line, which comes to this, that France will refuse any intervention whatsoever in European affairs, except in the case of a direct attack on France itself or on nearby Belgium or Switzerland. He is ready to sacrifice all the remaining countries of Europe, including Rumania and Poland. . . . Unfortunately, we must deal with him as minister of foreign affairs, but we must always have in mind that he will attempt to use our responses and proposals in support of his thesis on the impossibility of cooperation with us and of a modification of the Munich policy. In such a spirit would he also use the absence of a response from us.

Litvinov therefore proposed and asked for approval of what became the Soviet reply to Bonnet. To wit, that the Soviet government had suggested a six-power conference and agreed to the British proposal for a four-power declaration. While Poland and Romania had not asked for Soviet assistance, and although the Soviet Union had no treaty obligations with these two countries, the Soviet government was nevertheless willing "to listen to and to study" any concrete proposals.[13]

Litvinov duly instructed Surits to convey this reply to Bonnet. His instructions crossed with a cable from Surits indicating that Bonnet was pressing him for an answer to his proposal for negotiations. Yesterday he rang me up, today he called me in for a talk. "I found him in a state of complete prostration," said Surits. He showed me a pile of telegrams from various stations reporting the worsening situation: Italy had two million men under arms; German troops were reported moving toward the Polish frontier; the French fleet had been mobilized. War could break out in a matter of days. Bonnet is impatient for our reply, Surits reported; he sent instructions in this sense to Payart yesterday. He wants immediate discussions and is willing to sign a tripartite declaration without Poland.[14]

Surits was sending daily reports now of meetings with Bonnet or on the French political situation. "These last weeks I cannot complain about an absence of contact with the French government," he wrote. "In fact, the situation has become most peculiar in that these 'contacts' are beginning to be a burden. Bonnet is overpowering me by his pursuits and nearly daily meetings [with me]." At first Surits thought it was all show, to give the impression of constant contact and consultations in order to fool public opinion; but in the last week the situation had changed. "Bonnet for the first time, it seems to me, has finally understood that his policy has led the country to the brink of disaster and himself (which for him is probably more important) to political bankruptcy."

With each passing day in Paris a prewar atmosphere was growing stronger, Surits reported. Everyone was persuaded that war could not be avoided and that it would have to be conducted under conditions far worse than the previous autumn. First the occupation of Prague, then the invasion of Albania had transformed the public mood. "Throwing dust in everyone's eyes" no longer worked. French public opinion has turned around; press attacks against the USSR have all but ceased. France is not so finicky now about looking for Soviet aid. The old French arrogance is gone; they are supplicants: "people who need us, not . . . people whom we need." France is neck deep in rising danger; accommodation with the aggressors is no longer possible, and war is imminent. In fact, France and the Soviet Union needed each other. But Surits feared betrayal: we should negotiate but "not assume any obligations without reciprocal guarantees."[15]

Surits's letter crossed with one from Litvinov reiterating what he had written to Stalin on April 9, and full of mistrust for Bonnet and Halifax. Bonnet was just looking for a pretext to say that the Soviet Union was not prepared to act, as he had done during the Munich crisis. His willingness to sign a three-power declaration was meaningless; he knew full well that Britain would not agree to it, and he probably assumed that it would be unacceptable to Moscow as well.[16]

Whatever Litvinov's deep personal mistrust of the British and French governments, he could think dispassionately when the circumstances required it. Perhaps because of Surits's letter or a combination of circumstances, Litvinov contemplated a new proposal, his last as it turned out, to the French and British governments aimed at cooperation against Nazi Germany. Sargent and Cadogan wanted to "call . . . the Soviet bluff by asking . . . [for] a definite and detailed scheme showing the extent to which and the manner in which they [the Soviet] are prepared to cooperate with other governments. . . ." Litvinov decided to oblige them.

IV

The transition began when Litvinov rebuked Maiskii for statements he made in a meeting with Halifax on April 11. Halifax had advised that the British government was contemplating further guarantees to Greece and Romania. Discussion was wide-ranging, but Maiskii asserted that the only way to check aggression and guarantee the peace was through a broad multilateral undertaking rather than through bilateral or trilateral agreements. Halifax thought the British government was moving quickly toward a firm position against Nazi aggression, and he hoped the Soviet government would see it. Maiskii replied that the speed of British countermoves might have sufficed in the nineteenth century but was too slow to keep up with Hitler and Mussolini. It was necessary not only to catch up with the aggressors but to anticipate their actions and thwart them. Halifax left the meeting feeling frustrated: "Maisky's attitude during our conversation was quite friendly, but I could not feel at its conclusion that we had made any great progress towards the solution of the real difficulties of which His Majesty's Government are necessarily conscious, but which Maisky and the Soviet Government persistently appear to me to ignore."[17]

Two days later, on April 13, Litvinov recommended to Stalin that Maiskii take "a more reserved position" in his meetings with British officials, and he asked for approval of a draft cable to this effect. Stalin agreed, obviously because Litvinov reprimanded Maiskii for discounting the value of bilateral or trilateral agreements. "We also consider inappropriate your critique of English policy. You should be guided by our direct instructions, and not by articles from our press which may permit to itself greater liberties than an official Soviet representative." On the matters at hand, Litvinov instructed Maiskii to tell Halifax that the Soviet government was not indifferent to the fate of Romania and that it would like to know how Britain contemplated help by itself and by other countries for Romania. "We are ready," said Litvinov, "to take part in such assistance."[18]

On that same day the British government announced security guarantees for Romania and Greece, and the French did the same. In late March the British government had announced its intention to double its reserve forces. A week after the Anglo-French guarantees to Romania and Greece, a British Ministry of Supply was set up, and six days later a bill was introduced in the Commons for compulsory military service. It seemed that Britain and France were finally stiffening, but the new measures were long-term projects. They would take time to show results. And it was one thing to make guarantees, it was quite another to be in a position to protect Polish or Romanian frontiers against actual invasion. In London there were debates in the House of Commons on April 3 and 13. Many opposition speakers and some Conservatives wanted to know what was being done to bring in Russia. There were calls for a full-blown alliance with the Soviet Union, but still the government would not contemplate it. Channon noticed Churchill, Lloyd George, and a few others "in a triumphant huddle surrounding Maisky . . . , the Ambassador of torture, murder and every crime in the calendar."[19] Chamberlain was adamantly opposed to a Russian alliance, and Halifax only slightly less so, backed by Cadogan and Sargent. As Chamberlain put it to his sister Ida,

It doesn't make things easier to be badgered for a mt. of Parliament by the two oppositions and Winston who is the worst of the lot, telephoning almost every hour of the day. I suppose he has prepared a terrific oration which he wants to let off. I know there are a lot of reckless people who would plunge us into war at once but one must resist them until it becomes really inevitable.

Then Chamberlain turned to his meeting with Beck and their discussion of the Soviet Union.

I confess I very much agree with him for I regard Russia as a very unreliable friend with very little capacity for active assistance but with an enormous irritative power on others. Unhappily we have to strive against the almost hysterical passion of the Oppositions egged on by LlG who have a pathetic belief that in Russia is the key to our salvation. . . .[20]

The Foreign Office cabled its ambassador in Turkey on April 13, stating that "His Majesty's Government have no intention of concluding a bilateral agreement of mutual assistance with the Soviet government."[21] Halifax's assurances to Maiskii on April 6, for example, about bringing in the Soviet Union may have reflected his personal view but not the prime minister's nor even the official position of the Foreign Office. Soviet suspicions of Chamberlain, if not Halifax, were justified.

The next day, April 14, the British government invited the Soviet Union to make unilateral guarantees to Poland and Romania. It was the British way of bringing in "the Soviet" without making any commitments to it.[22] Maiskii nevertheless was positive with Halifax, so the latter recorded, about the British guarantees, and he informed the foreign secretary of the Soviet position on Romania. Halifax was anxious for a Soviet reply and asked for it quickly. In his report to Moscow, Maiskii mentioned seeing Vansittart after leaving Halifax. Vansittart confirmed that new instructions for Seeds asking for unilateral Soviet guarantees demonstrated that Anglo-Soviet relations were entering "a new phase" of consultations about real cooperation.[23] Litvinov could not be sure this was true, but he was willing to see.

On April 14 the French also took the initiative with the Soviet Union, without having first consulted with London. This was a new experience for them, not having done so since Barthou's time. Bonnet handed to Surits a general proposal for a supplement to the Franco-Soviet pact, by which each would agree to support the other in case either side went to war with Germany to support Poland or Romania. Typically, Bonnet's first draft of this proposal only mentioned Soviet aid for France, not French aid for the Soviet Union. Surits's account of the meeting is larded with sarcasm but does not mention Bonnet's neglect of the barest sort of reciprocity. Bonnet pressed Surits for an indication of the Soviet position; Surits would say only that the Soviet government might have a counterproposal.[24]

Seeds saw Litvinov on April 15 to speak to the British proposal. Litvinov gave Seeds "a friendly hearing," but he did not like a unilateral declaration that committed the Soviet Union but not anyone else. Litvinov put it somewhat differently in his record of conversation, stating that he did not hear anything in the ambassador's statement about what specific support Britain envisaged, both its own and Soviet, for Romania. The British government, observed Litvinov, "apparently preferred general declarations of principle to more precise obligations . . . agreed to beforehand."[25]

Litvinov met Seeds the following day to go over the same ground, but now he was rather more blunt. He wanted to know how far the other guarantors were willing to go and what precisely was expected of the Soviet government. And he wanted to know what Poland and Romania were proposing to do. For all Litvinov knew, these two could negotiate deals in Berlin and make the guarantors look like fools. Maybe the British government knows something we don't, said Litvinov, but we need to be completely informed before making any public declaration. Payart put it plainly: the Soviet Union did not intend to pull Anglo-French chestnuts out of the fire and did not wish to be left alone to face Nazi Germany. In Paris, Bonnet told Surits that the British proposal had caught him unawares, though the French government supported it.[26]

Litvinov did not tell Seeds that the Soviet government was contemplating a counterproposal to the British and French governments, of which Surits was apparently already aware when he met Bonnet on April 15. On that day Litvinov sent a proposal to Stalin for a tripartite alliance with France and Britain. We have British and French proposals now, said Litvinov; perhaps the British were sounding us out through the French. In any case, the British and

French governments were beginning to reveal their positions. "If we want to gain something from them," Litvinov said, "we also must disclose a little our own wishes. We ought not to wait for the other side to propose to us the very thing which we want." On the supposition that the Soviet government wanted to cooperate with France and Britain, Litvinov proposed a minimum four-point position. It can be summed up briefly: mutual assistance in case of aggression against any of the three signatories; support for *all states neighboring the Soviet Union, including the Baltic countries and Finland;* rapid agreement on the specific forms of mutual assistance; and agreement not to conclude a separate peace. We can expect "urgent and complex negotiations" with the French and "especially" the British, said Litvinov; we need to monitor British public opinion and try to influence it.[27]

The next day Litvinov discussed with Stalin his draft of the tripartite alliance with France and Britain. The resulting eight-point proposal was handed to Ambassador Seeds the following day, April 17. Litvinov explained the Soviet plan as an elaboration of Bonnet's proposal but also combining the British idea of guarantees to Poland and Romania.[28]

Sargent and Cadogan had dared Litvinov to produce specific proposals, and here they were. The Foreign Office was confounded, Cadogan thought the Soviet proposals "extremely inconvenient": they would "give little additional security" and would alienate our friends and provoke our enemies. "In order to placate our left wing in England, rather than to obtain any solid military advantage," noted Cadogan, the British government had asked for a Soviet unilateral declaration of support. "The assistance of the Soviet government would be available, if desired, and would be afforded in such manner as would be found most convenient." Cadogan had to admit, however, that the Soviet proposal put His Majesty's Government in a bind:

> ... there is great difficulty in refusing the Soviet offer. We have taken the attitude that the Soviet preach us sermons on "collective security" but make no practical proposals. They have now made such, and they will rail at us for turning them down. And the Left in this country may be counted on to make the most of this.... There is further the risk—though I should have thought

it a very remote one—that, if we turn down this proposal, the Soviet might make some "non-intervention" agreement with the German government.

Cadogan recommended that Litvinov's proposal be rejected, and it was—with "disdain," French Ambassador Corbin would say later.[29] Having rejected Litvinov's proposals, the second thought coming to the Foreign Office mind was to get to the French before they started negotiating separately with the Soviet government. They might actually be drawn into Litvinov's plans, and this would make things still worse for the British. So the Foreign Office asked the French government for consultations before it replied to the Soviet ambassador in Paris. Cadogan explained the British position to Corbin, who observed that "great care" would have to be taken in handling Litvinov's proposals. "A flat rejection," as Halifax put it to Phipps in Paris, "would enable the Russians to cause both Governments considerable embarrassment, [so that] it would be better if some practical counter-proposals could be devised."[30]

As the British feared, the French did show more interest. Bonnet "asked me to convey to you," Surits cabled Litvinov on April 18, "that his first impression is very favorable."[31] But then there were snags, as there usually were in Bonnet's dealings with the Soviet Union, not least because the British thought the French had responded too positively to Litvinov's proposals. Extensive discussions between the French and British considered a response to the Soviet offer. Léger told Phipps that Bonnet had at first thought the Soviet proposals "coincided" with French views. Now the French thought them too binding and too broad-ranging. *But* Léger thought the Soviet proposals, "stripped of certain obvious objections," could serve as the basis for agreement: "He felt that once France and Great Britain made certain requests of Russia they must be prepared to grant the requests for reciprocity in some form. . . ."[32] Bonnet saw Surits on April 22. We have some problems with the Soviet proposals, said Bonnet. The French government does not like the idea of guarantees for the Baltic states since there are no corresponding Soviet guarantees for Holland, Belgium, and Switzerland. Bonnet was just fishing. He told Surits the French government would study the proposals further and get back to him in a few days.[33]

The French government sought unsuccessfully to persuade the

British to move off their adamant opposition to a Soviet alliance. Bonnet handed Phipps the French reply to Litvinov's proposals: it said in effect that the Soviet concern for reciprocity of obligations was "a sine qua non," and had to be met to some degree. Public references to specific countries, especially Poland, should be avoided, and the agreement should refer only to "mutual and reciprocal engagements of assistance between the three Governments without naming any other state." The "formula proposed to [the] Soviet Government must therefore be in terms wide enough not to indicate specifically such or such a country, and precise enough to apply nevertheless to [the] most pressing and probable emergencies." What was more, the French government could not support the British proposal for a unilateral Soviet declaration of assistance because it simply would not be acceptable in Moscow. Even so, the French proposal, while engaging the Soviet Union to come to the aid of France and Britain if war ensued from their actions to protect the "status quo *in central or eastern Europe*" (emphasis added), did not require the French and British governments to come to the aid of the Soviet Union if it acted in similar circumstances. In other words, the French and British would decide the question of peace or war, and the Soviet Union would come along for the ride. Bonnet handed the French proposal for a trilateral agreement to Surits on April 25.[34]

The British thought the French had gone too far; the Soviet reckoned not far enough. Chamberlain "did not like" the French proposal; neither did Halifax or Cadogan. It was the usual story: Poland would decline any association with the Soviet Union.[35] The British ambassador in Warsaw, Kennard, warned that pressure on Poland would only make matters worse. Once the Soviet Union became a full member of an anti-German coalition, the Polish government would fear relegation to a secondary role. Moreover, the extraordinary publicity in the press and on radio about a possible agreement with the Soviet Union made Polish opinion anxious and played into the hands of Nazi propagandists exploiting fears of bolshevism. "Would it not be possible," pleaded Kennard, "even at this late hour for someone in authority to *insist* that the press and BBC control themselves?" (emphasis in the original). Cadogan thought that showing Kennard's letter to Chamberlain "might help."[36] Collier, Northern department head, commenting trenchantly in another context (about Romania), observed that "If Hitler decides to take immediate action, he can always find a pretext without referring to Russia!"[37]

Collier was one of Vansittart's men, and at times he boldly criticized the government. In a shocking comment on the minutes of the Committee on Foreign Policy, composed of senior cabinet ministers, he noted that if one "read between the lines," especially of Chamberlain's comments, one could not "help feeling that the real motive for Cabinet's attitude is the desire to secure Russian help and at the same time to leave our hands free to enable Germany to expand eastward at Russian expense." The Central department head, Strang, disputed this, but Cadogan, consistent with his earlier views, did not comment. Collier warned that the "Russians are not so naive as not to suspect this, and I hope that we ourselves will not be so naive as to think that we can have things both ways." Soviet support was worth having, whatever its shortcomings, and "we ought not to boggle at paying the obvious price—an assurance to the Russians, in return for their promise of help, that we will not leave them alone to face German expansion." Anything less would not only be cynical but doomed to failure.[38]

A shocking statement but true. It was a good thing Litvinov did not see it, though he needed no confirmation of Chamberlain's or Bonnet's bad faith. Litvinov considered Bonnet's proposal of April 25 to be "insulting," but he still wanted to hear more from Paris and London. Impatient to have the British response, Litvinov apparently told Seeds on April 25 that his proposals were not "hard and fast" but should serve as "a basis for discussion"—though two days earlier he had signaled Surits that the Soviet proposals taken as a whole were the "minimum" position. In fact, Seeds warned that a negative British reaction to Litvinov's proposals "would merely confirm them [the Soviet government] in the belief that we are trying to evade association with this country's efforts."[39] Where was the British reply? asked Litvinov. Was the Soviet Union to understand that the British government was withdrawing its call for a unilateral declaration in favor of the French tripartite accord?[40]

On April 28 Bonnet told Surits that the earlier French proposal was only semi-official and "his personal suggestion." "One has to conclude," Surits advised Litvinov, that the British had not agreed to Bonnet's "suggestion."[41] This was an understatement. Then, the following day, Bonnet rang up Surits and asked him again to come to see him.

Have you received anything from Moscow on my proposal? asked Bonnet.

No, replied Surits.

Bonnet mentioned that he had been "engaged constantly in negotiations with the English, but until now he still had not obtained an agreement." Then Bonnet went fishing for comments from Surits on his own tripartite proposal. The Soviet ambassador discreetly pointed out the absence of reciprocity in obligations. Feigning to notice, Bonnet blamed the problem on Léger and said he would have the wording changed at once to correct the deficiency.[42] This was careless diplomacy, to say the least, with war imminent in Europe. On April 28 Hitler reinforced the impressions of danger by denouncing in the Reichstag, the German legislature, the 1934 Polish-German nonaggression pact and the 1935 Anglo-German naval limitations agreement.

Litvinov wrote to Stalin on April 28 that Bonnet's original proposal lacked any pretense of reciprocity, but he was not entirely negative. Bonnet's proposal had a broader range covering all of "central and eastern Europe," not just Poland and Romania. We should not be in a hurry to answer the French, said Litvinov, before we have a reply from the British. Actually, what little good Litvinov saw in Bonnet's proposal proved false. Bonnet told Surits the following day that he had intended coverage only for Poland, Romania, and Turkey.[43]

On April 29 Halifax advised Maiskii that the British had been "too busy" to consider Litvinov's "very logical and well constructed" proposals. This statement was not disingenuous, it was false, as Litvinov was aware, having heard Bonnet say to Surits that he had been in constant negotiations with the British. Halifax also assured Maiskii that the British government would not leave the Soviet Union in the lurch in eastern Europe if it went to the assistance of victims of aggression. This may have been true, at least in Halifax's mind, but not everyone believed it, not even Collier in the Foreign Office. At the same time Bonnet told the British ambassador in

Paris that the French would go along with the British position on unilateral guarantees if the British could get the Soviet government to go along, a possibility that Bonnet doubted.[44] This marked the end of Bonnet's fortnight fling with an independent foreign policy toward the Soviet Union.

"Our negotiations with other countries are not going badly," Chamberlain wrote to his sister Hilda on April 29:

> Our chief trouble is with Russia. I confess to being deeply suspicious of her. I cannot believe that she has the same aims and objects that we have or any sympathy with democracy as such. She is afraid of Germany & Japan and would be delighted to see other people fight them. But she is probably very conscious of her military weakness and does not want to get into a conflict if she can help it. Her efforts are therefore devoted to egging on others but herself promising only vague assistance. Unfortunately she is thoroughly mistrusted by everyone except our fatuous oppositions and indeed it has been made pretty clear to us that open association with her would be fatal to any hope of combining Balkan powers to resist German aggression. Our problem therefore is to keep Russia in the back ground without antagonising her. . . .[45]

This was just the arrangement that the Soviet government was determined to thwart. On May 3 Litvinov sent a memorandum to Stalin on British policy. "The English are not in a hurry to reply to us," he said. They were evidently waiting for the Soviet reply to Bonnet and would repeat their proposal for unilateral guarantees. Litvinov categorically rejected both the British and the French proposals, recommending that the Anglo-French be disabused of any illusions on the Soviet position. He wanted integral acceptance of his proposals but recommended Soviet guarantees for Holland, Belgium, and Switzerland as a quid pro quo to obtain agreement for a guarantee of the Baltics and to meet Bonnet's objections.[46]

Litvinov was willing to bargain for his original proposals, but he would not be carrying on the negotiations. On May 3 he was replaced by Viacheslav Mikhailovich Molotov, Stalin's No. 2 man and chairman of the Council of People's Commissars. A brief cable sent to Soviet diplomatic posts said only that Litvinov had been replaced because of "a serious conflict" between him and Molotov "owing to the disloyal attitude of Comrade Litvinov to the Council of Commissars of the USSR."[47] Litvinov's departure caused speculation in the West that the Soviet Union might now entertain better relations with Nazi Germany and abandon collective security.

Payart reported that Litvinov's dismissal was not expected but was at least partially attributable to British stalling over Soviet proposals for a tripartite alliance. Added to earlier French and British "side-stepping," the cup of Soviet patience had finally run over. The immediate cause of the dismissal, speculated Payart, appeared to have been Halifax's last indication to Maiskii (on April 29) that the British government would again propose a Soviet unilateral guarantee, rejecting in effect Litvinov's eight-point tripartite alliance. "Litvinov was considered as the symbol of the policy of collective resistance to aggression. Even more, he brought to its defense in the councils of government the dynamism of his strong personality. It is to be feared that his disappearance . . . may signal . . . a withdrawal . . . into neutrality, or even an agreement . . . with Germany." But this option, Payart said a week later, seemed unlikely *for the moment* (emphasis in the original). The Soviet government still appeared committed to collective security, but Stalin would be taking a closer hand in Soviet foreign policy, and it would be subject to his *amour-propre* and to his impulses.[48]

As if to reinforce Payart's suppositions, Molotov reassured the French and British embassies that there would be no change in Soviet policy—unless, he added cryptically to Seeds, "other states changed theirs."[49] Seeds drew similar conclusions, and Soviet diplomats also assured their Western counterparts that Litvinov's departure did not signal a change in policy. Maiskii later said that the resignation was the result of a personal quarrel between Litvinov and Stalin.[50] All the evidence is not available to draw certain conclusions about Litvinov's dismissal; we still depend on the speculations of contemporaries. The Soviet-published documents give the impression, however, of a Litvinov still willing to negotiate and compromise with the untrustworthy French and British governments. Stalin may finally have lost patience and opted for the hard-nosed approach of Molotov.

V

There had been many warnings from the French embassy in Moscow about the dangers of a Nazi-Soviet rapprochement. Readers may wonder if these warnings were based in fact. Was there diplomatic activity between Moscow and Berlin after the recall of the Schnurre mission at the end of January? The answer is, very little. *Franco*-German economic discussions, which began in December 1938 at the time of Ribbentrop's visit to Paris, were more important than the brief flurry of activity created by the aborted Schnurre mission. Daladier thought about inviting Hermann Goering to Paris— Goering was responsible for the German four-year economic plan—and Bonnet was also interested in pursuing trade negotiations, which appeared on the verge of success in March. Hervé Alphand, a Commerce Ministry official, and Lucien Lamoureux, a former cabinet minister, were sent to Berlin to conduct negotiations.[51] In January–March 1939 the British also conducted negotiations with Nazi Germany. First political feelers, then contemplation of economic cooperation led the Foreign Office to send Ashton-Gwatkin to Berlin to sound out German officials and business people.[52] All this activity was cut short by the German occupation of Prague.

As for Nazi-Soviet relations, the ambassador Merekalov reported from Berlin in early March being invited to a lunch for the diplomatic corps hosted by Hitler. A brief conversation between Merekalov and Hitler was polite, though the ambassador complained about the hostility of the press. In fact, Litvinov thought the German and Italian presses had toned down their vitriol against the Soviet Union. "Germany itself would not mind," observed Litvinov, "using the Soviet trump in its game with England and France, but it has not decided on the corresponding political gestures which it wants, if possible, to substitute for an economic rapprochement. At the same time, fascist Germany never ceases to interest itself in our raw materials and its exports to the USSR."[53] A month later Litvinov wrote to Merekalov on the political situation: "I cannot tell you anything beyond that which you know from the newspapers—not from the German, of course, but from French, English, and Soviet." Hitler, it seemed, had been a little confused by the British declaration on Poland. Finally, Litvinov noted certain "enigmatic movements" of the German ambassador Schulenberg back and forth between Moscow and Berlin.[54] The following day Litvinov sent a brief cable asking Merekalov to go to the German Ministry of Foreign Affairs to request that Germany cease interference in the handing over from the Skoda arms factory in occupied Czechoslovakia of plans, models, and anti-aircraft artillery being manufactured under contract for the Soviet Union.[55]

Some historians have attributed great importance to the subsequent meeting between Merekalov and the state secretary of the German foreign ministry, Ernst Weizsäcker, on April 17, the day Litvinov finalized his proposals for an alliance with France and Britain. The meeting has been interpreted, based on Weizsäcker's account, as a Soviet opening to Germany which ultimately led to the August 1939 Nazi-Soviet nonaggression pact. Publication of Soviet documents in 1990 and 1992 indicates that there was no political opening, merely the execution of Litvinov's instructions to request a halt to German interference in the Skoda fulfillment of Soviet contracts. Merekalov made no report of offering political opinions except to say that the Soviet Union hoped that the threat of war would be ended. In this discussion Merekalov, according to his account, asked Weizsäcker a series of questions about Franco-German and German-Polish relations. Merekalov also complained about German press attacks on the Soviet Union, noting that they indicated no "change of line in the German press." In reply, "Weizsäcker threw up his hands and sighed." Merekalov then asked how Weizsäcker saw future German-Soviet relations. The state secretary made a joke about how bad they were, then said that "ideological" factors prevented an improvement, but that he hoped for the development of economic relations. Weizsäcker's report of the meeting, on which most historical accounts are based, indicates that Merekalov made a strong opening for better political relations. It is not impossible that Weizsäcker's account was correct, and that Merekalov concealed his own political observations, but if so, he was not acting on Litvinov's instructions.[56]

VI

The French and British governments would be sorry to see Litvinov go. His replacement, Molotov, was an entirely different sort of man—a ruthless, cold-blooded son of a bitch, a dog-loyal *oprichnik* who followed Stalin's orders to the letter. Molotov was the second most powerful man in the Soviet Union. Colorless bureaucrat to begin with, he was "comrade filing cabinet," according to Lenin. Unlike Litvinov, Molotov had not been outside the Soviet Union and spoke no foreign languages. Where Litvinov had stayed out of party politics, Molotov was in the thick of them as Stalin's henchman. He was in fact neck deep in the blood of the purges, having often signed the death warrants of the victims, many his former colleagues. Even in old age Molotov had little remorse. It was not a secret that he and Litvinov intensely disliked each other. Molotov recalled that "Litvinov remained among the living only by chance."[57] According to Churchill, who came to know Molotov during the war:

> He had lived and thrived in a society where ever-varying intrigue was accompanied by the constant menace of personal liquidation. His cannon-ball head, black moustache, and comprehending eyes, his slab face, his verbal adroitness and imperturbable demeanour, were appropriate manifestations of his qualities and skill. He was above all men fitted to be the agent and instrument of the policy of an incalculable machine. . . . I have never seen a human being who more perfectly represented the modern conception of a robot. And yet with all this there was an apparently reasonable and keenly polished diplomatist.[58]

On May 4, as Litvinov had anticipated, the British renewed their proposal for unilateral guarantees. What followed, however, was not so predictable. Potemkin had gone to Ankara to follow up on negotiations to improve relations with Turkey—an important Soviet ally during the interwar years—which had begun at the same time as those with the British and French. He saw the Turkish president, Ismet İnönü, who was critical of the French and British governments for failing to oppose German eastward expansion. Ismet reckoned that Anglo-French policy was intended to stay aloof, in the expectation that Nazi Germany would wear itself out at war in the east, so that ultimately the French and British could be arbiters of Europe.

Unfortunately they had miscalculated, and Austria, Czechoslovakia, and Albania had been swallowed up. The remaining independent states in eastern Europe, according to Ismet, had lost faith in Anglo-French support and were contemplating whatever accommodation they could make with Hitler. Britain and France had finally seen the danger and begun negotiations with Turkey and the Soviet Union. "In Ismet's opinion, the USSR should not decline [Anglo-French] offers of cooperation." He advised Potemkin that Moscow would do well to accept Bonnet's proposal or at worst the British concept of unilateral guarantees, then build on it. Acceptance, said Ismet, would not be incompatible with Soviet "dignity." An Anglo-Franco-Soviet alliance was critical. Ismet had told Weygand, who was visiting Turkey at nearly the same time as Potemkin, that France "could not defend itself against Germany without the support of the USSR."[59]

Would the Soviet government take Ismet's advice? Payart cabled to Paris that the British proposal was, to say the least, unfortunate "... at a time when we need to bring in the USSR and to take it at its word rather than to give it new reasons to withdraw on itself...."[60] On May 8 Seeds went to see Molotov to present the British proposal. Molotov was polite but skeptical, asking about British willingness for staff talks and a military agreement. And Molotov was confused by the different French and British proposals; he wanted an accounting for it. Seeds did not have an easy explanation. Then there were the usual questions about the Polish position, always the difficulty. Seeds gave the habitual reply of Polish apprehensions of offense to Nazi Germany. Molotov commented unfavorably to Seeds on the British delay in responding to Litvinov's proposals: the "Soviet government had always replied ... within three days, instead of three weeks." Seeds answered dryly, "I [take] off my hat to Soviet efficiency." Molotov "laughed heartily," though it was no laughing matter.[61] Payart did not buy the British or Polish argument of avoiding offense to Hitler; once it was decided to oppose Nazi Germany, it was necessary to take any measure required to make that policy effective.[62] Molotov also met Payart on May 11 to go over some of the same ground, but here Molotov emphasized the importance of effective cooperation as opposed to ineffective paper commitments.[63]

Molotov asked for advice from his ambassadors and from

Potemkin, who visited Bucharest, Sofia, and Warsaw after leaving Ankara. Potemkin replied from Warsaw on May 10: "Without the participation of the USSR France and England cannot guarantee real support to Poland and Romania against Germany." Potemkin repeated Ismet's blunt statement to Weygand that France could not sustain a war against Germany without the Soviet Union. And yet, "very characteristically," Britain had made proposals, asking for Soviet help without wanting to give anything in return, and wanting to dispose of Soviet support as bosses whenever it suited their interests, without taking into account those of the USSR. Even so, asked Potemkin, "should we simply reject the English proposal?" Potemkin argued that conditional Soviet acceptance would give the Soviet government certain advantages: international prestige, a way around open association with Poland and Romania, less binding Soviet commitments, and none before action by France and Britain. We could, said Potemkin, point out the defects of the British proposal while agreeing to it on conditions put forward in effect in Litvinov's proposals of April 17. "I ask you to take into account," wrote Potemkin (in case Molotov did not like his advice), "that I had to compose this reply on the run in conditions of haste."[64]

Potemkin might have worried a little less, for Surits submitted similar advice to Molotov. He went through all the drawbacks of British proposals, noting that the Soviet Union was treated as a kind of "blind companion" trailing after the French and British, not being able to count on their support even against the consequences of Soviet obligations to them. Having said all this, Surits advised not to reject out of hand the British proposals. That would serve the interests of Bonnet and Chamberlain, who would foist off responsibility for a rupture of negotiations on the Soviet Union in order to justify themselves before public opinion—which, Surits noted, supported an alliance with the USSR. In short, Surits recommended accepting Bonnet's last proposal (April 29) as a basis for discussion. Moscow would then, said Surits, "be declaring before the entire world our willingness to support our neighbors exposed to attack and we will put an end to all the fables about our double dealing with Germany." We will demonstrate our flexibility and our willingness to compromise and to accept reasonable counterproposals. And by accepting the Bonnet proposal as a basis for discussion, we will have on our side the vast majority of French public opinion, thus increasing pressure on the British and making it more difficult for Chamberlain to slip away in Parliament.[65]

Maiskii did not agree with his two colleagues. He opposed the acceptance of the British proposal, though he did not comment on Bonnet's. He reported a conversation with Halifax on May 9 at which the foreign secretary again tried to reassure the Soviet government against fear that the British would leave it to stand alone against Germany. Maiskii was not persuaded by Halifax's protestations; the British declaration was still a one-sided obligation, that is, that the Soviet Union would go to the aid of France and Britain if they became involved in hostilities, though not the other way around. But Halifax then said, according to Maiskii, "if you do not like this formula . . . propose another" which met each side's wishes for reciprocity. Maiskii gave full voice to Halifax's avowals of goodwill; indeed, he stressed that Halifax had twice stated the British government's desire for agreement with the Soviet Union. But Maiskii did not like it that the new British proposal was virtually unchanged from the original of April 14, and this so brief a time after Hitler had renounced the German-Polish nonaggression pact and the Anglo-German naval agreement (on April 28). And to reinforce his point, Maiskii added: " 'The appeasers' have raised their heads here again"—the *Times* had launched a big campaign "for one more try" to come to terms with Germany and Italy. "Personally, I consider that the [British] proposal . . . is unacceptable, but I think that it is not the last English word."[66] Perhaps it was just a coincidence that Oliver Harvey, Halifax's private secretary, remarked in his diary six days before Maiskii's dispatch to Molotov that " 'Appeasement' is raising its ugly head again. I keep hearing indirect reports that No. 10 is at it again behind our backs. There is the usual *Times* leader striking a defeatist note—'Danzig is not worth a war.' . . ."[67] Maiskii's reports were not unrepresentative either of Halifax's statements or of opinion in London.

Molotov thus had policy alternatives before him in early May 1939, and he seemed to waver. On May 10 he cabled Potemkin that he might delay his departure from Warsaw to talk to Polish Foreign Minister Beck. "The main question for us is to know how in Poland matters stand with Germany. You may hint that if Poland wishes, the USSR can give them support." According to Potemkin, Beck acknowledged that Poland could not hold out against Germany without Soviet support. This was scarcely a secret, but it was uncharacteristic candor coming from Beck. "For my part," said Potemkin, "I emphasized that the USSR would not refuse support to Poland if it so desired."[68]

The next day, Thursday, May 11, the Polish ambassador in Moscow, Grzybowski, called on Molotov to advise that his government objected to Bonnet's trilateral guarantee of Poland. Further, it would not participate in a mutual assistance pact with the Soviet Union. Grzybowski's only hedge was to say that his instructions reflected the circumstances of the moment and that in the future these issues might be seen in a different light. "All the conversation attested to the fact that Poland does not want in the given circumstances to tie itself to any agreement with the USSR or to an agreement on the participation of the USSR in a guarantee of Poland. . . ."[69] This, then, was the Polish reply to Potemkin's offer in Warsaw.

From London there was more news from Maiskii about a flareup of appeasement in Britain. He concluded, however, that public opinion was too hostile to Nazi Germany for a return to the Munich policy, however much Chamberlain might maneuver and wish to do so. The government would probably fall if it reverted to appeasement. Halifax saw Maiskii again on May 11, still pushing the British proposal of a Soviet unilateral guarantee. They went around on the issues of reciprocity, guarantees, and the British commitment to support the Soviet Union, but they resolved nothing. Maiskii reported, however, Halifax's wish to clear away suspicion and mistrust and obtain an agreement. He encouraged the Soviet government to elucidate its objections to the British proposal.[70] This it did in a Tass communiqué and an inspired editorial in *Izvestiia* on May 10–11. These public comments boded ill for the British proposal, though they were no surprise to the French.[71]

On May 14 Molotov reported the Soviet government's position. It reflected Maiskii's view, not that of Potemkin and Surits. The minimum Soviet position was a tripartite mutual assistance pact, a guarantee of the central and east European states, including the Baltics, and a concrete military accord. When Molotov spoke of the Baltic guarantee, Seeds "uttered deprecatory noises," tapping his fingers on the paper that explained the Soviet proposals. The British government did not wish to include the Baltic countries in a trilateral guarantee because of their opposition. Molotov listened politely but was not to be put off.[72]

Potemkin received Payart to advise him of the Soviet position. "England wants to have everything from us," said Potemkin, "without giving us a sufficient quid pro quo in exchange. What will happen, for example, if we are attacked by Germany through the Baltic states. No support from England would be assured to us. . . ." Asked about the discrepancies between the French and British proposals, Payart said the French government had put forward its proposals because it thought the British proposition would be unacceptable. Bonnet spoke to Surits in this same sense, insisting that he had not withdrawn his idea.[73] The British of course were vexed with Bonnet for putting forward a French proposal. "It has cut across our own negotiations," complained Seeds, ". . . for it is obvious that, when faced by two divergent proposals, only the fool (which the Russian is not) will not go all out for the more advantageous."[74]

On the Soviet side, Molotov had two policy options before him in May. He chose in effect to keep Litvinov's proposals on the table, and he rejected outright the British concept. Molotov ignored Bonnet's proposals, though these might have been taken up and transformed into something close to Litvinov's original program. The British were opposed to either concept because both envisaged a tripartite alliance. Chamberlain remained a major obstacle to agreement. Although Halifax was more flexible, he was influenced by Cadogan and Sargent, who opposed an alliance. Channon noted that Chamberlain in House debate showed "his dislike of the 'Bollos' and of Russia"; a Soviet alliance was "the pet scheme of the leftish clique in the Foreign Office." Strang, the Central department head, believed that Chamberlain resisted a Soviet alliance because it would signal the end of appeasement; he said "all at No 10 are anti-Soviet."[75] The prime minister was relieved by Litvinov's dismissal and threatened to resign "rather than sign [an] alliance with the Soviet." Even Corbin attributed the British cabinet's "reticence" to anti-communist animosity.[76]

May 14 was a crucial day in the negotiations to form an anti-Nazi alliance. There would be other opportunities for agreement, but this one was important. It was lost because anti-communism still determined policy at least in London, though perhaps less so in Paris, and because the Soviet government could not set aside its profound mistrust of the French and British governments which Munich and the other failures of collective security had engendered. Probably the only way to have persuaded Molotov and his colleagues of Anglo-French goodwill would have been the resignations of Chamberlain, Daladier, and Bonnet. *Les intentions se jugent aux actes,* deeds speak louder than words, was an axiom the Soviet government had long applied in its relations with France and Britain. Resignations and new leaders, such as Churchill, Mandel, and others, would have made a difference. But Churchill came only much later, and Mandel not at all.

CHAPTER FIVE

"The Russians Will Give Us More Trouble"

NEVILLE CHAMBERLAIN'S opposition to a Soviet alliance was critical to the failure of trilateral negotiations during the summer of 1939 and a major contributing factor to the beginning of the Second World War. Whenever Chamberlain relaxed and spoke his mind about the Soviet Union, his hostility and mistrust were conspicuous. "I am afraid the Russians will give us more trouble," Chamberlain wrote to Hilda on May 14, the day Molotov rejected the British proposal for a Soviet unilateral guarantee.

It is an odd way of carrying on negotiations. To reply to our reasoned & courteous despatch by publishing a tendentious & one sided retort in their press [on May 10–11]. But they have no understanding of other countries mentalities or conditions and no manners, and they are working hand in hand with our Opposition. The latter don't want to see anything that doesn't exalt or glorify Russia or perhaps they might understand that if an alliance which is incapable of giving much effective aid were to alienate Spain or drive her into the Axis camp we should lose far more in the west than we could ever hope to gain in the East. . . .[1]

The issue of Spanish hostility had been discussed a few days earlier in the cabinet. This was Franco's Spain, which in March 1939

144

had finally defeated the Republicans. Sir Ernle Chatfield, minister for coordination of defense, did not make much of Spanish enmity: a hostile Spain could be brought "to a stand-still" by blockade. The far greater danger was a Nazi-Soviet rapprochement; to avert it, Britain needed to get on better with Russia. But Halifax had heard nothing about the likelihood of "some secret agreement being concluded between Herr Hitler and M. Stalin." I find it "difficult to attach much credence to these reports," he said, "which might be spread by persons who desired to drive us into making a pact with Russia."[2] A pattern developed in the cabinet: those who opposed the Soviet alliance disparaged the dangers of not obtaining it; those who favored an alliance pointed to the hazards of failure, and since these actually materialized, one cannot say they were exaggerated. Even after Molotov's blunt reply to Seeds on the evening of May 14, rejecting unilateral guarantees, Sargent advised Chatfield that the Foreign Office was "still unwilling to accept the Russian proposal of a full-blown mutual guarantee treaty." It hoped that by giving a little ground, it could induce the Soviet government "to forego their full demand." "I gather," Channon recorded, "that it has now been decided not to embrace the Russian bear, but to hold out a hand and accept its paw gingerly."[3]

II

The French were more open to a Soviet alliance. On May 15 Bonnet instructed Corbin to press the British to respond quickly to Soviet overtures and to reexamine the French proposal of April 29 for a limited tripartite alliance.[4] True to practice, however, Bonnet did not press too hard. His expressions of impatience were also accompanied by the caveat that of course "the French government would be perfectly well satisfied with the British formula [for agreement] if the Soviet government could be persuaded to accept it." With regard to the discrepancies in British and French proposals to Moscow, Bonnet assured the British that Payart had been instructed not to give Molotov the impression there was "any difference of opinion" between London and Paris. But both Payart and Bonnet had already indicated to the Russians that there *had* been differences with London. Indeed, Payart was quite candid about it with Potemkin.[5]

Bonnet could not be true even to himself. Contrary to what some historians may say, the French government was not so quick to resume the diplomatic initiative. Bonnet instructed Payart "to take a back seat and let Sir W. Seeds make the running. . . ."[6] He later confided to the British ambassador that while an agreement with the Soviet Union was necessary, London and Paris should be careful not to allow themselves "to be dragged into war" by the Soviet government. The "best policy with the Soviet is to avoid giving them the impression that we are running after them." Bonnet sneered at cabinet ministers Reynaud and Mandel: "the [French] communists are unfortunately not the only people here who are under Soviet influence."[7] The Quai d'Orsay reiterated to Naggiar, back in Moscow in early June, that the French government would remain in the background. If the British failed to obtain Soviet agreement, the French government could put forward its own compromise solutions.[8]

Bonnet's pliancy allowed the British to take the lead in the negotiations, and it allowed Chamberlain to prevent any rush to agreement. Typical of the British government's attitude, Cadogan did not think much account needed to be taken of the French proposal for a tripartite alliance. Chamberlain suggested a fresh approach, which the Foreign Office was working up. "We must certainly remember to keep the French informed," noted Cadogan, but there was no need to seek their prior assent.[9] This attitude became less abusive during the summer, but the British continued to go their own way in spite of French concerns or objections.

III

Halifax sent Vansittart to see Maiskii to persuade him that the Soviet government should accept half a loaf, though in fact the British offered much less. Vansittart suggested that if the Soviet Union would give up a tripartite alliance and guarantees of the Baltic states, the British government would be willing to conduct staff talks. According to Maiskii, he told Vansittart that Molotov's proposals of May 14 (that is, a tripartite mutual assistance pact, guarantee of the central and east European states, including the Baltics, and a concrete military accord) were Moscow's minimum position, and that the British government should not hope for further Soviet concessions. According to Vansittart's account, Maiskii may have been a little less adamant than he reported, but in any case the ambassador forwarded to Moscow the latest British proposals. These were essentially a unilateral Soviet declaration, again, and a generally worded commitment "to concert together as to the methods by which such mutual support and assistance could, in case of need, be made most effective." To the Soviet government, hedged commitments, such as these, were not commitments at all. According to Maiskii, Vansittart promoted the new proposal as a tripartite alliance in fact, with the Baltic area eventually included in the coverage of an agreement. Not surprisingly, Vansittart's account does not refer to the new British proposal as a de facto alliance. Chamberlain was not ready for that, even in veiled form. Essentially Vansittart offered the same advice that Potemkin and Surits had earlier given to Molotov: accept the British proposals as a basis for discussion, then develop them further. Maiskii said that a positive reply from Moscow was unlikely.[10]

Molotov's proposals of May 14, Maiskii later reported, put the British government in "a difficult position" because public opinion strongly favored "an alliance with Russia." Every day there was new evidence of public support, and on May 19 another debate in the House of Commons on foreign policy was scheduled. Lloyd George and Churchill among others were expected to speak in favor of an alliance. What could the British government say in reply? asked Maiskii. As the German threat to Poland developed, the British would have to do something to back their guarantees. Even Chamberlain was beginning to show signs of movement, and the pace of British replies, contrary to usual practice, was speeding up. "I suppose that it [the British government] really wants to come to an agreement more quickly, but for the time being it still wishes to haggle and has not said its last word."[11]

In more colloquial language in his journal, Maiskii wrote that either Britain could conclude an alliance with the Soviet Union or face defeat in a war with Germany. But Chamberlain could still not psychologically digest an alliance with the Soviet Union "for it would once and for all throw him into the anti-German camp and would put an end to any projects to resurrect 'appeasement.' Therefore Chamberlain haggles with us like a gypsy, and again and again tries to palm off a lame horse on us. It won't happen! But he nevertheless does not lose hope." Parenthetically Maiskii wondered why Vansittart lent himself to Chamberlain's play. No doubt it was to drag the prime minister along into a more active policy, but "we will not accept the [British] formula, and this will only give Chamberlain an additional argument against [Vansittart]."[12] Maiskii's assessment was correct, but a more flexible Soviet policy might have brought the results anticipated by Potemkin, Surits, and Vansittart, and of course headed off the possibility of a Nazi-Soviet pact.

On the morning of Friday, May 19, Maiskii informed Van that the British formula remained unacceptable. According to Maiskii, Vansittart was not surprised but said he would again try to find an acceptable basis for agreement.[13] The debate in the House of Commons later that day made his work easier. Churchill and Lloyd George, among others, berated the government for failing to secure a Soviet alliance. "I beg His Majesty's Government to get some of these brutal truths into their heads," said Churchill. "Without an effective Eastern front, there can be no satisfactory defence of our interests in the West, and without Russia there can be no effective Eastern front." "For months," said Lloyd George, "we had been staring this powerful gift horse in the mouth." What was going on, why the delay in responding to Soviet proposals, why no pressure on Poland to cooperate? Channon thought Chamberlain gave as good as he got in the exchange. "I looked up at Maisky, the smirking cat, who leant over the railing of the Ambassadorial gallery and sat so sinister and smug (are we to place our honour, our safety in those blood-stained hands?)."[14]

The gift horse was still a gift horse, because Poland remained a convenient excuse to take no action. It's time this stopped, Maiskii told Corbin, the day before this latest parliamentary debate.[15] But Polish and Baltic objections were not the only factors troubling the British government. On May 20 Halifax met Bonnet and Daladier in Paris on his way to Geneva. The foreign secretary said the Soviet proposals went too far. We should take care not to provoke Germany, Halifax reiterated, and the Red Army cannot support France and Britain without crossing Polish and Romanian territory. Once again, passage rights were a stumbling block to agreement. It was one thing to go to the aid of the small countries of eastern Europe, said Halifax, it was quite another to go directly to the aid of the Soviet Union "whilst half the British population attributes as much to the Soviets as to the Nazis the responsibility for all the difficulties from which we have suffered for the last ten years." This would raise serious difficulties in Britain, and Chamberlain had to take these into consideration. Halifax may have been saying what Chamberlain wanted him to say, or he had not been keeping up with British public opinion. On May 10 Maiskii reported a recent opinion poll showing that 87 percent of those questioned supported an immediate Soviet alliance. The following month it was 84 percent.[16] Daladier made the counterarguments, much as Churchill and Lloyd George had done the day before in the House of Commons. Hitler counted on division and weakness. A solid eastern front backed by the Soviet Union was essential, said Daladier: "This is a question where bolshevism is irrelevant." Unfortunately, as was Daladier's custom, after putting up a fight he capitulated and agreed to press the British formula on the Soviet government.[17] It is ironic that Daladier made the realist's argument, since he had not always done so, nor would he do so in the future.

Chamberlain, unhappy with the situation, wrote to Hilda:

I have had a very tiresome week over the Russians whose methods of conducting negotiations include the publication in the press of all their despatches and continuous close communication with the opposition and Winston. I wish I knew what sort of people we are dealing with. They may be just simple straight forward people but I cannot rid myself of the suspicion that they are chiefly concerned to see the 'capitalist' powers tear each other to pieces while they stay out themselves. It appears that we shall have to take the fateful decision next week whether to enter into alliance with them or break off negotiations. Those who advocate the former say that if we dont agree Russia and Germany will come to an understanding which to my mind is a pretty sinister commentary on Russian reliability. But some of the members of the Cabinet who were most unwilling to agree to the alliance now appear to have swung round to the opposite view. In the end I think much will depend on the attitude of Poland & Roumania. If bringing Russia in meant their running out I should think the change was a very disastrous one.[18]

After leaving Paris, Halifax went on to Geneva where he saw Maiskii. The foreign secretary tried once more to shake Soviet determination for a formal alliance. Maiskii advanced the same arguments that Daladier had made the day before in Paris. The essential idea, said Maiskii, was to prevent war, and the only way to do this was "by organizing such a combination of forces that Germany would not dare to attack," or as Maiskii put it, a force so powerful that Hitler could see no possibility of victory. "Herr Hitler was not a fool and would never enter upon a war which he was bound to lose. . . . The only thing he understood was force." Maiskii concluded that the British government wished to avoid a tripartite alliance in order not "to burn its bridges to Hitler and Mussolini." Halifax reported that he had been unable to shake Maiskii and that "the choice before us is disagreeably plain": a breakdown of negotiations or agreement on a tripartite alliance.[19]

Chamberlain finally began to yield to the pressure. As Cadogan put it, the prime minister "has, I think, come to the view that it may be necessary to accept the Soviet principle of a triple pact, but he has come to this point very reluctantly and is very disturbed at all that it implies. . . ." Chamberlain "was anxious to leave no stone unturned," Cadogan noted, in averting a war over Danzig.[20] Whatever the metaphor, Cadogan's or Maiskii's not wanting "to burn the bridges," it came to the same thing and increased Soviet mistrust of British policy.[21] This was not the time to play the reluctant suitor with important potential allies. On May 22 Germany and Italy signed the Pact of Steel, which committed the two governments to support each other in the event of war. On the following day Hitler gathered his generals to tell them he would attack Poland at the first opportunity. There would be no repetition of the Czech arrangement.

On May 25 the British government, with the French in tow, offered only a limited mutual assistance pact to the Soviet Union. Its ignition clause depended on the consent of threatened third states, and the proposal was couched in the context of the discredited League of Nations. Chamberlain explained the strategy to his sister:

At the present time I am in a happier mood. The worst times for me and the only ones which really cause me worry are when I have to take a decision and dont clearly see how it is to come. Such a time was the early part of last week. Halifax had written from Geneva to say that he had been unable to shake Maisky in his demand for the 3 party alliance & Daladier had insisted that it was necessary.... It seemed clear that the choice lay between acceptance and the breaking off of negotiations.... There was no sign of opposition to the alliance in the press and it was obvious that refusal would create immense difficulties in the House [of Commons] even if I could persuade my Cabinet.

On the other hand I had and have deep suspicions of Soviet aims and profound doubts as to her military capacity even if she honestly desired & intended to help. But worse than that was my feeling that the alliance would definitely be a lining up of opposing blocs and an association which would make any negotiation or discussion with the totalitarians difficult if not impossible. The only supporter I could get for my views was Rab Butler and he was not a very influential ally.

In the circumstances, I sent for Horace Wilson to see if I could get any light from discussion with him and gradually there emerged an idea which has since been adopted. In substance it gives the Russians what they want but in form and presentation it avoids the idea of an alliance and substitutes a declaration of our *intentions* [emphasis in the original] in certain circumstances in fulfillment of our obligations under Art XVI of the [League of Nations] Covenant [on collective resistance to aggression]. It is really a most ingenious idea for it is calculated to catch all the mugwumps and at the same time by tying the thing up to Art XVI we give it a temporary character. I have no doubt that one of these days Art XVI will be amended or repealed and that should give us the opportunity of revising our relations with the Soviet if we want to.

As soon as I had this clearly worked out in my mind I recovered my equanimity and have retained it ever since. It still remains to be seen what the Russians have to say, but I think they will find it difficult to refuse.[22]

Public opinion was an important factor in calculating policy in London and Paris. Apart from Chamberlain's preoccupations about the British press and the House of Commons, Bonnet recorded: "There is today such a strong movement of public opinion in France and Great Britain in favor of an agreement with the USSR and such a conviction in the world and in France, among so many people, even among the most moderate, that the fate of Peace depends on it, that if negotiations fail, it is necessary at any price that the blame falls upon the USSR and not on us."[23] This recognition spread even to Seeds in Moscow, and he as much as told Potemkin that if talks did not succeed, "it would be impossible to blame" the British government.[24]

Chamberlain thought his League subterfuge would work, and that the Soviet government would be hard put to refuse. But Molotov, who was no fool, understood the prime minister's strategy at once: it would reduce the putative alliance to "a scrap of paper." Inadvertently agreeing with this assessment was Channon: ". . . our new obligation means nothing . . . a Geneva [based] alliance is so flimsy, so unrealistic and so impractical that it will only make the Nazis poke fun at us."

In a stormy meeting with Seeds and Payart on May 27, Molotov accused the British and French governments of bad faith. Given Chamberlain's boasting to his sister, how can one say the commissar was wrong? There was no plan in the Anglo-French proposals, said Molotov, for effective mutual assistance in the event of war. These proposals gave the impression that Britain and France were not really interested in an alliance. And then he turned to the references to the League of Nations. The USSR was not against the League, Molotov observed, but the League's mechanisms for assistance against an aggressor were wholly inadequate. "One of our cities is bombarded, we appeal to the League of Nations," and any state whatever, say Bolivia, could block assistance to us. I am obliged to ask myself why such League references apply in these proposals when no such stipulations appear in the British guarantee to Poland.[25] Halifax appears to have anticipated Molotov's reaction, for he sent further instructions to Seeds that the League references were intended only to satisfy British public opinion.[26] This is doubtful in view of public support for an alliance. Most people would not have cared a pin about the discredited League if it became an obstacle to agreement with the Russians.

Seeds and Payart tried their best to assure Molotov of British and French good faith, but they could not speak for Chamberlain or Bonnet, who did not have it. Seeds went back to see Molotov two days later, on May 29, to undo the damage. He was wasting his time. And Molotov raised again the issue of the Baltic states, which

the Soviet government wanted included in security guarantees provided under an alliance agreement. Seeds replied that the British
government was opposed to the imposition of guarantees on states
that did not want them. Molotov raised the precedent of Czechoslovakia, absorbed by Hitler, nominally with its consent. This could
happen in the Baltic. Would France and Britain, asked Molotov, "remain loftily unaffected were Belgium for example to compound with
Germany"? Seeds reckoned Molotov "totally ignorant of foreign affairs," a person "to whom the idea of negotiation—as distinct from
imposing the will of his party leader—is utterly alien." By Seeds's
lights, Molotov had a peasant's "foolish cunning." But the commissar was anything but foolish.[27]

Payart and then Naggiar, who returned to Moscow at the end of
May, saw Molotov differently. They reported deep Soviet mistrust of
Anglo-French proposals, which had been fed by the events at Munich. Even Payart did not find Seeds's defense of the British proposal
entirely convincing. As for Molotov, his mistrust manifested itself,
according to Naggiar, by an abruptness that disdained traditional
diplomatic usages. This "rude simplicity," so different from Litvinov's approach, showed signs of being intentional. Molotov was not
about to be satisfied by a limited reciprocity previously refused to
Litvinov and now perhaps offered after his departure. "The new
commissar . . . now intends to obtain more extensive advantages. . . ."[28] A striking remark, which recalls Litvinov's observation
in April that the longer the French and British waited to conclude
with the Soviet Union, the higher the price they would pay.

On May 31 Molotov spoke to the Supreme Soviet, reiterating the
main points of Soviet policy. He recalled the history of Anglo-French
concessions to the fascist states, culminating in the Munich settlement. This policy he juxtaposed to the consistent Soviet adherence
to collective security. He also recalled Stalin's speech of March 10,
restating that while the Soviet Union was committed to collective security, it would not pull other people's chestnuts out of the fire.
Molotov reported some signs of firmness in Anglo-French policy,
but it remained to be seen if the change in policy was serious. France
and Britain wished to organize a front against further aggression,
and the Soviet Union had agreed to negotiate, believing such a front
to be in the general interest. Reciprocity, equal obligations, and
guarantees to all the states on the Soviet western frontier must be the

basis of any agreement. As a cautionary note, however, Molotov added that these negotiations did not exclude the possibility of "commercial relations" with Italy and Germany.[29] All this Litvinov had said before, but Molotov lacked his predecessor's subtlety. This was not purblind peasant cunning, as Seeds had said, but justified mistrust of France and Britain, as Payart and Naggiar pointed out. Litvinov had also deeply mistrusted the French and British, but he had not permitted his mistrust to interfere with political flexibility—which the new commissar did not have, or did not wish to employ. The difficulty of the situation was that Soviet mistrust of Chamberlain and Bonnet was justified, but the Soviet remedy of a precise agreement covering every possible eventuality did not make for rapid agreement and ran the risk of failure.

As may now be evident, the negotiations were not well handled. While Chamberlain had complained about Soviet press leaks, there had in fact been very few in Moscow; most were coming from Paris and London. The situation was so bad that Naggiar cabled Bonnet to complain. The "spectacular publicity" surrounding the negotiations was making the Soviet government even more suspicious, as was the impression in Moscow that British concessions had been grudgingly extracted one by one.[30] The reader may wonder if the loquacious and well-connected Maiskii leaked any of this information, but Molotov long after noted that Maiskii was not kept informed of the details of the negotiations and could not have been responsible.[31]

On June 2 Molotov made counterproposals for ironclad, well-defined commitments and in effect returned to Litvinov's proposal of April 17 guaranteeing all the states between the Baltic and Black Seas.[32] The Soviet proposal specified a list of countries to be guaranteed, including the Baltics. Unlike the previous Anglo-French proposal, it did not condition assistance on the consent of affected third states. Moreover, Molotov's proposal, like Litvinov's, called for the conclusion of a military agreement "within the shortest possible time," specifying in detail the commitments of the contracting parties. Implementation of the alliance was linked to the conclusion of this military convention.[33] On the latter point Molotov explained to Seeds that the Soviet government had learned from its experience with the French. The Franco-Soviet mutual assistance pact "had turned out to be . . . a paper delusion." Without a military convention the political accord would be worthless. Back in London, Sargent commented, "The Russians have for years past been pressing for staff conversations to implement its [sic] Franco-Soviet pact, and the French largely at our instigation have always refused them." Molotov had a point. Do not take us for "simpletons and fools," he would later say.[34] Perhaps Molotov drove his point too far. Chamberlain, who was good at political finesse, might himself have been finessed if the Soviet government had pursued a more subtle policy. This is what Potemkin, Surits, and Vansittart had suggested.

Molotov's new proposals were thoroughly discussed in London. In the Committee on Foreign Policy, Halifax acknowledged that "it was true that we should go to the assistance of Holland if she was attacked by Germany without any request from Holland to do so...." Chamberlain was nevertheless opposed to a guarantee of the Baltic states, and his position prevailed.[35] Eden, then a backbench M.P., went to Halifax to suggest that he, Eden, go to Moscow to ease negotiations. The Foreign Office wanted to recall Seeds for consultations, but he fell ill and could not travel. Strang, not Eden, would go to Moscow instead. The French were in a hurry to obtain an agreement, Daladier more so than Bonnet.[36] Corbin went to see Halifax on June 7 to ask for information about British negotiations in Moscow. The French government should not have had to ask, but the British were taking the lead, and the French let them do it.[37]

Halifax informed Maiskii on June 8 of Strang's intended departure for Moscow. He indicated that the British government was still opposed to the guarantee of the Baltic states, the simultaneous signing of the political and military conventions of the alliance, and agreement not to conclude a separate peace. Halifax mentioned in passing that it had been suggested he visit Moscow, but as foreign secretary he did not wish to leave London. To this report Molotov replied quickly that without the Baltic guarantee *against direct or indirect aggression,* there could be no agreement. By "indirect aggression" Molotov meant the Czech precedent, which he had raised with Seeds on May 29, an internal coup d'état, or a change of policy directed or compelled by an aggressor. This was not a question of a "technical formula" but one of substance. If we can reach agreement on the substantive issues, said Molotov, it will not be difficult to find the appropriate wording. For Molotov it was a conciliatory position. He advised that on simultaneous conclusion of the political and military agreements, "this can be made more precise in the course of negotiations." In regard to the possibility of a visit to Moscow by Halifax, Molotov told Maiskii, "you can hint to him that in Moscow his visit would be welcomed."[38]

Maiskii saw Halifax first thing Monday morning, June 12, to carry out Molotov's instructions. Halifax said he understood the Soviet position "on the problem raised by direct or indirect aggression against the Baltic States," but the British government did not wish to impose unwanted guarantees. The wording of Maiskii's account of the meeting is somewhat more positive than that of Halifax. Whether Maiskii exaggerated Halifax's position, or whether the foreign secretary was hiding it from Chamberlain, the evidence does not indicate. According to Maiskii, Halifax said that "the British government was extremely interested in the rapid conclusion of an agreement." In the British account, Halifax hoped that linking political and military agreements would not cause delay. As instructed, Maiskii hinted at the desirability of a Halifax visit to Moscow. The foreign secretary again declined. "Halifax's well-known reserve is understandable," Maiskii said, "for a resolution of the question does not reside with him but with Chamberlain." Maiskii advised that he would use "indirect channels" to influence Halifax to make the trip to Moscow, but Molotov disapproved. "If Halifax really wants to come, then we will welcome it. [But] the hint which you gave him is sufficient for the time being."[39]

The actual instructions sent with Strang to Moscow were not positive in tone and were even peevish and nit-picking. A substantive reference to the League of Nations remained, though joint action did not hinge on League approval. In view of Molotov's hostility, why retain the reference to the League? As for Baltic guarantees, "Our object is, of course, to prevent our being dragged into war by Russia over a Baltic State without our having any voice in the matter." A reasonable position on the face of it, though Molotov might have made the same argument over Belgium. The Soviet government's insistence on the guarantee of the Baltic states had been advanced by Litvinov in April. This was nothing new. The Foreign Office also calculated that military talks would be prolonged and therefore did not want the political treaty made conditional on them.[40] This result was precisely what Molotov feared: an agreement with no force behind it. Each side in effect was adopting the same rigidity. After seeing the new British draft, Corbin commented to Cadogan that it was unlikely to succeed: ". . . Corbin said that he fully appreciated all the difficulties [of the British position] . . . but the fact remained that if the Russians were confronted with a document such as we had prepared they would be filled with the darkest suspicion. . . ."[41] In Moscow, Strang told Naggiar that his instructions were not to move toward the Soviet position but in fact to try to take back concessions made in the previous Anglo-French proposal of late May. "I have drawn the impression," said Naggiar, "that [Strang] came here with instructions to stay within the range of commitments already made and not to go beyond those accepted by our two governments in our proposal of 26 [sic] May. . . ."[42]

Maiskii characterized British policy as "bazaar technique": "But even in the bazaar, when asked a shilling one did not begin by offering twopence." Moscow had the impression that the British government was "at bottom opposed to a pact and was reluctantly and gradually being pushed against its will into making one." According to Maiskii, this impression "was one of the chief reasons for Russian suspiciousness and served to stiffen Moscow's attitude."[43] Once again Soviet suspicions were justified. Chamberlain wrote to Ida:

Meanwhile we dont get much further with the Bolshies. I wanted to get Seeds back, but he promptly went down with flu so we have got to send Strang out instead. I cant make up my mind whether the Bolshies are double crossing us and trying to make difficulties or whether they are only showing the cunning & suspicion of the peasant. On the whole I incline to the latter view, but I am sure they are greatly encouraged by the opposition and the Winston Eden LG group with whom Maisky is in constant touch.

You would hardly believe that anyone could be so foolish, but Anthony went to Halifax and suggested that we should send him as a special envoy to Moscow. He found a not unsympathetic answer, but when I suggested that to send either a Minister or an ex-Minister would be the worst of tactics with a hard bargainer like Molotoff, Halifax agreed and dropped the proposal. Nevertheless LlG repeated it to Butler & even suggested that if we did not approve of Anthony Winston should go! I have no doubt that the three of them talked it over together, and that they saw in it a means of entry into the Cabinet and perhaps even on the substitution of a more amenable PM!"[44]

Chamberlain must have felt like Br'er Rabbit struggling with the tar baby: the more he tried to get away, the more he got stuck. Ironically it was "Jedge" Stalin who in August "come long en loosed 'im."

Molotov was not the only one to mistrust Chamberlain and Bonnet; the British and French anti-appeasement opposition did not trust them either. In early June Churchill publicly questioned the Chamberlain government's good faith.[45] In mid-June Surits reiterated that French public opinion strongly favored a Soviet alliance. "I have met a great many and various people including military at numerous receptions these last few days. My general impression is that no one here will admit even the thought 'that negotiations with us can go wrong and not lead to agreement[']. . . ." Soviet prestige had never been higher; everyone recognized that "without the USSR nothing will turn out." But everyone wondered why the conclusion of such an important agreement had been delayed. The blame for the delay was being laid on the British, either because of conservatism or procrastination, or because of bad faith. Public opinion had swung round to accept the Soviet position on the Baltic states. The French and British had imprudently given guarantees to Poland and Romania. They had started negotiations with the Soviet Union only to "reinsure" these guarantees; now "all of a sudden as a result of their months of maneuvers, they find themselves before a tripartite agreement without reinsurance, without which the guarantees given by them will become a burden beyond their strength." They were caught between two evils now, said Surits, and they would choose the lesser evil of more flexibility on the Baltic question.[46] In early July Mandel told Surits that there should be guarantees of all countries threatened by aggression, and that he supported the Soviet position on the Baltic states. The Soviet government "has every right" to be mistrustful, said Mandel; it should insist on a "clear and explicit" agreement. "It is better to lose a few weeks than to allow any vagueness or reservations."[47]

IV

In this atmosphere of mistrust, is it any surprise that Stalin—suspicious, ruthless, and unscrupulous—began to contemplate the possibility of an agreement with Nazi Germany? We left the story of Nazi-Soviet relations in April 1939 when the Soviet ambassador, Merekalov, visited the German foreign ministry to discuss the fulfillment of Soviet contracts with the Skoda factories in defunct Czechoslovakia. The main purpose of the meeting was economic, but as Litvinov had reminded Payart in March, "there was a close interdependence between political and economic relations...."[48] The state secretary, Weizsäcker, was apparently hoping for, or sought to create, a political opening through this initiative.

On May 5, two days after Litvinov's dismissal, Schnurre told Astakhov that the suspended Skoda contracts would be honored. On the same day in Ankara, the new German ambassador to Turkey, Franz von Papen, met with his Soviet counterpart, A. V. Terent'ev. He gushed goodwill and sweet reason. In spite of strained relations between particular countries, Papen felt sure there would be no war "as long as no one [else] wants it." With regard to the Polish corridor and Danzig, "this is Germany's last demand." As for Nazi-Soviet relations, Papen was equally hopeful: "Personally I am deeply grieved that between both our great countries there is no proper cordiality in relations." "Papen does not see any questions," Terent'ev reported, "which could impede a rapprochement between the USSR and Germany and create insoluble conflicts between both governments." The Soviet ambassador felt obliged to respond at some length "on the basic principles of the foreign policy of the USSR," referring to Stalin's speech of March 10 and underlining that it was no fault of the Soviet government if Nazi-Soviet relations were unfriendly. Terent'ev made a return visit to Papen a few days later, where the latter again protested Germany's good intentions. What about Czechoslovakia? asked Terent'ev. Molotov and Stalin thought their ambassador a little too abrupt, and advised him to be more polite and to listen to any declarations Papen might wish to make.[49] Their admonishment to Terent'ev recalls Litvinov's to Maiskii in April.

Merekalov had returned to Moscow in late April, and the Soviet chargé d'affaires, Astakhov, took over in Berlin. On May 6 Astakhov submitted a press summary noting that the German papers were absorbed with Litvinov's dismissal and worsening German-Polish relations. The press was attempting to create the impression that Litvinov's departure represented a real turnabout in Soviet policy, away from collective security. Astakhov even observed that the press had published a biographical note on Molotov that was more or less "appropriate." "Normally any communication about us is given here with the addition of rude invective; this time the press restrained itself. But in the meantime all this does not provide, of course, the basis for any far-reaching conclusions." The German press also noted that German-Polish relations were worsening, and that German demands now went beyond the annexation of Danzig and an extraterritorial road across the Polish corridor to East Prussia. Germany wanted the entire corridor. "All the signs indicate" a new press campaign against Poland for Danzig. "The Germans are nevertheless trying in every way to create [public] confidence that Danzig will fall into their hands without war, since England will not fight for it, while in France they can trust in Bonnet."[50] German absorption of Danzig was a matter of concern in Moscow. The issues of German-Soviet and German-Polish relations were closely related to the Anglo-Franco-Soviet negotiations. If Germany went to war with Poland, the Soviet government needed to assure its security, one way or another.

There were further meetings between Astakhov and German officials, including one with Schnurre, on May 17. Without providing full details, it is sufficient to say that Astakhov's records of these meetings indicate that he was reserved and noncommittal. While the German press talked of a change in Nazi-Soviet relations, no change of substance had in fact occurred. Schnurre, however, in his account of their meeting on May 17, put into Astakhov's mouth the desire for improved relations—which in Astakhov's report comes from Schnurre. Astakhov gave the standard line dating back to the civil war period (1918–1921), that the Soviet government was ready to improve relations with any state willing to meet it halfway.[51]

Schnurre told Astakhov that he planned a trip to Moscow to see Mikoian about trade relations. A few days later, on May 20, Molotov saw the German ambassador Schulenberg to express his irritation: it was the first he had heard of Schnurre's proposed trip. He had the impression that Germany was playing games with the USSR instead of conducting serious economic negotiations. For such games, said Molotov, Germany should seek other partners. The Soviet Union was not interested. Schulenberg protested, but Molotov replied that for economic negotiations to succeed there must be corresponding political foundations. Schulenberg "again and again" vowed Germany's serious intent and noted that the "political atmosphere between Germany and the USSR" had improved significantly. Molotov was unpersuaded. When Schulenberg asked what Molotov meant by "political basis," the latter replied that it would be "necessary to think about it, both we and the German government." Am I to understand you, asked Schulenberg, that the time is not propitious for a visit by Schnurre? Molotov repeated that the creation of "political bases" must precede economic talks. According to Molotov, Schulenberg had not expected this rebuff. When Schulenberg pressed for a clearer meaning of political basis, Molotov by his account evaded a specific reply.[52]

Schulenberg gave a somewhat different story. On instructions from Ribbentrop, he said, he had "maintain[ed] extreme caution" in meeting Molotov. "As a result I contented myself with saying as little as possible, the more so as the attitude of M. Molotov seems to me quite suspicious." He was not going to be satisfied with a resumption of economic negotiations, ". . . he obviously wants to obtain from us more extensive proposals of a political nature." Schulenberg warned that Molotov might simply use German proposals as pressure on the French and British to conclude their negotiations with the Soviet government. "On the other hand, if we want to accomplish something here it may well be unavoidable that we sooner or later take some action."[53] As was often the case in accounts of these meetings, Schulenberg said he was cautious, though the Soviet account shows the ambassador pressing Molotov hard. There was one point of agreement, however: Molotov was reserved in responding to German overtures.

The Germans resumed their wooing on May 30 when Weizsäcker called in Astakhov for an hour-long meeting. Judging from Molotov's statements to Schulenberg, Weizsäcker said, the Soviet government was making economic negotiations dependent on improved political relations. This was new for the German government and contradicted what they had been hearing from Merekalov. Astakhov was evasive in reply, but it was clear from his report that

Weizsäcker was also pressing. Ironically the state secretary made, with his own differences, the realist argument for better German-Soviet relations: we do not have to like one another's political systems, but we have many other commodities in the German "shop" to sell to the Soviet Union. The implication was that these commodities were not just trade items.[54]

Astakhov appeared to want part of the action, because he asked Molotov to provide him with more information on negotiations in Moscow. If talks also touched upon political issues, "it would seem to me useful to bring them simultaneously to the attention of the German government in Berlin." Schulenberg was not a close confidant of Ribbentrop, who might take the ambassador's communications the wrong way. Moreover, if the Soviet Union wished to communicate unofficially with the Germans, it would be more expedient to do it in Berlin to provide for the necessary deniability.[55]

On the German side, the Weizsäcker-Astakhov meeting was intended to invite a Soviet reply. None was forthcoming, so Schulenberg, who met Astakhov in Berlin on June 17, raised the subject.

The German government had made the first step, Schulenberg said, and now expected a reply from the Soviet side.

"According to my information," replied Astakhov, "the commissar's reply was ready to give in Moscow." But "it is contained partially in the commissar's speech [of May 31]."

If I knew that Molotov intended a reply, said Schulenberg, I would immediately return to Moscow. The ambassador pressed for clarification, but Astakhov could not give it.

All I know is that "the reply must be given in Moscow."

The time was ripening for an improvement of relations, insisted Schulenberg, "and diplomats from both countries must act to influence the success of this process now beginning." The ambassador, taking up Weizsäcker's image of the German "shop full of commodities" for the right deal with the Soviet Union, specified that these included "political" advantages.[56]

V

While for the moment Molotov did not reply to these obvious German overtures, the *British* showed more interest in better relations with Berlin. Maiskii had noted more than once that Chamberlain—and Halifax, he might have added—did not wish to burn their bridges to Hitler. In public speeches, both carefully left open the possibility of new proposals from Berlin. On May 18 Halifax called in the German ambassador, Herbert von Dirksen, to vent his spleen about the disappearance of Czechoslovakia and to warn that an attack on a state guaranteed by Britain would mean war. Dirksen protested that Hitler would not challenge the British guarantees. Halifax eventually asked if Hitler could be persuaded to make a public statement renouncing force and committing himself to peaceful negotiations. Hitler did not make the requested speech, so on June 8 Halifax made one of his own in the House of Lords, repeating the message given to Dirksen that the way was open to negotiations if Hitler did not resort to force or the threat of force.[57] This was a week after Weizsäcker's meeting with Astakhov in Berlin. Chamberlain was also plainly interested in keeping the door open. He wrote to Ida:

> Both of us [Halifax and Chamberlain] have had in mind the danger that the German people may be deceived into thinking that we are planning to fall upon them as soon as we have concluded our combinations and both of us therefore were trying to make our position plain to them. Evidently the Nazis are afraid of our success since the word seems to have gone out to their own press and to the Italian press also to represent the 'move' as dictated by our difficulties with Russia. And of course our own opposition are busy doing their best to confirm that impression being apparently determined to stop every attempt to prevent a war. Well, the only thing is to go on and pay no attention to them hoping that something of what we say may get past the official barriers in Germany and Italy. I still believe that our best plan is to keep up contacts with Rome where I am certain war is looked upon with terror. . . .[58]

How ironic that at this point Chamberlain and Halifax appear to have been more interested in negotiations with Germany than was Molotov, if only Hitler would be "sensible." Trouble was that the Germans wanted to talk to Molotov, not to Chamberlain. On June 13 Weizsäcker saw the British ambassador in Berlin, Sir Nevile Henderson, to intimate that the conclusion of an Anglo-Soviet treaty would make more difficult an Anglo-German understanding.[59] This was a clever move while the Germans worked on Molotov to come around. Naggiar reported that Halifax's statement in the House of Lords and others in the Commons by Chamberlain and Sir John Simon had accentuated Soviet mistrust. The French also picked up rumors that the Nazi government wanted "to talk" with Moscow.[60]

VI

Meanwhile, Soviet negotiations with the French and British dragged on in June and July, haggling over conditions and endless wordings of a political agreement. The British instructions, to which the French agreed, meant that no agreement could be concluded as long as the Soviet government held fast to its position on the Baltic states. Seeds told Naggiar that he was discouraged and pessimistic. Talks would not succeed unless the French and British accepted Soviet conditions. At the same time Naggiar continued to complain about press leaks in Paris which could only come from inside sources.[61]

On June 15 Seeds, Strang, and Naggiar presented the Anglo-French position to Molotov based on the instructions sent out with Strang to stay within the late May proposals. The French had once again accepted the British position, despite misgivings. Molotov's reply the following day was simply a reiteration of what he had already said on previous occasions. The Soviet government was adamant on the guarantee of the Baltic states. If the Anglo-French did not wish to agree, then Molotov proposed a straight treaty of mutual assistance, operative only in the case of direct unprovoked attack on the signatories. "It seems to us that the English and French want to conclude a treaty advantageous for them and not advantageous for us, that is, they do not want a serious treaty, responding to the principles of reciprocity and equality of obligations."[62]

Several more meetings followed in mid-June; Seeds, with Strang and Naggiar supporting him, tried to bring Molotov around, to no avail. "I cant seem able to make any progress anywhere," Chamberlain complained to Hilda. "The Russians do nothing but issue press communiqués to the effect that our proposals are unsatisfactory. They are the most impossible people to do business with. . . ." In Moscow suspicion fell upon those who proposed weak formulas, warned Naggiar: "I do not cease to repeat it to Strang and his ambassador." British variants to blunt Soviet treaty proposals were useless and only fed Soviet suspicions. The Red Army would put at least one hundred divisions into the line, observed Molotov. In effect, he argued, a hundred divisions ought to be worth a Baltic guarantee. Strang wrote that the Anglo-French negotiating position was not strong. On June 22 Seeds concluded, as had Naggiar a few days earlier, that either the British and French governments accepted the Soviet position on the Baltic states or they negotiated a simple tripartite alliance against direct aggression.[63] Bonnet heard Naggiar's message and was in a hurry to come to agreement. Soviet mistrust was easily aroused on what in effect were secondary points—the League references, for example. Let's get these off the table and settle as quickly as possible, Bonnet told Corbin on June 17: see Halifax and impress on the Foreign Office the need for haste. Delays risk dangers which are superfluous to mention.[64] Bonnet was right, of course, but he still talked out of both sides of his mouth. On the same day Corbin told Cadogan that the French government would go along with British proposals. And it was a few days later that Bonnet, in a meeting with Phipps, sneered at Mandel and Reynaud for being under "Soviet influence."[65] Bonnet's conduct proved one of the laws of physics: for every action, there is an equal and opposite reaction.

On June 23 Halifax called in Maiskii to complain about the inconclusive negotiations and Molotov's "absolute inflexibility." According to Maiskii, Halifax accused the Soviet government of using "German methods"—naming a price and demanding 100 percent of it. This was delaying the conclusion of an agreement.

"Do you want a treaty, or not?" asked Halifax. "I looked at Halifax with astonishment," wrote Maiskii, "and replied that I did not consider possible even to discuss such a question." According to Halifax's account of the meeting, Maiskii said it had been a mistake for the Soviet government to state its "irreducible minimum" at the outset. It should have asked for more in the beginning in order to be able to make subsequent concessions. Maiskii saw no problem with a guarantee of the Baltic states and drew an analogy with the Americans' nineteenth-century Monroe Doctrine. Why shouldn't "the three European great powers" do something similar with regard to the Baltic states? The ambassador also hinted again that Halifax might want to go himself to Moscow to resolve the impasse, though the foreign secretary did not appear to appreciate the suggestion. Maiskii concluded that Halifax throughout the meeting was "vexed and discontented." Halifax concluded that their "conversation was carried on in a most friendly spirit" though with "a good deal of sparring."[66] These reports of meetings are sometimes at odds on substance, details, and atmosphere; yet such records were the basis for important policy decisions. It must make the historian cautious in their use, especially when only one account is available.

The British government was finally forced to make hard decisions. For Halifax's question, "Do you want a treaty or not?" applied equally well to the British government and in particular to its prime minister. On June 26 the question was faced head-on in the Committee on Foreign Policy. Halifax, the realist this time, faced Chamberlain, ever hesitant and unwilling to yield to the Soviet position. "The Russians were extremely suspicious," said Halifax, "and feared that our real object was to trap them into commitments and then leave them in the lurch. They suffered acutely from inferiority complex and considered that ever since the Great War the western powers had treated Russia with haughtiness and contempt." This was an accurate appraisal, and sounded a little like Maiskii's lecturing. For proof of it the reader need go no further than the reactions of Cadogan and Sargent to Litvinov's suggested visit to London and to his April proposals for a tripartite alliance. Chamberlain was not persuaded, and accused Molotov of "bazaar haggling," but it was the British who were haggling with weaker formulas and Molotov who held firm. At the end of the meeting Chamberlain found himself in the minority and had to go along with a concession to Molotov on the guarantee of the Baltic states. He insisted, however, that Holland and Switzerland be added to the list. It was more "bazaar haggling." One minister noted that "the importance of securing an agreement with Russia was much greater than the risk of offending the smaller states."[67] Of course this was the logic of power and great powers, and it had advocates in all three governments—Maiskii, Surits, Vansittart, Collier, Mandel, Léger, Naggiar, among others.

When the Soviet government thought it was not getting through to its British and French counterparts, it issued a Tass communiqué or a Soviet official signed an article in the Moscow press. Thus did Andre Zhdanov, the Communist party boss in Leningrad, publish a comment in *Pravda* on June 29, complaining about the inconclusive negotiations. From April 15 until the present, he wrote, negotiations had been going on for seventy-five days. Of these the Soviet government had required sixteen to reply to various British proposals. The rest of the time, fifty-nine days, had been wasted "in procrastination and delay." When the British wished to conclude pacts or issue guarantees, it found ways to do so quickly. So why the delay in the negotiations in Moscow? It raised questions about Anglo-French good faith and ulterior motives. The British and French governments did not want an agreement based upon reciprocity and equality of obligations; they wanted an agreement where "the USSR would play the part of a hired laborer bearing the brunt of the obligations on his shoulders." The British and French just wanted to talk about an agreement to prepare the ground for blaming the Soviet Union for the failure of talks and to justify a new deal with the aggressors. "The next few days," concluded Zhdanov, "will show whether it is the case or not."[68]

The message was heard in Paris and London. At the beginning of July the British government yielded on many of the sticking points: deletion of substantive League references, agreement to a no-separate-peace clause, and the guarantee and naming of the Baltic states. Still no agreement was reached. Seeds and Naggiar met Molotov on July 1 and 3. Molotov agreed to a secret protocol listing guaranteed states, but he bucked at the inclusion of Holland, Switzerland, and Luxembourg. He also asked for a reference in the treaty to "indirect aggression." The issue of a military convention and its linkage to a political agreement still remained unresolved. Molotov's concern about indirect aggression, that is, the Czech precedent, should have come as no surprise; he had raised it many times earlier, and indeed Chamberlain had first used the terminology in early April in the House of Commons. The concept, if not the terminology, also turned up in the Anglo-Polish protocol signed after Beck's visit to London in April (and was made explicit in the Anglo-Polish defense pact signed on August 25, 1939).[69] The same could be said of Soviet insistence on linking political and military agreements. And guarantees of Holland, Switzerland, and Luxembourg were not new either—though Chamberlain had raised them as an additional British demand. At the beginning of May Litvinov had recommended Soviet acceptance of guarantees to Holland, Belgium, and Switzerland in exchange for those of the Baltic states. Molotov now argued against them on narrow legal grounds: the Supreme Soviet had not approved these additional guarantees. Most readers will know, however, that it was Stalin, not the Supreme Soviet, who made these decisions. Molotov also conditioned the added guarantees on the conclusion of mutual assistance pacts with Poland and Turkey.[70] While Molotov's insistence on introducing indirect aggression into the treaty can be ascribed to previous Soviet carelessness, the refusal to guarantee the western European states was either peevish or obstructive. And while a Soviet-Turkish agreement was a realistic possibility, a Soviet-Polish mutual assistance pact was about as likely as hell freezing over.

The bogging down of the negotiations did not bother Chamberlain. At the beginning of July he wrote to Hilda:

> I have had another rather worrying and miserable week . . . the Russians continue to make fresh difficulties & even Halifax is beginning to get impatient with them while I grow more & more suspicious of their good faith. I had a 2 hour talk last week with Citrine, Morrison & Dalton [Labour and trade union leaders] in which I think I succeeded at last in convincing them that we had done all we could to get an agreement. But things are not made easier by these constant assertions in the British & French press that we are on the point of concluding an agreement when in fact we have never been in sight of it. My colleagues are so desperately anxious for it & so nervous of the consequences of failure to achieve it that I have to go very warily but I am so sceptical of the value of Russian help that I should not feel that our position was greatly worsened if we had to do without them. In any case we cant go on much longer on our present course.[71]

Sargent admitted to Corbin, also in early July, that the British guarantees to Poland and Romania had been a mistake. The Soviets, having thus obtained a measure of security, could hold out for their own terms. And they did: Molotov stuck tenaciously to the basic Soviet position laid out by Litvinov in April. The French and British had to negotiate or their guarantees would be worthless. Sargent's admission is "a little late," noted Naggiar; "to correct this error, Russia's price has to be paid."[72]

West European guarantees, "indirect" aggression and its definition, and the linking of military and political agreement remained
sticking points. The British were unenthusiastic about military conversations, and Halifax and other cabinet ministers doubted they
would lead to agreement. Halifax thought the British government
should play along on this issue. As he explained at a July meeting of
the Committee on Foreign Policy, military conversations might not
in the end be so important, but they would prevent the Soviet Union
"from entering the German camp." This was the old French argument justifying the Franco-Soviet pact. It was precisely to cut off the
eventuality of another scrap of paper that Molotov held to his position linking political and military agreements. On the issue of indirect aggression, or rather its definition, Halifax was adamant:
". . . by encouraging Soviet Russia in the matter of internal interference we should be doing incalculable damage to our interests both
at home and throughout the world." The British feared giving the
Soviet Union license to threaten Baltic independence or to spread
communism. The Soviet government feared German aggression
through the Baltic with or without consent. Meanwhile the Baltic
states looked on nervously. They preferred a year of Nazi occupation to a day of the Soviets—which is what worried the Soviet government.[73] The Baltic ambassadors made regular inquiries at the
Foreign Office; British ambassadors reported Baltic anxiety and
anti-Soviet hostility. In early June Estonia and Latvia signed nonaggression pacts with Germany, and German officers made inspection
trips to their frontier fortifications.

The French, on the other hand, cared less about the Baltic states
and more about the linkage between political and military agreements. And where Halifax would have settled for a simple tripartite
alliance against direct aggression, Bonnet opposed it since the military talks could fail and the political agreement would be lost.[74] The
French government remained impatient for an agreement and more
willing to make concessions in order to obtain it. But no sooner did
Bonnet send a trumpeting cable to London, insisting on the importance of an immediate agreement, than he sent further word that he
would defer to the British.[75]

In Moscow, Naggiar observed all this and became more and
more angry and alarmed. He and Seeds complained repeatedly
about press leaks revealing important details of the negotiations. It

was a veritable journalistic circus. In early July Bonnet eventually complained to the Foreign Office, claiming that most of the leaks were coming from London.[76] Naggiar reported that the Soviet government was suspicious of public statements by Chamberlain and others on British willingness to conciliate Germany. Bonnet called in Surits on July 7 to dispel Soviet doubts in Anglo-French good faith. According to Bonnet, these were "at the root of all the difficulties." He and Daladier had done their best, Bonnet said, to "put pressure" on the British to obtain their agreement, "first for the tripartite pact and then on the Baltic guarantee."[77] One can only imagine the reaction had Bonnet's comments reached London, or even the French embassy in Moscow. Apparently Bonnet had already put out this message for wider circulation, for a French journalist in Berlin reported a modified version of it to the Soviet press attaché.[78] In Moscow, Naggiar was ever more impatient. He asked for what amounted to plenipotentiary powers to conclude an agreement; if the cabinet did not like it, the Quai d'Orsay could disavow him. Bonnet queried the Foreign Office, but the British said no, and Bonnet did not insist.[79]

Naggiar worried less about the Baltic states than about the question of Poland and Romania. He reminded Paris repeatedly in July that their cooperation was vital to the success of an Anglo-Franco-Soviet alliance. Naggiar raised the issue of Red Army passage rights across Poland, as did the French military attaché Palasse. If the Polish government did not agree to it, there could be no effective eastern front. Poland and Romania could not hold out without Soviet support. And if the eastern front were broken, Germany and Italy could turn all their force against the west. This was not a question of Polish or Romanian security but of French security, quite apart from that of the Soviet Union. The Soviet government understood this point only too well and would not compromise itself against Germany without "precise and concrete military guarantees," as Coulondre had warned in October 1938 after Munich. New Anglo-French proposals for agreement risked provoking new Soviet counterproposals. If an accord were not reached, the Soviet Union could remain neutral or come to terms with Germany based on a partition of Poland and the Baltic states. It was time, said Naggiar, to recognize that relations between states were governed by equations of power. What was needed was a "classical" military alliance with concrete terms and conditions. No effort should be spared to obtain Polish and Romanian cooperation; no time should be lost in concluding an agreement on Soviet terms in spite of British and French reservations. Unfortunately, Naggiar noted later, "We did nothing in this regard, except at the last minute." This series of the French ambassador's cables is nothing less than a sweeping indictment of Anglo-French policy.[80]

According to Naggiar, the French and British governments were unprepared to make the necessary commitments. Bonnet wanted a political, not a military, agreement, which would require Polish cooperation. Poland did not want to give it, noted Naggiar, and the Anglo-French did not want to press for it. "We want a gesture," scribbled Naggiar, "the Russians want a concrete agreement involving the assent of Poland and Romania."[81] The Soviet government, having been disillusioned in the past, would accept nothing less than an ironclad military alliance.

The other alternative, a simple tripartite alliance, would leave Poland and Romania unprotected, according to Bonnet. And Molotov's insistence on tying political and military agreements together would enable the Soviet government to hold France and Britain to ransom. In August, when the danger of war was expected to increase, the Soviet could tighten the screw: either you agree to our terms or we break off talks and the political agreement—coveted by the French and British—falls to the ground. Any military agreement would hinge on the assent of the grudging Poles and Romanians.[82] Naggiar's notes aptly described the situation: the Quai d'Orsay calculated on the "psychological" effect on Hitler of an Anglo-Franco-Soviet political agreement. "The puerile idea is that we will force Hitler to back down with words, without the only reality which will cause him to reflect: the assent of Poland to a military accord with Russia."[83] A few days later Naggiar wrote again, "London and Paris continue not to want to understand what is essential in these negotiations: a military agreement which would permit Russia to make geographic contact with Germany to replicate the military conditions of 1914."[84]

Not wanting to understand caused mounting frustration in London. On July 19 Halifax and Chamberlain expatiated in the Committee on Foreign Policy on how "humiliating for us" it would be to make further concessions to Molotov when he would make none of his own.

> [Halifax] said that there should also be borne in mind the effect on Herr Hitler's mind of our going down on our knees to Soviet Russia to implore her assistance. Herr Hitler had a very low opinion of Russia and our action would confirm him in the idea that we were a weak and feeble folk. Considerations of this kind should be taken into account.

On the other hand, domestic pressures were building. A campaign to put Churchill in the cabinet had been under way for some time, and Chamberlain feared "considerable trouble" in the House of Commons over delays in concluding an agreement. The prime minister was in no hurry for military conversations, but Halifax feared that it might be "somewhat difficult to persuade the French to adopt our point of view." In any event, one cabinet member, Sir John Simon, sounding like Bonnet, thought that if talks were to break down, it would be important to have public opinion on "our" side. This was a motive that Maiskii had suspected for some time.[85] Once again Chamberlain explained his position to Hilda:

> I am glad to say that Halifax is at last getting 'fed up' with Molotoff whom he describes as maddening and we have accordingly sent a rather stiffer note to Seeds to the effect that our patience is pretty well exhausted. It would have been stiffer still if it had not been for the French and even they are beginning to feel that this delay is somewhat humiliating. If we do get an agreement as I rather think we shall I am afraid I shall not regard it as a triumph. I put as little value on Russia's military capacity as I believe the Germans do. I believe they would fail us in an extremity & even to talk with them has already got us into trouble with our friends. I would like to have taken a much stronger line with them all through, but I could not have carried my colleagues with me.[86]

When one British officer, General Sir Edmund Ironside, suggested that an agreement with the Soviet Union "was the one thing we could do," Chamberlain shot back, "the only thing we cannot do." Ironside concluded that Chamberlain's policy a month before the invasion of Poland was "not hurrying on getting in Russia."[87]

On July 10, five days before Chamberlain wrote to Hilda, Maiskii was skeptical of any cabinet shuffle in the British government. He did not think Churchill, Eden, or other popular politicians would be invited into the cabinet because it would mean the "final break with Germany" and the final renunciation of appeasement. There was no hiding, wrote Maiskii, that Chamberlain was still an appeaser. His concessions to a stiffer line against Hitler were half-hearted under the pressure of public opinion. Moreover, Chamberlain "intensely dislikes and fears Churchill." In fact, Churchill's entry into the cabinet would be only a prelude to Chamberlain's departure. The prime minister, observed Maiskii, did not wish to commit political suicide.[88]

As for the French, they were still just tagging along. Daladier wandered up to Surits on the reviewing stand during the July 14 Bastille Day parade. "Anything new from Moscow?" he asked. Nothing new, replied Surits. "We need to conclude quickly," Daladier said, "the more so, that now I do not see any serious disagreements."[89] Unfortunately this was not true. Molotov was as fed up as Halifax and Chamberlain. There is still disagreement over the definition of "indirect" aggression, Molotov advised Maiskii and Surits, and "our partners are resorting to all kinds of trickery and disgraceful subterfuge." They want to split the political and military agreements, while our position is to conclude "the whole treaty all at once." Otherwise the political convention will be only "an empty declaration."

> Only crooks and cheats . . . could pretend that our demands for the simultaneous conclusion of a political and military agreement are something new in the negotiations. . . . It is hard to understand just what they expect when they resort to such clumsy tricks. . . . It seems that nothing will come of the endless negotiations. Then they will have no one but themselves to blame.[90]

The British did not feel more kindly to the Soviet. "We give them all they want, with both hands," Cadogan wrote in his journal, "and they merely slap them away. Molotov is an ignorant and suspicious peasant." They're "dirty sweeps," Cadogan grumbled at the end of June.[91]

Surits agreed with Molotov, noting that because the vast majority of French opinion was impatient for agreement, the Anglo-
French negotiators felt compelled to claim that the Soviet side was
constantly raising new demands. Our partners do not want "a real
agreement" but are afraid of the public reaction if negotiations fail.
Maybe we should threaten to make the negotiations public, suggested Surits; a hint of this might compel the other side to change its
tactics.[92] Again, there was truth to Soviet suspicions. And it is also
true that the Soviet position had changed little since April, though
many historians have accepted the view that the Soviet side repeatedly made new demands. The Soviet requirement for the Baltic guarantee, the demand for a specific military convention as part of an
overall agreement, and the concern about indirect aggression were
not new issues. Even the Western guarantees were old hat; Bonnet
had raised this issue with Surits in April. Molotov's insistence on a
definition of indirect aggression was new, and his linking of the
British insistence on Western guarantees to mutual assistance pacts
with Poland and Turkey were new.[93] But most questions discussed in
Moscow were not. The same issues and the same disagreements kept
turning up like bad pennies.

Events began to move quickly, however, and temporarily calmed
Anglo-Soviet tempers. Anglo-French public opinion and the increas-
ing danger of war were the incentives. The putative guarantees to
Holland, Switzerland, and Luxembourg were dropped, as were the
Soviet conditions for mutual assistance pacts with Poland and
Turkey. On July 23 Molotov indicated that he was more or less satisfied with the political agreement; remaining difficulties over the
definition of "indirect aggression" could "easily" be settled later. He
wanted military conversations to start at once, and Naggiar and
Seeds both pressed for acceptance of Molotov's proposal. The
French and British governments agreed quickly—for a change—to
send military missions to Moscow. The British, unlike the French,
were not prepared to let the issue of "indirect aggression" be set
aside, and they conditioned agreement to it on the conclusion of a
military convention. As usual, the French went along with the
British position.[94]

In other ways the French position appeared to be stiffening, or so
Léger said to Phipps in July. Daladier was resolute and "firmly convinced of the necessity of showing an irreducible refusal to treat

with a régime [Nazi Germany] in whose word no confidence could be placed and with which any treaty must be valueless." Indeed, "so convinced was Daladier of the wisdom of an attitude of determined reserve that he had even given orders against any manifestations of friendship towards Germany such as mutual visits for athletic contests and such like: it was better for the time being to renounce the natural instinct to act 'en gentlemen.' . . ."[95] Léger offered no comment—or Phipps did not record it—on negotiations with the Soviet Union.

VII

In the meantime Soviet officials continued discussions with their German counterparts. The story was left off on June 17 when Astakhov saw Schulenberg, who made another pitch for better Nazi-Soviet relations. Three days later Astakhov recorded in his journal that the Berlin rumor mill was active. Among the canards, a German economic mission was preparing to go to Moscow. When asked about it, Astakhov had replied—so he reported—within the parameters of Molotov's May speech. Other rumors had the Germans planning to attack Poland at the beginning of September, and the British refusing to fight for Danzig. Astakhov also reported having dinner with two *Times* journalists and the British press attaché in Berlin, R. F. O. Bashford. After dinner they went to Bashford's flat to avoid being overheard at the Adlon Hotel, well known as a diplomats' meeting place and also for its electronic bugs. The British were pessimistic and discouraged. Poland was no match for Germany, they said, and would only serve as "cannon fodder." Their view of Romania was just as uncharitable. Bashford said it was impossible to negotiate with Hitler. Astakhov replied in effect that this was obvious to any ordinary Muscovite. He didn't understand why the British government couldn't get it. A few days later he noted a meeting with the Turkish ambassador who also asked about Nazi-Soviet negotiations. Astakhov did not record his reply.[96]

Schulenberg, who was back in Moscow, met Molotov at the end of June. On June 28 he came right to the point: "the German government wants not only normal relations but also an improvement of its relations with the USSR." I am acting, said Schulenberg,

on Ribbentrop's instructions as approved by Hitler. Molotov listened
skeptically to the ambassador, who insisted that the German government was serious. Schulenberg referred to recent nonaggression
pacts with Estonia and Latvia as proof of German good intentions.

Those pacts are not of direct interest to the USSR, replied Molotov: what about the recent abrogation of the German-Polish nonaggression pact?

Poland's fault, replied Schulenberg. Molotov recorded that he
had not wanted to get into a polemic with the ambassador. Schulenberg added: "No one in Germany, how should I say it, has
Napoleonic plans in regard to the USSR."

"It's impossible," replied Molotov, "to prohibit people from
dreaming; there must be people in Germany, inclined to dream."
Molotov added that there should be no doubt in the ambassador's
mind about the Soviet position: "The Soviet Union stood and stands
for the improvement of relations, or at least normal relations with
all countries, including Germany." Schulenberg went on, but Molotov could not resist an ironic comment about inconsistencies in the
German attitude toward the Soviet Union. Schulenberg suggested
that the Soviet government might "moderate" the tone of its press.
Molotov replied that the Soviet press gave no cause for German
complaint, which he could not say about the German papers. There
one could find plenty of evidence of hostility toward the Soviet
Union. Schulenberg's initial account of the meeting agreed on the
main points but left out the repartee. "Although there was no mis-
taking the strong distrust evident in all that Molotov said," Schulenberg reported, "he nevertheless described a normalization of
relations with Germany as being desirable and possible." This is not
exactly what Molotov's record stated.[97]

The meeting was not a great success from Schulenberg's point of
view, but on July 1 he returned to see Potemkin. Initially the discussion was about the freeing of Soviet citizens held by Spain in exchange for German nationals held by the Soviet government.
Schulenberg turned the conversation to his recent meeting with
Molotov. He had neglected to report Ribbentrop's avowal that the
anti-Comintern pact with Italy and Japan was directed not at the Soviet Union but against "international tendencies which the three
governments considered a danger to the existing social and political
order." Now the pact had evolved from this initial objective—even if

it retained its original name—and was aimed primarily against Britain. Schulenberg also let it drop that Germany might assist the Soviet Union in improving relations with Japan. This was no doubt to sweeten German offers since the Red Army was again involved in serious fighting with the Japanese Kwangtung army along the Manchurian frontier. "In response to Schulenberg's provocative chit-chat," Potemkin noted, "I limited myself to the dry observation that nothing prevented Germany from showing the seriousness of its intent to improve relations with the USSR." "As for Japan, until now it has done everything possible to demonstrate its hostility toward our country."[98] Again, from Schulenberg's point of view, the meeting was unsuccessful. What is more, he appeared to have violated Ribbentrop's new instructions not to pursue political questions "until further instructions." For the time being, "the talks should not be taken up again by us."[99]

Meanwhile the Narkomindel continued to receive discouraging reports from Rome and Berlin. L. B. Gel'fand, the Soviet chargé d'affaires in Rome, indicated that the Italians were just waiting for the next parcel of territory to fall into their laps. This in turn would enhance their ability to blackmail the French and British. They were banking on a resumption of "capitulationist" policies in Paris and London.

> The position of people like Bonnet and Chamberlain increases the certainty in Italian government circles that sooner or later they will succeed in obtaining some new territory. . . . French "soundings" about the possibility of concessions and negotiations with Italy, Chamberlain's speeches, and the British embassy's version of Anglo-Soviet negotiations, being spread around here, naturally strengthens the convictions of Mussolini and [Galeazzo] Ciano [the Italian foreign minister].

Rome and Berlin, at least until September, were apparently not planning any new ventures, reported Gel'fand: both Hitler and Mussolini feared war, but they counted on Polish capitulation. The British and French did not wish to fight for Danzig, but they did not want to admit it, for now. According to Ciano, they would come around. Anglo-Soviet negotiations were also attracting attention. Some thought the Soviet government held the peace of Europe in its hands; others that the talks would fail and that a Nazi-Soviet rapprochement might ensue. Gel'fand believed the Soviet position would be strengthened by an agreement with the British.[100] Astakhov reported Coulondre's fear that the Soviet talks would fail. In the diplomatic corps there was a black mood about Hitler's future intentions. Danzig was expected to be his next target, sometime in August.[101]

On July 19 Astakhov thought it was the quiet before the storm. All the Nazi chiefs were out of Berlin, and news about the Munich theatre festival had crowded out speculations on Danzig. While the Germans had not resumed "their flirtation with us," Astakhov reported, they did not miss an opportunity to say "obliquely" that they were ready to change policies and were only waiting for Moscow to come around. Anonymous letters received at the embassy said: don't come to terms with the British, be friends with Germany, let's make a deal on the division of Poland.[102] A British journalist asked Astakhov about rumors of Nazi-Soviet negotiations. Astakhov could only speculate, but he called the German foreign ministry to ask for information. Nothing new, came the reply.[103]

It was not quiet for long. On July 21 a member of Ribbentrop's staff went to see Astakhov to resume the wooing. And three days later Schnurre invited the Soviet chargé to pay a call on him. After discussing economic issues, Schnurre turned the conversation to Nazi-Soviet political relations. He proposed a three-step process of improved economic, cultural, and political relations. Schnurre also asked about the negotiations with Britain. He was convinced, reported Astakhov, that the Soviet Union would not agree since on it would fall the heaviest obligations in case of war; the British share would be "minimal."[104]

Schnurre saw Astakhov again two days later and was even more direct. "Tell me, what proof do you want?" asked Schnurre. "We are ready in practice to demonstrate the possibility of agreement on any questions, to give any guarantees." According to Astakhov's account, he remained noncommittal; in fact he thought the conversation had gone too far and turned it to generalities. He asked about German ambitions in the Ukraine, referring to *Mein Kampf*. That was written sixteen years ago, said Schnurre, "in completely different circumstances." "Now the Fuehrer thinks differently. Now the main enemy is England." This line would not have worked with Litvinov, but Astakhov asked for instructions. "I have no doubt," he wrote, "that if we would want it, we could draw the Germans into very far reaching negotiations, obtaining from them a string of assurances on questions of interest to us." Of course, what value these would have is another matter, wrote Astakhov, but the German interest in better relations was a useful trump to hold. It could do no harm, if played carefully.[105]

Molotov responded on July 28, approving of Astakhov's reserve in dealing with Schnurre and in promising to forward his declarations to Moscow. The following day Molotov, reflecting a little on Schnurre's démarches, conceded that an improvement of economic and political relations was possible. But until recently, he said, the Germans have only abused us and refused any improvement in political relations. If now they wish to change course, it will be up to them to say how, concretely, relations might improve. "The matter . . . depends entirely on the Germans. We of course would welcome any improvement of political relations between the two countries."[106] Molotov was beginning to show more interest in German overtures.

VIII

While the Germans continued their pursuit of Moscow, British officials carried on a corresponding flirtation with their German counterparts. Leading the British side were Hudson, whose talks had failed in Moscow in March, and Wilson, Chamberlain's closest adviser. It is unclear and in dispute how seriously these conversations should be taken, but the fact is that during June and July Wilson saw Helmuth Wohlthat, a senior official in charge of the German four-year economic plan, in London. He repeated more or less what Halifax had earlier said to the German ambassador: that Hitler had gone too far, and that it was up to him to renounce further resort to aggression. If he did, there might be Anglo-German cooperation; if he did not, there would be war. On July 18 Wilson saw Wohlthat again, reiterating what he had said in the earlier conversation and emphasizing that "the initiative must come from the German side." These were almost verbatim Molotov's words to Astakhov. On July 20 Wohlthat saw Hudson, who was acting on his own initiative. Hudson imprudently proposed a grandiose scheme for Anglo-German economic cooperation, colonial development, and a large British loan to Germany, subject of course to peaceful international conduct and disarmament. The news of Hudson's meeting leaked to the press on July 22 due to Hudson's indiscretion, and aroused suspicion that Chamberlain and his circle were at it again. Sharp questions filled the House of Commons on July 24, and Chamberlain had to admit that Wilson had also met Wohlthat more than once.[107] This public disclosure occurred just as German approaches to Astakhov resumed in Berlin.

Chamberlain was upset, unburdening himself, as he usually did, to one of his sisters. All the publicity of British contacts with the Germans "makes it impossible for me to enter into conversations with Germans on any subject." As for Hudson:

> He is a clever fellow with a persuasive tongue but he has a very bad reputation as a disloyal colleague who is always trying to advance his own interests at the expense of his friends. In particular it is a favourite device of his to take ideas on which other people have been working for years and put them forward as his own & as if nobody else had ever thought of them. The ideas which he put to Wohlthat for instance, as his own personal suggestions on an economic arrangement (not including a loan) are just those which we have been discussing in the Department for 12 months while the ideas on Colonies are those which I put together and which have actually been suggested to Hitler. . . . Unfortunately . . . Hudson was so pleased with himself that he has been talking to the press and the result is of course disastrous . . . so now the loan idea is given a semi-official air and all the busybodies . . . have put two & two together and triumphantly made five.
>
> One thing is I think clear, namely that Hitler has concluded that we mean business and that the time is not ripe for . . . [a] major war. Therein he is fulfilling my expectations. Unlike some of my critics I go further and say the longer the war is put off the less likely it is to come at all as we go on perfecting our defences, and building up the defences of our Allies. That is what Winston & Co never seem to realise. You dont need offensive forces sufficient to win a smashing victory what you want are defensive forces sufficiently strong to make it impossible for the other side to win except at such a cost as to make it not worth while. That is what we are doing. . . .

When the Germans catch on, Chamberlain concluded, "Then we can talk. But the time for talk hasn't come yet. . . ."[108]

This letter reveals Chamberlain's mind regarding relations with Germany and also indirectly with the Soviet Union. The prime minister's annoyance was generated as much by Hudson's stealing *his* and other colleagues' ideas as because of the press leakage. And Chamberlain's fatuous attitude toward the Germans is in striking contrast with Molotov's hard-nosed position. Both were leaving the door open to Hitler, but Molotov appears to have had fewer illusions.

"You dont need offensive forces sufficient to win a smashing victory . . . ," Chamberlain went on to say. This being the case, why was Chamberlain so hostile to an alliance with the Soviet Union? If one accepts the prime minister's logic, the acknowledged defensive strength of the Red Army should have been an important asset to Poland in particular and to the alliance in general. Most military sources rated the Red Army's defensive power as formidable, a point that seemed justified by a sound thrashing then being administered to the Japanese Kwangtung army by Soviet forces on the Manchurian frontier. Chamberlain's position on a Soviet alliance was illogical, given his views on a defensive military strategy, and incomprehensible, except insofar as his views were ideologically motivated.

In a letter to Hilda at the end of July, Chamberlain reiterated his observations on Hudson and relations with Nazi Germany just as Molotov was beginning to show more interest in German overtures.

> Hudson's gaffe has done a lot of harm and has clearly shown how completely he lacks the sense of responsibility—which a minister should have. I didn't want to add to my troubles by sacking him now, but—. In the meantime there are other and discreeter channels by which contact can be maintained for it is important that those in Germany who would like to see us come to an understanding should not be discouraged. . . . My critics of course think it would be a frightful thing to come to any agreement with Germany without first having given her a thorough thrashing. . . . But I dont share that view. Let us convince her that the chances of winning a war without getting thoroughly exhausted in the process are too remote to make it worth while.

But the corollary to that must be that she has a chance of getting fair and reasonable consideration & treatment from us & others if she will give up the idea that she can force it from us and convince us that she has given it up. . . ."[109]

Once again, Chamberlain's implication is that contacts with Germany were desirable, except that these had been found out and bungled by Hudson. The Soviet reaction to the leakage of these contacts, just at the moment when the Germans resumed their approaches, can easily be imagined. Maiskii reported the press revelations and was sure that Hudson had "voiced the prime minister's sentiments," though it was denied in the press. Otherwise Hudson would have been sacked. Maiskii did not believe Chamberlain's statement in the House of Commons that Hudson had acted without his knowledge, though this was true. If Chamberlain had been thinking about the negotiations in Moscow, he would have immediately dismissed Hudson, but of course he was not.[110]

Surits also drew negative conclusions from the press revelations. "Any honest advocate of an agreement with us is asking himself what confidence Moscow can have in the negotiations, when at the very moment of negotiations, a bridge is found toward an agreement with Germany and shameful advances are being made to Japan during a military conflict between the USSR and Japan."[111] This latter reference was to British efforts to avert a crisis over British rights at Tientsin in China, which the Japanese had blockaded. The British maneuvered out of danger, but not without embarrassment and loss of prestige. In hindsight, Surits's assessment may have been unfair, but at the time it seemed to him like one more British capitulation. Molotov later said that the Soviet government had concluded the nonaggression pact with Nazi Germany to avert an Anglo-German agreement, fears of which had been increased by the talks between Hudson and Wohlthat.[112]

There was in fact no possibility of an Anglo-German agreement, though Soviet mistrust of Chamberlain was well founded. Maiskii recognized that the prime minister was hemmed in by public opinion and Parliament but that he still possessed immense powers of persuasion and finesse. With more time and patience, Molotov might have obtained agreement with Britain. But time and patience were running out in Moscow, and the Germans had come a-courtin'.

CHAPTER SIX

Molotov Is
Suspicious

A T THE END OF JULY, Europe was at the crossroads. The British and French were preparing to send military missions to Moscow. Hitler had ignored British initiatives for improved relations while German officials courted the Soviet Union. Molotov showed interest in the German overtures, or at least a willingness to hear more. But Molotov was suspicious, as Schulenberg observed: he trusts neither us nor the British. Signs of German preparations for war against Poland were increasing. A crisis was imminent, and everyone feared the worst.

In France and Britain the anti-appeasers looked upon the staff talks in Moscow with a certain trepidation. Would they succeed? God help us if they don't. And who knew what Chamberlain or Bonnet would do? At the end of July, Seeds and Naggiar warned their governments that they'd better come to Moscow ready for business. "I am convinced," wrote Seeds,

> that the arrival in Moscow of a British military mission is the only proof of our sincerity which the Soviet government are likely to accept . . . every member of the Politbureau consider the present British government as imbued with a spirit of 'capitulating' if possible to [the] Axis Powers but that the most influential section thinks, nevertheless, we can be squeezed by our press and public and by Russian pressure, relentlessly applied, into an

agreement with this country. But such agreement must be absolutely water-tight and must clearly indicate military action.[1]

Naggiar sent a similar message a few days later. The Soviet government placed great importance on the staff talks; their success would determine the ultimate success of any agreement. Soviet authorities would not be satisfied with a superficial treatment of military obligations, a question which had preoccupied them since 1935 after the conclusion of the Franco-Soviet pact. We did not want a military convention, observed Naggiar; but now both Molotov and Potemkin are saying that without a staff accord there is no deal.[2]

Somehow the message did not get through. In anticipation of staff talks, the French and British governments made plans, though neither expected a quick agreement or perhaps any agreement. Negotiations would drag on, and eventually some general undertaking might be concluded. This did not trouble Halifax. As long as military conversations were ongoing, he reckoned that "we should be preventing Soviet Russia from entering the German camp." Chamberlain went along because "he did not attach any very great importance" to the talks. He told Admiral Sir Reginald Drax, head of the British mission to Moscow, that "the House of Commons had pushed him further than he had wished to go."[3]

For the British, the essential condition of a military agreement was Soviet acceptance of the British definition of "indirect aggression." British representatives were instructed "to go very slowly" in the military negotiations. If there were no agreement, at least time would be gained until the autumn or winter, delaying the outbreak of war.[4] Earlier in the summer Harvey, Halifax's private secretary, had recorded in his journal that the negotiations in Moscow were "in a proper mess—chiefly owing to [the] slowness and reluctance with which we first tackled Soviet Russia. This Government will never get anything done."[5] "Never get it done" was evident on August 2 when ministers briefed Drax on negotiations. From what he heard, Drax presumed that talks would likely fail: "On being asked to consider the possibility of failure, there was a short but impressive silence and the Foreign Secretary then remarked that on the whole it would be preferable to draw out the negotiations as long as possible. This looked an uninviting prospect but we agreed that it would be the best course."[6]

Complacency was illustrated in different ways. As is well known, the British government chose to send its mission to the Soviet Union by a chartered merchant ship, its modern flying boats being tied up in routine fleet maneuvers. One Foreign Office clerk thought the mission should be sent in a fleet of fast cruisers! It would signal to "the world in general and the Axis Powers in particular by some overt action that we really mean business by these conversations." The secretary of state was "considering" the suggestion, noted Sargent. Finally, Halifax "thought it might be . . . rather provocative to send a cruiser into the Baltic. . . ."[7] The talks seemed of so little importance that Halifax had "scarcely perused" British instructions. And the British delegation was told to avoid discussion of Soviet aid to Poland and Romania; the Soviet would have to negotiate directly with the Polish and Romanian governments. Such instructions were given in spite of knowing that the issue of passage rights was crucial to the Soviet Union.[8]

British complacency was not entirely shared by the French. They were impatient for the talks to begin and wanted to send their delegation more quickly to Moscow. As was their custom, however, after complaining about British travel plans they went along with them.[9] Instructions to the head of the French delegation, General Joseph Doumenc, were brief and vague, "almost useless," according to British General Hastings L. Ismay, though the much longer British instructions were no better. French generals seemed about as complacent as the British. According to Ismay, French instructions "deal . . . solely with what the French wish the Russians to do, and throw no light on what the French will do." "The Russians might have some questions to ask about the French and British contributions," observed Ismay. In reply, General Louis Jamet "smiled and shrugged his shoulders." When Ismay asked Doumenc what he would say in reply to Russian questions, he answered, "Very little, I shall just listen."[10] The French were showing their usual bad habits. Like the British instructions, the French said little about Soviet support for Poland and Romania, except to note that Poland was unlikely to agree to Red Army passage across its territory.[11] Doumenc complained to Léger that he was going to Moscow "empty-handed," not a good negotiating posture for supplicants. Léger agreed. Bonnet and Daladier, more rousing, urged Doumenc to come back with an agreement. Make promises, if you have to, said Bonnet. "What promises?" asked Doumenc. "Whatever you think necessary," replied Bonnet; if the negotiations failed, war was inevitable. *Au revoir et bonne chance!* bade Daladier.[12]

When Drax asked at the briefing if he should pay a call on Maiskii, Halifax replied, "if you can bear it. . . ." "Time was getting very short," as Drax noticed, and yet there was no sense of urgency about the talks in Moscow but rather a characteristic British arrogance toward the Russians. Maiskii left a record of his lunch with Drax. Conversation was mostly harmless until Maiskii asked why the delegation was not flying to Moscow or going in a fast cruiser. Drax gave a polite reply about too much baggage and putting officers out of their beds. "I could not believe my ears," wrote Maiskii. Drax volunteered that the delegations were traveling by chartered merchant ship, the *City of Exeter.* It makes thirteen knots, said Maiskii's aide. Maiskii was astonished and needled Drax. "Europe is beginning to burn under our feet," and the Anglo-French are going to Moscow in a freighter. "Staggering," wrote Maiskii. Chamberlain was still up to his tricks. "He does not need a tripartite pact, he needs negotiations on a pact, in order to sell more dearly this card to Hitler."[13]

Maiskii was not far wrong about Chamberlain, but surprisingly he remained optimistic about the outcome of the negotiations. Although profoundly mistrustful of the prime minister, he nevertheless thought an Anglo-Soviet bloc was gradually coming into being. Maiskii even mused about his seven years in London: "Slowly but irrepressibly, with zigzags, setbacks, failures, Anglo-Soviet relations are improving. From the Metro-Vickers affair [the Anglo-Soviet crisis in 1933 when Soviet authorities arrested British engineers working in the Soviet Union] we have come to the journey of the military mission to Moscow!" Over the remaining distance between the British and Soviet positions, sappers were closing the last span. Why was this? Maiskii asked himself: "because . . . the basic interests of the two countries now coincide." These interests were stronger than the ideological factors that divided them. Maiskii thought it ironic that Chamberlain should preside over the British government that built an Anglo-Soviet bloc against Nazi Germany. He concluded this entry with a reference to the eventual world proletarian revolution, but his thought was clear—the talks in Moscow would succeed.[14]

Mandel was not as optimistic when he saw Surits on August 2.

Doumenc was going to Moscow without detailed instructions, he said: "London and Paris (owing to the pressure of public opinion) want to avoid a breakdown of the talks, but there is no sign of any desire to achieve a serious agreement that should be put into effect immediately." The mission had not even been discussed in the French cabinet, an extraordinary situation given the importance of an agreement in Moscow.[15]

Gaffes in London did not reinforce the image of Anglo-French good faith. Butler, the parliamentary under secretary for the Foreign Office, made remarks in the House of Commons on July 31 to justify the government's position on indirect aggression. Butler cast suspicion on Soviet commitment to the independence of the Baltic states, which may have appeared justified in the light of future events, but at that moment, as the Anglo-French military missions were about to leave for Moscow, his statement was unhelpful, and perhaps intentionally so. Molotov was angry, and Tass issued a corrective: "Mr. Butler . . . misrepresented the position of the Soviet Government. In actual fact the differences of opinion do not concern the question of encroaching or not encroaching upon the independence of the Baltic States, since both parties are in favor of guaranteeing that independence; they concern the question of leaving no loopholes in the formula about 'indirect aggression' for an aggressor. . . ."[16]

Seeds and Naggiar met Molotov on August 2, and Butler's statement became a major topic of conversation. Seeds did not have a copy of Butler's statement and tried without success to soften the commissar's irritation. Molotov also complained about press leaks in the Paris and London press concerning confidential details of their negotiations. The nature of the information indicated that it was from government sources. "These methods," said Molotov, had a very negative effect on negotiations. Although Molotov did not suggest it, the leaks were probably intentional—to prepare public opinion for a failure of negotiations and to place the blame on the Soviet government. This was essential, as Bonnet had put it earlier.

Molotov also wanted to know if the military missions would be furnished with the necessary plenipotentiary powers. A telling question, as it turned out. Seeds concluded that "Molotov was a different man from what he had been at our last interview and I feel our negotiations have received a severe setback." Better let "the storm" blow over, Seeds recommended. Naggiar was just as critical and noted that he had been complaining about press leaks for two months without effect.[17] Seeds was more blunt in a private letter to Sargent.

> And now let me get off my chest a grouse against certain sinners amongst whom I strongly suspect your friends the C*b***t m*n**t**s [Cabinet ministers] to be leading culprits. Can nothing be done to make people at home.
> KEEP THEIR MOUTHS SHUT?
> During all these trying negotiations with extremely trying people, my position as negotiator has again and again been made unnecessarily arduous by a stream of indiscretions and leakages. To our shame, London has been worse than Paris. . . . In some cases my instructions entailing concessions to this government have been known here before I took action. . . . I am placed in an impossible position . . . when, for example, a London newspaper publishes our proposal for a secret annex to the treaty almost at the same moment as we suggest it to the Soviet government![18]

Butler went to see Maiskii to patch things up. The ambassador was conciliatory: ". . . he trusted not too much would be made out of the incident." As well he might have thought, in view of his confidence in the success of negotiations in Moscow.[19]

Naggiar saw Potemkin to exchange delegate lists for the upcoming talks. Nothing could better demonstrate the seriousness of Soviet intentions, said Potemkin, than the composition of the Soviet delegation, which would be headed by the commissar for defense, Voroshilov, and included the chief of the general staff of the Red Army, B. M. Shaposhnikov. Doumenc and Drax were not of the same stature. Naggiar also forwarded Molotov's question concerning the powers of the Anglo-French delegations. And a few days later Naggiar asked again about the positions of the Polish and Romanian governments on passage rights.[20]

The Soviet delegation had full powers to negotiate and sign a military convention with the Anglo-French delegation. Shaposhnikov prepared a detailed paper including various contingencies and force levels which the Red Army would use to meet its obligations. More significant, however, were the personal instructions for

Voroshilov, head of the Soviet delegation. Among these were the following: "first of all," identify the plenipotentiary powers of the Soviet delegation and ask for those of the French and British side. "If it turns out that they do not have penipotentiary powers to sign a convention, express astonishment, take them by the hands and politely ask for what purposes did their governments send them to the USSR." If they reply that they came to discuss the preparation of a military convention, ask if they brought with them concrete defense plans in the case of aggression against their future allies. If not, ask the British and French on the basis of what plans they propose to conduct negotiations with the Soviet side. "If the French and British nevertheless insist on negotiations, then lead negotiations to a discussion of specific issues of principle, mainly passage of our troops across the Vilenskii [i.e., Vilna] corridor and Galicia [in Poland] and also across Romania."

> If it becomes clear that free passage of our troops across the territory of Poland and Romania is excluded, then declare that without this stipulation agreement is impossible since without free passage across the said territories defense against aggression in any contingency is doomed to fail, and we do not contemplate participating in an undertaking which is doomed beforehand to failure.[21]

Soviet instructions anticipated every weakness of the Anglo-French delegations, and their scornful tone foretold no good result. Staff talks were on a collision course for failure at the very moment when German overtures became more pressing, from the lowest to the highest authorities of the Soviet government. Anglo-French policy was inept, something which cannot be said of German initiatives during the same period.

II

The Soviet press attaché, A. A. Smirnov, was at the German foreign ministry on July 31 and met the deputy head of the press bureau, B. von Stumm.

Germany had "no aggressive plans against the Soviet Union," Stumm said.

"We haven't forgotten what Hitler wrote in his book [*Mein Kampf*]," replied Smirnov.

"Ach, that," exclaimed Stumm, "there's a big difference between what is said and what is done in practice. The book was written in prison, a long time ago, hastily . . . what's written in that book is out of date, and we shouldn't take it seriously."[22] But *Mein Kampf* with its visions of eastern conquest was never far from the Soviet mind.

On August 2 Astakhov saw Weizsäcker on routine business. After going through the usual German lines about better relations, Weizsäcker said that Ribbentrop would like to see him, which was a surprise for Astakhov. Ribbentrop confided that Germany was anxious for better trade relations. The Soviet Union had many raw materials that Germany needed, said Ribbentrop, and "we have many manufactured products which you need." Getting quickly to the point, Ribbentrop noted that the conclusion of an economic agreement could be the beginning of an improvement in political relations. There was no reason for enmity between the two nations, he said, if they agreed not to interfere in each other's internal affairs. "National socialism is not an item for export, and we are far from contemplating its imposition on anyone at all. If your country also holds a similar view, then a further rapprochement is possible." Astakhov replied with equivalent flimflam, and then with the familiar line that the Soviet government did not consider ideological or internal differences incompatible with friendly international relations. Ribbentrop reacted positively to this reply, noting that there were no serious obstacles to better relations. Germany and the Soviet Union should be able to agree on all territorial questions between the Black and Baltic seas, he emphasized several times.

Ribbentrop then turned to the question of the "so-called western European democracies." He didn't pay much attention to their protests. "We have sufficient power to treat these with contempt and disdain. We believe in our strength. . . . There is no war which Adolf Hitler would lose." As for Poland, one way or another Danzig "will be ours," and a resolution of this problem would not be long in coming. Germany did not take seriously Polish military power; a campaign against Poland would be an affair of a week or ten days. Of course Germany hoped this would not be necessary. And on and on he went. Astakhov described it as a lengthy, at times bombastic monologue. Ribbentrop asked that his observations on Nazi-Soviet relations be forwarded to Moscow. Astakhov agreed, adding, "I do not doubt that my government is ready to welcome any improvement of relations with Germany."[23]

On Ribbentrop's orders, Schulenberg went to see Molotov on August 3 to follow up on the conversation in Berlin. This was the day after Molotov had seen Seeds and Naggiar about Butler's statement in the House of Commons. By now the German suggestions were familiar, but Schulenberg went over them again, offering a variation of Schnurre's proposals for a three-step improvement in relations—economic, press, cultural. These would be the preconditions for an improvement of political relations. Molotov replied along the lines of his last meeting with Schulenberg at the end of June, though without the sarcasm. He hoped for the conclusion of an economic agreement, but political problems remained. The anti-Comintern pact was impossible for the Soviet government to ignore, since it encouraged Japanese aggression in the Far East. And Molotov reminded the ambassador that the German government refused to participate in international conferences at which there was a Soviet presence. How did the ambassador reconcile these hostile acts with the present overtures of the German government? asked Molotov.

"[I don't] intend to try to justify past German policy," replied Schulenberg, "[I] only want to find a way to improve future relations." Molotov responded favorably and reiterated what he had said before, that "the Soviet government always stood and now stands ready for a normalization and an improvement of relations with Germany and with other countries." Schulenberg added that his government would respect Soviet interests in the Baltic region and in Poland. Germany would not renounce its claim to Danzig but hoped the question could be settled peacefully, unless another path was imposed on it. Molotov observed that it depended first on Germany whether this "other path" became necessary. Schulenberg protested: Polish "dirty tricks" were provoking Germany.

The ambassador reiterated that he did not wish to review past German policy; it was necessary now to look for ways to improve relations. I agree, Molotov replied, but we cannot forget past German policy. Schulenberg's account gave a rather more positive gloss to this conversation than did Molotov's. "In today's conversation . . . Molotov abandoned his habitual reserve and appeared unusually open." Otherwise their accounts largely coincided, which was not always the case in German and Soviet records of meetings. "From Molotov's whole attitude," concluded Schulenberg,

> it was evident that the Soviet government are, admittedly, increasingly prepared for improvement in German-Soviet relations, although the old mistrust of Germany persists. My general impression is that the Soviet Government are at present determined to conclude an agreement with Britain and France, if they fulfill all Soviet wishes. Negotiations, however, may still last a long time yet, especially since mistrust of Britain is also great. I believe that my statements made an impression on Molotov; it will, nevertheless, require considerable effort on our part to cause a reversal in the Soviet Government's course.[24]

This was the same day, incidentally, that Potemkin saw Naggiar to tell him that the composition of the Soviet military delegation should be taken as a sign of Soviet commitment to staff conversations. Molotov cabled Astakhov on August 5 that it would be desirable to continue general discussions with Germany. Much would depend on how trade negotiations developed.[25]

On this same day, August 5, Astakhov met Schnurre to pass on Molotov's instructions. Schnurre was testy in reply, asking if the chargé had any other authority than to receive German views. Astakhov replied in the negative but said he thought that Molotov's position was a step forward. Schnurre was not so sure: Molotov "had been too much concerned with the past." Schulenberg was relatively optimistic about the negotiations: "we have . . . given the Soviets something to think about." But Molotov was suspicious. "At every word and at every step," Schulenberg wrote, "one can sense the great distrust towards us. . . . The unfortunate part of it is that the mistrust of such people is very easily kindled and can only be allayed slowly and with difficulty."[26]

On August 8 Astakhov wrote again to Moscow about the specific German agenda for improving political relations. Among these were press and cultural relations, but the most important related to territorial issues along the Soviet western frontier, from the Baltic to the Black Seas. Based on what he had heard from informal sources, the Germans would be prepared

to declare their "disinterestedness" (at least political) in the fate
of the Baltics (except Lithuania), Bessarabia, Russian Poland
(with modifications in favor of the Germans) and to renounce
aspirations in the Ukraine. For this they would want to have
from us confirmation of our disinterestedness in the fate of
Danzig, and also former German Poland . . . , and (in the way of
discussion) Galicia.

Such discussions could only occur "in the absence of an Anglo-
Franco-Soviet military-political agreement." Astakhov did not put
any faith in long-term German respect for such commitments; any
understanding would be for the near term "in order at this price to
neutralize us in the case of war with Poland."[27]

On August 10 Schnurre invited Astakhov to discuss routine business, after which he turned the talk to political questions.

The German government is most interested in the question of
our position on the Polish problem [Astakhov reported]. If an
attempt to settle peacefully the question of Danzig proves impossible, and Polish provocation continues, then war is possible.
The German government would want to know what will be the
position of the Soviet government in this case.

In case of war Germany would reclaim its old borders, but not beyond. The German government "is ready," Schnurre said, "to do
everything possible not to threaten us and not to harm our interests,
but it wants to know what these interests would be. . . ." Astakhov
reported saying nothing definite in reply. In a final comment,
Schnurre noted that the conclusion of an agreement by the Soviet
Union with France and Britain would be a poor beginning to negotiations with Germany.[28] In his own account, Schnurre indicated that
Astakhov had no instructions to discuss Poland or negotiations in
Moscow. But while Astakhov reported saying nothing definite,
Schnurre indicated that the Soviet chargé was willing to talk on his
own initiative. "Negotiations with Britain had begun at a time when
there had still been no sign of any disposition on the part of Germany to come to an understanding." The Soviet government had entered into the talks "without much enthusiasm, but what choice did
we have in the circumstances? Now the situation had changed," said
Astakhov: "But one could not now simply break off something

which had been begun for well-considered reasons." The outcome of the negotiations was uncertain, and it was quite possible that Soviet options would remain open.[29]

Astakhov's communications to Moscow were important in defining the details of a possible territorial modus vivendi. But Astakhov's cable of August 10 appears to have been particularly important in alerting Moscow for the first time to direct German warnings that war was imminent and that the Soviet government would have to make up its mind quickly where it stood. Moreover, Schnurre and other German officials told Astakhov that an agreement with France and Britain would be incompatible with an understanding with Germany and that the Soviet government would therefore have to choose between the two options. Gel'fand in Rome later noted that August 10 was a crucial date when Germany also started to put heavy pressure on the Italian government to declare its intentions.[30] On August 11 Molotov replied tersely to Astakhov's letter of August 8: "The list of objectives mentioned in your letter of 8 August interests us. Negotiations on them require preparations and some transitional stages from a trade-credit agreement to other questions. We prefer to conduct negotiations on these questions in Moscow."[31] The Soviet government was taking the German bait.

While the Germans pressed and threatened Soviet officials, the British were making last-ditch efforts to persuade Hitler to come around and avoid war with Poland. Lord Kemsley, owner of the *Sunday Times* and an ardent appeaser, met Hitler at the end of July. The conversation was amiable: Hitler wanted colonies and the "cancellation" of the Versailles treaty. He suggested, on Kemsley's prodding, that each side, German and British, should put its demands on paper so that discussion might then ensue. On his return to London, Kemsley met with Wilson; then Halifax and Chamberlain agreed to take up Hitler's suggestion, and a letter was prepared and sent through discreet channels. Wilson also met the German ambassador on August 3, the same day Molotov saw Schulenberg. Wilson passed the message that if Hitler relaxed tensions, general discussions might follow. According to Wilson, Dirksen proposed an agenda of items that would interest Hitler; according to Dirksen, Wilson confirmed what he had suggested to Wohlthat in July, including a nonaggression treaty and trade negotiations. Wilson also warned, again according to Dirksen, that if news of these negotiations leaked,

Chamberlain might be forced to resign. The Wilson-Dirksen agenda resembled in some ways what the Germans had offered to Molotov. Chamberlain was keen, but not Hitler. The Fuehrer wanted a deal with the Soviet Union to free his hands for war with Poland, a deal which the British, unlike Molotov, could not conclude.[32]

III

The Anglo-French delegations arrived in Leningrad in the early morning of August 10 and in Moscow August 11, the same day Molotov sent his cable to Astakhov showing interest in German proposals. A German joke asked, "Why do the British send an Admiral in charge of their Mission to Moscow?" Reply: "They have recently had so many diplomatic shipwrecks that they think an Admiral may be better able to keep them off the rocks."[33]

On arrival in Moscow the missions went to their respective embassies. According to Doumenc, Naggiar did not hide his disquiet and his helplessness to influence events. Negotiations with Molotov had been largely without result "because Paris and London wrangled constantly only to yield too late. . . ."

"Did you bring something clear on passage across Poland?" asked Naggiar. Doumenc replied that Daladier had given him instructions *not* to agree to any military accord stipulating Red Army passage rights across Poland. Doumenc must indicate to the Soviet government that it was being asked only to provide military supplies to Poland and other such aid as the Polish government might eventually request. "If the Russians do not want to conclude on this basis," added Daladier, "I have another card to play, and I will play it if necessary." Doumenc did not say or Daladier did not name his other card.

"They haven't read . . . or understood my dispatches," Naggiar complained: passage rights were a key issue and could not be avoided. Doumenc said that Drax's instructions were to delay an agreement. Naggiar was appalled, telling Doumenc that these instructions would kill the negotiations.[34] As the ambassador noted in retrospect, "I recommended a well-defined military agreement and they send from Paris and London two missions instructed to agree to nothing in this regard. As improbable as this seems, it is nevertheless true."[35] The evidence from Naggiar and Doumenc, apart from other sources, qualifies what is assumed to have been French determination to conclude a Soviet alliance. In 1946 Daladier claimed that Soviet insistence on Red Army passage came as an "extraordinary" surprise to the French government, but it was not a surprise at all.[36]

After repeatedly warning of the need to deal with the passage issue, Naggiar was at his wit's end. He immediately cabled Paris that British instructions were at variance with what had been agreed by the three governments. They were exceedingly dangerous unless the British "secretly hoped for the failure of the talks." The Soviet government was already highly suspicious of Anglo-French motives; it would now become more so. Naggiar asked Bonnet to intervene in London.[37]

In Paris the Quai d'Orsay, reacting to Naggiar's cable of August 12, asked the British Foreign Office "to relax the instructions" to Drax. Seeds also cabled Halifax with the same request: the "French general has instructions to do his utmost to conclude military agreement at the earliest possible date, and such instructions clearly do not tally with those given to Drax." Seeds asked if the government definitely wanted progress in the talks, "beyond vague generalities." If not it would be a pity, "as all indications so far go to show that Soviet military negotiators are really out for business."[38] The deputy chiefs of staff agreed with Seeds, and the Foreign Office advised that Drax's instructions could be loosened, though not completely. But Halifax was puzzled by Seeds's comment on Doumenc's instructions, since the French mission had shown no impatience to conclude while in London. *C'est très juste,* quite so, noted Naggiar.[39]

The talks began in Moscow on Saturday, August 12, after a banquet and concert the evening before. Negotiations ran into early trouble when Voroshilov, following his instructions, put his written powers on the table and asked for those of Doumenc and Drax. Doumenc provided a vague letter of authority from Daladier. Drax, "a trifle non-plussed," as he put it—"extremely embarrassed and coughing," according to Doumenc—had to reply, "after a long pause," that he had none: "Marshal Voroshilov appeared very disappointed that the British and French missions had not been given plenipotentiary powers." Voroshilov finally agreed to proceed while Drax hurriedly cabled London asking for written instructions by return air mail! The Foreign Office complied; Drax would have power to discuss and to negotiate, but still not to sign. "It was an astonishing thing," Drax later wrote, "that the Government and the Foreign Office should have let us sail without providing us with Credentials or any similar document." Doumenc registered the same observation.[40]

The French and British had planned to keep the negotiations to generalities. Not Voroshilov. Once again following his instructions, he wanted to discuss operational plans, and he would not let the British and French dodge the issues. On Sunday, August 13, after listening to a report by Doumenc, Voroshilov asked how they envisaged the role of the Soviet Union in the event of aggression against the prospective allied powers, and in particular Poland and Romania. As Doumenc put it, "The Marshal, with a sort of apparent easygoing directness, put us against the wall." No equivocation, no maneuvers, no diplomatic retreat was possible.[41]

The following day, August 14, Voroshilov repeated his question. Doumenc, respecting Daladier's instructions, answered that each ally would defend its own territory, asking for help if necessary.

"What if they do not ask for it . . . in good time?" asked Voroshilov. "It will mean they have put up their hands, that they will have surrendered." Doumenc responded evasively; Drax noted that Poland and Romania would "soon ["in two weeks," according to Doumenc's account] become German provinces" if they did not accept Soviet military support. The marshal allowed his counterparts to dance around the issue a little longer, then he cut them short.

> I want a clear answer to my very clear question concerning the joint action of the Armed Forces of Britain, France and the Soviet Union against the common enemy . . . should he attack. That is all I want to know. . . . Do the French and British General Staffs think that the Soviet land forces will be admitted to Polish territory in order to make direct contact with the enemy in case Poland is attacked?

Doumenc and Drax, discountenanced, still tried to dodge, but Voroshilov would not tolerate it. "I want a straight answer. . . . Your opinion is that Poland and Romania will ask for our help. I doubt if it would turn out like that. They might ask for aid . . . or they might not, or they might ask for it too late." If so, "their forces will be destroyed. These troops should be used as an additional allied asset; it is in the interest neither of England, nor of France, nor of the USSR that they should be destroyed."[42]

After five years of discussion and evasion—since 1934 in fact—Voroshilov, as Doumenc observed, had cornered his would-be allies. The British asked for a fifteen-minute break. Leaving the conference room, Drax was stunned. He thought it was the end of their mission. "We . . . thought we could obtain Russian support without dealing with very legitimate questions," Doumenc wrote. Naggiar, however, was not ready to call it quits. I told you so, he cabled Paris. But it was still not too late to extort an answer from the Poles and Romanians. Seeds cabled London, supporting Naggiar. Britain and France were the "petitioners in this matter," said Seeds; the onus was on London and Paris to obtain an answer from Warsaw.[43]

The Anglo-French delegation informed their Soviet counterparts on the following day, August 15, that they had referred Voroshilov's questions to Paris and London for reply. General discussions continued while replies were awaited: the Soviet delegates offered one hundred divisions to buttress the defense of Poland. Doumenc had to be inventive, since the French had no offensive plans to go to the aid of the Poles, though to admit it was scarcely possible. Voroshilov let these discussions go on until August 17 when he finally interrupted them, declaring that operational planning could not begin until there was an answer to his "cardinal question," as he put it, on Red Army passage rights. The French and British governments still had not replied, so further meetings were put off until August 21.

In London the deputy chiefs of staff, whom Chamberlain had tried at times to manipulate or finesse, would no longer acquiesce. "In view of the speed with which events are moving, it is possible that this report will be to a large extent out of date before there is time to circulate it, but we feel that it may be of advantage to put on record," they said pointedly, "certain general observations on the broad question of the use of Polish and Roumanian territory by the Russian forces." Voroshilov could have written the report. It was "no time for half-measures," said the deputy chiefs; the "strongest pressure" should be brought to bear on Poland and Romania; "the Russians should be given every facility for rendering assistance and putting their maximum weight into the scale on the side of the anti-aggression powers."

> It is perfectly clear that without early and effective Russian assistance, the Poles cannot hope to stand up to a German attack . . . for more than a limited time. The same applies to the Roumanians except that the time would be still more limited.
>
> The supply of arms and war material is not enough. If the Russians are to collaborate in resisting German aggression against Poland or Roumania they can only do so effectively on Polish or Roumanian soil; and . . . if permission for this were withheld till war breaks out, it would then be too late. The most the Allies could then hope for would be to avenge Poland and Roumania and perhaps restore their independence as a result of the defeat of Germany in a long war.
>
> Without immediate and effective Russian assistance . . . the longer that war would be, and the less chance there would be of either Poland or Roumania emerging at the end of it as independent states in anything like their original form.

Who can say now that the deputy chiefs were wrong? The "unpalatable truth," they said, had to be presented "with absolute frankness" in Warsaw and Bucharest. A treaty with the Soviet Union was "the best way of preventing a war"; if it failed, Poland and Romania could pay the price of a possible Soviet-German rapprochement.[44] While this drama unfolded, the Foreign Office was still producing papers on indirect aggression. "This would be comical if it was not tragic," scribbled Naggiar.[45]

In Paris, Voroshilov's ultimatum and Naggiar's cables prompted the Quai d'Orsay to pressure the Polish government to accept Red Army passage across Polish territory. The Poles had heretofore refused to cooperate. Moscow might think Poland afraid and put up the price of its help. "Bargaining with the Soviet government . . . was like doing a deal in an oriental bazaar," noted a Polish official; "the essential thing was to show no interest in what you really wished to buy."[46]

On August 15 Bonnet summoned the Polish ambassador in Paris, Łukasziewicz, who said Beck would certainly reject out of hand a Soviet demand for passage.[47] Bonnet sent instructions to Noël to see Beck, and the French military attaché, General Félix-Joseph Musse, was ordered back to Warsaw. In the midst of a full-blown crisis, commented Naggiar, "the military attaché was on holiday in Biarritz." It was worse than that: neither Noël nor Musse was prepared to apply the full rigor of his instructions. Noël feared to compromise his personal position in Warsaw. Musse was vulnerable to Polish influence and questioned Soviet good faith as much as did the Poles.[48]

Noël met Beck on August 18; the Polish government was adamant that it would not accord passage rights. To do so would make war inevitable, and, in any event, the Soviet government could not be trusted nor the Red Army relied upon to give real help to Poland. Doumenc wanted to send a senior officer to Warsaw to help with negotiations, but Paris blocked it for fear of undesirable publicity. He sent instead a subaltern, Captain André Beaufre, who could not hope to influence Noël or Musse. Typical of the negotiations, Beaufre missed his plane back to Moscow, prompting Naggiar to more sarcastic marginalia. With such messengers, he thought, there was no chance of success. The Soviet would let the British and French cut their throats, Drax reported, over the question of passage rights. Naggiar signaled that if the Poles did not agree, the talks in Moscow would fail.[49]

The Foreign Office sent instructions to Kennard in Warsaw to support the French, though he had no greater success. "We have done our best," Kennard said, but the Polish government would not budge. "Passage of Russian forces has been the rock on which every proposal for a collective alliance in Eastern Europe has since foundered." Quite apart from centuries-old national animosities, "strong internal political reasons" dictated the Polish position—that is, large Ukrainian and Belorussian minorities in eastern Poland.

> It is almost unthinkable that the present political structure of Eastern Galicia could survive the entry of Russian troops especially as Communism makes a certain appeal to young Ukrainians. In Vilna area large White Russian population is politically immature and is easily influenced by Soviet propaganda.[50]

Noël submitted similar conclusions to Paris. The Foreign Office sent additional instructions, but Kennard replied that he had already used his best arguments and had decided "to refrain from further action."[51] The Quai d'Orsay directed Noël to try again. On August 21, in response to Naggiar's urging, the French government authorized

Doumenc—though the British never sent similar instructions to Drax—to sign the best agreement he could get in Moscow. "Too late," noted Naggiar.[52]

IV

On August 12 Astakhov reported Molotov's instructions (of the previous day) to Schnurre: the Soviet government was prepared to consider political negotiations after appropriate preparations and transitional stages from a trade agreement. What about the Polish question? asked Schnurre. Astakhov could say nothing definite. He advised Molotov that time was running out, and that the Germans were not interested in progressing by stages. They wanted to discuss "territorial-political" issues "in order to free their hands in case of a conflict with Poland. . . ." More than that, the Germans were worried about negotiations with the Anglo-French, and they were willing to make offers to prevent an agreement—disinterestedness in the Baltic, Bessarabia, eastern Poland, not to speak of the Ukraine. In exchange the Germans wanted only "the promise of non-interference in a conflict with Poland." In a further letter on the same day, Astakhov warned that war in Poland was coming fast. He did not need to say that the Soviet government had to move quickly to protect its security.[53]

On Sunday, August 13, as the military talks in Moscow were getting down to serious business, Schnurre returned with an even more pointed message to Astakhov: "Events are moving very fast, and we cannot lose time." The Soviet Union would have to decide whether it was a friend or foe of Germany.[54] On Tuesday, August 15, Schulenberg proposed to Molotov a meeting with Ribbentrop in Moscow to settle outstanding differences, and he read a long letter from Ribbentrop expressing the German government's desire for better relations. Molotov dropped his previous reserve and suspiciousness. Would the German government be prepared to sign a nonaggression pact? asked Molotov. Would it be willing to exercise its influence on Japan to end fighting on the Manchurian frontier? Although Molotov was evasive on the date of a visit by Ribbentrop—this would require "adequate preparation"—he was interested in the German overture. Schulenberg was more optimistic about the conclusion of an agreement, unlike his impression after the August 3 meeting with Molotov.[55] It was also on August 15 that Doumenc and Drax promised Voroshilov to ask for instructions on Red Army passage rights across Poland and Romania.

The next day Astakhov cabled that he had information from the Italian chargé d'affaires that the Germans were no longer discussing the Danzig question in isolation but as part of the general problem of Poland, whose future looks "extremely sombre." The situation "is so tense that the possibility of a world war is by no means excluded. All this must be decided at most in the course of the next three weeks."[56] War was imminent. Did the Soviet government want to be in it with partners as uncertain as Britain and France? Doumenc and Drax had been dancing around Voroshilov's hard questions for several days. It made a bad impression on the Soviet government, which had its own back to the wall on the question of peace or war.

On Thursday, August 17, Schulenberg told Molotov that the German government was interested in a nonaggression pact. He asked for clarification of the Soviet position on the Baltic states; Molotov evaded a direct reply. This would have to be worked out by both governments. Schulenberg reiterated that the German government was in a hurry and did not intend "to tolerate Polish provocations." The ambassador asked for Soviet agreement to a meeting with Ribbentrop either that week or next, and he asked for a quick reply. Molotov handed Schulenberg an aide-mémoire proposing a nonaggression pact or a reaffirmation of the Berlin neutrality treaty of 1926, with a protocol defining German and Soviet foreign policy interests. I should add, said Molotov, that Comrade Stalin is informed and agrees with these proposals. But before political negotiations could begin, the trade agreement had to be completed. "This will be the first step, which we need to take on the path of improved relations." Regarding the timing of Ribbentrop's visit, Molotov appreciated the German government's willingness to send a high-ranking official to Moscow, unlike the British who had sent only Strang. Before his arrival, necessary preparations had to be made; the Soviet Union did not wish prematurely to create a public "storm."[57] Schulenberg's account of the meeting corresponded with Molotov's and indicated that Soviet policy had come a long way in two weeks while Voroshilov still waited for an answer from Paris and London on passage rights. Molotov's gratuitous slap at the Strang mission was a good indication of the Soviet frame of mind.

The Soviet mood was worrying the Turks. The Turkish ambassador in Moscow, A. Kh. Aktai, saw Molotov on the same day as Schulenberg to convey the Turkish president Ismet İnönü's hopes that an agreement with France and Britain would soon be concluded. This agreement was essential for the preservation of peace, and it was in the general interests of Turkey and the Soviet Union. "The negotiations have dragged out," replied Molotov, "but not by any fault of ours. We have done and are doing everything possible, but not all in this regard depends on us."[58] In view of Molotov's proposals to Schulenberg, this was a disingenuous reply to a long-standing ally.

On Saturday, August 19, while the Soviet government continued to wait for an Anglo-Soviet reply to Voroshilov, Schulenberg went in the afternoon to see Molotov. The ambassador excused his insistence for a meeting, but the situation was "unusual" and "quick methods" were needed to come to agreement. "In Berlin they fear war between Germany and Poland." The slightest incident could set off hostilities. Schulenberg always used this preface to ask for agreement from Molotov; it played to Soviet fears. Germany needed to know where the Soviet Union would stand in the event of war. Ribbentrop was in a hurry, according to Schulenberg: there was general agreement on all issues. "Hitler is ready to take into account everything that the USSR may desire." The ambassador insisted on quick assent for Ribbentrop's trip to Moscow. According to the Soviet account of the meeting, Molotov indicated that he would report Schulenberg's communication to the Soviet government. He was positive about the German foreign minister's eventual visit, but before he could arrive, agreement had "more or less" to be settled. And the trade negotiations had not yet been concluded. This one-step-at-a-time, so-many-questions approach exasperated the German ambassador, who insisted on agreement for the date of Ribbentrop's arrival in Moscow. Molotov played a little with Schulenberg, asking innocently if the German rush was related to German-Polish relations. Schulenberg responded in the affirmative, reminding Molotov that the German government wanted to consider Soviet interests "before the onrush of events." The game continued a little longer, Molotov delaying, Schulenberg pressing almost desperately. At the end of the afternoon the game was apparently concluded, because Molotov called the ambassador back, handing him a draft nonaggression pact and informing him that Ribbentrop could come to Moscow on August 26–27. "Molotov did not give reasons for his sudden change of mind," reported Schulenberg; "I assume that Stalin intervened." If this was true, was Molotov still holding out for the French and British? The available evidence does not provide an answer.[59]

In Berlin, Soviet representatives stalled on the signing of the trade agreement while Molotov and Schulenberg sparred in Moscow. Schnurre said the stalling had nothing to do with the agreement itself. "The reasons put forward by the Russians are transparent pretexts. It is obvious that they have received from Moscow, for political reasons, instructions to delay the conclusion of the treaty." On August 20 Hitler, anxious to settle so he could move against Poland, sent a cable to Stalin insisting on an earlier meeting. Stalin agreed on the following day.[60] On August 21 Tass announced the signature of a Soviet-German trade agreement; on August 22 that Ribbentrop was expected in Moscow on the morrow to conclude a nonaggression pact.[61]

V

The announcement of the trade agreement came as the Anglo-French delegations met Voroshilov for the last time. They still did not have an answer from Paris and London on passage rights, but Drax could finally present his written credentials. He suggested putting off further meetings for three or four days, but Voroshilov proposed adjournment *sine die*. There was nothing to discuss until Paris and London replied. Voroshilov left open the possibility of a resumption of talks and the conclusion of an agreement, but in view of the discussions between Molotov and Schulenberg, this was mere courtesy. And the Soviet government had a good idea of the Polish response to Anglo-French démarches. The Soviet ambassador in Warsaw reported that the Polish press was full of derisive comments about cooperation with the Soviet Union. Doumenc and Drax tried to keep discussions going, but Voroshilov said no.[62]

Doumenc met Voroshilov privately on the evening of August 22 in a final attempt to salvage the situation. The French government, he said, had authorized him to sign an agreement consenting to Red Army passage across Poland.

"And the British government?" asked Voroshilov. Doumenc did not know.

What about the Polish and Romanian governments? Doumenc could not say. "I am persuaded," replied Voroshilov, "that the Poles would want to participate directly in our talks had they given their consent to the passage of Soviet troops. They would certainly have insisted. . . . As this is not the case, I doubt that they were informed."

"That is possible," conceded Doumenc.

"Let's wait until everything becomes clear."

"I will wait with pleasure, but I would not want to wait for nothing. I will be frank with the Marshal," said Doumenc. "It has already been announced that someone must soon arrive and for me such visits are not a pleasure."

"That is true. But the fault for this lies with the French and British sides. The question of military cooperation with the French has been a matter of importance for us for several years," replied Voroshilov, "but it was not resolved. . . ." And then he raised the issue of Czechoslovakia. Doumenc replied unpersuasively. But the main message was that Voroshilov did not wish to continue talks, though he left the door open a little, perhaps out of courtesy, or simply because the Soviet government never liked to close off an option.[63]

Seeds went to see Molotov on the same evening after Doumenc's visit to Voroshilov. The meeting was stormy. Molotov angrily rejected Seeds's accusation of bad faith. He would not allow the British "to stand in judgment of the Soviet government."

You should have warned us, accused Seeds.

The British government does not advise us of changes in *its* policy, replied Molotov.

This is different, retorted Seeds.

The British government was not serious, said Molotov. The "height of insincerity had been reached when military missions arrived in Moscow empty-handed" and unwilling to deal with the question of Red Army passage across Poland and Romania. You were only "playing with us," accused Molotov. Finally the Soviet government had decided—"either yesterday or the day before," surmised Seeds—to accept the German proposals.

Seeds denied that the British mission had arrived "empty-handed"—though Doumenc had used the same expression when discussing his instructions with Léger in Paris. Molotov waved off Seeds's explanation. The passage issue had been raised "on several occasions in the past," and the French could never bring themselves "to give a clear answer."[64] Who can say that Molotov was wrong? Even in 1935, noted Naggiar, the Soviet Union had proposed definite treaty obligations "to which we responded with vague formulations."[65] Payart paid a call on Potemkin in early September. He sometimes wore his feelings on his sleeve, as he did on this occasion, regretting the nonaggression pact. I always was and remain, said Payart, an advocate of Franco-Soviet cooperation, but I must admit my sorrow at the loss of one of my "illusions." "I replied to these lamentations," wrote Potemkin, "that the governments of France and England must take on themselves the responsibility for the failure of the attempts to reach a Soviet-Anglo-French political agreement."[66]

The best the Poles would finally do was to agree on August 23 that in the event of German aggression, some form of Polish-Soviet cooperation would not be excluded, or was possible. This was not enough, noted Naggiar. The Polish refusal to conclude with the Soviet Union was a political "illness," according to Noël.[67] Bonnet sent a cable on the same day intended for Bucharest, stating *falsely* that the Poles had agreed to passage rights and the Romanian government should do the same. "Inexact," noted Naggiar, and an act of desperation. "It was in April that we should have moved in Bucharest and Warsaw."[68] Coulondre in Berlin cabled to Naggiar that he had confidential information from a high German official that nothing specific had been decided between the German and Soviet governments. They had agreed only on extremely general terms. There was still time to act in Moscow.[69]

VI

In fact, it was too late. Ribbentrop arrived in Moscow the same day, August 23, and signed a nonaggression pact in the early hours of the following morning. The pact included a secret protocol, the terms of which are well enough known but can be summarized. "In the event of territorial-political reconstruction," Finland, Estonia, Latvia, Bessarabia, and Poland east of the Narev, Vistula, and San Rivers would fall within the Soviet "sphere of interest." Lithuania and the rest of Poland were assigned to Germany. "The question of whether it is in the interests of both parties to preserve the independence of the Polish government and what will be the borders of this government can only be finally clarified in the course of further political developments." Both sides agreed to keep the protocol "strictly secret."[70]

Ribbentrop had wanted to add some flowery passages about German-Soviet friendship, but Stalin declined. The two nations had been dumping "buckets of shit" over each other for years; it would take time before Soviet public opinion got used to the idea. After business was concluded, vodka glasses were raised, jokes exchanged, and photographers called in to record the event. Apparently Stalin drank water, not vodka. "I had to toast Hitler . . . ," remembered Molotov: "That's diplomacy."[71]

The Anglo-French had been warned many times over the years of the danger of a German-Soviet rapprochement. Litvinov, for one, had done so repeatedly. So had Alphand, Coulondre, Payart, and Naggiar. How many times did I say it? remarked Alphand: "Implement the [mutual assistance] accord with the USSR, or the Russians will come to terms with the Germans."[72] It had been no use. The French and British governments did not take such warnings seriously—or, in any event, seriously enough.

In Warsaw, Beck was untroubled by the sudden turn of events which simply confirmed his suspicions of the Soviet government. "Really not much had changed," Beck told Noël. When Naggiar saw this report, he noted, "One cannot imagine anything more insane."[73] The British Foreign Office took the sudden turnabout with less equanimity. Sargent complained about the lapse in British intelligence: how could they have been taken so unawares? This was an ironic twist since he had previously derided the danger of a German-Soviet rapprochement as Litvinov's "empty threat." Collier had been monitoring the potential danger for years and had often clashed with Sargent. And the reversal of Soviet policy had occurred so quickly that intelligence sources might not have had enough time to pick it up. The U.S. State Department passed information to the British ambassador in Washington only on August 17, when it was probably too late to matter. The Soviet government had issued a press release on July 22 indicating that German-Soviet trade negotiations were resuming. Schnurre had objected, implicitly to avoid premature disclosure. If the Anglo-French had remembered Potemkin's warning in February that economic negotiations often led to political discussions, they might have been more concerned. Or, as Litvinov had reminded Payart in March, "there was a close interdependence between political and economic relations. . . ." In fact, the French and British should not have needed such warnings; the linking of economic and political negotiations was long-standing Soviet policy.[74]

In Paris, Daladier calculated that the German army would march into Poland in a matter of days. He condemned the Poles' "folly" as much as the Soviets' "duplicity," though in the latter case he had little room for criticism.[75] In September the president of the French Senate, Jules Jeanneney, asked Daladier if "Russian-German collusion" had caught the general staff off guard. "No," replied Daladier, "we have for a long time considered it a possibility, but all the same, what deceit by Stalin. He was amusing our military mission in Moscow with interminable demands." Passage rights, for example, across Poland; they were tough to obtain, explained Daladier, but the Poles finally consented. Then, this proved insufficient for the Russians.[76] Daladier's explanation to Jeanneney was untrue, but like Bonnet he was anxious to put the blame on the Soviet government for the failure of negotiations.

After Bonnet received the news from Moscow, he called in Surits to complain. The nonaggression pact had produced "a painful impression" in the French cabinet. They were all "stupefied" that the Soviet government would conclude with Germany while the Anglo-French military mission was in Moscow. Bonnet claimed that the Polish government had consented to passage rights, though Surits would have doubted it or known better. Bonnet also cabled Naggiar to invoke the consultative clause of the 1935 Franco-Soviet mutual assistance pact. "A little late," thought Naggiar.[77] Bonnet finally launched a flirt with Rome to enlist Italian mediation, like that before Munich, to avert a German invasion of Poland. Apart from this, the French ran out of ideas. In London the Chamberlain government sought a way out up to the last minute, but to no avail.

VII

What is one to make of these extraordinary events? Stalin may have considered it simple reciprocity to pay back the British and French governments in their own coin for the lack of response to collective security. Naggiar thought so. *Après Munich, c'est la réponse du berger à la bergère,* he noted—after Munich it was the Soviet tit for tat.[78] It was not a question of whether Stalin trusted Hitler more than the Anglo-French; Stalin trusted no one. It was a question of buying time or of *sauve qui peut*—a stampede to safety. His decision was akin to that of the Anglo-French in 1938 not to go to war over Czechoslovakia. It was encouraging the "crocodile" to stalk other prey.

Did the Soviet government have another option to protect its security other than the conclusion of a nonaggression pact with Germany? Surits and Potemkin offered one in May, but Molotov did not take it up. The British government was divided and hesitant. The French were more responsive, but they were unable to persuade the British to go along, and went along with London instead. And what is one to say of Poland: a reef on which collective security foundered, an aggressor in 1938 and a victim in 1939. Could the Soviet Union refuse a nonaggression pact with Nazi Germany when the French and British governments opposed an "all-in" alliance and when Poland scorned Soviet support right up to the end?

Should the Soviet government have waited for the British? The anti-appeasers in Britain, notably Churchill, would eventually win out, as Maiskii himself predicted on occasion. Was the Soviet position too inflexible in spite of Anglo-French complacency and reticence? The answer must be that the Soviet position was both inflexible and justified. Finesse might have obtained what the Soviet wanted, as Surits and Potemkin suggested, if Molotov had had the patience to play out the game. Stalin did not have it. War was imminent, and the Germans told Molotov to choose his friends. Here is how Molotov put it in his reminiscences:

If we hadn't moved toward the Germans in 1939, they would have invaded all of Poland right up to our old border. That's why we came to an arrangement with them. They had to agree. They took the initiative on the nonaggression pact. We couldn't defend Poland because it didn't want to deal with us. Inasmuch as Poland would not deal, and war was close at hand, give us just that part of Poland that we believe indisputably belongs to the Soviet Union.[79]

In view of British reticence and French weakness, was the Soviet western option too dangerous? Chamberlain did not want an alliance with the Soviet Union. By his own account, public opinion and Parliament pushed him further than he wanted to go, and even then he opposed the alliance and was not sorry when negotiations failed. As the Germans courted Molotov, Chamberlain held out the offer of negotiations to Hitler, if only he would stop his threats and rein in his army. Yes, British policy was evolving in 1939, but Chamberlain, Wilson, and Halifax (perhaps at times to a lesser extent), among others, were recalcitrant and moving grudgingly toward a stiffer policy. And what can one say of the French? No one trusted Bonnet, and Daladier was a "bull with snail's horns." Mandel, who saw Surits regularly, encouraged a tough Soviet stand so that the French government could not slip away from a real alliance.

A long-standing mythology has developed concerning the Nazi-Soviet nonaggression pact. It was already being developed in the summer of 1939, when the British and French leaked information to the press to prepare public opinion for a possible failure of negotiations and to place the blame on the Soviet Union. According to the mythology, the Soviet government had "colluded" with Nazi Germany and cunningly, actively sought a nonaggression pact. During negotiations in 1939 Molotov kept making fresh demands on the French and British to give the Germans time to catch up. The Soviet demand for passage rights came as a "surprise" at the talks in Moscow. The nonaggression pact "caused" the Second World War.

After the war Daladier even accused the French communists of treason for the nonaggression pact, but he also bore a heavy responsibility for what happened in August 1939.[80] And so did Chamberlain, especially Chamberlain. Anglo-French complacency in preparing for the military conversations in Moscow is incomprehensible except as a reflection of anti-Soviet hostility, unwillingness to abandon last hopes of accommodation with Hitler, and, in the case of the French, a lack of determination which disposed them to follow the British line in spite of misgivings. The Anglo-French strategy of delay, generalities, and avoidance of the question of passage rights flew in the face of Soviet expectations for operational plans, detailed commitments, Polish cooperation, and quick agreement. Unless one considers Anglo-French policymakers—Chamberlain, Halifax, Daladier, Bonnet—to have been fools, which they certainly were not, their policies toward the Soviet Union in 1939 were less a blunder than a calculated risk which went wrong.

The same was true of Soviet policy. Although we do not have all the evidence from the Soviet side, what we do have indicates that the Germans actively courted the Soviet government beginning in May, while "the Soviet" stood off until the end of July or the beginning of August. The key determinants of Soviet policy appear to have been disbelief in the good faith of France and Britain, crucial security concerns over the Baltic states, fear of imminent war in Poland (confirmed directly by the Germans), and the German demand that the Soviet Union declare its position before war broke out. It seems incredible that the Soviet government could have abandoned its deep, long-standing hostility to Nazi Germany and its commitment to collective security during a fortnight in August, but that is what the available evidence shows. It is also untrue that Molotov kept heaping fresh demands on Seeds and Naggiar. The basic Soviet position was marked out and known in 1935. There was little difference in Litvinov's original offer and the various iterations of it produced by Molotov. Neither "indirect" aggression, nor the Baltic guarantee, nor passage rights, nor a military convention were new issues or fresh demands. Daladier lied through his teeth when he said he was surprised by the Soviet demand for passage rights. Not only was he not surprised, he anticipated that the issue would be raised and he instructed Doumenc not to agree to it.

And how quickly Litvinov was forgotten during the summer of 1939. Not even four months after his dismissal, it must almost have seemed as though he had not been the most important Soviet diplomat of the interwar years. Collective security, Litvinov's policy, was cast away like an old sock. A member of the French embassy in Moscow gave a good account of Stalin's policy: "It would appear a well-established fact that the Soviet government abandons its ideologies for realities . . . hatred of fascism, defense against the aggressors, are for it not objectives, but means." The objectives of Soviet policy were state security and the recovery of the tsars' lost territories. Soviet policy was "detached from any moral concern"; it derived from "the school of Machiavelli in its purest form."[81] In view of Stalin's easy shifts in domestic politics from opposing positions, and his murderous elimination of rivals and innocents, why should he not apply the same rules of conduct in foreign policy?

The Soviet government wanted to buy time, keep clear of the fighting, and see the war brought to an early end, if its propaganda is to be believed. Stalin made the same mistake as the French and British: he thought he could do business with Hitler, or at least put off the inevitable confrontation until the Soviet Union was stronger. In hindsight it is easy to see that Stalin should have stuck with Litvinov and collective security and given the French and British governments more time to come around. But hindsight is always clear; at the time it was not a good bet that the British and French would come around. Not Chamberlain certainly, not the French, who had no Clemenceau, and not the Poles, who were blind and intractable. Stalin had to choose between fighting sooner or later; he chose to fight later, if at all. It was a calamitous miscalculation. Mandel, who had figured out Hitler early on, knew *at the time* what should have been done. "We sat and twiddled our thumbs," he said, "until Poland was crushed. We should have fought at the start." This was not hindsight; it was good advice, and Stalin should have followed it. In 1942 Molotov admitted, "We were both at fault."[82]

"A Situation of Delicacy and Danger"

IN AUGUST 1939 the world seemed suddenly to turn on its head. What appeared to be certainties and solid points of reference disappeared into the air like puffs of smoke in the breezes of a late summer's day. In the course of a fortnight in August the stunning reversal occurred, and the two archenemies composed their differences. "Yesterday it was there. Today it is gone," noted American journalist William Shirer from Berlin: "There will be no long [German] front against Russia to hold this time." In France and Britain there was shock, anger, and humiliation, especially knowing of Nazi *Schadenfreude* over the turnabout which cleared the way for a German invasion of Poland. With "Russia in the bag," Nazis boasted, the British will not dare to fight.[1]

The Soviet volte-face changed everything. Until August 1939 the Soviet Union held the high political ground in the effort to resist Nazism. It was a small piece of high ground, awash in blood spilled in the Stalinist purges, but it was high ground nevertheless. When Molotov signed the nonaggression pact, the high ground was swamped. Foreign communists were stunned, and many quit their parties in disillusionment. The Soviet Union had extended a hand to fascism. It was shocking. In France and Britain, anti-communist rhetoric that had diminished during the spring and summer while negotiations went on in Moscow, now erupted again. In late August the French government banned the communist daily *L'Humanité*, and the following month it outlawed the French communist party and arrested Communist deputies. It was an anti-communist roundup. If someone was imprudent enough to say too loudly *"Vivent les Soviets"* in the local café, it was *hé hop*, eighteen months in jail, *ferme*, no parole for the unfortunate perpetrator. In Britain Labour was bitter against Stalin, but the cabinet, while feeling double-crossed, was less affronted. Having claimed that a Soviet alliance was "not much more than an unnecessary luxury," A. J. P. Taylor observed, the British government had "to appear undismayed."[2] In fact, Anglo-French officials put on a brave face but saw their strategic plans for a long grinding war and strangling blockade of Nazi Germany gravely compromised.

In the early morning of September 1 almost sixty German divisions invaded Poland. On September 2 Chamberlain spoke in the House of Commons not of a declaration of war but of further negotiations. There was consternation in the House, which thought that Chamberlain was about to "do another Munich." An opposition leader rose to speak. One M.P. shouted "Speak for England," and the House rumbled its approval. In France it was worse; the government took three days before it could muster up determination enough to issue an ultimatum to Germany. And it did so reluctantly, trailing the British. Where's the French army? the Poles wanted to know. After years of criticizing the Soviet Union for its inability to sustain offensive operations, the French high command launched the *drôle de guerre*, the phony war, not a general offensive, and let Poland be crushed in a fortnight—about what Drax had predicted to Voroshilov a few weeks before.

The second front in the east collapsed before it was ever organized, but on the western front it was only the Bore War. While the Luftwaffe remorselessly bombed Poland, it was the *guerre de confettis*, the confetti war, in the west. The British dropped ineffectual propaganda leaflets on the few German divisions manning the Siegfried line against France. German soldiers might symbolically have used the leaflets for toilet paper. Not the British intention, to be sure, but the Anglo-French were reluctant to provoke the enemy.[3]

Pas de conneries, no screwing around, was a popular French attitude, or *we'll pay the price*.[4] "Some Funkstick in the Air Ministry," later complained Churchill, was afraid that retaliation against the enemy would provoke counterretaliation. "Don't irritate them, dear!" replied a sarcastic Churchill, who had taken a seat in the British War Cabinet.[5] The German army played on these anxieties: "We won't shoot if you don't" was a message broadcast to French troops at the front. *"Pas méchants,"* not so bad, these Germans, thought many French soldiers.[6] Meanwhile Poland disappeared. Maiskii was astonished by the rapidity of the Polish collapse. *La Pologne est foutue,* Poland's fucked, reckoned the French commander-in-chief Gamelin: we'll have to dig in and hope for better luck. What happened to the Poles, however, won't happen to us. "France is not Poland!"[7] The British attitude was similar but also more creative.

Creativeness and patience were much in need because on September 17 the Red Army occupied eastern Poland. Poland was finished anyway, but in London and Paris it seemed like a stab in the back. The Anglo-French had no room to talk, and the Soviet government, not unexpectedly, took a different view of the circumstances. The Soviet Union felt no debts of obligation to Poland. Readers will remember that Soviet-Polish relations before the war had been cold or hostile, and when the Soviet government sought to improve relations with France or to promote collective security, Poland was there, as an obstacle. Apart from preventing German invasion forces from driving up against Soviet frontiers, the Polish collapse offered Moscow the additional and satisfying advantage of recovering Ukrainian and Belorussian territories captured by the Poles during the Russo-Polish war of 1919–1920. Perhaps this is why Molotov telephoned Schulenberg on September 8 to congratulate the German army on its entry into Warsaw.[8] "That's diplomacy," Molotov might have said again. But it was more like a Russian's perverse satisfaction at Poland's distress. At the end of September, Ribbentrop went again to Moscow to sign further agreements with Molotov, coldly renegotiating their respective spheres of interest in Poland and the Baltic and developing trade relations. Molotov swapped ethnic Polish territory for Lithuania as easily as American kids swapped baseball cards. The Soviet government imposed mutual assistance pacts on the Baltic states in September and October allowing, *inter alia,* for the stationing of Soviet troops in those countries. The Baltic governments had no choice but to agree to Soviet terms. No one could or would help them to resist.[9]

The fate of Poland rankled in London and Paris, but there was nothing the British or French governments could do. It was an uncomfortable moral position, though in war morality has little purchase on the minds of war-makers. In protesting against the Soviet occupation, the French were somewhat more aggressive than the British, though even they held to the position that we had to "swallow our feelings" because of "the extreme importance of not getting on the wrong side of the Russians. . . ." Seeds, the British ambassador in Moscow, also advised caution in dealing with the ugly situation. "I beg respectfully to express my opinion," he said, "that the attitude of H. M. Government . . . has been much better adapted [than the French] to a situation of delicacy and danger."[10]

Danger concentrated the Foreign Office mind most effectively. The British government almost immediately adopted a cautious policy toward the Soviet Union.[11] But the British government went further than mere passive caution; it actually sought to encourage an Anglo-Soviet rapprochement. The British initiative broke a pattern of twenty years: it had been the needy and isolated Soviet Union that had sought better or at least businesslike political and economic relations while the French and British had often rejected Soviet overtures.

II

In September 1939 circumstances were different: the British became the suitor while "the Soviet" stood off, relieved to have avoided being drawn into the war and anxious to take advantage of the destabilization of Europe without compromising its declared position as a neutral. Surprisingly, those policymakers in the Foreign Office who only months before had rejected Soviet overtures—Sargent, Cadogan, Butler, Halifax, even Chamberlain—now contemplated a more flexible policy.

What choice did they have? In their political reflections immediately after the Soviet turnabout in August, the Foreign Office concluded that it was best to wait out the situation. According to Sargent, Russia was reverting back to its "historic national policy" and abandoning its "international ideals." The recovery of territories lost during the last war and access to the ice-free sea were now its main objectives. Molotov had tried to obtain French and British acquiescence in the Soviet annexation of the Baltic states (as Sargent saw it), but, having encountered difficulties, turned to Herr Hitler for satisfaction. "It is a dangerous game," noted Sargent, "for there is every prospect of the two thieves falling out sooner or later, and Hitler has on the whole better cards than Stalin."[12] The Poles, who were then doomed but did not know it, had a simpler explanation for all of what had happened. "The man in the street," observed the British ambassador in Warsaw, Kennard, "who knows little of possible military implications, has taken the news with a half-amused shrug." "Isn't Vasily a swine!" they were saying.[13]

A Foreign Office clerk later summed up the position in response to a letter of complaint about British policy from a private citizen, one Miss J. F. Tuke: "It would not be difficult to put up a debating case for our failure to treat Soviet aggression against Poland as we treated German aggression against that country. . . . It is quite true that our attitude towards the Soviet Govt. is dictated by funk—fear of their combining with Germany if we annoy them. . . . Our policy towards the Soviet Union being in fact an immoral one thrust upon us by necessity, the less we say about it the better."[14] So a brief letter of acknowledgment was sent to Miss Tuke, and the Foreign Office got on with the realist's policy that Vansittart had promoted unsuccessfully since 1934.[15]

Not just diplomats in London and Paris had to get used to new European realities; some Soviet diplomats did also. Maiskii had taken it for granted that an Anglo-Franco-Soviet alliance would be concluded in August. He was not quite sure what to make of his government's volte-face, noting in his journal: "Our policy obviously represents a kind of sudden reversal, the reasoning behind which is for the present still not entirely clear to me." While he waited for information from Moscow, Maiskii observed confusion and anger in London. Labour politicians were furious: the Soviet government had betrayed its first principles. "This will pass," observed Maiskii, and anyway the Tories were taking the Soviet reversal with more serenity. Indeed they were even trying to calm the Labour outcry.[16] Maiskii did not mention the British communists, but they were equally dismayed by the Soviet turnabout. When the Comintern in

Moscow ordered that a new line be followed in favor of peace and against the "imperialist" war, the British Communist party lost half its membership.[17]

In the higher altitudes of diplomacy, these defections did not matter: Soviet officials laid responsibility for the new situation on the Anglo-French and the Poles for the failure of the Moscow talks to achieve an anti-Nazi alliance. It was a legitimate argument and effective with some French and British emissaries because of their embarrassment over delays and hesitations in the negotiations. But in general Western public opinion laid the blame on the Soviet Union for the pact with Nazi Germany. At the time, the Foreign Office was not so confident of the position. Louis Fischer, a well-known American journalist and historian previously "infected with Bolshevik ideas" but then "disillusioned and disappointed," asked the British for privileged information for a story condemning Soviet policy. Halifax refused, calculating that the "left" could scarcely be more disillusioned, and that "it might not impossibly cause ourselves some embarrassment...."[18] Halifax need not have worried; most Western historians still roundly condemn the Soviet Union for the pact with Hitler.

In September events moved quickly: Labour indignation dissipated, and Labour politicians were soon pressing for an improvement of relations with the Soviet Union. The British government was willing to examine the possibilities. So was Maiskii. The Soviet ambassador had worked long, hard, and somewhat deviously to improve Anglo-Soviet relations. As a former Menshevik, he appreciated deviousness as an essential quality for survival in Bolshevik Russia. This was especially true during the Stalinist purges when no one knew who would be arrested next. During his years in London, Maiskii cultivated a network of relationships within the British elite. In the autumn of 1939 he used every opportunity to meet the principal representatives of this far-flung network. His purpose was to defuse British hostility over the Nazi-Soviet nonaggression pact and the Soviet occupation of eastern Poland.

Maiskii met Lord Strabolgi in Parliament on September 20, a few days after the Soviet advance into Poland. Strabolgi was an early trader in the Soviet Union and a well-known advocate of good Anglo-Soviet relations. Over tea in the House of Lords, Maiskii gave the usual Soviet line of unrequited overtures to the West repeatedly spurned since 1933.

Did Maiskii know what "double-crossing" meant? Strabolgi asked, because that was how the British felt about the failed negotiations in Moscow.

Maiskii was quick to defend Soviet policy; he had been doing it for many years and knew the position well. "It was only when his Government was convinced that the British and French were not in earnest about the Pact under negotiation that they decided to enter into a political arrangement with Germany." After a long disquisition on this point, Maiskii insisted that the Soviet government did not want Nazi Germany to win the war and did not want to see it on the shores of the Black Sea. When Strabolgi then replied that the Soviet Union ought not to have signed the nonaggression pact, Maiskii returned to his earlier points. Sending the Anglo-French military mission to the Soviet Union on a slow merchant ship had made, to say the least, a poor impression in Moscow.

Was it not in Soviet interests, asked Strabolgi, to see "the capitalist imperialisms of France and Britain" eliminated?

No, answered Maiskii, "because [we] would then only have a greater and stronger Germany, another capitalist Empire, as [our] neighbour." Strabolgi pressed on, asking if the Soviet government would cooperate in blocking German expansion into the Balkans. Maiskii replied that some form of cooperation might be possible.[19]

Maiskii had a similar conversation with Ernest Remnant, a longtime habitué of the corridors of power when Anglo-Soviet relations were strained. This conversation, with Strabolgi's, was reported to the Foreign Office and prompted Halifax to invite Maiskii in for a talk.[20]

What were Soviet intentions, asked Halifax, in view of the recent changes in Soviet policy? Halifax remarked dryly that "the Soviet government had been impressing upon us that the main principle of their policy was to assist European States to defend their independence against aggression." He had listened to many of M. Litvinov's speeches in Geneva along these same lines. "I should be greatly obliged if [you] could help to clear up our doubts," Halifax said, concerning Soviet policy in general and in regard to the future of Poland in particular.

The Soviet Union was neutral, Maiskii responded, but Halifax wondered aloud whether the Soviet government could clarify the apparent obscurities in its policy and in particular provide a "clearer definition of [its] neutral status." For instance, was the Soviet Union prepared to negotiate a war trade agreement? What was the Soviet position regarding Polish frontiers?

Halifax reported that Maiskii "displayed evident embarrassment" in response to his questions. Maiskii, in his account of the meeting, indicated that the foreign secretary was also uncomfortable. "Halifax was very strained and ill-at-ease, he spoke slowly in a forced tone of voice, weighing his words carefully, he often stopped and gazed for a long time at the ceiling. . . . I felt, that, looking at me, Halifax was silently putting the question: are you an enemy or not?" Clearly this was just the question that the British government sought to answer. Maiskii's report of the meeting was similar to that of Halifax, leaving out the foreign secretary's sarcastic references to previous Soviet policy and his own embarrassment, if he had any. Maiskii promised to refer these questions to his government, and he did so at once.[21]

One might allow that both Halifax and Maiskii were embarrassed by the situation, though neither may have cared to admit it. It had been two months since Maiskii had seen Halifax, and the Soviet position was not easy to defend. Nor was the British, in view of the bungled Anglo-Franco-Soviet negotiations during the spring and summer. On the other hand, there may have been slight humor in Maiskii's many meetings with British officials. One can easily imagine the ambassador and the foreign secretary rushing off to their respective studies and secretaries to write down their recollections of this and future meetings. Historians should be grateful for their industry.

In reply to Maiskii, the remorseless Molotov was terse and unhelpful. "England, if it really wishes, could enter into negotiations on trade with the USSR, but the USSR will remain and intends to remain neutral in the war in western Europe, assuming, of course, that England itself in its relations with the USSR does not force it onto the path of involvement in this war." The fate of Poland, Molotov added, depended on many factors and contradictory forces. It was impossible at the moment to predict the outcome.[22]

The next day, September 27, Maiskii conveyed Molotov's brief message to the Foreign Office. Halifax could not resist another arid comment on the irreconcilability of present and previous Soviet policies. What sort of action by us, asked Halifax, might compel the Soviet Union to abandon its neutrality? The ambassador "was unable to give any clear answer."[23]

Maiskii appears to have wanted to open a narrow alley to the British, being little supported by Moscow, and to encourage the Foreign Office to make overtures to the Soviet government. The discussion in London on whether to do so was divided. Seeds in Moscow thought of "driv[ing] a wedge between the two aggressors."[24] The Foreign Office saw it in similar terms and contemplated sending a mission to Moscow. "I shd. do everything in practice," Cadogan said, "to try and induce the Soviet to be as inconvenient as possible to Germany and later, if possible, to assist us and our friends." Another mission to Moscow, however, did not seem appropriate. The position was reinforced by Vansittart, who now had little influence: ". . . I hope we shall not come so low. We have just received a most resounding kick in the pants. We may get something even worse and more damaging; but at least there are a few pickings of compensation in the opinion of other countries. Even those we shall sacrifice if we abase ourselves to go to Moscow. By all means let us refrain from hostility or hostilities, and wreathe our wry smiles as we may. But not *that*!"[25] The realist was now disillusioned and embarrassed by his earlier efforts to bring about an Anglo-Soviet rapprochement.

While Maiskii worked to improve relations with Britain, Surits lay low in Paris. The French were not so disposed to resume courtship of the Soviet Union, even though Daladier replaced Bonnet as foreign minister. Bonnet was merely shifted to the Ministry of Justice, and Daladier was more ideologue than realist. It was against the French communists that he showed his greatest mettle. While Mandel and Herriot were said to want a new diplomatic effort toward the Soviet Union and the dispatch of a high-profile representative to Moscow, nothing happened. Surits reported that the French, apart from military "gymnastics" on the western front, had given no support to the Poles, and rumors circulated in Paris of an effort to end the war, with the Germans setting up a puppet Polish government as a way out for France and Britain. Surits suspected that the lack of fighting by the French was merely preparation for negotiations, that they were more disposed to join "some anti-Soviet coalition."[26] Molotov must have asked himself: if the French would do nothing for the Poles, would they have done anything more for us?

After the Soviet seizure of eastern Poland, Daladier called in Surits to protest. Was this a defensive action to deny Polish territory to Germany, or an action taken in cooperation *with* Germany? Was the Soviet Union about to annex Ukrainian and Belorussian territory? What were Soviet intentions? Was the Soviet government acting in alliance with Germany or not? Daladier asked Surits to inform Moscow that France and Britain intended to wage war until the end. "I don't intend to submit," he said, "to the admonitions of various Lavals and Flandins." Lying to Surits about the talks in Moscow, as he had to Jeanneney, Daladier added, no doubt to be conciliatory, that the French government had forced the Poles to yield on passage rights, but too late. A few weeks later, after making a speech rejecting Nazi peace offers, Daladier was heard to say: "It wasn't me who wrote this speech. It's much too hard. I only want to do one thing: to stop everything." Clemenceau used to say that to lead in war it took "males" with "balls," *des couilles*.[27] Daladier did not have them.

In the days following the Soviet occupation of eastern Poland, Surits reported that the French government intended to hold a restrained position, even discouraging the Polish government in exile from declaring a state of war with the Soviet Union. "People of the Mandel type" tended to see in Soviet action in Poland a defense of purely Russian, even traditional tsarist national interests and in effect a defeat for Hitler. Not impressed, Molotov eventually instructed Surits to tell Daladier that the "insulting tone of his questions" regarding Poland was unappreciated and did not merit a reply except for the one he had already given to Maiskii for Halifax.[28]

The Mandel-like view of things was also to be found inside the British government. Although the Soviet Union was not about to do anything for the *beaux yeux* of Britain, its actions in eastern Europe were not entirely inconsistent with British interests.[29] Churchill, then first lord of the admiralty, recognized the position in a well-known, often cited speech on October 1: while Britain might have hoped for different circumstances, with Poland and the Soviet Union as allies, Russian armies stood in Poland to block any further Nazi advance in the east. It was hard to understand the contradictions in Soviet

policy. "Russia is a riddle . . . ," said Churchill in his famous epigram, "but perhaps there is a key." That key was "a cold policy" of
"Russian national interest." "It cannot be in accordance with the interest or the safety of Russia that Germany should plant herself
upon the shores of the Black Sea, or that she should overrun the
Balkan States. . . ."[30] Here was Maiskii's line repeated in essence by
a minister in the War Cabinet. The ambassador hoped the line
would play well, and there were signs it did. After a row at the outset of war over the British blocking delivery of machine tools con-
tracted by the Soviet Union, the British and Soviet governments
concluded a barter arrangement in early October: Soviet timber for
British rubber and tin.[31] Trade was often a good way to improve political relations.

On October 6 Churchill invited Maiskii to the Admiralty for one
of his habitual nocturnal meetings. Churchill pursued his line on
Anglo-Soviet relations: they were strained and were driven by mutual suspicions. The British government suspected that the Soviet
Union had concluded a military alliance with Nazi Germany.
Churchill did not believe it, but suspicions were widespread in
political and even in government circles. On the other hand, he recognized that the Soviet Union suspected all sorts of British machina-
tions in the Baltic and the Balkans, and that this suspicion affected
relations between the two countries. Churchill freely admitted that
negotiations for a tripartite pact had been badly handled. "But the
past is the past," he said. He was "more interested in the present
and the future." Then Churchill brought out a familiar refrain not
heard much since the Anglo-Soviet rapprochement of the mid-
1930s. The basic interests of the Soviet Union and Great Britain, he
said, were nowhere in conflict and were rapidly coming to coincide.
While some "sentimentalists" in the Liberal and Labour parties had
"shed tears" about a Soviet protectorate over the Baltic states, he
had rather see them under Soviet than under German control.
"Stalin is playing a big game, and playing it with good luck. He
must be pleased. But I do not see why we should be displeased."
Churchill went on at some length, asking for Maiskii's suggestions.
The ambassador evaded an answer, or so he said, but asked if
Churchill spoke for the government. Churchill affirmed that in general he did.[32]

The minister for health, Walter Elliot, took up Churchill's line two days later. Like Churchill, Elliot indicated that the British government sought better relations and asked Maiskii if he could suggest some ideas on how the British might approach the Soviet government. Maiskii said he had eluded such questions, but he asked Moscow for immediate instructions. In the circumstances, advised Maiskii, my responses to these queries "could have great practical significance."[33]

Eden, who had come into the cabinet with Churchill as Dominions secretary, then met Maiskii a few days later (October 13) over breakfast. British and Soviet interests were not in conflict, Eden said, following Churchill's line: all members of the government agreed on the need to improve relations and eliminate suspicions. Eden suggested the dispatch of a high-profile mission to Moscow to resume trade negotiations and the replacement of Ambassador Seeds by a representative of greater authority who would enjoy Soviet confidence and who could establish better Anglo-Soviet relations. Maiskii was impressed by these British initiatives: "While by no means exaggerating my recent conversations . . . I nevertheless must note that if three ministers in the course of one week ask my advice about measures for a possible improvement of Anglo-Soviet relations, the given question, obviously, is being . . . discussed in government circles." Maiskii again requested instructions. "I am in a difficult position," he said, "and I might unintentionally make some mistake . . . [which] could have one or another practical consequences." In particular, Maiskii asked if the time would be appropriate for an improvement in Anglo-Soviet relations and if it would be expedient for the British government to send a high-profile delegation to Moscow.[34]

Eden's account of his conversation with Maiskii had different emphases than those of the ambassador. Like Halifax, Eden referred to earlier Soviet policy. "Peace is indivisible," Litvinov had said, but now Maiskii replied, ". . . the situation is somewhat different." Once again Maiskii blamed the change in Soviet policy on five years of failed collaboration with the French and British governments. The British would know "how deep at all times were the suspicions in the minds of our respective Governments of each other." Eden professed still to be confused by present Soviet policy. "In a world such as this where wild beasts [are] loose," replied Maiskii, every country ha[s] to take certain precautions for its own safety." Eden again rejoined, and eventually Maiskii's wife, who was present, "interjected that her husband had always been anxious for improved Anglo-Russian relations and that recent events had been a disappointment to him." Maiskii insisted that Soviet professions of a desire for neutrality were genuine; this would not change unless the British took unfriendly action. Eden noted that "Maisky implied several times during the conversation that if we would make some further advance now we should not be rebuffed, though he was always vague as to the form which any such action might take."[35] And here is the dissonance in the two accounts of this meeting: Eden said that Maiskii had implicitly encouraged a British approach which would not be rebuffed. But Maiskii advised Molotov that he had offered no advice while asking if the moment was right for an improvement of relations. Eden himself reckoned that Maiskii wanted better relations, but he did not think the ambassador was "very well informed on all details of Soviet policy." This was not quite it: Maiskii was ahead of his government, whose policy he was trying to finesse into an opening to the British.

In mid-October Maiskii's efforts produced positive results in London but not in Moscow. While Molotov was slow to reply to Maiskii's urgent requests for instructions, Halifax was prepared to move forward. "During the last few days I have been thinking a good deal about what possible means there may be by which we could improve our political contacts with Russia." The opportunities seemed almost "nonexistent," Halifax told Oliver Stanley, president of the Board of Trade; but "if it was possible to find means through which the present position . . . could be remedied, it might be of great usefulness."

> I find it difficult to believe that the Soviet Government have thrown in their lot with Herr Hitler, to such an extent as would make it difficult or uncongenial for them to double-cross him, and obviously if we could persuade them in any way to double-cross him, or to have the appearance of doing so, it would be of great potential significance.

And Halifax went on: "It so happened that Sir Stafford Cripps came to see me last night upon other matters." During the conversation Cripps, a maverick Labour man, turned to the subject of the Soviet Union and pressed hard for a trade mission to Moscow. "I told him," said Halifax, "that with the general purpose of encouraging the Russians to double-cross the Germans, I was in warm sympathy. . . ." But Halifax wanted assurances that London could "pull off a pretty good agreement," which was another way of saying that he did not care to be "exposed to humiliation and merely serve the purpose of giving Stalin another scalp." "I [am] naturally suspicious after my Russian experiences of the last few months." Cripps thought some dangers could be avoided by first exploring the ground with Maiskii. The ambassador was "very keen on it," said Cripps. And so Halifax again saw Maiskii.[36]

"Today [16 October] Halifax invited me in to see him," reported Maiskii; "he said that the British government would like to improve Anglo-Soviet relations . . . and he is ready to discuss different means of achieving these ends. . . ." Halifax thought that trade negotiations would be the best way to proceed, and he suggested that they take place in London. Although saying nothing definite, the foreign secretary implied that if the basis of an agreement could be reached, a British delegation would go to Moscow to conclude negotiations.[37] Halifax's account of the meeting does not entirely square with Maiskii's, for in the British account it is the ambassador who states that the Soviet government was "prepared to do more in the direction of improving trade, if we [the British government] so desired," and it is Halifax who says that "we are considering these possibilities and that [he] hoped, if any such opportunities did, in fact, exist, that we might be able to take advantage of them." Halifax also raised the issue of the difficulty in a trade agreement of British goods sent to the Soviet Union finding their way to Germany.[38] On this important point Maiskii was silent.

Interesting silences and transposed voices often characterized the British and Soviet accounts of these important meetings. Thus the initiative for an improvement of relations appears to shift from one side to the other, according to the British or Soviet account. It was safer for both sides. Maiskii had to fear for his life if he erred, while Western politicians had merely to fear right-wing displeasure or ridicule if they went too far in courting the Soviet Union. Anglo-Soviet and indeed Western-Soviet relations had often been like this before the war. "After you Alphonse; but no sir, after you" was the well-worn refrain of Western-Soviet dialogue.

III

There was more to this meeting. While Halifax's report is short and limited to trade matters, Maiskii's indicates that other issues were discussed, including Soviet-Turkish negotiations and affairs in the Baltic area. Then,

> Halifax briefly touched upon the prime minister Neville Chamberlain's last statement in Parliament [on October 12, rejecting Nazi offers for a peace settlement made by Hitler on October 6], and, underlining British determination to wage "war to the finish," at the same time he gave me to understand that if Hitler put forward some new, more acceptable proposals, the British government would be ready to examine them.[39]

The same subject came up in a conversation on the following day between Maiskii and Butler, who was to become the principal Foreign Office go-between with Maiskii.

> The general orientation of the British government, in Butler's words, comes to this, that it would be ready to conclude peace even tomorrow, would it be assured that the arrived-at agreement has a stable character ("would assure peace and tranquility for 20–25 years," as Butler put it). Such confidence, in the opinion of the British government, could be created through guarantees of the peace treaty by all the great powers and in particular the USA and the USSR. For the sake of achieving a solid peace of this kind the British government would be ready to make significant concessions to Germany even in the colonial area.

Butler then qualified the position by noting that inasmuch as such a peace was at present impossible, "Great Britain will continue the war." But he reckoned that in the next phase of the war new offers might be made "possibly with greater chances of success."[40] In Butler's account of the meeting there is not a word about the prospects of peace with Nazi Germany—not surprising since such discussions were unpopular in the autumn of 1939.[41] Before the war Butler had been a loyal executor of Chamberlain's policy of appeasement. His conversation with Maiskii, therefore, was consistent with the British government's prewar position. Moreover, these private talks took place in the context of public discussions in Britain about the prospects for an early peace. Lloyd George made a speech in the House of Commons on October 3 suggesting that the government keep the door open to a peace initiative, especially if it came from a neutral power, and he mentioned the Soviet Union, among others.[42] Although Lloyd George was roundly condemned in the press, it appears as though the Foreign Office may have taken his advice under cover of Chamberlain's statement in Parliament on October 12. Even now, appeasement in Britain was not dead.

Molotov, who had not yet responded to Maiskii's urgent requests for instructions on Anglo-Soviet relations, promptly queried Maiskii about Butler's statements. At the same time he informed the German ambassador Schulenberg of the conversation in London. In a two-sentence cable Molotov asked Maiskii if Butler "had hinted to you about the desirability of our mediation in the spirit of the conclusion of peace with Germany in certain conditions. I await an answer."[43] Molotov's question was serious and consistent with the new Soviet position calling for an end to the war. Since issues arising from the disintegration of Poland had been resolved, said a joint Nazi-Soviet communiqué published at the end of September, there was no need for a continuation of the war.[44]

Maiskii hastened to answer Molotov's inquiry: "Characterizing the orientation of the British government on war and peace, Butler clearly stated the point of view of Chamberlain and Halifax. At one point he even referred to his conversation with them. I do not have the impression that Butler is directly hinting at the desirability of our mediation. He spoke rather along the lines of an explanation . . . of British government policy. . . ." But Maiskii thought that from all Butler had said, the British government would not oppose Soviet mediation and guarantees of a peace treaty. The ambassador went on along these lines, referring to a recent conversation with Lloyd George, who nevertheless noted that the German sinking of the British battleship Royal Oak inside the main British base at Scapa Flow (on October 14), among other German raids, had aroused instinctive British defiance.[45] When Schulenberg later asked for more information on British interest in a peace settlement, Molotov replied that according to Maiskii, there was nothing definite.[46]

Maiskii's accounts of wistful but impossible thoughts of peace by British ministers could scarcely have impressed the suspicious Molotov with the British government's determination to fight to the finish. And Maiskii's reports sometimes captured indiscretions: British ministers should have kept to themselves their anxieties and lack of confidence in victory.[47] Maiskii, for one, had no high regard for the composition of the British cabinet. With the exception of Churchill and Eden, "Munichites" remained in the most important posts: Chamberlain, Halifax, Simon, Hoare, among others. It was the same old government of Tory ". . . 'appeasers,' " observed Maiskii, "ever so faintly touched up in anti-Hitlerite colors. . . ."[48] Soviet attitudes were contradictory: on the one hand, Molotov now appeared to favor a peace settlement; on the other, Maiskii was disdainful of the appeasers and seemed to be looking for signs of British determination to fight. The Soviet government would not risk the nonaggression pact for any important agreement with the British—trade or otherwise—unless it could be persuaded that the British were a partner and possibly even an ally worth having. The phony war, however, did not inspire confidence, and it did not go unnoticed by Maiskii or in Moscow.

"It's a strange war," Maiskii wrote in his journal on October 24: there was no action at the front. The French military communiqués repeated stock phrases like "The night passed quietly" or "The day was marked by routine patrols." The Anglo-French hoped for success in a long war of attrition, wrote Maiskii, while Hitler hoped for the "rottenness of democracy." "I hear continually here at each step: 'Ultimately only Russia will profit from the war' or 'When the western capitalist countries will have clawed at one another's throats, communism will triumph.' . . ." Maiskii reckoned the spread of revolution more likely now than at any time since Karl Marx wrote *The Communist Manifesto*. The belligerents were hesitating to come to death blows, thought Maiskii, but unless a miracle occurred, all-out war was not far off.[49]

The British government continued to hold similar opinions about war as a generator of communist revolution; it was a spoken and unspoken assumption of the interwar years. A Foreign Office paper written a week before Maiskii's journal entry noted that the Soviet objective is "to hold the balance between the belligerents with a view of bolshevising Europe at little cost to herself when both sides become exhausted." One senior Foreign Office official, R. A. Leeper, blamed it all on Hitler: "He has . . . enabled Stalin to get into a stronger position for introducing the Bolshevik virus into Europe at the beginning of the war instead of having to wait until the end when the European nations had weakened themselves in a life and death struggle."[50] "After all," said Sargent, "the fundamental principle of Bolshevism is the extension of communism." "I agree generally," rejoined Halifax. Sir Arthur Rucker, Chamberlain's principal private secretary, put it this way in mid-October: "Communism is now the great danger, greater even than Nazi Germany . . . [it] is a plague that does not stop at national boundaries, and with the advance of the Soviet into Poland the states of Eastern Europe will find their powers of resistance to Communism very much weakened. It is thus vital that we should play our hand very carefully with Russia, and not destroy the possibility of uniting, if necessary, with a new German government against the common danger." And Tory diarist Channon had a similar view.[51]

IV

These widely held British views did not stop either Maiskii or Halifax from attempting to improve Anglo-Soviet relations. In fact, Maiskii was a busy man in October 1939, seeing British ministers, officials, and politicians almost every day. There appears to have been no more talk of Soviet mediation of a peace conference, but a great deal of discussion continued about possible trade negotiations. Maiskii privately made fun of the obvious British interest in a rapprochement with the Soviet Union, but in his meetings with British officials he advised them to get on quickly with trade negotiations. To Moscow, Maiskii reported the further statements by British officials indicating their desire to improve Anglo-Soviet relations.[52]

And still Molotov did not reply to his ambassador's request for instructions, even after Maiskii had another meeting with Halifax on October 25.[53] Halifax advised that the cabinet had approved the opening of negotiations with the Soviet Union to reach a trade agreement and that Oliver Stanley would lead the British side. As Halifax put it, "I said that my interest in the matter was primarily political, in that I was concerned, if possible, to effect some improvement in the relations between this country and the Soviet Government, or at least to prevent any further deterioration in them." Maiskii's account confirmed the main point. But there were the usual nuances in their separate accounts of the meeting. Halifax reported on Maiskii's enthusiasm at the prospect of negotiations, an enthusiasm the ambassador understandably fails to mention in his cable to Moscow.[54] Maiskii then met Stanley; both of them prepared records of conversation. The accounts largely concur, though once again Maiskii did not report to Moscow the pleasure he expressed at the prospect of a beginning of negotiations. According to Stanley's account, the ambassador "claimed that he had the authority of his Government to state that they were willing to discuss a trade agreement with us. . . ."

Maiskii's declaration was technically true based on Molotov's cable to Maiskii of September 26, but it was really making a silk purse out of a sow's ear because of Molotov's continued silence in response to Maiskii's requests for instructions. The ambassador's attempted finesse did not entirely escape the notice of British ministers. "M. Maisky . . . left upon me an impression of personal goodwill," observed Stanley, "but of complete dependence upon Moscow and lack of any personal authority." As Stanley reported to the cabinet: "The next move [is] with M. Maisky. . . ."[55] Could he persuade Molotov to go along?

On November 11 Molotov finally replied to Maiskii. During Litvinov's years as foreign commissar, the Soviet government would have jumped at the lavish British expressions of interest in better relations, but not now.

> When an opportunity arises, you can say that the Soviet government is sympathetic with their wishes [of Churchill, Eden, etc.], but inasmuch as actual British policy is not defined by these gentlemen, the Soviet government does not see at the present time encouraging possibilities in this regard. The facts indicate that in reality British power is hostile to the Soviet Union. We feel [this hostility] in all corners of Europe . . . not to mention in the Far East. An improvement of Anglo-Soviet relations requires that British policy move toward a more favorable disposition [to the Soviet Union].[56]

Molotov's cable left Maiskii overextended. He had to backtrack with his many counterparts, but he did not request, as he normally should have done, a meeting with Halifax to explain the new position. He went instead to go-betweens.

On the following day Cripps met Maiskii to ask unofficially why there was a delay in the Soviet response to British proposals to begin trade negotiations. Maiskii repeated Molotov's line that Stanley, Eden, and the others had no great practical influence—a somewhat obtuse statement since Halifax had stated that he spoke on behalf of the cabinet. According to Maiskii's account, he said the Soviet government was regrettably too preoccupied with other international business to examine British offers.[57] Two days later Maiskii talked to Churchill in the spirit, so he said, of Molotov's cable, but one wonders just how accurate was the ambassador's representation of his instructions. Churchill put a favorable gloss on the Soviet desire for better relations, when in fact Molotov had said only that the British would have to take the initiative in improving them. This was a line Molotov had used with Schulenberg, but here it had a different meaning. Maiskii put the blame for the present state of affairs on hostile British policies in order to divert attention from Soviet indifference to British overtures.[58] In any event, there is no report of Churchill's conversation in the Foreign Office files, which perhaps explains why the Foreign Office continued to wonder when it might have a Soviet reply to its proposals.

The cabinet discussed the Soviet silence in mid-November, and could only speculate on the reasons for it based on erroneous assumptions advanced to Halifax by Cripps. The Foreign Office did not care to give the impression of being in too much haste to start negotiations for fear that the Soviet would play even harder to get, but British patience began to run out.[59] Meanwhile Maiskii continued his line with Elliot, saying, according to Elliot, that he had "been in close communication with his own Government who were anxious for better relations with Great Britain." In Maiskii's account of the same meeting, he reported that he had spoken with the minister along the lines of Molotov's cable of November 11. "Elliot was very glad [to hear] of our positive attitude to an improvement in Anglo-Soviet relations." These were the same refrain and the same sharp practices that Maiskii had employed in his earlier meeting with Churchill. In Maiskii's account, Elliot talked about mutual suspicions, but Maiskii was not allaying them in London, whatever his desire to improve Anglo-Soviet relations.[60] Indeed, his overextended position had forced him into a disingenuousness which Foreign Office officials assumed was also that of the Soviet government. Such was not the case if one is to judge by Molotov's instructions.

Surits did not encounter similar problems in Paris because the French were less interested than the British in improving relations. In October Surits indicated that French opinion inclined toward the Mandel-Churchill line on Poland and the Baltic, and there were signs that the French wished to resume contacts. But in November, as relations went downhill in London, so they did also in Paris. "To a far greater degree than ever before," reported Surits, "our relations with France are now burdened with considerations of internal [French] politics. In Quai d'Orsay circles, they are saying that Daladier, given these considerations, cannot reveal his 'generally favorable view of Soviet foreign policy.' This 'unwillingness to reveal' takes the form very nearly of a boycott of our embassy." No French minister or high official could accept an invitation to the Soviet embassy without authorization, this was given only with difficulty. Repression against French communists had gone so far that it had aroused dissent in the cabinet, either because it would damage the French war effort or relations with the Soviet Union.[61]

In London the cabinet finally lost patience on November 23 and authorized Halifax to call in Maiskii to discover if there was any news from Moscow. Butler seemed to want to prepare the ground, seeing Maiskii a few days before his discussion with the foreign secretary (on November 27) and repeating many of the lines of Churchill and other ministers.[62] According to Maiskii's account, Halifax was more blunt: do you want trade negotiations or not? The British government had been perfectly clear that it wanted an improvement of Anglo-Soviet relations, but the long silence from Moscow raised doubts as to whether the Soviet government was serious about negotiations. Maiskii replied that such doubts were unfounded—not an accurate representation of Molotov's position, but necessary in order to save Maiskii's policy. He had to keep the British interested in negotiations. But he neatly threw back at Halifax the reproach over delays, noting that the British government had been in no particular hurry to negotiate, a point that the foreign secretary admitted was true. According to Halifax, Maiskii replied "vaguely and with some embarrassment," as well he might have done. Halifax assumed that the ambassador was "merely voicing the party line," but it appears more the case of Maiskii trying to escape a very sticky wicket. Maiskii portrayed himself as direct and challenging in the interview, though Halifax saw a slippery, vague, and slightly embarrassed emissary.

Halifax complained about the recent harshness of the Soviet press, which suggested an unfriendly or even hostile position toward Britain. Maiskii replied that it was paying off the British press in its own coin and that it reflected the general Soviet impression that the British government was everywhere working against Soviet interests. "I told M. Maisky," said Halifax, "that . . . H.M.G. looked after their own interests and nothing more." According to Maiskii, Halifax "suddenly reddened (which with him never happens), he became very agitated and all but vehemently began to argue that Soviet government's suspicion . . . had no basis whatever."[63] Halifax's account implicitly supports Maiskii's version, but this exchange was one that had occurred many times over the previous twenty years. It was pot calling kettle black. "Hard words break no bones," said Soviet officials, but they were just as sensitive about the harshness of the British press.[64]

V

Halifax also raised with Maiskii the question of Finland. The Soviet government had been trying since the beginning of 1939 to conclude an agreement with Finland providing for better security around Leningrad and in the Baltic Sea. The Finnish frontier was only twenty miles from the city, within reach of hostile guns. The Finnish government feared and disliked its Soviet neighbor and had proved unwilling to buckle under to Soviet demands for a cession of territory near Leningrad in exchange for other less desirable territory on its eastern borders. Negotiations were conducted under increasing tensions as the Finns mobilized their army in October 1939 and spat defiance at Moscow. Molotov interpreted these acts as provocative, and even in the British Foreign Office some clerks found the Finns to be "most tiresome," just as they had been during British negotiations in Moscow in the summer. The Soviet government made its own preparations for war. In light of a shooting incident on the Russo-Finnish frontier on November 26, Halifax warned Maiskii that if hostilities broke out an improvement of Anglo-Soviet relations would be "very difficult," a warning only implied in Maiskii's account.[65]

It was not the first time the Finnish question had arisen or the first time the Foreign Office had issued a warning about worsening Soviet-Finnish relations. In late September Collier, still head of the Northern department, had drawn attention to the likelihood of increased Soviet pressure on Finland. He recommended encouraging Finnish resistance "because anything which increases Russian preoccupation in any part of the world improves our position in bargaining with the Soviet Government. . . ." Collier suggested inquiring if the Finnish government "would welcome assistance in the . . . [inter alia] supply of British war material to . . . Finnish forces. . . ." The Foreign Office took up Collier's proposal and the service departments so notified. This was all music to the ears of the British ambassador in Helsinki, Thomas Snow, who was an anti-red incendiary, against any Finnish concessions.[66] The Soviet government was aware of Snow's encouragement of Finnish defiance, and the Soviet embassy in Helsinki reported the Finnish military buildup and the highly visible and suspicious presence of numerous British nationals in the Finnish capital.[67]

Halifax warned Maiskii even in October that Finnish-Soviet hostilities would make impossible an improvement of relations, while Maiskii's account said only that Halifax had expressed the hope that Soviet-Finnish negotiations would have a successful outcome "without any shocks." Although the ambassador replied that he saw no reason to fear the outbreak of hostilities with Finland, he does not appear to have reported Halifax's apparent direct warning, perhaps because he preferred to avoid irritating Moscow with unpleasant facts which might dash his hopes of improved relations.[68] But Molotov had other sources of information and was aware of British activities perceived to be hostile to Soviet interests. His reference to these activities was not without foundation, while Halifax's denial of them was not entirely true.

Churchill saw the problem, having even discussed it with Maiskii in November. It was only clerks and lower government *bureaux* who had been guilty of indiscretions, said Churchill. What did you expect, he asked, after the Nazi-Soviet pact and the suspicions it had engendered?[69] Shortly afterward Churchill raised the issue in the War Cabinet, reiterating his view that it was in British interests to see the Soviet Union hold a strong position in the Baltic and that it would be a mistake "to stiffen the Finns against making concessions to the U.S.S.R." Halifax replied that Finland should not be encouraged to yield to demands contrary to its interests. Collier picked up on this exchange, did not agree with Churchill's estimate of the situation, and persuaded Halifax to take a harder line.[70]

Finland was not the only source of Soviet suspicions of Britain. Turkey and the Caucasus were others. Even before the outbreak of war between Finland and the Soviet Union on November 30, the British government had begun to contemplate subversive activities in the Caucasus with the connivance of Turkish military and intelligence authorities.[71] Bombing of the Soviet oil fields around Baku was mooted at the end of October, though the Foreign Office did not think it was a "practicable" idea. The papers on these topics were all in green, top-secret jackets for good reason; in fact, some papers are still withheld from the files, until 2016. The idea of raiding Baku nevertheless continued to be studied by the Joint Intelligence Subcommittee of the chiefs of staff.[72] The Soviet government also picked up information on British activities in Turkey and Romania perceived to be directed against the Soviet Union.[73]

Butler saw Maiskii on November 29 to reinforce Churchill's earlier statements that the British government was not pursuing a "Machiavellian" policy toward the Soviet Union, but in Moscow these declarations had no credibility.[74] In hindsight Maiskii asserted that British policy was to extend the right hand of friendship and at the same time, with the left, to "sow the seeds of anti-Soviet intrigue in all the corners of the world."[75] This view was only partially correct but entirely persuasive in Moscow. It hardly mattered, for later that day, after Maiskii met Butler, the Narkomindel summoned the Finnish minister in Moscow to inform him that the Soviet government was breaking off diplomatic relations. While the phony war continued in the west, a real war broke out between Finland and the Soviet Union the following day. It was a surprise to Maiskii.[76]

VI

The Russo-Finnish War got Maiskii off one petard only to hoist him upon another. The British government immediately abandoned any interest in negotiations with the Soviet Union, the ambassador no longer had to worry about reconciling Moscow's disinterest in better relations with his own encouragement of them. But the war also threatened any Anglo-Soviet relations at all. Seeds, in Moscow, thought they should be broken off and a blockade thrown up around the Soviet Union. This was nothing compared to Snow's imprudent recommendation in early November, even before war broke out, that Japan should be encouraged to attack the Soviet Union! The Foreign Office thought Snow's proposal to be risible and tried to take a more restrained approach.[77] Public opinion risked forcing Britain out of a position of restraint. It was the same in France: the Paris press commenced a vicious campaign against the Soviet invasion, and the French government gave off the distinct impression of preferring to down the Bolsheviks rather than to fight "Colossus Germany."[78]

The Foreign Office itself reckoned the Soviet not quite an enemy but nearly so. The British press almost unanimously condemned the Soviet attack on Finland. The communist *Daily Worker* was the only cuckoo. Maiskii was taken aback by the virulence of public reaction. The question here, Maiskii noted in his journal, is "who is Enemy No. 1—Germany or the USSR?" There were all sorts of rumors going round London about new peace feelers to Hitler. But in spite of the anti-Soviet fury, there was no talk of a diplomatic rupture, unlike in France. Maiskii thought the British smarter than the French, and did not think it would come to a break. But "beyond the near future, I could not guarantee." Relations were outwardly correct, observed Maiskii, but around the embassy and trade mission there was a "cold emptiness." With few exceptions, "all our 'friends' " had run for cover. "But it's not the first time. They'll be back." "I am an old hand," he wrote, "facing the storm is nothing new for me." One thing for sure: "The sooner the business in Finland is finished, the sooner things will settle down." The British were great lovers of *faits accomplis.*[79]

Maiskii was not too far wrong: Cadogan likened the Foreign Office position to that of "a posse of police [who] can't deal with a whole mob all at once. They have to crack the nearest heads...." By this Cadogan meant Nazi Germany. For the moment the Foreign Office knew who was "Enemy No. 1."[80] On the other hand, "anti-Bolshevik feelings" had to be satisfied, and the Foreign Office did so

through inspired articles in the press. There was "the clear understanding," however, that "anti-Bolshevik propaganda [should not]
get out of control . . . or degenerate into a clamour for war against
the Soviet Government."[81]

In France the atmosphere was more tense. "The French are completely out of control," reported Surits: Finland had become a member of the Allied coalition, and "aid for Finland" was openly
discussed. Rumors were circulating of imminent British naval operations against the Soviet Union. Nearly the entire French press was
shouting that the USSR was easy pickings and riven with internal
dissent. "Our embassy has become a plague zone and is surrounded
by a swarm of plainclothes cops."[82] Actually, Surits understated the
situation in France. *Il faut casser les reins à l'URSS* was heard at the
highest levels of the French government. "We'll sweep them
away . . . drive them from the field" said some French generals and
politicians. According to Léger, the French government did not intend to break diplomatic relations or declare war, ". . . but will if
possible destroy the Soviet Union—using cannon if necessary." Such
talk was commonplace in the posh bistros of Paris. No one was arrested for café bluster *against* the Soviet Union. Finland was the
cause sacrée; with a good cigar and a Pernod, it was glorious to
imagine aloud the crushing of the enfeebled reds. Not everyone in
Paris was as keen, but such attitudes were reminiscent of October
1918 when the French general staff confidently planned to invade
southern Russia to drive off the Bolsheviks.[83] Finland was a fever:
the French had got it, and the fever was catching in London too.

On December 14 the Soviet Union was thrown out of the League
of Nations. Molotov, a hardened Bolshevik, took it amiss.[84] Maiskii
reported that the French were agitating for a rupture of relations
and that the idea was receiving a far more favorable hearing in
British governing circles. Events seemed to demonstrate to the
British that the Soviet Union had a closer relationship with Nazi
Germany than previously supposed. According to this thinking, it
might be a lesser evil to see open Soviet involvement in the war on
the side of Nazi Germany. The Soviet Union would then be unable
to stand aside in the war to pick up the pieces after the exhaustion
of the capitalist powers. According to the same scenario, the United
States would almost certainly come into the war on the Anglo-
French side. In this regard, U.S. public opinion had swung strongly

to the Finnish side, which was particularly encouraging to the British. A rupture of relations between Moscow and London would be the first step toward driving the Soviet Union into the war, "in the worst-case scenario on the side of Germany, in the best case (you can never tell), one on one against all the bourgeois world, including Germany, for the hope of some kind of deal with Germany until now has not been given up here." This was a minority position, said Maiskii, the majority position still favored a "neutral" Soviet Union. "How long, however, the majority will hold its . . . position depends on many circumstances which now are difficult to fore-see."[85]

At the end of December 1939 the Soviet Union found itself almost completely isolated. Its relations with France, Britain, and the United States were severely strained. A few months before, it had been involved in serious fighting with Japan on the Manchurian frontier. The Red Army had thrashed the Japanese, but the situation was still uncertain. Relations with Italy, Turkey, and even its ally China were under stress. It had been expelled from the League of Nations. And what can one say of Soviet relations with Nazi German? Two scorpions in the night had warily agreed to share a prey, keeping one eye on the prey and one eye on each other with stingers raised high to strike.

Maiskii was worried, but Molotov, in a chilling reply to him, was angry and defiant. First, he said, Soviet action against Finland "is to be explained by the fact that we can no longer tolerate the existence of a hostile Finnish government at the very gates of Leningrad, threatening the security of the Soviet Union."

> We have decided to put an end to this situation and we will liquidate it by any means in spite of everything. Secondly, rumors about some political, or even military agreement of the Soviet Union with Germany against the Anglo-French do not correspond to reality. We have no such agreement with Germany, and talk of it is either the product of panic or provocation. Third, if they calculate on weakening the Soviet Union by supporting Finnish resistance, nothing will come of it. We will liquidate the Mannerheim-Tanner gang, and we will not be stopped by it in spite of its accomplices and well-wishers. If they attempt to drag the Soviet Union into a larger war, then they should be aware

that our country is thoroughly prepared for it. Being roused to war, the Soviet Union will wage it until the end with all its might.[86]

Maiskii must have anticipated Molotov's cable, which appears to have crossed with one of his relating a Christmas Eve conversation with Lloyd George. "Anglo-Soviet relations," said the former prime minister, "have entered a very dangerous period." The British government was now taking a line that would logically lead to a rupture of relations. Lloyd George's message was simple: don't play into the hands of those who want a rupture. Not everyone stood for this position; some people such as Churchill were against it. "The position can still be set right." On the Finnish issue the Soviet Union was justified, said Lloyd George, in asking for dispositions to assure its security. But the question had gone outside these narrow bounds: it was becoming one of opposing systems: capitalism versus socialism. Finland was now a magnet for all the "reactionary powers." "If I was in your place," Lloyd George told Maiskii, I would end the Finnish war as soon as possible, for each week will bring new dangers of complications and new efforts to create an anti-Soviet bloc. And I would end the Finnish war without using the "German methods" applied in Poland, for this will only give ammunition to anti-Soviet "provocateurs." Maiskii protested this last point, but Lloyd George only laughed: "Excuse me, an old man, understanding a thing or two about international political and military affairs. I don't want to offend you. But from my personal experience, I know that war is war. And especially in this war, which, in my view is the last great struggle of capitalism for its right to existence."[87] On the same day Harvey, Halifax's private secretary, wrote in his diary about the dangers of an anti-Bolshevik "crusade" allied with Germany *sans* Hitler. "Many here would be foolish enough to fall into such a trap, the P. M. and Horace Wilson first of all. . . ."[88]

"End the Finnish war" was good advice. The position of the Soviet Union had changed dramatically. From being the proponent of collective security and the defender of small countries threatened by aggression, Moscow had moved to a pact with Hitler and its own aggression against a small country. War in Finland, which was supposed to provide added security to the Soviet Union, had had the opposite effect. The Soviet high command had underestimated its adversaries: the Finns fought effectively and blocked the Soviet offensive with heavy losses. The Soviet government was diplomatically isolated and risked war with France and Britain. Anti-communism was on the rise again. "Wild beasts" were on the loose, as Maiskii put it, and "every country had to take . . . precautions for its own safety." In taking precautions, the Soviet government found itself dangerously overextended. Soviet prestige and perceptions of its power were damaged. Now it rode the tiger and hung on for dear life.

Maiskii's role in London in this autumn of 1939 was risky but was intended to establish better relations with Britain. Some historians criticize Maiskii's conduct before the war, but basically he was a *Litvinovets,* a Litvinov man. For him anti-Nazism and collective security were more than Stalin's old sock. So he tried to maneuver his government into better relations with Britain. This was not so easily done with Stalin and Molotov, who stuck to the German nonaggression pact.

If the British government had pursued the policy of autumn during spring and summer, it might well have achieved an alliance with the Soviet Union. Wiser policy came only with increased danger. But when the Winter War with Finland broke out, the beasts of anti-communism were let loose again, leading to imprudent contemplation of military action against the Soviet Union and some misapprehension as to who was "Enemy No. 1." It was worse in France. In September–October the French government did not follow the British lead to improve relations with Moscow, though it avoided any worsening of them. But when the Winter War broke out, it was hard to hold back the anti-communists from hurling themselves against the Soviet Union.

CHAPTER EIGHT

Epilogue:
Anglo-Soviet Relations
Are Like a
Taut String

NINETEEN THIRTY-NINE was a long year, and the Winter War was unfinished business. Its outcome would be crucial in determining the direction of the Second World War. Maiskii's reports in December captured the mood in London and in the British Foreign Office. The French and British governments carried on a dangerous contemplation of plans to bomb the Soviet oil fields around Baku. In Paris Jeanneney, president of the French Senate, feared that public opinion might forget who was the real enemy. French appeasers, the "defeatists," preferred this other war to the actual war with Nazi Germany. "Watch out," warned Jeanneney. "There's no rush to make yet another enemy."[1]

The British idea was to tighten the blockade against Germany by denying it Soviet oil. It scarcely seemed to matter that the French and British air forces did not have the means to destroy or disrupt Soviet oil production, or that Germany received relatively little oil from Soviet sources. In any event, Sargent preferred to keep the way open to Moscow: developments in Finland might cause a Nazi-Soviet quarrel.[2] But could the Foreign Office maintain control of the agenda? The Foreign Office had lost it once before in 1927 when the government broke off diplomatic relations with Moscow. And the Foreign Office itself was divided.

Vansittart, who for years had advocated a realist's policy toward the Soviet Union, seemed to lose a wheel in the heat and after-heat of the Russo-Finnish War. There was plenty of "common ground," he thought, between the Nazis and the Soviet: Baku was their "Achilles-heel." Vansittart was bitter over past failures, including his own. "We really ran after Russia," but we were had by "Soviet duplicity." "Let us never again forget it or haunt any more garden paths . . . if one plays cards once with a sharper it is one's misfortune; if one plays twice it is one's fault." Vansittart had caught the Finnish fever: "We should strike at Russo-Germany or Teutoslavia—call the combination what we will or they will—before its gets too strong."[3] Cadogan viewed war with the Soviet Union with near-equanimity and thought the bombing of Baku not a bad idea: "I shd. say that, if there were a reasonable chance of success, it ought to be tried. . . . We should have to pick a quick quarrel with the Soviet I suppose, before we launched our bombers. . . ."[4] Daladier, still French premier, talked about the Baku raids as partly a matter of "internal politics": ". . . those elements among the upper classes . . . owing to their fear of bolshevism, would be glad to make peace with Germany before she is thoroughly beaten." The right might also keep Daladier in power if he sent French troops to Finland. In early March Daladier told the Finnish minister in Paris, Harri Holma, that if Finland kept fighting, France would send fifty thousand men to help "in the blink of an eye." The Finnish government had only to ask. One blink and Daladier's government would have been saved; one blink and France and Britain would have been at war with the Soviet Union. Foreign Office official Harvey, then in Paris, recorded in his diary that Chamberlain did not wish to see Germany beaten up too badly for fear it would "open the door to Bolshevism."[5] Such statements were not far off Maiskii's reports of them to Moscow. To bomb Baku seemed like a wonderful idea—clean, useful, and easy to carry out against the hated reds. It would be cathartic revenge for the nonaggression pact, a double-cross which had ruined the Allied blockade, and for the occupation of eastern Poland which had underlined Allied weakness. "It's jolly good to look at the map. And finish the foe in a day," noted one

British wag. And this was just the problem. Even Cadogan, who could so easily contemplate action against Baku, doubted whether there were enough Blenheim bombers to do the job.[6] "The only charitable conclusion," A. J. P. Taylor observed, "is to assume that the British and French governments had taken leave of their senses."[7]

"Teutoslavia" was an emotional and dangerous assessment of the Soviet-German relationship. It was also inaccurate. Molotov met the German ambassador many times in the autumn and winter of 1939–1940, but not for running after Nazi Germany or agreeing to every German demand, though he agreed to some. Discussions concerned border incidents between Soviet and German ground and naval forces, the settlement of frontier disputes, the evacuation of citizens of German descent from the Baltic states, and the transshipping across Germany of war materiel for Finland. When Schulenberg invited Molotov to visit Berlin, the commissar was in no hurry. I am too busy, he said. When Schulenberg asked Molotov to send a Soviet ship west of the British Isles to obtain weather information to assist German air attacks on Britain, Molotov first delayed and then declined the German request. He also declined to provide safe harbor to German ships on the Kamchatka peninsula off the Bering Sea. Soviet negotiators concluded an important trade agreement with Germany in February 1940, but the bargaining was hard. "Don't take us for fools," they warned.[8] The Soviet government was attempting to pursue its own interests, taking advantage of the war, without being pulled into the Axis or involved in the fighting any more than it already had been in Finland. It was a dangerous, shortsighted policy which failed, but it was similar, as A. J. P. Taylor noted, to the shortsighted Anglo-French policy which had failed earlier on.[9] One wonders why the deeply suspicious Molotov did not doubt a government so unaccustomed to keeping international agreements. The Foreign Office eventually concluded that it was Stalin's funk. Molotov claimed in his old age that they knew war was coming but thought they could put it off for just a little longer. "We weren't fools. No one ... considered us fools."[10]

II

At the same time, Maiskii seemed to get his wits back about him, once he had escaped his overextended position with Molotov. He did what he did best: he attempted to rebuild broken bridges. He warned Molotov in January 1940 of the dangerous strain in relations with the British government, and he worked to calm British emotions wrought up by the Finnish war. Anglo-Soviet relations had worsened since December: they're like a taut string, said Maiskii, and if more tension is put on the string, it will certainly break. The most immediate danger was the situation in Finland, "and the sooner this situation is brought to a satisfactory conclusion, the better the chances that Anglo-Soviet relations can survive the present crisis."[11] Maiskii also worked on Butler: it was necessary to isolate the Finnish question. "It['s] essential," Maiskii said (according to Butler's account), "that those who [are] responsible for big decisions . . . keep cool heads."[12] Once again there is a shade of difference between Maiskii's report and Butler's, for, according to the ambassador, the advice about keeping cool heads came from Butler's mouth, not his. It was no doubt preferable from Maiskii's point of view that Butler should tell Molotov to maintain his composure. Whatever the provenance, it was good advice for London too, because some clerks in the Foreign Office had their own difficulties in keeping cool. They preferred hostile relations with the Soviet; the "possibility of eventual Anglo-Soviet cooperation against Germany" seemed to them to be "illusory."[13]

The Foreign Office disliked Maiskii's methods, but Butler listened to his arguments. And the two kept talking. In mid-February, Butler brought up the Finnish question. The British government wanted "to save Finland" but not to the extent of a break with the Soviet Union. The best way out would be a peaceful solution. Maiskii talked again about "localizing" the Finnish conflict but commented that Butler's concept of it—the dispatch of warplanes, supplies, and volunteers—was not what he had in mind. Butler observed that the government was under heavy public pressure to act but might curtail its support for Finland if it could be assured that Norway and Sweden were not threatened. Maiskii dismissed this concern with a laugh, but Butler was not entirely persuaded, asking if the latest Nazi-Soviet economic agreement signaled the formation of an alliance. It was only a trade agreement, replied Maiskii, but Butler again was not persuaded.[14]

This conversation drew a reply from Molotov, and if Butler had offered a slackening of support for Finland as a lure in exchange for Soviet guarantees of Sweden and Norway, the commissar took the bait. He informed Maiskii that the Soviet government had no intention of disturbing Norway or Sweden if they did not enter the war, nor was it opposed to a negotiated settlement with Finland. Molotov even suggested British mediation to settle the conflict. But Molotov did not like Butler's insinuation that the Soviet Union had become a Nazi ally. "You can communicate the following to Butler about our relations with Germany:

> First, we consider ridiculous and slanderous not only the assertion but even the simple suggestion that the USSR has allegedly entered into a military alliance with Germany. Even simpletons in politics do not enter so clumsily into a military alliance with a belligerent power, understanding all the complexity and all the risk of such an alliance. On what basis does Butler think that the Soviet Union is governed by people not possessing even that understanding which is accessible to any simpleton in politics?
>
> Second, the trade agreement with Germany is only an agreement for a commercial transaction by which exports from the USSR to Germany amount to 500 million marks; the said treaty is economically profitable for the USSR since the USSR will receive from Germany a large quantity of armaments, machine tools, equipment, the sale of which was invariably refused to us by both England and France.
>
> Third, as the USSR has been neutral, so it will remain neutral unless of course England and France attack the USSR and compel it to take up arms. The widely circulated rumors about a military alliance of the USSR with Germany are being warmed up not only by various elements in Germany itself, in order to confuse England and France, but also by various agents of England and France themselves, wishing to use the supposed "passage of the USSR into the German camp" for their special purposes in the realm of internal politics.[15]

Maiskii duly repeated the message to Butler on the following day, without Molotov's acerbity.[16]

A few days earlier, on February 16, Molotov had welcomed a visit from Cripps on a world tour, who flew a long way from China to meet the foreign commissar in Moscow. As happened more often than not, there were differences in the Soviet and British records of the meeting. According to the Soviet account, Molotov indicated that if the British government really wished to improve relations, the Soviet Union would meet it halfway. And Molotov vented the usual Soviet grievances against the British, which he and Maiskii had many times raised in the past. The Cripps version confirmed this position but then added the menace that if an improvement of relations did not take place, ". . . Russia would have to proceed in other directions with trade and political agreements." There is no such threat recorded in the Soviet record of the meeting. Was Cripps here playing the role of a British Maiskii? The evidence does not provide an answer, but Cripps pressed Halifax to consider resuming negotiations: "I have no doubt whatever that there is at the moment [the] opportunity of doing something to draw Russia away from Germany and that this opportunity may not still exist in a few months or weeks time."[17]

Foreign Office reaction was at first largely derisive and negative. The British government was not interested in conveying unfavorable terms to the Finns and therefore refused to mediate. It was all a ruse, thought the Foreign Office clerks; Stalin was afraid of raids on Baku. Let him continue to worry. "For most purposes the Soviet Govt. are already our enemy."[18] On March 13 the Russo-Finnish War ended. Soviet terms were relatively generous considering that the Finnish army was beaten. But hostility's momentum carried on. The French government "picked a fight" with Moscow, demanding the recall of the Soviet ambassador on a pretext, just as it had done in October 1927 to expel the *polpred*, Kh. G. Rakovskii, who would die forgotten in 1941 at the hands of an anonymous Stalinist executioner. As Cadogan saw it, the French were making it hard to contemplate a flirt with Maiskii. They still seemed to want a raid on Baku.[19]

Butler kept up an unsung but important fight to entice the Foreign Office into resuming its courting of the Soviet, however homely and disagreeable the target of their future affections. "I am becoming very alarmed," said Butler: ". . . There is a certain noble purity about British policy which tends—provided right is on our side and the human brain dictates the logic of an action—to add one enemy after another to those opposed to us." Butler's position is the more remarkable because less than a year before he had been Chamberlain's only supporter in resisting pressure for an Anglo-Franco-Soviet alliance. He was, and is, sometimes dismissed as a weakling appeaser, but in these circumstances he held his ground in an unpopular cause. And this was not the only one, for he continued to maintain his earlier position that a truce in the war should not be excluded if the nonbelligerent powers became involved in peace negotiations.[20]

Maiskii also kept up his equally unsung part. "The Finnish difficulty [is] now removed," the ambassador told Butler; we should try to move toward a "better understanding."

But the war has "left many bitter wounds."

"We must now bandage them and heal them."

Butler was responsive: he told Maiskii that he hoped for an improvement of Anglo-Soviet relations. He repeatedly told his Foreign Office colleagues that British interests required better relations with the Soviet: "Labour is very averse to war with Russia." Whatever the Foreign Office might think, Russia held a place, in spite of Finland, "in the minds of many working men." It would also keep Hitler off balance and uncertain about his eastern frontiers. "I feel that a reckless alienating of the Soviet Union [will] do more harm than good . . . "; Britain needed Russian cooperation if it was to close the blockade around Nazi Germany. To Maiskii, Butler said that Halifax would gladly see him if the ambassador had important questions to discuss.[21]

Events moved quickly away from confrontation, even if riled clerks and senior officials in the Foreign Office saw no need to propitiate the Soviet government. Moscow, they advised, was just throwing "dust in our eyes."[22] Halifax, however, agreed with Butler's position, and he was not alone. On March 27 Lord Chatfield, minister for the coordination of defense, asked Halifax to reopen the question of negotiations with Moscow.[23] On the same day, with exquisite timing, Maiskii went to see Halifax to advise that the Soviet government was prepared to accept Stanley's invitation of the previous October for trade talks.[24] It was hard to reject the offer out of hand, and the War Cabinet approved the possibility of resuming trade negotiations. At nearly the same time the Soviet government declined to accord transit rights to Germany through Vladivostok, considered by the British to be "a bad gap" in the blockade. And in early April the Soviet government temporarily suspended shipments of raw materials to Germany because of the latter's failure to deliver agreed-upon commodities to the Soviet Union.[25] Yet Molotov made a vitriolic speech against France and Britain at the end of March. The usual contradictions marked both Soviet and British policy, but it may also have been camouflage to hide from German notice Soviet feelers in London.

The conjuncture of circumstances seemed briefly to be right for a resumption of negotiations. To irritated clerks in the Foreign Office, it looked like Maiskii had pulled another fast one: ". . . M. Maisky has been seeing a good deal of Mr. Lloyd George of late, which . . . bodes no good . . . and we know that Lord Beaverbrook and Low, the cartoonist, are both [his] friends. . . ." Fitzroy Maclean suggested some "inspired articles . . . emphasizing the closeness and sinister character of Soviet-German co-operation." To Sargent, however, the idea did not seem so opportune, "seeing that we are on the point of again exploring the possibility of a trade agreement with Russia. . . ."[26]

III

If the moment was propitious, nothing came of it. But the debate inside the British government about Soviet intentions went on until the German invasion of the Soviet Union in June 1941. In the interim the Foreign Office thought the Soviet wanted to keep Britain "in play." But this was also what the British government, in its lucid moments, wanted to do in Moscow. Neither side liked the other, and who could blame them? The clerks and many higher officials in the Foreign Office were dismissive of Soviet intentions and strength. As in the prewar period, there were often ideological underpinnings to these attitudes, but as with the French, these were cloaked in technical arguments about Soviet weakness and the Soviet "alliance" with Nazi Germany.[27] Because of ideological assumptions about the spread of communism in the event of victory over Nazi Germany, some British officials did not want an alliance with the Soviet Union, even after June 1941. At the end of 1940 Cadogan could still rail in his diary against the 1936 French Popular Front and the "Red" government in Spain: ". . . millions of people in Europe (I would not exclude myself) think that these things are awful."[28] The Soviet government also saw weakness and lack of will on the British side, and the Bore War did nothing to reassure them. But it came to an end in April 1940 when Germany invaded Norway, getting there just as the British started to mine Norwegian waters.

The end of the Bore War marked the beginning of many black weeks for the Anglo-French alliance. The Norwegian campaign was a fiasco, though worse was to come. In May the Germans launched their armored offensive through the Ardennes, crushing the Anglo-French armies and leading to the miraculous evacuation at Dunkirk. The only positive development for the Allied cause was the appointment of Churchill as prime minister in May. Now there would be no more fear of provoking Nazi Germany, though Churchill had few divisions and fewer guns to "bleed and burn" the enemy. In the east the Soviet government reacted to the French collapse by annexing the Baltic states, Bessarabia, and Bukovina. The Germans immediately began shifting divisions to the Soviet frontier while the British government sent Cripps to be ambassador in Moscow.

It was also at this time, as France collapsed, that the French government made one last, dying effort to move closer to the Soviet Union. It was a sad event. Eirik Labonne, the resident general in Tunis, was hurriedly named ambassador to replace Naggiar, recalled at the beginning of the Winter War. In 1927 Labonne had been in the thick of Anatole de Monzie's attempt to obtain a debts-credit settlement with the Soviet Union. This effort, as with others, was blocked by the French government itself.[29] But when a French government did think about improving relations with the Soviet Union, it sent one of its Russophiles, like Alphand or Coulondre, to Moscow. Labonne came from the same Herriot-Monzie school, though it was too late for him to do any good. When Labonne arrived in Moscow on June 12 the French armies were in headlong retreat, and when Labonne met Molotov on June 14, German forces were occupying Paris. Labonne had instructions to initiate political discussions with the Soviet government, based on the mutual interest "to correct the alarming disequilibrium" opening up between Anglo-French and German forces. The French government, as did the British, thought they had noticed some faint signs of Soviet interest in resuming contacts. Labonne was to work with Cripps to this end.[30]

During a two-hour conversation Labonne asked Molotov whether the Soviet government would be willing to discuss cooperation to counter German dominance. Molotov was polite but evasive. He reminded Labonne that for a long time France had pursued a policy toward the Soviet Union "which one could not characterize as friendly." Labonne acknowledged the point—he knew from first-hand experience in 1927—but said that circumstances had changed because of French misfortune. This change of attitude is sudden, replied Molotov, but I recognize that new situations can lead to new policies. With August 1939 in mind, one wonders whether the irony here was intended. The commissar asked about rumors of a French separate peace, to which Labonne could only reply that much would depend on future international support of French resistance. At the end Molotov promised to consult his government.[31] The Foreign Office was cautiously interested, but nothing came of it. The French asked for armistice negotiations on June 18 and capitulated to Germany four days later. Coulondre had commented in 1935 that improvements in Franco-Soviet relations were like "an enchanted forest" which always moved farther away as one approached. "We have only ourselves to blame," Coulondre observed, "since for years we have missed opportunities because we did not know how to make the necessary effort in time."[32]

IV

France was done for, and Britain faced Nazi Germany alone. If ever the British and Soviet governments needed each other, it was now. But in the blackest days just before the French collapse, Maiskii was unsympathetic when Butler reminded him that the broken European military equilibrium should be a concern to the Soviet Union. It's a little late for bringing it up, replied Maiskii: if Britain and France had pursued different policies earlier on, we might not have come to this pass.[33] Well, yes it was true, and Butler was scarcely in a position to talk. But the Soviet government had options too, however much a Sophie's choice: the Nazi-Soviet nonaggression pact was no more predetermined than Anglo-French appeasement, whatever the revisionist historians now say about the latter.

After the French surrender, Labonne withdrew from all diplomatic contacts, but Cripps, who had arrived in Moscow at the same time, carried on. On July 1 he met Stalin to convey the British government's interest in better relations. Cripps took up Labonne's approach, but without success. Stalin reassured him that the Soviet Union had not formed a "bloc" with Germany against Britain; "we have only a pact of nonaggression." Beyond that, Stalin offered little encouragement. The Soviet Union was not prepared to work for the reestablishment of the prewar European equilibrium, nor did Stalin think that Germany could establish hegemony over Europe without control of the seas, which was beyond its reach.[34]

The Soviet reply should not have surprised the British, given the military situation in western Europe. France had surrendered two weeks earlier, and the British army was "literally naked," having left its guns and lorries on the beaches of Dunkirk. But Maiskii reported that there was no panic in Britain, and that for this Churchill's parliamentary speeches had played an important role. "There's growing [here] a stubborn will," Maiskii reported, "a cold British hatred and determination to fight to the end." Maiskii conceded that people around Chamberlain feared the consequences of a long war, and would conclude peace with Germany at the first opportunity. But this was not a position openly declared, and even Chamberlain was taking a hard line. Maiskii did not overplay the defeatist tendency: Churchill's support in Labour circles was strong; they saw in him the one man who could "win the war."[35]

Churchill confirmed to Maiskii in July that the British government was determined to fight to the finish: "The fate of Paris does not await London." This was brave talk by a brave prime minister, but could the British hold out? The beaten French and victorious Germans did not think so. There's no use hiding the truth, Maiskii reported, "the danger is very great." Even Churchill would not predict victory, but he warned Maiskii that if the British were beaten, Hitler would turn all his might against the Soviet Union.[36]

In August Cripps saw Molotov to reiterate Churchill's warning that Germany could turn against the Soviet Union if its hands were freed in the west. Cripps complained that the Soviet government applied two standards in its neutrality toward Nazi Germany and Britain. Molotov admitted that this was true: "We have a nonaggression pact with Germany to which the USSR attaches great importance"; we do not have a similar agreement with Britain. It was a point of difference to which the Soviet Union could not close its eyes. Molotov agreed that an improvement in trade relations was possible, but he complained about "new surprises," unfriendly acts by the British government against Soviet interests in the Baltic (the British seizure of Baltic assets in Great Britain after the absorption of the Baltic states into the Soviet Union). It was not for the Soviet Union therefore to take the initiative in improving trade relations.[37] Cripps's account of the meeting gave a more positive gloss to Molotov's statements, which admitted the possibility of an improvement of political relations (absent in the Soviet record). And Cripps was more optimistic about improved relations if Britain could show itself capable of resisting an expected German invasion and if it would make concessions to the Soviet government.[38]

Although these Soviet policy explanations appear to have been candid and direct, some British officials took Molotov's statements rather badly. Vansittart did not. He had calmed down since the heated atmosphere of the Finnish war and saw again the value of better relations with the Soviet Union. He did not think, however, that concessions to the Soviet would bring it around. Concessions will not work "until we both become and remain militarily stronger." It was the eve of the Battle of Britain, and the threat of German invasion was on everyone's mind. The British had to prove they could beat off the Nazis. When Britain is a first-rate military power, said Vansittart, "Russia will come our way quick enough."

> Her interest will dictate it. Until that is remedied, there is nothing doing. It was the terrible exhibition of military weakness and blindness that we have offered during the last decade which caused Russia to double-cross us last year. We were simply not a tempting proposition. And it was this same notorious inefficiency which encouraged Fascism in France and is at the bottom of all the anti-British feeling in France ever since I can remember,

and that is a very long time. We shall never have a reliable friend anywhere until we are thought both reliable and worth while ourselves. On the other hand, we shall always have friends provided we do not slip back into our old abominable habits.[39]

Vansittart's explanation had merit, and the British kept up their warnings about the German threat to Soviet security. Those who faced the Nazi peril "were better advised if they clung together," Butler told Maiskii in October.[40] But Cripps did not like lecturing the Russians about the German danger, since he thought Molotov "fully alive to the position." Vansittart, relishing the irony of the situation, did not agree:

> . . . the obvious is not always the same to all people, and . . . one has frequently to deal with people who do not wish to see the obvious in any circumstances. In dealing with the mythical habits of the ostrich it is often essential to go on pegging away at the obvious, and sometimes . . . it is necessary to convince people that we have seen the obvious. We have not always done so, and we cannot take it for granted that people always credit us with this quality.

Vansittart could not help but remember the 1930s and his own role in trying to alert his government to the obvious danger.

> One of M. Maisky's most constant complaints against His Majesty's Government before 1939 was that they had not seen that it was inevitable that Germany would make war upon them. I was of course a very obvious person for him to select for this kind of talk. But it carries with it the corollary that Sir Stafford Cripps is now just as much entitled to reproach the Soviet Government with failing to see that it is obvious that Germany is going to make war on *them*."[41] (emphasis in the original)

The Soviet government was not unaware of the threat. Immediately after the fall of France, Soviet intelligence and diplomatic sources sent plentiful evidence of a vast military buildup in the east. In the autumn of 1940 the Soviet government calculated that ninety-four German infantry and armored divisions were now on its eastern frontiers, up from trifling numbers in the spring. This was an open secret: even William L. Shirer, the American journalist in Berlin, was aware of the buildup, though not of its scope.[42]

Who was Cassandra now? Molotov apparently failed to recognize the irony of the situation. Churchill told Maiskii that the two nations had to forget about the past and get on with the present and future. But Molotov liked to remember past Anglo-French duplicity in order to justify present Soviet policy. He did not remember everything, however, for he chose to forget or dismiss Litvinov's many early warnings of inevitable war. The price for doing so was unspeakably high, a point which may have troubled even the cold-blooded Molotov. Memories died hard: in 1942 Molotov and Litvinov, then Soviet ambassador in Washington, could still rage at one another over the Soviet abandonment of collective security.[43] While Molotov admitted to Strang in London that "we were both at fault" in 1939, he was not about to admit it to Litvinov. Not that, not to him.

V

In this story neither side was virtuous, but there were individuals whose foresight and courage stand out. There are not just the usual villains but also, dare one say it, heroes who are largely unknown now but who should be recognized. Litvinov, who figures little at the end of this tale, was perhaps the most intrepid, fighting unsuccessfully for collective security in an intolerable atmosphere of suspicion and murder at home. He was the West's preferred Soviet emissary, but his policies were spurned and derided by the French and British governments and thus became increasingly discredited in Moscow. Essentially Litvinov looked at Hitler and Nazi Germany and applied Occam's razor, that the simplest explanation was the most appropriate. For the Anglo-French, Litvinov was the red stormcrow, warning of the Nazi danger only to conceal the greater danger of communist revolution. Litvinov suffered the rejection of his policies in the West while watching his own friends and colleagues disappear in the purges. He stayed at his post—what choice did he have?—until dismissed in 1939. The reader may still notice his shadow, however, as the British and Soviet governments tried to cope with the terrible dangers of the early war period. And there was Maiskii, disliked by British Foreign Office officials because of his use of an influential network of connections in Britain, who nevertheless fought, deviously and at times dangerously, for an Anglo-Soviet rapprochement. Unlike Molotov and Stalin, Maiskii appears not to have forgotten Litvinov's anti-Nazi dictums. In May 1942 Eden praised Maiskii for his role in building bridges between Britain and the Soviet Union.[44] The foreign secretary was perhaps more right than he knew.

Vansittart needed no prodding from Maiskii or Litvinov to recognize early on the Nazi threat to peace. Like Litvinov, Vansittart was not rewarded for his foresight but was put out of the way in 1938 because of his eloquent persistence in pointing out the weaknesses of British foreign policy. He too figures little at the end of this story, though he occasionally returns to recall British failures in the 1930s, and to point out the irony and danger of the post-August 1939 Soviet position. Butler and Cripps also fought uphill to overcome the bloody-minded or ideologically driven opposition in the Foreign Office to a rapprochement with the Soviet Union. Butler in particular pursued a more complicated line of policy than some historians have supposed.

VI

Interwar anti-communism was an important cause of the Second World War. Not the only one, to be sure; German resistance to the Versailles treaty, Anglo-French discord and military weakness, the depression of the 1930s were others. But the root of failure of Anglo-Franco-Soviet cooperation against Nazism was anti-communism. The war-revolution nexus was the dominant spoken and unspoken assumption of Anglo-French policymakers toward the Soviet Union in the interwar years. This assumption did not go unchallenged; on the contrary, readers have heard the voices of Herriot, Mandel, Churchill, Vansittart, and Collier, among others. But anti-communism prevailed at crucial times: in 1934–1935 when Laval succeeded the assassinated Barthou and gutted the Franco-Soviet pact; in 1936 when Eden blocked a promising Anglo-Soviet rapprochement; and in 1939 when Chamberlain sabotaged a Soviet alliance and Daladier and Bonnet—wedded to London and to their own anti-communism—went along for the ride. When Chamberlain said he did not believe in Soviet military power or the danger of a Nazi-Soviet rapprochement, it was to remove the risk, as he saw it, of having to make concessions to the Soviet Union.[45] We can get along without the Soviet Union, said Chamberlain, though much evidence to the contrary emerged when the danger was greatest. Churchill and Lloyd George, for example, derided such arguments.

Fear of victory over fascism drove appeasement as much as fear of Nazi power and virility. Victory over Nazism could not be achieved without a Soviet alliance and without an increase of Soviet prestige and a risk of spreading communism into Europe. This is what happened in the end anyway, many will argue: Chamberlain's fears were proved right after all. Not exactly. The ideologues' 1930s scenario, as it actually developed after 1945, was the result of the failure of collective security and the ensuing Nazi-Soviet nonaggression pact. In the scenario that never happened, victorious French and Polish armies would have stood with British, U.S., and Soviet forces, and—especially the Poles—would have blocked unwanted communist expansion in Europe. Soviet prestige would have grown, but Soviet communism would not have expanded into the military void created by the Polish and French debacles.

The Soviet government could have done more to help itself. The grotesque and bloody purges of the 1930s did not cause the failure of the Anglo-Soviet and Franco-Soviet rapprochements of the mid-1930s, because these failures preceded the purges. But they offered an ideal pretext to the anti-communists who opposed closer relations with the Soviet Union. The early purges were aimed against the "old Bolsheviks," and with a few exceptions, the French and British did not care a pin for their fate. The purges of the Red Army high command were another matter. It was further fuel to the fire of the anti-communists for it appeared to, and certainly did, weaken Soviet military power at a crucial point in the lead-up to war. Even so, the Red Army conducted an impressive mobilization on its western frontiers during the Munich crisis. And the Soviet armed forces gave a good account of themselves against Japanese border intrusions in the far east in 1938–1939, though these successes received little attention from British and French policymakers. In the long war envisioned by Anglo-French military planners, even the weakened Red Army could play a crucial role.

The Munich crisis and failure of Anglo-Franco-Soviet negotiations in 1939 led directly to the Nazi-Soviet nonaggression pact. Many Western historians have argued a contrary position—that the nonaggression pact caused the failure of the negotiations for a tripartite anti-Nazi alliance; Hitler and Stalin colluded because there really was no difference, or not much, between Nazism and communism. Lines like these became familiar in the post-1945 cold war. This cold war ideology tended to overshadow Anglo-French culpability and responsibility for the path to war in 1939. It has inclined some contemporary historians to overlook the strength of anti-communism during the interwar years and its destructive influence on the foreign policies of France and Britain. Indeed, anti-communism helped to compromise Western security against Nazi Germany.

None of this minimizes Soviet responsibility for what occurred between August 1939 and June 1941. In fact, Litvinov's warnings to the French and British came home to haunt the Soviet government itself. It would have taken the foresight and courage of a Litvinov to be receptive to British overtures in 1939 and after, and then to sell them to Stalin. For this role Molotov lacked the independence of mind and sophistication of his predecessor; he was not the kind to put behind him the mistrust developed and nurtured over twenty-odd years. The events of 1939 and 1940 did not take place in a vacuum, as the participants in this drama often remembered: they were part of the early cold war which the West and Soviet Russia had waged since the Bolshevik revolution in November 1917.

The Winter War inflamed anti-communist opinion in Britain but especially in France, where the French Communist party had already been banned and many party members arrested. The end of the Finnish war in March, combined with the beginning of German offensive operations in the west in April, allowed cooler heads to prevail. The Soviet government was lucky to escape this bungled adventure without graver consequences than those it had suffered: heavy military losses, diminished prestige, and strained relations in the West. The British government—and even the French at the end—resumed the realist's policy toward the Soviet Union. British overtures were not embraced by the Soviet government. Stalin had made his bed with the Nazi-Soviet pact and was obliged to stay in it for fear of provoking a war for which the Soviet Union was not ready. If Molotov's reminiscences are correct, the Soviet government was prepared to delay war for as long as possible. Even a few months mattered.

In the end, neither side, Anglo-French or Soviet, was in a position to reproach the other for its appeasement of Nazi Germany, or its hostility the one toward the other. The British and French feared the spread of communism or collusion with Nazi Germany, the Soviet Union, a capitalist war-making bloc against it which might include Nazi Germany. Each side could point to the other's contradictory policies, and each side had good reasons for mistrust. After August 1939 France had a minor role to play, first because of its domestic anti-communist campaign, then because of its collapse in June 1940. The British went on courting Moscow, but without success. Finally, each had to prove to the other its ability to survive the Nazi onslaught—the British in 1940 and the Soviet Union in 1941.

The British government sought to draw the Soviet Union away from Nazi Germany but succeeded only just in keeping it "in play." The Soviet government was less interested than Britain in a rapprochement—perhaps not interested at all—mindful of the dangerous impact this could have on its German relationship; but it too wanted to keep the British "in play." Like the British, it only just succeeded in doing so. This was enough, for ultimately Nazi Germany's unslakable thirst for conquest brought about the rapprochement that Britain and the Soviet Union were incapable or unwilling to achieve on their own.

Notes

Acknowledgments

1. A.J.P. Taylor, *The Origins of the Second World War* (Middlesex, 1964); Sidney Aster, *1939: The Making of the Second World War* (London, 1973); and D. Cameron Watt, *How War Came* (London, 1990).

2. E.g., M.J. Carley, "Five Kopecks for Five Kopecks: Franco-Soviet Trade Relations, 1928–1939," *Cahiers du monde russe et soviétique*, vol. 33, no. 1 (January–March 1992), 23–58; Carley, "End of the 'Low, Dishonest Decade': Failure of the Anglo-Franco-Soviet Alliance in 1939," *Europe-Asia Studies*, vol. 45, no. 2 (1993), 303–341; Carley, "Down a Blind-Alley: Anglo-Franco-Soviet Relations, 1920–1939," *Canadian Journal of History*, vol. 29, no. 1 (April 1994), 147–172; Carley, "Generals, Diplomats, and International Politics in Europe, 1898–1945," *Canadian Journal of History*, vol. 30, no. 2 (August 1995), 289–321; Carley, "Fearful Concatenation of Circumstances: The Anglo-Soviet Rapprochement, 1934–1936," *Contemporary European History*, vol. 5, no. 1 (March 1996), 29–69; Carley "Prelude to Defeat: Franco-Soviet Relations, 1919–1939," *Historical Reflections*, vol. 22, no. 1 (Winter 1996), 159–188; and Carley, "The Early Cold War, 1917–1939," *Relevance*, vol. 5, no. 4 (Fall 1996), 6–11.

Preface

1. E.g., Lewis B. Namier, *Diplomatic Prelude, 1938–1939* (London, 1948).

2. See, e.g., Maurice Cowling, *The Impact of Hitler: British Politics and British Policy, 1933–1940* (London, 1975); Margaret George, *Warped Vision: British Foreign Policy, 1933–1939* (Pittsburgh, 1965); Keith Middlemas, *Diplomacy of Illusion: The British Government and Germany, 1937–1939* (London, 1972); Taylor, *Origins*; and Neville Thompson, *The Anti-Appeasers: Conservative Opposition to Appeasement in the 1930s* (Oxford, 1971).

3. E.g., Robert Manne, "The Foreign Office and the Failure of Anglo-Soviet Rapprochement," *Journal of Contemporary History*, vol. 16, no. 4 (1981), 725–755.

4. Gaines Post, Jr., *Dilemmas of Appeasement: British Deterrence and Defense, 1934–1937* (Ithaca, N.Y., 1993); W.K. Wark, "Appeasement Revisited," *International History Review*, vol. 17, no. 3 (August 1995), 545–562; but see also Keith Neilson, "Pursued by a Bear: British Estimates of Soviet Military Strength and Anglo-Soviet Relations, 1922–1939," *Canadian Journal of History*, vol. 28, no. 2 (August 1993), 189–221.

5. G.C. Peden, *British Rearmament and the Treasury, 1932–1939* (Edinburgh, 1979).

6. Henry Channon, a Tory M.P., made this statement in September 1936, recorded by Harold Nicolson, *Diaries and Letters, 1930–1939* (New York, 1966), p. 273.

7. William D. Irvine, *French Conservatism in Crisis: The Republican Federation of France in the 1930s* (Baton Rouge, 1979), p. 179.

8. Marc Bloch, *Strange Defeat: A Statement of Evidence Written in 1940* (New York, 1968), *passim*; Pertinax (André Géraud), *Les Fossoyeurs*, 2 vols. (New York, 1943), *passim*; Jean-Baptiste Duroselle, *La Décadence, 1932–1939* (Paris, 1985), pp. 12–27; and Eugen Weber, *The Hollow Years: France in the 1930s* (New York, 1994), *passim*.

9. René Girault, "Les Décideurs français et la puissance française en 1938–1939," in R. Girault and Robert Frank, eds., *La Puissance en Europe, 1938–1940* (Paris, 1984), pp. 34–40.

10. Stephen A. Schuker, "France and the Remilitarization of the Rhineland, 1936," *French Historical Studies*, vol. 14, no. 3 (Spring 1986), 299–338; Elisabeth du Réau, *Édouard Daladier, 1884–1970* (Paris, 1993); Martin Alexander, *The Republic in Danger: General Maurice Gamelin and the Politics of French Defence, 1933–1940* (Cambridge, England, 1992); William D. Irvine, "Domestic Politics and the Fall of France in 1940," *Historical Reflections*, vol. 22, no. 1 (Winter 1996), 77–90; Robert J. Young, *France and the Origins of the Second World War* (New York, 1996); and Schuker, "Two Cheers for Appeasement," unpublished paper, presented at Society for French Historical Studies conference, Boston, March 1996.

11. Weber, *Hollow Years*, p. 6.

12. E.g., R.A.C. Parker, *Chamberlain and Appeasement: British Policy and the Coming of the Second World War* (London, 1993). Cf. Paul Kennedy, "Appeasement," in Gordon Martel, ed., *The Origins of the Second World War Reconsidered* (Boston, 1986), pp. 140–161.

13. Earl of Birkenhead, *Halifax* (London, 1965), p. 440.

14. E.g., V. Ia. Sipols, *Diplomaticheskaia borba nakanune vtoroi mirovoi voiny* (Moscow, 1989), pp. 262–267; or I.K. Kobliakov, *USSR: For Peace Against Aggression, 1933–1941* (Moscow, 1976), pp. 144–156.

15. Watt, *How War Came*, pp. 338, 452.

16. E.g., Duroselle, *Décadence*, pp. 416–417, and *passim*; Robert J. Young, *In Command of France: French Foreign Policy and Military Planning, 1933–1940* (Cambridge, Mass., 1978), pp. 236–237, 240–241; and Young, "A.J.P. Taylor and the Problem with France," in Martel, *Origins*, pp. 97–118.

17. K. Feiling, *The Life of Neville Chamberlain* (London, 1947), p. 403; and John Charmley, *Chamberlain and the Lost Peace* (London, 1989), p. 181.

18. Geoffrey Roberts, *The Unholy Alliance: Stalin's Pact with Hitler* (Bloomington, Ind., 1989), pp. 225–226; and Watt, *How War Came*, p. 120.

19. On Tory anti-bolshevism, see George, *Warped Vision, passim*; Thompson, *Anti-Appeasers*, pp. 38–40 and *passim*; and Cowling, *Impact of Hitler, passim*. On Chamberlain's anti-bolshevism, see Aster, *1939*, pp. 184–185 and *passim*; and Parker, *Chamberlain, passim*.

20. Taylor, *Origins*, p. 318.

21. Taylor, *Origins*, p. 319; Dimitri Volkogonov, *Staline* (Paris, 1991), p. 268; Roy Medvedev, *Let History Judge: The Origins and Consequences of Stalinism* (New York, 1989), p. 728.

22. G. Gorodetsky, "The Impact of the Ribbentrop-Molotov Pact on the Course of Soviet Foreign Policy," *Cahiers du monde russe et soviétique*, vol. 31, no. 1 (January–March 1990), pp. 27–28.

23. See *inter alia* Gerhard Weinberg, *The Foreign Policy of Hitler's Germany: Starting World War II, 1937–1939* (Chicago, 1980), *passim*; Adam Ulam, *Expansion and Coexistence* (New York, 1968), pp. 257–279, or, more recently, Aleksandr M. Nekrich, *Pariahs, Partners, Predators: German-Soviet Relations, 1922–1941* (New York, 1997), *passim*. T.J. Uldricks notes that this view "makes 98 per cent of all Soviet diplomatic activity a brittle cover for the remaining covert 2 per cent" (Uldricks, "A.J.P. Taylor and the Russians," in Martel, *Origins*, p. 178). See V. Ia. Sipols, "A Few Months Before August 23, 1939," *International Affairs* (June 1989), pp. 124–136; Geoffrey Roberts, "The Soviet Decision for a Pact with Nazi Germany," *Soviet Studies*, vol. 44, no. 1 (1992), 57–78; Roberts, *The Soviet Union and the Origins of the Second World War: Russo-German Relations and the Road to War, 1933–1941* (London, 1995); Roberts, "The Alliance That Failed: Moscow and Triple Alliance Negotiations, 1939," *European History Quarterly*, vol. 26, no. 3 (1996), 383–414; and Ingeborg Fleischhauer, *Pakt: Gitler, Stalin i initsiativa Germanskoi diplomatii, 1938–1939* (Moscow, 1991), pp. 19–40.

24. "«Kruglyi stol»: vtoraia mirovaia voina—istoki i prichiny," *Voprosy istorii*, no. 6 (June 1989), 3–33.

Chapter 1. "A Long List of Disappointments"

1. Coulondre, no. 569, confidential, Nov. 16, 1937, *Documents diplomatiques français* [hereafter *DDF*], 2ᵉ série, 18 vols. (Paris, 1963–), pp. 433–435; and Coulondre, no. 228, Nov. 29, 1937, *ibid.*, pp. 550–552.

2. Daniel Lévi, French chargé d'affaires in Moscow, no. 109, April 5, 1938, *DDF*, 2ᵉ, IX, 225–227.

3. Vansittart's minute, March 13, 1939, N1389/57/38, London, Public Record Office, Foreign Office [hereafter PRO FO] 371 23677.

4. John Carswell, *The Exile: A Life of Ivy Litvinov* (London, 1983), p. 113.

5. Untitled, handwritten memorandum by R.A. Leeper, June 17, 1933, N4812/5/38, PRO FO 371 17241.

6. Paul-Émile Naggiar's undated minute on his dispatch no. 161, July 19, 1939, Paris, Ministère des Affaires étrangères [hereafter MAE], Papiers Naggiar/8.

7. William C. Bullitt, U.S. ambassador in Moscow, no. 340, strictly confidential, Oct. 5, 1934, 500.A15A4/2588, Washington, D.C., National Archives, Record Group [hereafter NA RG] 59 (1930–1939), box 2396; and "Memorandum of Conversation with Litvinov," by Hugh R. Wilson, U.S. representative in Geneva, Nov. 21, 1934, 500.A15A4/2618, *ibid.*

8. William Manchester, *The Caged Lion: Winston Spencer Churchill, 1932–1940* (London, 1989), p. 114.

9. Anthony Eden, *Facing the Dictators* (Boston, 1962), p. 271; Norman Rose, *Vansittart: Study of a Diplomat* (London, 1978), *passim*; and also the special issue on Vansittart in *Diplomacy & Statecraft*, vol. 6, no. 1 (March 1995), with articles by B.J.C. McKercher, Charles Morrisey and M.A. Ramsay, M.L. Roi, Simon Bourette-Knowles, and John R. Ferris.

10. Rose, *Vansittart*, p. 94.

11. Robert G. Vansittart, *The Mist Procession: The Autobiography of Lord Vansittart* (London, 1958), p. 478.

12. Vansittart's minute, Feb. 9, 1935, C1076/55/18, PRO FO 371 18825.

13. Vansittart to Sir Maurice Hankey, secretary to the cabinet, April 16, 1936, C2842/4/18, PRO FO 371 19902; Vansittart's minute, June 19, 1936, C4342/4/18, PRO FO 371 19907.

14. Vansittart's minutes, May 17, 1935, C3943/55/18, PRO FO 371 18840; June 15, 1935, C4564/55/18, PRO FO 371 18845; July 5, 1935, C5178/55/18, PRO FO 371 18847; and Nov. 9, 1935, C7647/55/18, PRO FO 371 18851.

15. Vansittart, *Mist Procession*, pp. 454–455; I.M. Maiskii, *Vospominaniia sovetskogo diplomata, 1925–1945gg.* (Moscow, 1971), pp. 222, 290–291, 300; and Sidney Aster, "Ivan Maisky and Parliamentary Anti-Appeasement, 1938–39," in A.J.P. Taylor, ed., *Lloyd George: Twelve Essays* (London, 1971), pp. 317–357.

16. Maiskii to Narkomindel (commissariat for foreign affairs), June 15, 1935, *Dokumenty vneshnei politiki*, 23 vols. (Moscow, 1958–) [hereafter *DVP*], XVIII, 397–398; Maiskii to Narkomindel, Dec. 9, 1935, *ibid.*, 585–586; "Record of a conversation . . . with . . . Churchill," Maiskii, April 3, 1936, *DVP*, XIX, 211–217; and Maiskii, *Vospominaniia*, pp. 300–302. For a fuller account of Churchill's meetings with Maiskii in 1935–1936, see Carley, "Fearful Concatenation of Circumstances," *passim*.

17. Eden's minutes, Jan. 15, and Jan. 10, 1936, N479/20/38, PRO FO 371 20338.

18. Eden to Phipps, private, Feb. 28, 1936, N1693/20/38, PRO FO 371 20339; and Eden's minute, May 21, 1936, N2514/16/38, PRO FO 371 20338.

19. Anthony Adamthwaite, *Grandeur and Misery: France's Bid for Power in Europe, 1914–1940* (London, 1995), p. 186.

20. On Paul-Boncour's role, see Carley, "Five Kopecks for Five Kopecks," *passim*.

21. Telford Taylor, *Munich: The Price of Peace* (New York, 1979), pp. 580–581.

22. "Record of a conversation . . . with the ambassador of France in the USSR Alphand," Litvinov, Sept. 22, 1933, *DVP*, XVI, 527–529.

23. "Record of a conversation . . . with the ambassador of France in the USSR Alphand," Stomoniakov, July 5, 1933, *DVP*, XVI, 411–416.

24. As early as 1921 the Soviet government paid the semi-official *Le Temps*, among other Paris papers, more than 520,000 francs to achieve "the establishment of diplomatic and economic relations between Russia and France" (untitled memorandum, strictly secret, not signed, not dated [but 1921], AVPRF, fond 4, opis' 32, delo 53620, papka 259, listy 56–58).

25. The above account is based on Eugen Weber, *Action Française: Royalism and Reaction in Twentieth-Century France* (Stanford, 1962), pp. 295–344; and D.W. Brogan, *The Development of Modern France, 1870–1939*, 2 vols. (Gloucester, Mass., 1970), II, 651–661, and *passim*.

26. "Record of a conversation . . . with the ambassador of France in the USSR Alphand," Stomoniakov, Feb. 13, 1934, *DVP*, XVII, 140–142; and "Record of a conversation . . . ," Litvinov, Sept. 22, 1933, *DVP*, XVI, 527–529.

27. Dovgalevskii to Narkomindel, Feb. 24, 1934, *DVP*, XVII, 165–166.

28. Alphand, nos. 444–446, Oct. 12, 1934, *DDF*, 1re série, 13 vols. (Paris, 1964–1984), VII, 718–719; and Litvinov to M.I. Rozenberg, Soviet chargé d'affaires in Paris, Oct. 19, 1934, *DVP*, XVII, 824.

29. Édouard Herriot, *Jadis: D'une guerre à l'autre, 1914–1936* (Paris, 1952), pp. 437–438; and Jean Szembek, *Journal, 1933–1939* (Paris, 1952), pp. 85–86.

30. Alphand, no. 552, Dec. 20, 1933, MAE Z-Europe, 1918–1940, followed by the geographic subheading, volume, and folio number, thus MAE Z-URSS/1003, ff. 45–47; and Alphand, no. 283, July 20, 1934, enclosing "Réception chez Vorochilov," Colonel Edmond Mendras, French military attaché in Moscow, nd, MAE Z-URSS/967, ff. 168–170.

31. Payart, no. 377, Sept. 26, 1935, MAE Z-URSS/961, ff. 280–281.

32. Szembek, *Journal*, pp. 141–142; and Potemkin to Narkomindel, Nov. 22, 1935, *DVP*, XVIII, 562–564.

33. Sargent's minute, Jan. 2, 1936, C1/1/17, PRO FO 371 19855.

34. Potemkin to N.N. Krestinskii, deputy commissar for foreign affairs, Feb. 23, 1935, *DVP*, XVIII, 130–133; Litvinov to Potemkin, April 2, 1935, *ibid.*, 259; and Potemkin to Narkomindel, April 10, 1935, *ibid.*, 282–283.

35. "Remis au ministre par l'ambassadeur des Soviets, Pro memoria," March 5, 1935, MAE Z-URSS/973, ff. 29–33; and René Massigli, deputy political director, to Paul Bargeton [?], political director, Paris, April 15, 1935, MAE Z-URSS/974, f. 26.

36. Note, directeur politique [Bargeton], March 19, 1935, MAE Z-URSS/973, ff. 107–110; and "Note de M. [Jules] Basdevant sur la négociation du traité franco-soviétique du 2 mai 1935," Dec. 21, 1935, MAE Z-URSS/980, ff. 171–176.

37. Litvinov to Potemkin, Oct. 29, 1935, *DVP*, XVIII, 541; Litvinov to Potemkin, Nov. 4, 1935, *ibid.*, 667; and N. Lloyd Thomas, British chargé d'affaires in Paris, to Eden, no. 1310, Oct. 14, 1936, C7262/92/62, PRO FO 371 19880.

38. Litvinov to Potemkin, Jan. 13, 1936, *DVP*, XIX, 26–27; "Record of a conversation ... with ... Alphand," Litvinov, Jan. 14, 1936, *ibid.*, 27–28; and Litvinov to Potemkin, Feb. 23, 1936, *ibid.*, 38–39.

39. Potemkin to Litvinov, June 26, 1935, *DVP*, XVIII, 415–421; Note, Directeur politique [Paul Bargeton], MAE, June 24, 1935, MAE Z-URSS/1004, ff. 172–174; and also "Note sur les avantages et les inconvénients de l'alliance russe," État-Major de l'Armée [EMA], 2ᵉ Bureau, April 24, 1935, Château de Vincennes, Paris, Service historique de l'armée de terre [hereafter SHAT], 7N 3143.

40. Alphand, nos. 36–40, Jan. 25, 1936, MAE Bureau du chiffre [hereafter BC], Télégrammes à l'arrivée de Moscou, 1936.

41. Litvinov (Paris) to Narkomindel, immediate, Feb. 2, 1936, *DVP*, XIX, 58–59.

42. Potemkin to Narkomindel, highest priority, Feb. 26, 1936, *DVP*, XIX, 102–103; Litvinov to Maiskii, March 9, 1936, *ibid.*, 130; Krestinskii to Potemkin, March 22, 1936, *ibid.*, 182–183; Potemkin to Krestinskii, March 26, 1936, *ibid.*, 189–195.

43. See, e.g., John Michael Sherwood, *Georges Mandel and the Third Republic* (Stanford, 1970).

44. Eden's minute, Aug. 25, 1936, C5939/1/17, PRO FO 371 19858; and Sir George Clerk, British ambassador in Paris, to Eden, no. 1164, Sept. 8, 1936, C6328/1/17, PRO FO 371 19859.

45. Nicolson, *Diaries*, p. 270; Thomas Jones, *A Diary with Letters, 1931–1950* (London, 1954), p. 231; Sargent's minute, Aug. 12, 1936, *Documents on British Foreign Policy* [hereafter DBFP], 2ⁿᵈ series, 19 vols. (London, 1947–1984), XVII, 90–91; and Parker, *Chamberlain*, p. 82.

46. Vansittart's memorandum, Sept. 17, 1936, *DBFP*, 2ⁿᵈ, XVII, 269–271.

47. Potemkin to Narkomindel, immediate, Sept. 17, 1936, *DVP*, XIX, 428–429.

48. "Compte-rendu du général [Victor-Henri] Schweisguth sur un entretien avec M. Léger," Oct. 9, 1936, SHAT 7N 3143; and N. Lloyd Thomas, British chargé

d'affaires in Paris, to Vansittart, private and confidential, Oct. 26, 1936, W14793/9549/41, PRO FO 371 20583.

49. Minute by Collier, head of the Northern department, Nov. 5, 1937, N4924/272/38, PRO FO 371 21103.

50. Neilson, "Pursued by a Bear," *passim*; and Neilson, "The Role of the Soviet Union in British Foreign and Defence Policy, 1930–1939," paper delivered at the meeting of the Canadian Historical Association, St. Catherines, Ontario, June 2, 1996.

51. "URSS, Manoeuvres de Russie blanche de septembre 1936," Schweisguth, Oct. 5, 1936, SHAT 7N 3184.

52. Alexander, *Gamelin*, pp. 242, 296, and *passim*.

53. See Carley, "Fearful Concatenation of Circumstances," *passim*; and Carley, "Prelude to Defeat," *passim*.

54. Coulondre, nos. 507–520, Nov. 12, 1936, MAE BC, Télégrammes à l'arrivée de Moscou, 1936; Coulondre, no. 355, Nov. 16, 1936, MAE Z-URSS/1005, ff. 14–22; and R. Coulondre, *De Staline à Hitler, souvenirs de deux ambassades, 1936–1939* (Paris, 1950), pp. 31–32.

55. Schweisguth notes, Oct. 22 and Dec. 4, 1936 (comments by General Marie-Eugène Debeney), Paris, Archives nationales [hereafter AN], Papiers Schweisguth, 351AP/3; and minute by deputy chief of staff General Paul-Henri Gérodias on Jean Payart, French chargé d'affaires in Moscow, no. 308, Sept. 27, 1936, SHAT 7N 3124.

56. "Record of a conversation of the People's commissar for foreign affairs . . . with the ambassador of France to the USSR, Coulondre," Litvinov, Nov. 10, 1936, *DVP*, XIX, 550–551; cf. Coulondre, nos. 507–520, Nov. 12, 1936, *DDF*, 2ᵉ, III, 748–751.

57. Lord Chilston, British ambassador in Moscow, no. 648, Nov. 20, 1936, N5722/307/38, PRO FO 371 20349.

58. Schweisguth notes, June 24, 1936, AN Papiers Schweisguth, 351AP/3; and "Compte-rendu d'une conversation entre M. Hirschfeld, chargé d'affaires de l'URSS, et le général Schweisguth," nd (but June 30, 1936), AN Papiers Schweisguth, 351AP/5.

59. "URSS, Manoeuvres de Russie blanche de septembre 1936," Schweisguth, Oct. 5, 1936, SHAT 7N 3184.

60. Litvinov (Geneva) to Narkomindel, Oct. 5, 1936, *DVP*, XIX, 461–462; Potemkin to Narkomindel, Sept. 17, 1936, *ibid.*, 428–429; and Potemkin to Narkomindel, Sept. 19, 1936, *ibid.*, 430–432.

61. Daladier to Delbos, no. 1411 2/EMA SAE, Oct. 13, 1936, SHAT 7N 3143; and the dossier entitled "Cession de matériel à l'URSS (July–September 1936)," AN Papiers Daladier, 496AP/7.

62. Schweisguth notes, June 25, 1936, AN Papiers Schweisguth, 351AP/3; and Girshfel'd to Narkomindel, Oct. 8, 1936, *DVP*, XIX, 465–466.

63. Schweisguth notes, Oct. 27 and 31, Nov. 7, Dec. 22, 1936 and Jan. 5, 1937, AN Papiers Schweisguth, 351AP/3; cf. Maurice Vaïsse, "Les Militaires français et l'alliance franco-soviétique au cours des années 1930," *Forces armées et systèmes d'alliances: Colloque international d'histoire militaire et d'études de défense nationale* (Montpellier, 1981), II, 696–697; and Young, *In Command of France*, pp. 147–149.

64. Potemkin to Narkomindel, Nov. 9, 1936, *DVP*, XIX, 549; and Litvinov to Potemkin, Nov. 14, 1936, *ibid.*, 775.

65. "Record of a conversation . . . with . . . Chautemps," Potemkin, Jan. 19, 1937, *DVP*, XX, 43–46.

66. Schweisguth notes, Jan. 8 and Feb. 8, 1937, AN Papiers Schweisguth, 351AP/3.

67. Schweisguth notes, Feb. 8 and March 19, 1937, AN Papiers Schweisguth, 351AP/3.

68. Schweisguth notes, Feb. 8, 1937, AN Papiers Schweisguth, 351AP/3. Young and Vaïsse report the lack of French interest in staff talks but allude only to French duplicity (Young, *In Command of France*, pp. 148–149; and Vaïsse, "Les Militaires français," p. 696).

69. "Visite du général Semenoff . . . ," very secret, Feb. 17, 1937, SHAT 7N 3186.

70. Potemkin to Narkomindel, Feb. 17, 1937, *DVP*, XX, 88–89; and "Entretien avec M. Potemkine . . . le 17 février 1937 . . . , Notes prises par Léon Blum," AN Papiers Daladier, 496AP/7.

71. "Compte rendu au ministre," very secret, Feb. 23, 1937, AN Papiers Daladier, 496AP/7.

72. Schweisguth notes, Mar. 19, 1937, AN Papiers Schweisguth, 351AP/3.

73. "Conversation du général Schweisguth avec le général Séménoff . . . ," very secret, Mar. 19, 1937, SHAT 7N 3186.

74. Schweisguth notes, April 8 and 23, 1937, AN Papiers Schweisguth, 351AP/3.

75. Schweisguth notes, April 25, May 14, 26, 27, 1937, AN Papiers Schweisguth, 351AP/3; Vansittart's minute, May 13, 1937, C3620/532/62, PRO FO 371 20702; and "Extract from a record of conversation at a lunch given by the Secretary of State to MM. Delbos & Léger on May 15, 1937," C3685/532/62, *ibid*.

76. Potemkin to Surits, May 4, 1937, *DVP*, XX, pp. 227–228.

77. Relating two conversations at the end of June 1937 with the French journalist Pertinax (Lord Chilston, British ambassador in Moscow, to Collier, July 27, 1937, N3932/45/38, PRO FO 371 21095).

78. Surits to Litvinov, Nov. 27, 1937, *DVP*, XX, 630–634.

79. Coulondre, no. 569, Nov. 16, 1937, *DDF*, 2ᵉ, VII, 433–435; Coulondre, no. 288, Nov. 29, 1937, *ibid*., 550–552; Coulondre, no. 306, Dec. 15, 1937, *ibid*., 715–719; and Coulondre, nos. 20–29, Jan. 12, 1938, *ibid*., 878–879.

80. Carley and R.K. Debo, "Always in Need of Credit: The USSR and Franco-German Economic Cooperation, 1926–1929," *French Historical Studies*, vol. 20, no. 3 (Summer 1997), 315–356; Carley, "Five Kopecks for Five Kopecks," *passim*; and Carley, "Fearful Concatenation of Circumstances," *passim*.

81. Coulondre, no. 308, Dec. 27, 1937, and enclosed report of the interview, *DDF*, 2ᵉ, VII, 785–788.

82. "Memorandum by Mr. Sargent . . . ," Feb. 7, 1935, *DBFP*, 2ⁿᵈ, XII, 501–502; and Sargent's minute, April 1, 1935, C2656/55/18, PRO FO 371 18833.

83. Sargent's minute, Mar. 22, 1935, N1313/53/38, PRO FO 371 19456.

84. Alexander, *Gamelin*, pp. 242, 247, and *passim*; and P.M.H. Bell, *France and Britain, 1900–1940: Entente & Estrangement* (London, 1996).

85. "Secretary of State," Vansittart, Mar. 31, 1936, C2702/4/18, PRO FO 371 19900.

86. Minutes by Stanhope, Apr. 6, 1936, and by Vansittart, Mar. 30, 1936, C2202/4/18, PRO FO 371 19896.

87. Carley, "Generals, Statesmen," pp. 310–311.

88. Post, *Dilemmas of Appeasement*, pp. 290–291 and *passim*.

89. Winston S. Churchill, *The Gathering Storm* (Boston, 1948), p. 391.

90. Alexander, *Gamelin*, pp. 242, 249, 255, 263–264, 271–272.

91. Post, *Dilemmas*, p. 207, n. 44; and Alexander, *Gamelin*, p. 296.

92. Anthony Adamthwaite, "French Military Intelligence and the Coming of War, 1935–1939," in Christopher Andrews and Jeremy Noakes, eds., *Intelligence and International Relations, 1900–1945* (Exeter, 1987), p. 194; and Douglas Porch, *The French Secret Services: From the Dreyfus Affair to the Gulf War* (New York, 1995), pp. 145–146.

93. Robert J. Young, "French Military Intelligence," in Ernest R. May, ed., *Knowing One's Enemies: Intelligence Assessment Before the Two World Wars* (Princeton, 1986), pp. 302–309.

94. Alexander, *Gamelin*, pp. 212, 282. Alexander quotes from Robert J. Young, "The Aftermath of Munich: The Course of French Diplomacy, October 1938 to March 1939," *French Historical Studies*, vol. 8, no. 2 (Fall 1973), 304–322.

95. Peter Jackson, "French Military Intelligence and Czechoslovakia, 1938," *Diplomacy & Statecraft*, vol. 5, no. 1 (March 1994), 81–106.

96. Carley, "Low, Dishonest Decade," p. 311; and Churchill, *Gathering Storm*, p. 322.

97. "The Proposed Eastern Pact," Sargent, Jan. 28, 1935, C962/55/18, PRO FO 371 18825.

98. Sargent's minute, Aug. 12, 1936, *DBFP*, 2nd series, XVII, 90–91.

99. Phipps to Sargent, Apr. 4, 1935, C2892/55/18, PRO FO 371 18834; and Sargent's minute, Apr. 12, 1935, *ibid.*

100. "Record of a Discussion which took place between the Prime Minister and a deputation from both Houses of Parliament on July 28, 1936," 106 pp., PRO PREM1/193.

101. "Extract from Cabinet Conclusions," 56 (38), Nov. 22, 1938, N5798/328/38, PRO FO 371 22295.

102. Christopher Andrew, *Secret Service: The Making of the British Intelligence Community* (London, 1987), p. 579; Wesley Wark, "Something Very Stern: British Political Intelligence, Moralism and Grand Strategy in 1939," *Intelligence and National Security*, vol. 5, no. 1 (January 1990), 155, 167; and Peter Jackson, "Recent Journeys Along the Road Back to France, 1940," *The Historical Journal*, vol. 39, no. 2 (1996), 502.

103. Alexander, *Gamelin*, p. 292; Young, "French Military Intelligence," pp. 297, 302; Adamthwaite, "French Military Intelligence and the Coming of War," pp. 197–198; and du Réau, *Daladier*, p. 348.

104. Chilston to Halifax, no. 307, July 2, 1937, N3374/97/38, PRO FO 371 22289.

Chapter 2. "Thou Art Weighed in the Balance and Found Wanting"

1. Manchester, *Caged Lion*, p. 299.

2. Churchill, *Gathering Storm*, pp. 326–328; and Manchester, *Caged Lion*, pp. 368–371.

3. Surits to Narkomindel, Feb. 15, 1938, *DVP*, XXI, 77–78; Surits to Narkomindel, immediate, Feb. 22, 1938, *ibid.*, 84; and Coulondre, nos. 250–260, Mar. 13, 1938, *DDF*, 2e, VIII, 772–774.

4. Surits to Narkomindel, Mar. 15, 1938, *DVP*, XXI, 126–127; and Maiskii to Narkomindel, highest priority, Mar. 18, 1938, *ibid.*, pp. 132–134.

5. Excerpt from Osusky to Kamil Krofta, Czech foreign minister, Dec. 11, 1937, *Dokumenty po istorii miunkhenskogo sgovora, 1937–1939* [hereafter *DIMS*] (Moscow, 1979), pp. 19–20; and excerpt from Osusky to Krofta, Mar. 4, 1938, *ibid.*, pp. 38–40.

6. Maiskii to Narkomindel, Mar. 24, 1938, *DVP*, XXI, 151–153.

7. Maiskii to Narkomindel, May 13, 1938, *DVP*, XXI, 253–255

8. Chamberlain to Ida, Mar. 20, 1938, University of Birmingham, Neville Chamberlain papers [hereafter Chamberlain papers], NC18/1/1042.

9. Maiskii to Narkomindel, immediate, May 11, 1938, *DVP*, XXI 246–247.

10. Chamberlain to Hilda, Apr. 10, 1937, NC18/1/1001, Chamberlain papers; Chamberlain to Hilda, Feb. 27, 1938, NC18/1/1040, *ibid.*; and Chamberlain to Ida, Apr. 9, 1939, NC18/1/1093, *ibid.*

11. Chamberlain to Ida, Dec. 12, 1937, NC18/1/1031, Chamberlain papers.

12. Parker, *Chamberlain*, pp. 1–11; Taylor, *Munich*, pp. 548–555; Taylor, *Origins*, p. 277 and *passim*.

13. Hugh Ragsdale, "Soviet Military Preparations and Policy in the Munich Crisis: New Evidence," *Jahrbücher für Geschichte Osteuropas*, forthcoming, 1999; Joseph Paul-Boncour, *Entre deux guerres: souvenirs sur la IIIᵉ République*, 3 vols. (Paris, 1946), III, 58–62; Maurice Gamelin, *Servir*, 3 vols. (Paris, 1946), II, 279; and extract from Potemkin to Surits, April 4, 1938, *DIMS*, pp. 80–83.

14. Litvinov (Geneva) to Narkomindel, May 14, 1938, *DIMS*, pp. 100–102; and Litvinov to S.S. Aleksandrovskii, Soviet ambassador in Prague, May 25, 1938, *ibid.*, pp. 121–123.

15. Anthony Adamthwaite, *France and the Coming of the Second World War, 1936–1939* [hereafter *France*] (London, 1977), pp. 103ff; Sherwood, *Mandel*, pp. 211, 213; and Parker, *Chamberlain*, pp. 140–141.

16. Churchill, *Gathering Storm*, p. 301; and Vansittart's minute, Jan. 3, 1940, C20885/90/17, PRO FO 371 22915.

17. Phipps, no. 717 saving, Sept. 28, 1939, C15288/25/17, PRO FO 371 22910.

18. Coulondre, nos. 324–327, Apr. 24, 1938, *DDF*, 2ᵉ, IX, 471–472.

19. Coulondre, no. 134. confidential and urgent, Apr. 28, 1938, *DDF*, 2ᵉ, IX, 553–555.

20. Excerpt of a letter from Osusky to Beneš, June 8, 1938, *DIMS*, pp. 134–135.

21. Oliphant's minute, Apr. 26, 1938, N1984/26/38, PRO FO 371 22286.

22. Coulondre, no. 121, Apr. 15, 1938, enclosing Palasse's report, *DDF*, 2ᵉ, IX, 390–394; and "Note pour le colonel Palasse . . . ," no. 1356 2/EMA-SAE, signed General Henri-Fernand Dentz, deputy chief of staff, May 30, 1938, SHAT 7N 3186. Cf. Young, "French Military Intelligence," p. 297.

23. Taylor, *Munich*, p. 394.

24. "Note d'audience du Ministre," May 22, 1938, *DDF*, 2ᵉ, IX, 846–847; and Bonnet to Léon Noël, French ambassador in Warsaw, no. 390, May 23, 1938, MAE Papiers 1940, Varsovie, Télégrammes, départs, 1938–1940.

25. Noël, no. 293, May 31, 1938, *DDF*, 2ᵉ, IX, 973–979.

26. Surits to Narkomindel, highest priority, May 25, 1938, *DVP*, XXI, 286–287.

27. Noël, no. 433, very confidential, Apr. 26, 1938, *DDF*, 2ᵉ, IX, 509–510; and Noël, nos. 472–474, May 10, 1938, *ibid.*, 673.

28. "From notes of a conversation . . . with the president of the Czechoslovak Republic," Aleksandrovskii, May 18, 1938, *DIMS*, pp. 103–107.

29. Noël to Bonnet, no. 556, June 3, 1938, *DDF*, 2ᵉ, IX, 1011–1012.

30. Litvinov to Surits, June 5, 1938, *DIMS*, p. 132; and Coulondre to Bonnet, nos. 419–421, June 8, 1938, *DDF*, 2ᵉ, IX, 1025–1026.

31. Girshfel'd to Litvinov, immediate, June 8, 1938, *DVP*, XXI, 315–316.

32. Girshfel'd to Narkomindel, June 14, 1938, *DVP*, XXI, 333.

33. Pertinax, *Les Fossoyeurs*, II, 43; Geneviève Tabouis, *They Called Me Cassandra* (New York, 1942), p. 207; and Gamelin, *Servir*, II, 360.

34. Noël, no. 293, May 31, 1938, *DDF*, 2e, IX, 973–979; and Coulondre, *De Staline à Hitler*, pp. 21, 197.

35. Parker, *Chamberlain*, pp. 141–146; and Taylor, *Munich*, pp. 508–510.

36. J.C. Cairns, "Reflections on France, Britain and the Winter War Prodrome, 1939–1940," *Historical Reflections*, vol. 22, no. 1 (Winter 1996), 211–234; Adamthwaite, *France*, pp. 95–98; and Jules E. Jeanneney (Jean-Noël Jeanneney, ed.), *Journal politique, septembre 1939–juillet 1942* (Paris, 1972), entry of May 9, 1940, pp. 44–45.

37. Kurt Bräuer, German chargé d'affaires in Paris, to German foreign ministry, no. 433, Sept. 7, 1938, *Documents on German Foreign Policy* [hereafter *DGFP*], series D, 7 vols. (London, Paris, and Washington, D.C., 1949–1956), II, 712–714; and William Bullitt, U.S. ambassador in Paris, to Cordell Hull, secretary of state, rush, Sept. 27, 1938, Orville H. Bullitt, ed., *For the President Personal and Secret: Correspondence Between Franklin D. Roosevelt and William C. Bullitt* (Boston, 1972), pp. 292–293.

38. Maiskii to Narkomindel, immediate, Aug. 6, 1938, *DVP*, XXI, 424–427.

39. Maiskii to Narkomindel, immediate, Aug. 10, 1938, *DVP*, XXI, 428–430.

40. Maiskii to Narkomindel, immediate, Aug. 17, 1938, *DVP*, XXI, 435–437.

41. Excerpt from Osusky to the Czech foreign ministry, July 22, 1938, *DIMS*, pp. 150–151.

42. Surits to Litvinov, July 27, 1938, *DVP*, XX, 392–402; and Surits to Narkomindel, July 17, 1938, *ibid.*, 728.

43. "Record of a conversation . . . with . . . Krofta," Aleksandrovskii, July 27, 1938, *DVP*, XXI, 402–405.

44. Fierlinger to Czech foreign ministry, June 18, 1938, *DIMS*, pp. 139–140.

45. Coulondre, no. 193, July 12, 1938, *DDF*, 2e, X, 362–363; and Coulondre, nos. 419–421, June 8, 1938, *DDF*, 2e, IX, 1025–1026.

46. Coulondre, nos. 336–337, Apr. 25, 1938, MAE BC, Télégrammes à l'arrivée de Moscou, 1938–1939; and Coulondre, nos. 578, July 26, 1938, *ibid.*

47. Coulondre, no. 223, July 27, 1938, *DDF*, 2e, X, 519–520.

48. Coulondre, nos. 592–594, Aug. 2, 1938, *DDF*, 2e, X, 565; Coulondre, nos. 606–610, Aug. 8, 1938, MAE BC, Télégrammes à l'arrivée de Moscou; Coulondre, nos. 624–626, Aug. 13, 1938, *ibid.*; and Palasse to Daladier, no. 493/S, Aug. 21, 1938, *DDF*, 2e, X, 763–765. There are several favorable estimates by Palasse of the result of fighting between Red Army and Japanese forces in SHAT 7N 3123, but followed in October by Palasse's report of the disappearance of Marshall V.K. Bliukher, the Soviet commander-in-chief in the Far East (Palasse, no. 506/S, Oct. 14, 1938, SHAT 7N 3123). Cf. Jonathan Haslam, *The Soviet Union and the Threat from the East: Moscow, Tokyo and the Prelude to the Pacific War* (Pittsburgh, 1992), pp. 114–121.

49. Maiskii to Narkomindel, immediate, Sept. 2, 1938, *DVP*, XXI, 473–475.

50. Litvinov to Aleksandrovskii and A.F. Merekalov, Soviet ambassador in Berlin, Aug. 22, 1938, *DIMS*, pp. 174–175.

51. Krofta to Osusky and Masaryk, Aug. 25, 1938, *DIMS*, p. 178; Roger Cambon, French chargé d'affaires in London, no. 2096, Aug. 26, 1938, *DDF*, 2e, IX, 831; and Bonnet to Coulondre (Payart), nos. 493–494, Aug. 27, 1938, *ibid.*, 843.

52. "From a note of conversation . . . with the French chargé d'affaires in the USSR," Potemkin, Aug. 29, 1938, *DIMS*, pp. 182–183; and Payart, nos. 640–642, Aug. 30, 1938, *DDF*, 2e, IX, 874–875.

53. Bonnet to Payart, nos. 498–502, Aug. 31, 1938, *DDF*, 2ᵉ, IX, pp. 899–900; and "Record of a conversation . . . with the French chargé d'affaires in the USSR," Potemkin, Sept. 1, 1938, *DIMS*, pp. 185–187.

54. Litvinov to Aleksandrovskii, Sept. 2, 1938, *DIMS*, pp. 187–188.

55. Payart, nos. 653–659, Sept. 2, 1938, *DDF*, 2ᵉ, IX, 934–935; Payart, no. 661, Sept. 4, 1938, MAE BC, Télégrammes à l'arrivée de Moscou; Litvinov to Surits, Sept. 2, 1938, *DVP*, XXI, 471; and Victor de Lacroix, French minister in Prague, nos. 1854–1856, Aug. 31, 1938, *DDF*, 2ᵉ, X, 905. Cf. Jonathan Haslam, *The Soviet Union and the Struggle for Collective Security in Europe, 1933–1939* (New York, 1984), pp. 178–181.

56. Surits to Narkomindel, immediate, Sept. 3, 1938, *DVP*, XXI, 477.

57. Maiskii to Potemkin, Sept. 5, 1938, *DIMS*, pp. 190–191.

58. Churchill, *Gathering Storm*, pp. 294–295.

59. Hugh Dalton, *The Fateful Years: Memoirs 1931–1945* (London, 1957), pp. 179–185.

60. "Record of a conversation . . . with the French chargé d'affaires in the USSR," Potemkin, Sept. 5, 1938, *DIMS*, pp. 192–193.

61. Payart, no. 249, Sept. 5, 1938, *DDF*, 2ᵉ, X, 16–18.

62. "Note de la Direction politique: mise en oeuvre éventuelle du pacte soviéto-tchécoslovaque," Sept. 6, 1938, *DDF*, 2ᵉ, XI, 43–45.

63. Aleksandrovskii to Narkomindel, Sept. 7 1938, *DIMS*, pp. 195–196; and excerpt "From a record of a conversation . . . with the British ambassador in the USSR," Potemkin, Sept. 8, 1938, *ibid.*, pp. 197–198.

64. "Record of a conversation . . . with the French ambassador in the USSR," Potemkin, Sept. 11, 1938, *DIMS*, pp. 205–207.

65. Coulondre, nos. 670–677, Sept. 11, 1938, *DDF*, 2ᵉ, XI, 153–155.

66. Litvinov (Geneva) to Narkomindel, Sept. 11, 1938, *DIMS*, pp. 207–208.

67. Cf. Litvinov (Paris) to Narkomindel, highest priority, Oct. 2, 1938, *DVP*, XXI, 555–556.

68. "Notes du Ministre, Conversation avec M. Litvinov," Geneva, Sept. 11, 1938, *DDF*, 2ᵉ, XI, 159–160; and "Note du Ministre, Conversation avec M. Comnène," Geneva, Sept. 11, 1938, *ibid.*, 161. Cf. Dov B. Lungu, *Romania and the Great Powers, 1933–1940* (Durham, N.C., and London, 1989), pp. 130–135.

69. Robert Rhodes James, ed., *Chips: The Diaries of Sir Henry Channon* (London, 1967), entries of Sept. 9, 10, 13, 16, 1938, pp. 164–167.

70. Fierlinger to Czech foreign ministry, Sept. 15, 1938, *DIMS*, p. 215.

71. Coulondre, nos. 687–690, Sept. 15, 1938, *DDF*, 2ᵉ, XI, 245–246.

72. Potemkin to Litvinov (Geneva), Sept. 15, 1938, *DVP*, XXI, 495–496; and "Record of conversation . . . with Fierlinger," Potemkin, Sept. 15, 1938, *ibid.*, 494–495.

73. Maiskii to Litvinov, immediate, Oct. 13, 1938, *DVP*, XXI, 584–585. Cf. Igor Lukes, *Czechoslovakia Between Stalin and Hitler: The Diplomacy of Edvard Beneš in the 1930s* (New York, 1996), p. 197. Lukes gives a somewhat different account of this meeting, based on a Czech source or Czech translation. This is a curious scholarly procedure since Payart's account in French and Litvinov's in Russian have both been published, and may be compared. Moreover, in a book with such categorical conclusions, it is surprising how little Lukes refers to the *DDF* or *DVP* collections.

74. Masaryk to Czech foreign ministry, Sept. 14, 1938, *DIMS*, pp. 211–212; G.A. Astakhov, Soviet chargé d'affaires in Berlin, to Narkomindel, Sept. 15, 1938, *ibid.*, pp. 216–217; Fierlinger to Czech foreign ministry, Sept. 13, 1938, *ibid.*, pp.

209–210; and William L. Shirer, *The Collapse of the Third Republic: An Inquiry into the Fall of France in 1940* (New York, 1969), pp. 358–359.

75. Litvinov (Geneva) to Narkomindel, Sept. 15, 1938, DIMS, pp. 213–214.

76. Fierlinger to Czech foreign ministry, Sept. 19, 1938, DIMS, p. 236.

77. Coulondre, nos. 694–696, Sept. 17, 1938, DDF, 2ᵉ, XI, 278–279.

78. Pierre Arnal, secretary general of the French delegation at the League of Nations, to Bonnet, no. 144, Sept. 18, 1938, DDF, 2ᵉ, XI, 299–300.

79. *Channon Diaries*, entry of Sept. 14, 1938, p. 166.

80. Adamthwaite, *France*, pp. 202, 239–240; and Alexander, *Gamelin*, pp. 163–167.

81. Fierlinger to Czech foreign ministry, Sept. 20, 1938, DIMS, pp. 240–241; cf. Taylor, *Munich*, pp. 778–791; Shirer, *Collapse*, pp. 363–369; and Dalton, *Fateful Years*, p. 185.

82. Émile Charvériat, member of French delegation at League of Nations, to Bonnet, no. 156, Sept. 21, 1938, DDF, 2ᵉ, pp. 398–399; and Litvinov's speech to the assembly of the League of Nations, Sept. 21, 1938, DVP, XXI, 501–509.

83. Litvinov (Geneva) to Narkomindel, "immediately . . . send to the Kremlin," Sept. 23, 1938, DIMS, pp. 278–279.

84. Litvinov (Geneva) to Narkomindel, highest priority, Sept. 23, 1938, DVP, XXI, p. 520; cf. Haslam, *Collective Security*, pp. 187–188.

85. Surits to Narkomindel, immediate, Sept. 24, 1938, DVP, XXI, 527–528; and Surits to Narkomindel, Sept. 24, 1938, *ibid.*, p. 528.

86. Dalton, *Fateful Years*, p. 190.

87. Masaryk to Czech foreign ministry, Sept. 24, 1938, DIMS, p. 284; S.B. Kagan to Narkomindel, Sept. 24, 1938, *ibid.*, pp. 284–286; and Gilbert, *Prophet of Truth*, p. 985.

88. Voroshilov to N.N. Vasil'chenko, Sept. 25, 1938, DIMS, p. 293; G. Jukes, "The Red Army and the Munich Crisis," *Journal of Contemporary History*, vol. 26 (1991), 195–214; Hugh Ragsdale, "Soviet Actions during the Munich Crisis of 1938," resumé of a paper given at the Kennan Institute, Washington, D.C., June 1998; and Ragsdale, "Soviet Military Preparations and Policy in the Munich Crisis: New Evidence," *Jahrbücher für Geschichte Osteuropas*. Cf. Lukes, *Czechoslovakia*, p. 268, n. 111. Lukes doubts whether there was a mobilization, or if there was, how extensive it might have been. He even questions whether the alleged mobilization related to the Czech crisis at all. These are puzzling conclusions, perhaps explained by the desire of a Czech emigré to carry on the cold war against the Czech communist left. His book's impressive research in Czech archives conceals a political tract and a somewhat hagiographical and antiquarian treatment of Beneš.

89. Sherwood, *Mandel*, pp. 207, 211; Taylor, *Munich*, p. 879; Shirer, *Collapse*, pp. 379–380; and Vansittart's minute, Jan. 3, 1940, C20885/90/17, PRO FO 371 22915.

90. Osusky to Czech foreign ministry, Sept. 26, 1938, DIMS, p. 298.

91. Alexander, *Gamelin*, p. 167; *Channon Diaries*, entry of Sept. 23, 1938, p. 168; and "Note sur la situation actuelle du 12 octobre 1938, Avis du General Vuillemin," EMA, SHAT 5N 579.

92. Surits to Narkomindel, Sept. 27, 1938, DIMS, p. 300. Unless otherwise noted, see Parker, *Chamberlain*; Duroselle, *Décadence*; and Taylor, *Munich* for more details of these events.

93. Shirer, *Collapse*, pp. 384–385; Sherwood, *Mandel*, p. 211; Taylor, *Munich*, p. 879; and Charles Micaud, *The French Right and Nazi Germany, 1933–1939* (New York, 1964 reprint), p. 172.

94. "Notes du Directeur politique," Sept. 22, 1938, DDF, 2ᵉ, XI, 448–449; and

Aleksandrovskii to Narkomindel, by telephone, Sept. 22, 1938, *DVP*, XXI, 515–516.

95. "Record of a conversation . . . with the Polish chargé d'affaires in the USSR Jankowski," Potemkin, Sept. 23, 1938, *DVP*, XXI, 516–517.

96. "Record of a conversation . . . with the French ambassador in the USSR," Potemkin, Sept. 23, 1938, *DIMS*, pp. 269–270; and Coulondre, nos. 713–716, Sept. 23, 1938, *DDF*, 2ᵉ, XI, 486–487.

97. Coulondre, nos. 718–719, Sept. 23, 1938, MAE BC, Télégrammes à l'arrivée de Moscou; and Coulondre, nos. 724–727, Sept. 27, 1938, *ibid.*

98. Bonnet to Coulondre, nos. 541–542, Sept. 24, 1938, MAE BC, Télégrammes à l'arrivée de Moscou; Bonnet to Coulondre, nos. 551–554, Sept. 26, 1938, *ibid.*; Coulondre, nos. 724–727, Sept. 27, 1938, *ibid.*; Noël, nos. 929–931, Sept. 24, 1938, *DDF*, 2ᵉ, XI, 495–496; and Bonnet to Noël, nos. 650–651, Sept. 25, 1938, *ibid.*, 529–530.

99. Coulondre, no. 720, Sept. 24, 1938, MAE BC, Télégrammes à l'arrivée de Moscou; Coulondre, nos. 724–727, Sept. 27, 1938, *ibid.*; "Note du directeur politique, Démarche de l'attaché militaire soviétique," Sept. 26, 1938, *DDF*, 2ᵉ, XI, 581; and Bonnet to Coulondre, no. 555, Sept. 28, 1938, *ibid.*, 632.

100. Parker, *Chamberlain*, pp. 178–179; *Channon Diaries*, entry of Sept. 28, 1938, p. 171; Maiskii to Narkomindel, Sept. 28, 1938, *DIMS*, p. 310; and Maiskii to Narkomindel, Sept. 29, 1938, *ibid.*, pp. 319–320.

101. Parker, *Chamberlain*, pp. 179–181.

102. Bonnet to Noël, no. 685, Oct. 1, 1938, *DDF*, 2ᵉ, XI, 739.

103. Coulondre, no. 742, Oct. 1, 1938, MAE BC, Télégrammes à l'arrivée de Moscou.

104. Churchill, *Gathering Storm*, pp. 322–323.

105. Manchester, *Churchill*, p. 359; and Parker, *Chamberlain*, pp. 179–181.

106. Manchester, *Caged Lion*, p. 371; Churchill, *Gathering Storm*, pp. 326–328; Gilbert, *Prophet of Truth* 996–1001; Taylor, *Munich*, p. 903; Dalton, *Fateful Years*, p. 198; and *Channon Diaries*, entries of Sept. 30 and Nov. 2, 1938, pp. 173, 175.

107. Sherwood, *Mandel*, p. 212; Shirer, *Collapse*, pp. 403–405; Manchester, *Caged Lion*, pp. 358–359; du Réau, *Daladier*, pp. 280–281, 285; and Serge Berstein and Jean-Jacques Becker, *Histoire de l'anti-communisme, 1917–1940* (Paris, 1987), pp. 309–319.

108. Maiskii to Narkomindel, Oct. 2, 1938, *DIMS*, pp. 342–344.

109. Litvinov (Paris) to Narkomindel, highest priority, Oct. 2, 1938, *DVP*, XXI, 555–556.

110. Coulondre, no. 744, Oct. 4, 1938, *DDF*, 2ᵉ, XI, 18–19; Coulondre, nos. 745–748, Oct. 5, 1938, MAE BC, Télégrammes à l'arrivée de Moscou; and Coulondre, nos. 758–761, Oct. 12, 1938, *ibid.*

111. Coulondre, no. 265, Oct. 4, 1938, MAE Papiers 1940, Cabinet Bonnet/16, ff. 327–333.

112. Surits to Litvinov, Oct. 12, 1938, *DVP*, XXI, 575–581.

113. Maiskii to Narkomindel, immediate, Oct. 11, 1938, *DVP*, XXI, 571–574; Maiskii to Narkomindel, immediate, Oct. 13, 1938, *ibid.*, 584–585.

114. R.H. Hadow, Foreign Office, to Phipps, no. 2124, Sept. 19, 1938, N4454/26/38, PRO FO 371 22287; Phipps, no. 1139, immediate, Oct. 6, 1938, N4901/26/38, *ibid.*; Phipps, no. 345, Oct. 7, 1938, N4914/26/38, *ibid.*, Collier's minute, Oct. 8, 1938, *ibid.*; Collier's minute, Oct. 28, 1938, N5164/97/38, PRO FO 371 22289; and Maiskii to Narkomindel, immediate, Oct. 26, 1938, *DVP*, XXI, 608.

115. "Record of a conversation . . . with Coulondre," Litvinov, Oct. 16, 1938, *DVP*, XXI, 589–590.

116. Coulondre, no. 283, Oct. 18, 1938, AN Papiers Daladier, 496AP/11.

117. Surits to Narkomindel, Oct. 18, 1938, *DVP*, XXI, 740; and Litvinov to Surits, Oct. 19, 1938, *ibid.*, 594.

118. Litvinov to Surits, Oct. 22, 1938, *DVP*, XXI, 600–601.

119. Coulondre, nos. 770–773, Oct. 19, 1938, MAE BC, Télégrammes à l'arrivée de Moscou; Litvinov to Surits, Oct. 19, 1938, *DVP*, XXI, 741; and Litvinov to Surits, Nov. 4, 1938, *ibid.*, 618–619.

120. Chilston to Halifax, no. 442, Oct. 18, 1938, N5164/97/38, PRO FO 371 22289.

121. "S. of S.," Vansittart, Oct. 19, 1938, PRO FO 800 314, ff. 195–196.

122. Maiskii to Narkomindel, immediate, Oct. 13, 1938, *DVP*, XXI, pp. 584–585.

123. Parker, *Chamberlain*, pp. 182–188.

124. Maiskii to Narkomindel, immediate, Oct. 19, 1938, *DVP*, XXI, 594–596.

125. Maiskii to Narkomindel, immediate, Oct. 25, 1938, *DVP*, XXI, pp. 605–606.

126. Maiskii to Narkomindel, immediate, Nov. 13, 1938, *DVP*, XXI, 637.

127. Litvinov to Surits, Nov. 4, 1938, *DVP*, XXI, 618–619.

128. "Record of a conversation . . . with . . . Payart," Litvinov, Nov. 20, 1938, *DVP*, XXI, 642–643.

129. Payart, nos. 787–794, Nov. 23, 1938, *DDF*, 2^e, XII, 726–727.

Chapter 3. "1939 Will Be the Decisive Year"

1. Charmley, *Chamberlain*, p. 144; and Cowling, *Impact of Hitler*, p. 281.

2. Adamthwaite, *France*, pp. 256–257.

3. Minutes by Sargent, Alexander Cadogan, permanent under secretary (Vansittart's successor), and Halifax, Oct. 21–25, 1938, C12637/55/17, PRO FO 371 21600.

4. Adamthwaite, *France*, pp. 265–266; and Phipps, no. 1326, Nov. 16, 1938, C14025/55/17, PRO FO 371 21600.

5. "Conversations franco-britanniques du 24 novembre 1938, comptes rendus," *DDF*, 2^e, XII, 754ff., especially 777.

6. "Record of a conversation . . . with Lloyd George," Maiskii, Dec. 6, 1938, *DVP*, XXI, 661–662; and "Record of a conversation . . . with . . . Vansittart," Maiskii, Dec. 8, 1938, *ibid.*, 663–664.

7. Surits to Narkomindel, Dec. 8, 1938, *DVP*, XXI, 662–663.

8. Tabouis, *They Called Me Cassandra*, p. 379; cf. Duroselle, *Décadence*, pp. 386–389.

9. Litvinov to Surits, Dec. 10, 1938, *DVP*, XXI, 666–667.

10. For example, Raymond Patenôtre and César Campinchi (Surits to Narkomindel, Dec. 22, 1938, *DVP*, XXI, 688–689).

11. "Note sur la situation actuelle," very secret, Colson, nd, but covered by Gamelin to Daladier, no. 936/DN.3, Oct. 26, 1938, SHAT 5N 579.

12. Palasse, no. 507/S, Oct. 18, 1938, SHAT 7N 3123.

13. John Harvey, ed., *The Diplomatic Diaries of Oliver Harvey, 1937–1940* (London, 1970), entry of Nov. 18, 1938, p. 222.

14. Bullitt to Roosevelt, personal and confidential, Feb. 1, 1939, *For the President*, pp. 305–308; and Bullitt to Roosevelt, personal and secret, May 20, 1938, *ibid.*, pp. 261–264.

15. Tabouis, *They Called Me Cassandra*, pp. 386–387.

16. Maiskii to Litvinov, Jan. 10, 1939, Ministerstvo inostrannykh del SSSR, *God krizisa: dokumenty i materialy* [hereafter *God krizisa*], 2 vols. (Moscow, 1990), I, 179–182.

17. Cowling, *Impact of Hitler*, p. 169.

18. Harold Caccia's memorandum, Jan. 3, 1939, and attached minutes, Jan. 5–21, 1939, N57/57/38, PRO FO 371 23677.

19. *Channon Diaries*, entry of Dec. 5, 1937, p. 141.

20. Maiskii to Narkomindel, Jan. 20, 1939, V.M. Falin, et al., eds., *Soviet Peace Efforts on the Eve of World War II (September 1938–August 1939)* [hereafter *SPE*], 2 vols. (Moscow, 1973), I, 178–180.

21. Merekalov to Narkomindel, Jan. 5, 1939, *God krizisa*, I, 167–168; and Mikoian to Merekalov, Jan. 8, 1939, *ibid.*, 177.

22. Merekalov to Narkomindel, Jan. 12, 1939, *God krizisa*, I, 185–186. Cf. Anthony Read and David Fisher, *The Deadly Embrace: Hitler, Stalin, and the Nazi-Soviet Pact, 1939–1941* (New York, 1988), pp. 49–51; and Fleischhauer, *Pakt*, pp. 79–80. Schulenberg invited Merekalov to dine at his residence in Moscow on November 15 and December 2, 1938. Schulenberg intended to set in motion an improvement of German-Soviet relations (Fleischhauer, *Pakt*, pp. 67, 69, 75–76).

23. "Record of a conversation . . . with . . . E. Wiehl," Merekalov, Jan. 20, 1939, *God krizisa*, I, 191–192.

24. Collier's minutes of Jan. 24, 28, 30, 1939, N492/243/38, PRO FO 371 23686; N464/243/38, *ibid.*; N511/92/38, PRO FO 371 23680; and Payart, nos. 34–37, Jan. 27, 1939, *DDF*, 2ᵉ, XIII, 805.

25. Merekalov to Narkomindel and Narkomvneshtorg [commissariat for external trade], Jan. 28, 1939, *God krizisa*, I, 200–201.

26. Excerpt from Litvinov to Merekalov, Feb. 4, 1939, *God krizisa*, I, 213.

27. Payart, nos. 50–52, Jan. 31, 1939, MAE BC, Télégrammes à l'arrivée de Moscou.

28. Payart nos. 53–58, Feb. 1, 1939, MAE BC, Télégrammes à l'arrivée de Moscou.

29. Payart, nos. 66–67, 72–78, Feb 5–6, 1939, MAE BC, Télégrammes à l'arrivée de Moscou; and Potemkin to Surits, Feb. 4, 1939, *DVP*, XXII, bk. 1, 98–100.

30. Merekalov to Narkomindel, Feb. 6, 1939, *God krizisa*, I, 215; and "Record of a conversation . . . with . . . Schulenberg," Potemkin, Feb. 18, 1939, *ibid.*, 231. Cf. Fleischhauer, *Pakt*, pp. 83–91.

31. "Record of a conversation . . . with . . . Seeds," Litvinov, Feb. 19, 1939, *God krizisa*, I, 233–234; and Seeds, no. 24, Feb. 19, 1939, N902/57/38, PRO FO 371 23677.

32. "Record of a conversation . . . with . . . Naggiar," Potemkin, secret, Feb. 9, 1939, *DVP*, XXII, bk. 1, 116–117; Litvinov to Surits, Feb. 10, 1939, *ibid.*, 119; and Naggiar, nos. 82–88, Feb. 9, 1939, MAE Papiers Naggiar/10.

33. Surits to Litvinov, secret, Feb. 11, 1939, *DVP*, XXII, bk. 1, 122–128; and Surits to Narkomindel, Feb. 10, 1939, *SPE*, I, 209.

34. Litvinov to Maiskii, Feb. 19, 1939, *God krizisa*, I, 231–232.

35. Naggiar, no. 134, Feb. 24, 1939, MAE Papiers Naggiar/10.

36. Maiskii to Narkomindel, Mar. 2, 1939, *God krizisa*, I, 246–248.

37. Litvinov to Maiskii, Mar. 4, 1939, *God krizisa*, I, 248–250. Cameron Watt says that Litvinov and Maiskii, ideologically blinkered, did not notice the gradual change in British policy, but clearly they did (*How War Came*, p. 120).

38. Haslam, *Threat from the East, passim*.

39. "Secretary of State," Hudson, Mar. 8, 1939, N1389/57/38, PRO FO 371 23677.

40. Maiskii to Narkomindel, highest priority, very secret, Mar. 8, 1939, *DVP*, XXII, bk. 1, 169–171. Cameron Watt mistakenly says that the Hudson mission was only "a narrow exercise in trade promotion" (*How War Came*, p. 119).

41. Butler's untitled note, Mar. 9, 1939, N1342/57/38, PRO FO 371 23677.

42. Maiskii to Narkomindel, immediate, very secret, Mar. 9, 1939, *DVP*, XXII, bk. 1, 172–173.

43. "From the report of the central committee VKP (b), 18th congress of the VKP (b)," Mar. 10, 1939, *God krizisa*, I, 258–264; and Seeds, no. 93, Mar. 20, 1939, *DBFP*, 3rd series, 9 vols. (London, 1949–1957), IV, 411–419.

44. E.g., Watt, *How War Came*, pp. 110–111; and Fleischhauer, *Pakt*, pp. 96–104.

45. Maiskii to Narkomindel, immediate, very secret, Mar. 14, 1939, *DVP*, XXII, bk. 1, 183–184.

46. *Channon Diaries*, entry of Mar. 15, 1939, p. 186; and Astakhov to Litvinov, secret, Mar. 17, 1939, *DVP*, XXII, bk. 1, 200–201.

47. Excerpts from Astakhov's journal, Mar. 14–16, 1939, *DVP*, XXII, bk. 1, 184–188.

48. Chamberlain to Hilda, Feb. 5, 1939, NC18/1/1084, Chamberlain papers; and David Dilks, ed., *The Diaries of Sir Alexander Cadogan, 1938–1945* (London, 1971), entry of Mar. 26, 1939, p. 163.

49. Aster, *1939*, pp. 61–65; and *Channon Diaries*, entry of Mar. 18, 1939, p. 187.

50. Parker, *Chamberlain*, pp. 200–205.

51. Maiskii to Narkomindel, immediate, very secret, Mar. 17, 1939, *DVP*, XXII, bk. 1, 196–197.

52. Maiskii to Narkomindel, Mar. 18, 1939, *God krizisa*, I, 292–293.

53. Litvinov to Maiskii and Surits, Mar. 18, 1939, *God krizisa*, I, 293–294; Litvinov to Maiskii and Surits, Mar. 18, 1939, *ibid.*, 294; Litvinov to Maiskii and Surits, Mar. 19, 1939, *ibid.*, 295; and "To the general secretary TsK VKP (b) I.V. Stalin," secret, Litvinov, Mar. 18, 1939, *DVP*, XXII, bk. 1, 201–202.

54. Maiskii to Litvinov, Mar. 19, 1939, *God krizisa*, I, 296; Maiskii to Litvinov, Mar. 19, 1939, *ibid.*, 296–297; and Aster, *1939*, pp. 69–74, 82.

55. Surits to Narkomindel, Mar. 20, 1939, *God krizisa*, I, 307–308; and "Conversation du 20 mars avec Monsieur Souritz," Bonnet, MAE Papiers 1940, Cabinet Bonnet/16, f. 102.

56. "To the general secretary TsK VKP (b) I.V. Stalin," secret, Litvinov, Mar. 20, 1939, *DVP*, XXII, bk. 1, 209–211; and Litvinov to Maiskii, secret, Mar. 19, 1939, *ibid.*, 206–208.

57. Maiskii to Narkomindel, highest priority, very secret, Mar. 20, 1939, *DVP*, XXII, bk. 1, 211–212.

58. Bonnet to Naggiar, no. 52, Feb. 25, 1939, MAE Papiers Naggiar/9; and Bonnet to Naggiar, no. 53, Feb. 25, 1939, *ibid.*

59. Surits to Narkomindel, Mar. 15, 1939, *SPE*, I, 246–247.

60. "To the general secretary TsK VKP (b)," secret, Litvinov, Mar. 20, 1939, *DVP*, XXII, bk. 1, 208–209.

61. "Record of an Anglo-French Conversation . . . , on March 21, 1939, at 5 p.m.," *DBFP*, 3rd, IV, 422–427.

62. Cadogan's minute on a note by Sargent, Mar. 20, 1939, C3775/3356/18, PRO FO 371 23061.

63. Litvinov to Maiskii, Mar. 20, 1939, *God krizisa*, I, 305; "Record of a conversation . . . with . . . Seeds," Litvinov, Mar. 21, 1939, *ibid.*, 308–310; Litvinov to Maiskii and Surits, Mar. 22, 1939, *ibid.*, 314; Seeds to Halifax, no. 39, Mar. 21, 1939, *DBFP*, 3rd, IV, 429; and Seeds, no. 42, Mar. 22, 1939, C3821/3356/18, PRO FO 371 23061.

64. Surits to Narkomindel, highest priority, very secret, Mar. 22, 1939, *DVP*, XXII, bk. 1, 218–219.

65. Naggiar's undated, *post facto* minute on his dispatch no. 161, July 19, 1939, MAE Papiers Naggiar/8.

66. Raymond Brugère, French minister in Belgrade, no. 97, Mar. 1, 1938, MAE Z-URSS/988, f. 59; Payart, nos. 171–175, Mar. 15, 1939, MAE Papiers Naggiar/10; and Coulondre (Berlin), no. 1203, May 4, 1939, *DDF*, 2e, XVI, 109–111.

67. Maiskii to Narkomindel, highest priority, very secret, Mar. 22, 1939, *DVP*, XXII, bk. 1, 219 (cf. Lungu, *Romania*, pp. 153–161); and *Channon Diaries*, entry of Mar. 22, 1939, p. 188.

68. Phipps, no. 114, Mar. 18, 1939, C3455/3356/18, PRO FO 371 23060.

69. W. Jędrzejewicz, ed., *Diplomat in Berlin, 1933–1939: Papers and Memoirs of Jozef Lipski* (New York, 1968), pp. 504–507; cf. Anita Prażmowska, *Britain, Poland, and the Eastern Front, 1939* (Cambridge, England, 1987), pp. 48–49, 60; and Weinberg, *Hitler's Germany*, p. 193.

70. Noël, no. 19, Jan. 4, 1939; and no. 74, Jan. 12, 1939, MAE Z-URSS/1019.

71. Payart, no. 313, Aug. 20, 1934, MAE Z-URSS/981, ff. 6–10; Jules Laroche, French ambassador in Warsaw, nos. 483–486, June 5, 1934, MAE Z-URSS/965, ff. 63–65bis; Chilston, no. 110 confidential, Mar. 9, 1935, N1313/53/38, PRO FO 371 19456; Kennard to Collier, Apr. 6, 1937, N1926/45/38, PRO FO 371 21095; and Kennard to Sargent, Nov. 30, 1938, *DBFP*, 3rd, III, 373–375.

72. Phipps, no. 114, Mar. 18, 1939; and minute by F. K. Roberts, C3455/3356/18, PRO FO 371 23060.

73. R.I. Campbell, British chargé d'affaires in Paris, no. 155 saving, Mar. 22, 1939, C3784/3356/18, PRO FO 371 23061; "Record of conversation between M. Léger and Mr. Campbell on March 18th," C3962/3356/18, *ibid.*, and "Record of an Anglo-French Conversation . . . ," Mar. 21, 1939, *DBFP*, 3rd, IV, 422–427.

74. "Record of an Anglo-French Conversation . . . , on March 21, 1939, at 5 p.m.," *DBFP*, 3rd, IV, 422–427.

75. Chamberlain to Ida, Mar. 26, 1939, NC18/1/1091, Chamberlain Papers.

76. Phipps to Halifax, no. 373, Mar. 28, 1939, *DBFP*, 3rd, IV, 535.

77. "Record of a conversation . . . with . . . Hudson," Litvinov, Mar. 23, 1939, *God krizisa*, I, 317–319; and "Statement by the People's Commissar for Foreign Affairs . . . ," Mar. 23, 1939, *SPE*, I, 280–281.

78. Seeds, no. 43, Mar. 23, 1939, C3880/3356/18, PRO FO 371 23061.

79. Seeds, no. 107, Apr. 3, 1939, C5121/3356/18, PRO FO 371 23063.

80. Seeds, no. 106, Mar. 31, 1939, N1865/92/38, PRO Treasury [hereafter T] 160 1005/F10070/030/4.

81. "Record of a conversation . . . with . . . Hudson and . . . Seeds," Litvinov, Mar. 25, 1939, *God krizisa*, I, 324–327.

82. "Record of a conversation . . . with . . . Hudson," Potemkin, Mar. 27, 1939, *God krizisa*, I, 335–337.

83. Litvinov to Maiskii, Mar. 28, 1939, *God krizisa*, I, 340–341.

84. Foreign Office to Seeds, no. 32, by telephone, most immediate, Mar. 27, 1939, PRO T 160 1005/F10070/030/4.

85. Litvinov to Maiskii, highest priority, Mar. 28, 1938, *God krizisa*, I, 339–340; "Record of a conversation . . . with . . . Cadogan," Maiskii, secret, Mar. 29, 1939, *DVP*, XXII, bk. 1, 238–240; Cadogan's untitled memorandum, Mar. 29, 1939, N1721/92/38, PRO FO 371 23681; and Maiskii to Narkomindel, Mar. 29, 1939, *God krizisa*, I, 346–347.

86. *Cadogan Diaries*, entry of Feb. 24, 1939, p. 151.

87. Litvinov to Surits, Mar. 29, 1939, *God krizisa*, I, 342–343.

88. Aster, *1939*, pp. 88–95.

89. Aster, *1939*, pp. 99–101.

90. "Record of a conversation . . . with . . . Cadogan," secret, Maiskii, Mar. 29, 1939, *DVP*, XXII, bk. 1, 238–240; and Cadogan's untitled note, Mar. 29, 1939, C4692/3356/18, PRO FO 371 23062.

91. Maiskii to Narkomindel, Mar. 31, 1939, *God krizisa*, I, 351–353; Litvinov to Maiskii, Apr. 1, 1939, *ibid.*, 354–355; Halifax to Seeds, no. 232, Mar. 31, 1939, *DBFP*, 3rd, IV, 556–558; and Seeds, no. 51, *ibid.*, 574–575.

92. Maiskii to Narkomindel, Apr. 1, 1939, *DVP*, XXII, bk. 1, 243–244.

93. E.g., Birkenhead, *Halifax*, p. 434; Prażmowska, *Britain, Poland, and the Eastern Front*, p. 52; and Aster, *1939*, pp. 94–95.

94. Maiskii to Narkomindel, Apr. 1, 1939, *DVP*, XXII, bk. 1, 243–244.

Chapter 4: "Russia Has 100 Divisions"

1. "Commercial Relations with the Soviet Union," Waley, nd (but to cabinet on Feb. 8, 1939), PRO T 160/1005/F10070/030/4.

2. Palasse to Dentz, no. 1955, June 14, 1938, SHAT 7N 3186.

3. "The Red Army," Firebrace, under cover of Seeds, no. 81, Mar. 6, 1939, *DBFP*, 3rd, IV, 188ff.

4. Maiskii to Litvinov, Apr. 2, 1939, *SPE*, I, 308–310; and Aster, *1939*, p. 157.

5. Litvinov to Maiskii, Apr. 4, 1939, *SPE*, I, 311–313.

6. Manchester, *Caged Lion*, pp. 407–409.

7. Litvinov to Merekalov, secret, Apr. 4, 1939, *DVP*, XXII, bk. 1, 252–253.

8. "Record of a conversation . . . with . . . Grzybowski," secret, Potemkin, Mar. 31, 1939, *DVP*, XXII, bk. 1, 242–243; "Memorandum of a conversation . . . ," Litvinov, Apr. 1, 1939, *SPE*, I, 302–305; "Memorandum of a conversation . . . ," Litvinov, Apr. 2, 1939, *ibid.*, 305–306; and excerpts from notes of a conversation with Grzybowski, Litvinov, Apr. 4, 1939, *God krizisa*, I, 357–359.

9. Maiskii to Narkomindel, Apr. 6, 1939, *God krizisa*, I, 361–363; Halifax to Seeds, no. 255, Apr. 6, 1939, *DBFP*, 3rd, V, 53–54; minutes by Sargent, Cadogan, Halifax, Apr. 6–8, 1939, C5430/3356/18, PRO FO 371 23063; and Aster, *1939*, pp. 159–160.

10. Payart, nos. 235–239, Apr. 2, 1939, MAE Papiers Naggiar/10.

11. Surits to Narkomindel, Apr. 4, 1939, *SPE*, I, 316–317; Surits to Narkomindel, immediate, very secret, Apr. 6, 1939, *DVP*, XXII, bk. 1, 257; and Bonnet to Payart, nos. 110–113, Apr. 6, 1939, MAE Papiers Naggiar/9.

12. Surits to Narkomindel, Apr. 7, 1939, *SPE*, I, 320–321; Surits to Narkomindel, Apr. 8, 1939, *ibid.*, 321–322; Bonnet to Payart, nos. 116–121, Apr. 9, 1939,

MAE Papiers Naggiar/9; and W.H.B. Mack (British embassy in Paris) to Central department, FO, Apr. 11, 1939, C5261/15/18, PRO FO 371 22969.

13. "To the general secretary of the TsK VKP (b) I.V. Stalin," secret, Litvinov, Apr. 9, 1939, *DVP*, XXII, bk. 1, 261–262.

14. Litvinov to Surits, Apr. 10, 1939, *God krizisa*, I, 366; and Surits to Narkomindel, highest priority, Apr. 10, 1939, *ibid.*, 367.

15. Surits to Narkomindel, Apr. 11, 1939, *God krizisa*, I, 368–370.

16. Excerpts from Litvinov to Surits, Apr. 11, 1939, *God krizisa*, I, 370–372.

17. Maiskii to Narkomindel, Apr. 11, 1939, *God krizisa*, I, 373–375; and Halifax to Seeds, no. 230, Apr. 11, 1939, C5068/3356/18, PRO FO 371 23063.

18. "To the general secretary TsK VKP(b) I.V. Stalin," secret, Litvinov, Apr. 13, 1939, *DVP*, XXII, bk. 1, 270; and Litvinov to Maiskii, very secret, Apr. 13, 1939, *ibid.*, 270–271.

19. *Channon Diaries*, entry of Apr. 3, 1939, p. 192.

20. Chamberlain to Ida, Apr. 9, 1939, NC18/1/1093, Chamberlain papers.

21. Parker, *Chamberlain*, pp. 218–223.

22. Parker, *Chamberlain*, p. 223.

23. Maiskii to Narkomindel, highest priority, very secret, Apr. 14, 1939, *DVP*, XXII, bk. 1, 273–274; and Halifax to Seeds, no. 284, Apr. 14, 1939, *DBFP*, 3rd, V, 209–210.

24. Bonnet to Payart, nos. 129–136, Apr. 15, 1939, MAE Papiers Naggiar/9; Surits to Narkomindel, Apr. 14, 1939, *God krizisa*, I, 380–381; and Halifax to Phipps, no. 919, Apr. 17, 1939, *DBFP*, 3rd, V, 225.

25. Seeds, no. 65, Apr. 15, 1939, *DBFP*, 3rd, V, 215; and "Record of a conversation . . . with . . . Seeds," Litvinov, Apr. 15, 1939, *God krizisa*, I, 281–382.

26. Seeds, no. 66, Apr. 16, 1939, C5382/3356/18, PRO FO 371 23063; "Record of a conversation . . . with . . . Seeds," Litvinov, Apr. 16, 1939, *God krizisa*, I, 384–385; Surits to Narkomindel, Apr. 15, 1939, *ibid.*, 382; and Payart, nos. 282–287, Apr. 17, 1939, MAE Papiers Naggiar/10.

27. "To the general secretary TsK VKP(b) I.V. Stalin," secret, Litvinov, Apr. 15, 1939, *DVP*, XXII, bk. 1, 277–278; cf. Roberts, "Alliance That Failed," pp. 392–393.

28. "To the general secretary, TsK VKP(b), secret, Litvinov, Apr. 17, 1939, *DVP*, XXII, bk. 1, 283; "Proposals transmitted by . . . Litvinov to . . . Seeds," Apr. 17, 1939, *ibid.*, 283–284; and Seeds, no. 69, Apr. 18, 1939, *DBFP*, 3rd, V, 228–229.

29. Cadogan's note, Apr. 19, 1939, C5460/15/18, PRO FO 371 22969; and Corbin, no. 409, May 25, 1939, *DDF*, 2e, XVI, 562–566.

30. Halifax to Phipps, no. 981, Apr. 20, 1939, *DBFP*, 3rd, V, 260; also Halifax to Phipps, no. 945, Apr. 19, 1939, C5532/3356/18, PRO FO 371 23064.

31. Surits to Narkomindel, Apr. 18, 1939, *God krizisa*, I, 388.

32. Phipps to Sargent, Apr. 20, 1939, *DBFP*, 3rd, V, 260–262.

33. Surits to Narkomindel, very secret, Apr. 22, 1939, *DVP*, XXII, bk. 1, 307.

34. Phipps, no. 188, Apr. 24, 1939, *DBFP*, 3rd, V, 294–295; Surits to Narkomindel, Apr. 25, 1939 (two cables), *God krizisa*, I, 399–401; and Surits to Narkomindel, Apr. 25, 1939, *SPE*, I, 357–358.

35. Foreign Office to Phipps, no. 186, Apr. 28, 1939, C5838/3356/18, PRO FO 371 23064; minutes by Cadogan and Halifax, Apr. 22, 1939, C5842/3356/18, *ibid.*; and minutes of the Committee on Foreign Policy, Apr. 25, 1939, C6202/3356/18, *ibid.*

36. Kennard to Cadogan, Apr. 18, 1939, C5859/3356/18, PRO FO 371 23064; Kennard, no. 38 (saving), Apr. 19, 1939, C5676/3356/18, *ibid.*; and Kennard, no. 116, Apr. 18, 1939, C5682/3356/18, *ibid.*

37. Collier's minute, May 3, 1939, C5749/3356/18, PRO FO 371 23064.

38. Collier to Strang, Apr. 28, 1939, C6206/3356/18, PRO FO 371 23064.

39. Litvinov to Surits, Apr. 23, 1939, *God krizisa*, I, 397; Litvinov to Surits, Apr. 26, 1939, *ibid.*, 403; and Seeds, no. 76, Apr. 25, 1939, *DBFP*, 3rd, V, 319.

40. Litvinov to Surits, Apr. 27, 1939, *God krizisa*, I, 408.

41. Surits to Litvinov, very secret, Apr. 28, 1939, *DVP*, XXII, bk. 1, 316–317.

42. Surits to Narkomindel, Apr. 29, 1939, *God krizisa*, I, 413; and Phipps, no. 258 saving, May 3, 1939, *DBFP*, 3rd, V, 406.

43. "To the general secretary TsK VKP (b) I.V. Stalin," secret, Litvinov, Apr. 28, 1939, *DVP*, XXII, bk. 1, 315–316; and excerpt from Surits to Litvinov, Apr. 29, 1939, *God krizisa*, I, 414.

44. Maiskii to Narkomindel, Apr. 29, 1939, *God krizisa*, I, 410–412: and Phipps, no. 192, Apr. 30, 1939, C6213/3356/18, PRO FO 371 23064.

45. Chamberlain to Hilda, Apr. 29, 1939, NC18/1/1096, Chamberlain papers.

46. "To the general secretary TsK VKP(b) I.V. Stalin," secret, Litvinov, May 3, 1939, *DVP*, XXII, 1, 325–326.

47. Stalin to Surits, Maiskii, and others, very secret, May 3, 1939, *DVP*, XXII, bk. 1, 327.

48. Payart, nos. 326–329, May 4, 1939, MAE Papiers Naggiar/10; and Payart, nos. 351–356, May 10, 1939, *DDF*, 2e, XVI, 265–266.

49. Payart, nos. 346–349, May 9, 1939, MAE Papiers Naggiar/10; Seeds, no. 87, May 8, 1939, C6804/3356/18, PRO FO 371 23065; "Memorandum of a conversation . . . [between Molotov and Seeds]," May 8, 1939, *SPE*, II, 25–26; and "Record of a conversation . . . of Molotov with . . . Payart," May 11, 1939, *God krizisa*, I, 449–451.

50. Merekalov to Narkomindel, immediate, very secret, May 4, 1939, *DVP*, XXII, bk. 1, 332; Potemkin (Bucharest) to Narkomindel, highest priority, very secret, May 8, 1939, *ibid.*, 344; Seeds, no. 143, May 12, 1939, *DBFP*, 3rd, V, 542–546; Coulondre, no. 1203, May 4, 1939, *DDF*, 2e, XVI, 109–111; and "Conversation between Lord Strabolgi and Mr. Maisky . . . 20th September 1939," private and confidential, C14877/13953/18, PRO FO 371 23103.

51. Adamthwaite, *France*, pp. 294–297.

52. Parker, *Chamberlain*, pp. 195–197.

53. Excerpts from Merekalov's journal, secret, Mar. 1–3, 1939, *DVP*, XXII, bk. 1, 160–162; and Litvinov to K.A. Mikhailov, Soviet ambassador in Afghanistan, Mar. 9, 1939, *ibid.*, 173–174.

54. Litvinov to Merekalov, secret, Apr. 4, 1939, *DVP*, XXII, bk. 1, 252–253.

55. Litvinov to Merekalov, Apr. 5, 1939, *God krizisa*, I, 360.

56. "Record of a conversation . . . of A.F. Merekalov with . . . Weizsäcker," secret, Astakhov, Apr. 17, 1939, *DVP*, XXII, bk. 1, 291–293; Merekalov to Litvinov, Apr. 18, 1939, *God krizisa*, I, 389; "Memorandum by the State Secretary," Berlin, Apr. 17, 1939, *DGFP*, VI, 266–267; cf. Geoffrey Roberts, "Infamous Encounter?: The Merekalov-Weizsäcker Meeting of 17 April 1939," *Historical Journal*, vol. 35, no. 4 (1992), 921–926; Roberts, *Origins*, pp. 69–71; and Fleischhauer, *Pakt*, pp. 119–129.

57. Steven Merritt Miner, "His Master's Voice: Viacheslav Mikhailovich Molotov as Stalin's Foreign Commissar," in G.A. Craig and F.L. Loewenheim, eds., *The Diplomats, 1939–1979* (Princeton, 1994), pp. 65–67; and Albert Resis, ed., *Molotov Remembers: Inside Kremlin Politics, Conversations with Felix Chuev* (Chicago, 1993), p. 69.

58. Churchill, *Gathering Storm*, p. 368.

59. Potemkin (in Ankara) to Narkomindel, highest priority, very secret, May 5, 1939, *DVP*, XXII, bk. 1, 332–335.

60. Payart, no. 338, May 8, 1939, MAE Papiers Naggiar/10.

61. Seeds, no. 87, May 8, 1939, C6804/3356/18, PRO FO 371 23065; Seeds, no. 142, May 9, 1939, *DBFP*, 3rd, V, 483–487; and "Record of a conversation . . . of Molotov with . . . Seeds," May 8, 1939, *God krizisa*, I, 435–436.

62. Payart, nos. 339–342, May 8, 1939, MAE Papiers Naggiar/10.

63. "Record of a conversation of . . . Molotov with . . . Payart," May 11, 1939, *God krizisa*, I, 449–451; and Payart, nos. 362–366, May 12, 1939, *DDF*, 2e, XVI, 327–328.

64. Molotov to Surits, very secret, May 8, 1939, *DVP*, XXII, bk. 1, 342; Molotov to Maiskii, May 8, 1939, *ibid.*, bk. 2, 546; Potemkin (Warsaw) to Molotov, highest priority, very secret, May 10, 1939, *ibid.*, pp. 352–354.

65. Surits to Molotov, highest priority, very secret, May 10, 1939, *DVP*, XXII, bk. 1, 354–355.

66. Maiskii to Narkomindel, highest priority, very secret, May 9, 1939, *DVP*, XXII, bk. 1, 348–349; cf. Halifax to Seeds, no. 351, May 9, 1939, C6812/3356/18, PRO FO 371 23065.

67. Harvey, *Diplomatic Diaries*, entry of May 3, 1939, p. 286.

68. Molotov to Potemkin, highest priority, very secret, May 10, 1939, *DVP*, XXII, bk. 1, 352; Potemkin to Molotov, May 10, 1939, *God krizisa*, I, 444; and Payart, nos. 371–374, May 14, 1939, *DDF*, 2e, XVI, 358–359.

69. "Record of a conversation . . . of V.M. Molotov with the Polish ambassador in the USSR, V. Grzybowski," May 11, 1939, *God krizisa*, I, 448–449.

70. Maiskii to Narkomindel, highest priority, very secret, May 11, 1939, *DVP*, XXII, 1, 357–358; and Halifax to Seeds, no. 366, May 11, 1939, C6922/3356/18, PRO FO 371 23065.

71. "On the International Situation," *Izvestiia*, May 11, 1939, *SPE*, II, 34–37; and Payart, nos. 359–360, May 11, 1939, MAE Papiers Naggiar/10.

72. Seeds, no. 93, May 15, 1939, C7065/3356/18, PRO FO 371 23066; Seeds, no. 148, May 16, 1939, C7328/3356/18, *ibid.*; and "Record of a conversation . . . of Molotov with . . . Seeds," Molotov, May 14, 1939, *God krizisa*, I, 460.

73. "Record of a conversation . . . with . . . Payart," Potemkin, May 14, 1939, *God krizisa*, I, 460–461; Surits to Narkomindel, May 15, 1939, *ibid.*, 464–465; and Payart, nos. 369–370, May 14, 1939, MAE Papiers Naggiar/10.

74. Seeds to Oliphant, May 16, 1939, C7614/3356/18, PRO FO 371 23066.

75. Harvey, *Diplomatic Diaries*, entries of May 3, 16, 24, 1939, pp. 286, 290, 292; *Channon Diaries*, entries of May 5, 15, 1939, pp. 197, 199; and Cowling, *Impact of Hitler*, p. 272.

76. Cowling, *Impact of Hitler*, p. 302; Aster, *1939*, pp. 184–185; *Cadogan Diaries*, entry of May 20, 1939, p. 182; and Corbin, no. 409, May 25, 1939, *DDF*, 2e, XVI, 562–566.

Chapter 5. "The Russians Will Give Us More Trouble"

1. Chamberlain to Hilda, May 14, 1939, NC18/1/1099, Chamberlain papers.

2. Extract from cabinet conclusions, May 10, 1939, C7106/3356/18, PRO FO 371 23066.

3. Sargent to Chatfield, May 15, 1939, C7246/3356/18, PRO FO 371 23066; and *Channon Diaries*, entry of May 16, 1939, p. 199.

4. Bonnet to Payart, nos. 167–171, May 16, 1939, MAE Papiers Naggiar/9.

5. "Record of a conversation . . . with . . . Payart," Potemkin, May 14, 1939, *God krizisa*, I, 460–461; Surits to Narkomindel, May 15, 1939, *ibid.*, 464–465.

6. Memorandum, by Strang, May 16, 1939, C7206/3356/18, PRO FO 371 23066; and Phipps, no. 307 saving, May 18, 1939, C7264/3356/18, *ibid.*

7. Phipps, no. 217, June 1, 1939, C7916/3356/18, PRO FO 371 23067; and Phipps, no. 344 saving, June 7, 1939, C8137/3356/18, *ibid.*; and Phipps to Halifax, June 22, 1939, *DBFP*, 3rd, VI, 150–151.

8. Bonnet to Naggiar, nos. 218–219, June 14, 1939, MAE Papiers Naggiar/9.

9. Minutes by Strang and Cadogan, May 17–18, 1939, C7266/3356/18, PRO FO 371 23066.

10. Maiskii to Narkomindel, very secret, May 17, 1939, *DVP*, XXII, bk. 1, 378–379; and Vansittart's minute, May 16, 1939, C7268/3356/18, PRO FO 371 23066.

11. Maiskii to Narkomindel, highest priority, very secret, May 17, 1939, *DVP*, XXII, bk. 1, 379–380.

12. Excerpt from Maiskii's journal, secret, May 18, 1939, *DVP*, XXII, bk. 1, 382–383.

13. Maiskii to Narkomindel, highest priority, very secret, May 19, 1939, *DVP*, XXII, bk. 1, 383.

14. Manchester, *Caged Lion*, pp. 459–462; Parker, *Chamberlain*, p. 229; and *Channon Diaries*, entry of May 19, 1939, p. 199.

15. Corbin, nos. 1560–1565, May 18, 1939, *DDF*, 2e, XVI, 426–427.

16. Maiskii to Narkomindel, May 10, 1939, *God krizisa*, I, 444–447; and Parker, *Chamberlain*, p. 233.

17. "Notes prises au cours de l'entretien franco-britannique du 20 mai 1939 . . . ," AN Papiers Daladier, 496AP/13; and Halifax to FO, no. 8 L.N., May 21, 1939, C7551/3356/18, PRO FO 371 23066.

18. Chamberlain to Ida, May 21, 1939, NC18/1/1100, Chamberlain papers.

19. Halifax (Geneva) to Cadogan, no. 10, May 22, 1939, *DBFP*, 3rd, V, 630–634; and Maiskii (Geneva) to Narkomindel, May 21, 1939, *God krizisa*, I, 487–488.

20. Cadogan to Halifax, May 23, 1939, C7469/3356/18, PRO FO 371 23066; and Manchester, *Caged Lion*, p. 471.

21. Cf. Maiskii to Molotov, May 10, 1939, *God krizisa*, I, 444–447; and Maiskii to Narkomindel, May 21, 1939, *ibid.*, 487–488.

22. Chamberlain to Hilda, May 28, 1939, NC18/1/1101, Chamberlain papers. Cf. Watt, *How War Came*, p. 247.

23. "Visite de Monsieur Souritz du 26 mai 1939 . . . ," MAE Papiers 1940, Cabinet Bonnet/16, ff. 266–268. N.B., the same note in the AN Papiers Daladier, 496AP/13, has a different, less negative conclusion.

24. "Record of a conversation . . . with . . . Seeds," secret, Potemkin, May 20, 1939, *DVP*, XXII, bk. 1, 384–385.

25. *Channon Diaries*, entry of May 24, 1939, p. 201; Molotov to Surits, May 26, 1939, *God krizisa*, I, 500; "Record of a conversation of . . . Molotov with . . . Seeds and . . . Payart," Potemkin, May 27, 1939, *ibid.*, 508–511; Payart, nos. 400–405, May 27, 1939, MAE Papiers Naggiar/10; and Seeds, no. 103, May 27, 1939, C7682/3356/18, PRO FO 371 23066. Cf. Watt, *How War Came*, pp. 247–248.

26. Halifax to Seeds, no. 120, May 25, 1939, *DBFP*, 3rd, V, pp. 680–681.

27. Seeds, no. 105, May 30, 1939, *DBFP*, 3rd, V, 722–723.

28. Payart, nos. 406–407, May 29, 1939, MAE Papiers Naggiar/10; Payart, nos. 408–414, May 30, 1939, *DDF*, 2ᵉ, XVI, 599–600; and Naggiar, nos. 416–422, May 31, 1939, MAE Papiers Naggiar/10.

29. "The International Situation and the Foreign Policy of the USSR . . . ," Molotov, May 31, 1939, *SPE*, II, 67–75; and Seeds, no. 108, May 31, 1939, C7886/3356/18, PRO FO 371 23067.

30. Naggiar, nos. 424–427, June 1, 1939, MAE Papiers Naggiar/10.

31. "Conversation of the people's commissar for foreign affairs, V.M. Molotov, with the ambassador of Great Britain in the USSR, Sir S. Cripps," secret, Feb. 1, 1941, *DVP*, XXIII, bk. 2, part 1, 376–378.

32. Bonnet to Naggiar, nos. 198–205, June 2, 1939, MAE Papiers Naggiar/9; and MAE internal note, Direction politique, July 5, 1939, MAE Papiers 1940, Cabinet Bonnet/16, ff. 280–297.

33. "Draft agreement . . . ," June 2, 1939, *SPE*, II, 75–76.

34. Seeds, no. 161, May 30, 1939, C7937/3356/18, PRO FO 371 23067 (and Sargent's minute on this cable); and Seeds, no. 181, June 20, 1939, C8840/3356/18, PRO FO 371 23069.

35. Meeting of the Committee on Foreign Policy, Monday, June 5, 1939, C8138/3356/18, PRO FO 371 23067.

36. Phipps, no. 344 saving, June 7, 1939, C8137/3356/18, PRO FO 371 23067; and Phipps, no. 224, June 8, 1939, C8212/3356/18, *ibid.*

37. Halifax to Phipps, no. 1400, June 7, 1939, C8213/3356/18, PRO FO 371 23067.

38. Maiskii to Narkomindel, immediate, very secret, June 8, 1939, *DVP*, XXII, bk. 1, 442–443; and Molotov to Maiskii, highest priority, very secret, June 10, 1939, *ibid.*, 449.

39. Maiskii to Narkomindel, highest priority, very secret, June 12, 1939, *DVP*, XXII, bk. 1, 459–460 and fn. on 460; and Halifax to Seeds, no. 450, June 12, 1939, *DBFP*, 3ʳᵈ, VI, 50–51.

40. "Instructions for Sir W. Seeds," FO, June 12, 1939, *DBFP*, 3ʳᵈ, VI, 33–41.

41. Record of a meeting with Corbin, Cadogan, June 8, 1939, C8405/3356/18, PRO FO 371 23068.

42. See Naggiar's handwritten notes on his nos. 481–483, June 14, 1939, MAE Papiers Naggiar/10; and Naggiar, nos. 502–506, June 16, 1939, *ibid.*

43. "Mr. [W.N.] Ewer's [diplomatic correspondent, *Daily Herald*] account of his talk with M. Maisky," nd (but June 9, 1939), C8701/3356/18, PRO FO 371 23068.

44. Chamberlain to Ida, June 10, 1939, NC18/1/1102, Chamberlain papers.

45. Manchester, *Caged Lion*, p. 471.

46. Surits to Narkomindel, very secret, June 19, 1939, *DVP*, XXII, bk. 1, pp. 486–487.

47. Surits to Narkomindel, highest priority, very secret, July 7, 1939, *DVP*, I, 529–530.

48. Payart, nos. 185–190, March 17, 1939, MAE Papiers Naggiar/10.

49. Merekalov to Narkomindel, very secret, May 5, 1939, *DVP*, XXII, bk. 1, 338; "Record of a conversation . . . with . . . von Papen," secret, Terent'ev, May 5, 1939, *ibid.*, 336–337; "Record of a conversation . . . with . . . von Papen," secret, Terent'ev, May 9, 1939, *ibid.*, 350–352; and L.A. Bezymenskii, "Sovetsko-Germanskie dogovory 1939g.; novye dokumenty i starye problemy," *Novaia i Noveishaia Istoriia*, no. 3 (1998), p. 15.

50. Astakhov to Molotov, secret, May 6, 1939, *DVP*, XXII, bk. 1, 339–341.

51. Roberts, *Soviet Union*, pp. 73–75; Astakhov to Potemkin, May 12, 1939, *God krizisa*, I, 457–458; Schnurre's memorandum, May 17, 1939, *DGFP*, D, VI, 535–536; and Astakhov to Narkomindel, very secret, May 17, 1939, *DVP*, XXII, bk. 1, 381.

52. "Record of a conversation . . . with . . . Schulenberg," secret, Molotov, May 20, 1939, *DVP*, XXII, bk. 1, 386–387; cf. Roberts, *Soviet Union*, p. 75.

53. Schulenberg to Weizsäcker, May 22, 1939, *DGFP*, D, VI, 558–559; and Schulenberg to Weizsäcker, May 20, 1939, *ibid.*, 547.

54. Astakhov to Narkomindel, highest priority, very secret, May 30, 1939, *DVP*, XXII, bk. 1, 405–406; "Record of a conversation . . . with . . . Weizsäcker," Astakhov, May 30, 1939, *God krizisa*, I, 518–522; Weizsäcker to Schulenberg, May 27, 1939, *DGFP*, D, VI, 597–598; memorandum by Weizsäcker, May 30, 1939, *ibid.*, 604–607.

55. Astakhov to Molotov, secret, June 14, 1939, *DVP*, XXII, bk. 1, 464.

56. "Record of a conversation . . . with . . . Schulenberg," secret, Astakhov, June 17, 1939, *DVP*, XXII, bk. 1, 483–486.

57. Aster, *1939*, pp. 226–234; and Parker, *Chamberlain*, pp. 260–262.

58. Chamberlain to Ida, June 10, 1939, NC18/1/1102, Chamberlain papers.

59. Henderson to Halifax, no. 688, June 13, 1939, *DBFP*, 3rd, VI, 59–62.

60. Naggiar, no. 484, June 15, 1939, MAE Papiers Naggiar/10; and "Note rédigée par un des fonctionnaires de la délégation française au Conseil de la Société des Nations," June 16, 1939, *DDF*, 2ᵉ, XVI, 866–867.

61. Naggiar, nos. 463–470, June 11, 1939, MAE Papiers Naggiar/10.

62. Molotov to Maiskii and Surits, June 16, 1939, *God krizisa*, II, 34–35.

63. Chamberlain to Hilda, June 17, 1939, NC18/1/1103, Chamberlain papers; Strang to Sargent, June 21, 1939, C9010/3356/18, PRO FO 371 23069; Naggiar, nos. 525–527, June 21, 1939, MAE Papiers Naggiar/10; Naggiar, nos. 528–533, June 22, 1939, *DDF*, 2ᵉ, XVI, 937–938; Seeds, no. 139, June 23, 1939, C8928/3356/18, PRO FO 371 23069; and Naggiar, nos. 507–518, June 17, 1939, MAE Papiers Naggiar/10.

64. Bonnet to Corbin, nos. 1188–1192, June 17, 1939, *DDF*, 2ᵉ, XVI, 878–879.

65. Cadogan's untitled note on a meeting with Corbin, June 17, 1939, C8773/3356/18, PRO FO 371 23069; and Phipps to Halifax, June 22, 1939, *DBFP*, 3rd, VI, 150–151.

66. Excerpt from Maiskii's journal, secret, June 23, 1939, *DVP*, XXII, bk. 1, 496–497; and Halifax to Seeds, no. 488, June 23, 1939, C8979/3356/18, PRO FO 371 23069.

67. Cabinet, Committee on Foreign Policy, Monday, June 26, 1939, C9315/3356/18, PRO FO 371 23069; and Aster, *1939*, pp. 270–271.

68. "The English and French Governments do not want an Equal Agreement with the USSR," Zhdanov, *Pravda*, June 29, 1939, *SPE*, II, 116–119.

69. Carley, "Low, Dishonest Decade," p. 317; and Prażmowska, *Britain, Poland, and the Eastern Front.* pp. 161–164, 193–194.

70. Molotov to Maiskii and Surits, July 3, 1939, *God krizisa*, II, 82; Seeds, no. 150, July 3, 1939, C9286/3356/18, PRO FO 371 23069; Naggiar, nos. 590–599, July 1, 1939, MAE Papiers Naggiar/10; Naggiar, nos. 608–614, July 3, 1939, *ibid.*

71. Chamberlain to Hilda, July 2, 1939, NC18/1/1105, Chamberlain papers.

72. Naggiar's minute on Bonnet to Naggiar, nos. 333–338, July 5, 1939, MAE Papiers Naggiar/9; see also Payart's earlier, nos. 383–388, May 24, 1939, *ibid./*10;

Naggiar, nos. 442–445, June 3, 1939, *DDF*, 2ᵉ, XVI, 655–656; and Naggiar, nos. 543–549, June 22, 1939, *ibid.*, 951–952.

73. Naggiar, nos. 449–454, June 6, 1939, MAE Papiers Naggiar/10; and Seeds, no. 139, June 23, 1939, C8928/3356/18, PRO FO 371 23069.

74. Committee on Foreign Policy, July 10, 1939, C9761/3356/18, PRO FO 371 23070.

75. Bonnet to Corbin, no. 1517, July 19, 1939, AN Papiers Daladier, 496AP/13; and Kirkpatrick's minute, July 21, 1939, C10292/3356/18, PRO FO 371 23071.

76. Naggiar, nos. 601–603, July 2, 1939, MAE Papiers Naggiar/10; Bonnet to Corbin, nos. 1356–1359, July 4, 1939, *DDF*, 2ᵉ, XVII, 154–155; and Seeds to Sargent, personal letter, Aug. 3, 1939, C11927/3356/18, PRO FO 371 23073.

77. Surits to Narkomindel, highest priority, very secret, July 7, 1939, *DVP*, XXII, bk. 1, 529–530.

78. Excerpt from the Soviet press attaché in Berlin A.A. Smirnov's journal, secret, June 26, 1939, *DVP*, XXII, bk. 1, 509–510.

79. Naggiar, nos. 580–586, June 29, 1939, MAE Papiers Naggiar/10; Naggiar, no. 589, July 1, 1939, *ibid.*; Naggiar, nos. 642–644, July 7, 1939, *ibid.*; and Bonnet to Naggiar, nos. 444–448, July 15, 1939, *ibid./9*.

80. Naggiar, nos. 629–639, July 5, 1939; Naggiar, nos. 674–683, July 11, 1939; Naggiar, nos. 686–691, July 13, 1939; Naggiar, nos. 699–703, July 15, 1939; Naggiar, no. 707, July 16, 1939, Naggiar, nos. 723–737, July 18, 1939, *ibid./10*; and "Note," Palasse, no. 599/S, July 13, 1939, SHAT 7N 3186. Cameron Watt mistakenly states that Paris was ill-served by Naggiar, who failed to appreciate the possibility of the Soviet Union choosing a German rapprochement (*How War Came*, p. 611).

81. Naggiar's minutes on Bonnet's nos. 423–428, 430–436, July 11, 1939, MAE Papiers Naggiar/9.

82. Naggiar, nos. 543–549, June 22, 1939, MAE Papiers Naggiar/10; Bonnet to Naggiar, nos. 252–259, June 24, 1939, *ibid./9*; Bonnet to Naggiar, nos. 360–363, July 5, 1939, *ibid.*; and Corbin to Sargent, July 11, 1939, C9972/3356/18, PRO FO 371 23070.

83. Naggiar's minute on Bonnet, nos. 505–511, July 25, 1939, MAE Papiers Naggiar/9.

84. Naggiar's minute on Bonnet, no. 548, July 30, 1939, MAE Papiers Naggiar/9.

85. Committee on Foreign Policy, July 19, 1939, C10267/3356/18, PRO FO 371 23071; and Maiskii to Narkomindel, highest priority, very secret, June 28, 1939, *DVP*, XXII, bk. 1, 510.

86. Chamberlain to Hilda, July 15, 1939, NC18/1/1107, Chamberlain papers.

87. Ian Colvin, *The Chamberlain Cabinet* (New York, 1971), p. 229; and Parker, *Chamberlain*, pp. 240–241.

88. Maiskii to Molotov, secret, July 10, 1939, *DVP*, XXII, bk. 1, 535–537.

89. Surits to Narkomindel, highest priority, very secret, July 14, 1939, *DVP*, XXII, bk. 1, 543.

90. Molotov to Maiskii and Surits, July 17, 1939, *SPE*, II, 140–141.

91. *Cadogan Diaries*, entries of June 20, 28, 1939, pp. 189–190.

92. Surits to Narkomindel, very secret, July 19, 1939, *DVP*, XXII, bk. 1, 544–545.

93. Surits to Narkomindel, very secret, April 22, 1939, *DVP*, XXII, bk. 1, 307.

94. Seeds, no. 170, July 24, 1939, C10319/3356/18, PRO FO 371 23071; Nag-

giar, nos. 744–751, July 23, 1939, MAE Papiers Naggiar/10; excerpt from Maiskii to Narkomindel, July 25, 1939, *God krizisa*, II, 134; Corbin to Halifax, July 19, 1939, C10291/3356/18, PRO FO 371 23071; and Kirkpatrick's minute, July 21, 1939, C10292/3356/18, PRO FO 371 23071.

95. Phipps, no. 929, July 21, 1939, C10410/90/17, PRO FO 371 22912.

96. Excerpts from Astakhov's journal, secret, June 20, 24, 1939, *DVP*, XXII, bk. 1, 492–494, 502.

97. "Record of a conversation . . . with . . . Schulenberg," Molotov, June 28, 1939, *God krizisa*, II, 65–67; Schulenberg to German foreign ministry, secret, urgent, June 29, 1939, *DGFP*, D, VI, 805–807; and Schulenberg to German foreign ministry, most urgent, July 3, 1939 [a more detailed account of the meeting], *ibid.*, 834–836.

98. "Record of a conversation . . . with . . . Schulenberg," secret, Potemkin, July 1, 1939, *DVP*, XXII, bk. 1, 514–516.

99. Weizsäcker to Schulenberg, June 30, 1939, *DGFP*, D, VI, 813.

100. Gel'fand to Molotov, secret, July 1, 1939, *DVP*, XXII, bk. 1, pp. 520–523.

101. Astakhov to Narkomindel, very secret, July 8, 1939, *DVP*, XXII, bk. 1, 531.

102. Astakhov to Molotov, July 19, 1939, *God krizisa*, II, 108–109.

103. Excerpts from Astakhov's journal, July 20–26, 1939, *DVP*, XXII, bk. 1, 547–551.

104. Excerpts from Astakhov's journal, July 20–26, 1939, *DVP*, XXII, bk. 1, 547–551; and "Record of a conversation . . . with . . . Schnurre," secret, Astakhov, July 24, 1939, *DVP*, XXII, bk. 1, 554–556.

105. "Record of a conversation . . . with . . . Schnurre," Astakhov, July 26, 1939, *God krizisa*, II, 136–139, and Astakhov to Potemkin, July 27, 1939, *ibid.*, 139–140. Cf. Roberts, *Soviet Union*, pp. 83–84.

106. Molotov to Astakhov, July 28, 1939, *God krizisa*, II, 145; and Molotov to Astakhov, July 29, 1939, *ibid.*, 145. Cf. Roberts, *Soviet Union*, pp. 80–81; and Fleischhauer, *Pakt*, pp. 211–220.

107. Aster, *1939*, pp. 244–251; Watt, *How War Came*, pp. 394–403; and Parker, *Chamberlain*, pp. 264–265.

108. Chamberlain to Ida, July 23, 1939, NC18/1/1108, Chamberlain papers.

109. Chamberlain to Hilda, July 30, 1939, NC18/1/1110, Chamberlain papers.

110. Maiskii to Narkomindel, July 24, 1939, *God krizisa*, II, 118–119.

111. Surits to Narkomindel, July 25, 1939, *God krizisa*, II, 135.

112. Molotov to Terent'ev, very secret, Sept. 3, 1939, *DVP*, XXII, bk. 2, 12.

Chapter 6. Molotov Is Suspicious

1. Seeds, no. 172, July 23, 1939, C10325/3356/18, PRO FO 371 23071.

2. Naggiar, nos. 774–780, July 28, 1939, MAE Papiers Naggiar/10.

3. Committee on Foreign Policy, July 10, 1939, C9761/3356/18, PRO FO 371 23070; and Admiral Sir Reginald Drax, "Mission to Moscow, August 1939," Churchill Archives Centre, Cambridge, England, Drax Papers, 6/5, f. 7.

4. Cabinet conclusions, July 26, 1939, C10629/3356/18, PRO FO 371 20371; Drax, "Mission to Moscow, August 1939," Churchill Archives, Drax Papers, 6/5, f. 6; and "Rapport de mission à Moscou," Capt. de corvette Williaume, August 1939, SHAT 7N 3185.

5. Harvey, *Diplomatic Diaries*, entry of July 1, 1939, p. 301.

6. Drax, "Mission to Moscow, August 1939," Churchill Archives, Drax Papers, 6/5, f. 6.

7. "Anglo-French-Soviet Negotiations," Skrine Stevenson, FO, July 25, 1939, C10634/3356/18, PRO FO 371 23071; Sargent's minute, July 28, 1939, *ibid.*; and Committee on Foreign Policy, Aug. 1, 1939, C10826/3356/18, PRO FO 371 23072.

8. "Extract from the minutes of a meeting of the Committee of Imperial Defence . . . ," Aug. 2, 1939, C10952/3356/18, PRO FO 371 23072; and "Anglo-Franco-Soviet Negotiations," C.P. 172 (39), secret, Strang, July 27, 1939, C10507/3356/18, PRO FO 371 23071.

9. F.K. Roberts's minute, Aug. 2, 1939, C10822/3356/18, PRO FO 371 23072.

10. "Cabinet extract . . . Major General H.L. Ismay's conversations in Paris on 29 July 1939," C10811/3356/18, PRO FO 371 23072.

11. Gamelin to Doumenc, no. 1522/DN.3, July 27, 1939, SHAT 7N 3186.

12. Doumenc, "Souvenirs de la mission en Russie, août 1939," ff. 11–12, SHAT 7N 3185. Cameron Watt and Duroselle quote or refer to this exchange (from excerpts in the *DDF*), but they do not mention Doumenc's important comment that he was leaving for Moscow empty-handeed—*les mains vides* (Watt, *How War Came*, p. 452; and Duroselle, *Décadence*, p. 428).

13. Excerpt from Maiskii's journal, secret, Aug. 4, 1939, *DVP*, XXII, bk. 1, 580–581.

14. Excerpt from Maiskii's journal, secret, Aug. 5, 1939, *DVP*, XXII, bk. 1, 582–583.

15. Surits to Narkomindel, Aug. 3, 1939, *SPE*, II, 168–170.

16. "Tass statement on One of the Reasons for the Delay in Negotiations with Britain," Aug. 2, 1939, *SPE*, II, 167.

17. Seeds, no. 185, Aug. 2, 1939, C10821/3356/18, PRO FO 371 23072; Seeds, no. 188, Aug. 3, 1939, C10886/3356/18, *ibid.*; Naggiar, nos. 810–819, Aug. 2, 1939, MAE Papiers Naggiar/10.

18. Seeds to Sargent, Aug. 3, 1939, C11927/3356/18, PRO FO 371 23073.

19. Butler's untitled minute, Aug. 4, 1939, C11018/3356/18, PRO FO 371 23072.

20. Naggiar, nos. 820–822, Aug. 3, 1939, MAE Papiers Naggiar/10; and Naggiar, nos. 840–841, Aug. 8, 1939, *ibid.*

21. "Instructions for . . . Voroshilov . . . ," secret, Aug. 7, 1939, *DVP*, XXII, bk. 1, 584.

22. Excerpt from Smirnov's journal, secret, July 31, 1939, *DVP*, XXII, bk. 1, 564–565.

23. "Record of a conversation . . . with . . . Ribbentrop and . . . Weizsäcker," secret, Astakhov, Aug. 2, 1939, *DVP*, XXII, bk. 1, 566–569; Astakhov to Narkomindel, Aug. 3, 1939, *God krizisa*, II, 157–158; Astakhov to Narkomindel, highest priority, Aug. 3, 1939, *ibid.*, 159; and Ribbentrop to Schulenberg, most urgent, Aug. 3, 1939, *DGFP*, VI, 1049–1050.

24. "Record of a conversation . . . with . . . Schulenberg," secret, Molotov, Aug. 3, 1939, *DVP*, XXII, bk. 1, 570–572; and Schulenberg to German foreign ministry, most urgent, Aug. 4, 1939, *DGFP*, D, VI, pp. 1059–1062. Cf. Roberts, *Soviet Union*, pp. 84–85.

25. Molotov to Astakhov, Aug. 5, 1939, *God krizisa*, II, 175.

26. Schnurre's memorandum, secret, Aug. 5, 1939, *DGFP*, D, VI, 1067–1068; and Schulenberg to Martin Schliep, German foreign ministry, Aug. 7, 1939, *ibid.*, 1075–1077.

27. Astakhov to Molotov, secret, Aug. 8, 1939, *DVP*, XXII, bk. 1, 585–587. Cf. Roberts, *Soviet Union*, pp. 86–87.

28. Astakhov to Narkomindel, very secret, Aug. 10, 1939, *DVP*, XXII, bk. 1, 595–596.

29. Schnurre's memorandum, Aug. 10, 1939, *DGFP*, D, VII, 17–20. Cf. Fleischhauer, *Pakt*, pp. 225–237.

30. Gel'fand to Molotov, secret, Aug. 28, 1939, *DVP*, XXII, bk. 1, 672–676.

31. Molotov to Astakhov, August 11, 1939, *God krizisa*, II, 184.

32. Parker, *Chamberlain*, pp. 266–268; and Aster, *1939*, pp. 254–258.

33. Drax, "Mission to Moscow, August 1939," Churchill Archives, Drax Papers, 6/5, f. 10.

34. Naggiar's minute on his cable, nos. 860–863, August 12, 1939, MAE Papiers Naggiar/10; Doumenc, "Souvenirs," ff. 56–57, SHAT 7N 3185; and the little-noted confirmation of Daladier's instructions in L. Noël, *L'Agression allemande contre la Pologne* (Paris, 1946), p. 423.

35. Naggiar's retrospective minute on his cable no. 707, July 16, 1939, MAE Papiers Naggiar/10.

36. Namier, *Diplomatic Prelude*, pp. 204–206; cf. Watt, *How War Came*, pp. 452–453.

37. Naggiar, nos. 860–863, Aug. 12, 1939, MAE Papiers Naggiar/10.

38. Seeds, no. 196, Aug. 12, 1939, C11275/3356/18, PRO FO 371 23072; and Strang's minute, Aug. 14, 1939, *ibid.*

39. Halifax to Seeds, no. 209, August 15, 1939, C11275/3356/18, PRO FO 371 23072; Chatfield to Drax, no. 1, August 15, 1939, *ibid.*; and Bonnet to Naggiar, no. 585, August 15, 1939, MAE Papiers Naggiar/9.

40. Seeds, military mission no. 1, Aug. 12, 1939, C11276/3356/18, PRO FO 371 23072; Instructions, Aug. 15, 1939, *ibid.*; Drax, "Mission to Moscow, August 1939," ff. 14–15, Churchill Archives, Drax Papers, 6/5; and Doumenc, "Souvenirs," ff. 65–66, SHAT 7N 3185.

41. Doumenc, "Souvenirs," ff. 67–68, SHAT 7N 3185; "Record of the evening meeting of the military missions of the USSR, Britain, and France," Aug. 13, 1939, *SPE*, II, 196–202.

42. "Record of the meeting of the military missions of the USSR, Britain, and France," Aug. 14, 1939, *SPE*, II, 202–210; and André Beaufre, *1940: The Fall of France* (London, 1967), pp. 109–113, 118. Beaufre's published account is taken word for word from Doumenc's "Souvenirs," ff. 74–80, 90, and *passim*, SHAT 7N 3185.

43. Doumenc, "Souvenirs," f. 76, SHAT 7N 3185; Naggiar, nos. 869–872, Aug. 14, 1939, MAE Papiers Naggiar/10; and Seeds, mission no. 3, Aug. 14, 1939, C11323/3356/18, PRO FO 371 23072.

44. "Committee on Imperial Defence, Deputy chiefs of staff subcommittee," meeting of Aug. 16, 1939, C11506/3356/18, PRO FO 371 23072.

45. Naggiar's minute on Bonnet to Naggiar, no. 601, Aug. 18, 1939, MAE Papiers Naggiar/9.

46. Quoting an unnamed Polish foreign ministry official (C.J. Norton, British chargé d'affaires in Warsaw, no. 205, July 21, 1939, C10460/3356/18, PRO FO 371 23071).

47. "Conversation du Ministre des Affaires étrangères avec M. Lukachiecvicz," Bonnet, Aug. 15, 1939, AN Papiers Daladier, 496AP/13.

48. Doumenc, "Souvenirs," ff. 96–97, SHAT 7N 3185.

49. Colson to Doumenc, no. 2388-EMA/2-SAE, Aug. 15, 1939, SHAT 7N 3186; Naggiar, nos. 873–874, Aug. 15, 1939, MAE Papiers Naggiar/10; Noël to Naggiar, nos. 5–15, Aug. 18, 1939, *ibid./9*; Charles-Jean Tripier, French minister in

Riga, Aug. 20, 1939, *ibid.*; and Drax to Chatfield, Aug. 16, 17, 1939, C12064/3356/18, PRO FO 371 23073.

50. Kennard, no. 279, most secret, Aug. 19, 1939, C11585/3356/18, PRO FO 371 23073; Kennard, no. 273, most secret, Aug. 18, 1939, C11582/3356/18, *ibid.*; and Roger Cambon, French chargé d'affaires in London, no. 2642, Aug. 21, 1939, AN Papiers Daladier 496AP/13.

51. Kennard, no. 282, Aug. 21, 1939, C11701/3356/18, PRO FO 371 23073; and Noël, nos. 1203–1212, Aug. 20, 1939, DDF, 2ᵉ, XVIII, 217–220.

52. Naggiar, nos. 895–901, Aug. 20, 1939, MAE Papiers Naggiar/10; Bonnet to Naggiar, no. 615, Aug. 21, 1939, MAE Papiers Naggiar/9; Seeds, mission no. 9, Aug. 22, 1939, and Strang's minute of the same day, C11729/3356/18, PRO FO 371 23073; Bonnet to Noël, nos. 612–620, Aug. 19, 1939 AN Papiers Daladier 496AP/13; and Bonnet to Noël, nos. 624–627, Aug. 20, 1939, *ibid.*

53. Astakhov to Molotov, secret, Aug. 12, 1939, DVP, XXII, bk. 1, 597–598; Astakhov to Molotov, Aug. 12, 1939, *God krizisa*, II, 186–188; and Schnurre to Schulenberg, Aug. 14, 1939, DGFP, D, VII, 58–59.

54. "Record of a conversation . . . with . . . Schnurre," secret, Astakhov, Aug. 13, 1939, DVP, XXII, bk. 1, 603–604; cf. Roberts, *Soviet Union*, pp. 87–88.

55. "Record of a conversation . . . of Molotov with . . . Schulenberg," secret, Aug. 15, 1939, DVP, XXII, bk. 1, 606–608; Schulenberg to German foreign ministry, most urgent, secret, Aug. 16, 1939, DGFP, D, VII, 76–77.

56. Astakhov to Narkomindel, immediate, very secret, Aug. 16, 1939, DVP, XXII, bk. 1, 608–609.

57. "Record of a conversation of . . . Molotov with . . . Schulenberg," secret, and annexed aide-mémoire, Aug. 17, 1939, DVP, XXII, bk. 1 609–612; and Schulenberg to German foreign ministry, most urgent, secret, Aug. 18, 1939, DGFP, D, VII, 114–116.

58. "Record of a conversation . . . of Molotov with . . . A. Kh. Aktai," secret, Aug. 17, 1939, DVP, XXII, bk. 1, 612–613.

59. "Record of a conversation of . . . Molotov with . . . Schulenberg," secret, Aug. 19, 1939, DVP, XXII, bk. 1, 615–617; and Schulenberg to German foreign ministry, most urgent, secret, Aug. 20, 1939, DGFP, D, VII, 149–151. Cf. Roberts, *Soviet Union*, p. 90.

60. Sipols, "A Few Months Before August 23, 1939," *passim*; and Schnurre's note, Aug. 19, 1939, DGFP, D, VII, 132–133. Cf. Fleischhauer, *Pakt*, pp. 249–265.

61. Astakhov to Narkomindel, highest priority, very secret, Aug. 19, 1939, DVP, XXII, bk. 1, 619–620; and "Communication on Soviet-German Relations," *Izvestiia*, Aug. 22, 1939, *ibid.*, p. 626.

62. "Record of the Meeting of the Military Missions of the USSR, Britain and France," Aug. 21, 1939, SPE, II, 254–259; and N.I. Sharonov, Soviet ambassador in Warsaw, to Narkomindel, very secret, Aug. 19, 1939, DVP, XXII, bk. 1, 619.

63. "Record of a conversation between the head of the Soviet military mission K.E. Voroshilov with the head of the French military mission J. Doumenc," Aug. 22, 1939, *God krizisa*, II, 307–311.

64. Seeds, no. 211, Aug. 22, 1939, C11740/3356/18, PRO FO 371 23073.

65. Naggiar's minute on his cable reporting Seeds's meeting with Molotov, nos. 941–943, Aug. 23, 1939, MAE Papiers Naggiar/10; and Naggiar, no. 944, Aug. 23, 1939, *ibid.*

66. "Record of a conversation . . . with . . . Payart," secret, Potemkin, Sept. 2, 1939, DVP, XXII, bk. 2, 7–9.

67. Naggiar's minute on Noël to Naggiar, no. 21, Aug. 23, 1939, MAE Papiers Naggiar/9; Naggiar, nos. 946–947, Aug. 23, 1939, MAE Papiers Naggiar/10; and Noël, nos. 1203–1212, Aug. 20, 1939, DDF, 2ᵉ, XVIII, 217–220.

68. Bonnet to Adrien Thierry, French minister in Bucharest, nos. 565–568; Naggiar, nos. 637–641; and elsewhere, Aug. 23, 1939, and Naggiar's minutes, MAE Papiers Naggiar/9; and Roberts to Cadogan, Aug. 23, 1939, C11814/3356/18, PRO FO 371 23073.

69. Coulondre to Naggiar, nos. 1–4, Aug. 23, 1939, MAE Papiers Naggiar/9.

70. German-Soviet nonaggression pact and secret protocol, signed by Ribbentrop and Molotov, Aug. 23, 1939, *DVP*, XXII, bk. 1, 630–632.

71. Read and Fisher, *Deadly Embrace*, pp. 252–259; and *Molotov Remembers*, p. 12.

72. Hervé Alphand, *L'Étonnement d'être* (Paris, 1977), p. 20.

73. Noël, nos. 1223–1227, Aug 22, 1939, AN Papiers Daladier 496AP/13; and Naggiar's minute on Bonnet to Naggiar, nos. 619–624, Aug. 23, 1939, MAE Papiers Naggiar/9.

74. Collier's memorandum, Aug. 26, 1939, and Sargent's minute, Sept. 3, 1939, N3335/243/38, PRO FO 371 23686; cf. Sargent's minute, Apr. 3, 1936, C2401/4/18, PRO FO 371 19898; "Record of a conversation...with... Schnurre," Astakhov, July 24, 1939, *God krizisa*, II, 120–122; Potemkin to Surits, secret, Feb. 4, 1939, *DVP*, XXII, bk. 1, 98–100; Payart, nos. 185–190, Mar. 17, 1939, MAE Papiers Naggiar/10; Andrew, *Secret Service*, pp. 592–598; and D. Cameron Watt, "An Intelligence Surprise: The Failure of the Foreign Office to Anticipate the Nazi-Soviet Pact," *Intelligence and National Security*, vol. 4, no. 3 (July 1989), 512–534.

75. Campbell (Paris), no. 543 saving, Aug. 23, 1939, C11815/3356/18, PRO FO 371 23073.

76. Jeanneney, *Journal politique*, p. 6.

77. Surits to Narkomindel, highest priority, very secret, Aug. 25, 1939, *DVP*, XXII, bk. 1, 652; and Naggiar's minute on Bonnet to Naggiar, nos. 627–630, Aug. 23, 1939, MAE Papiers Naggiar/9.

78. Naggiar's comment on his cable nos. 965–972, Aug. 25, 1939, MAE Papiers Naggiar/10.

79. *Molotov Remembers*, p. 9.

80. Henri Amouroux, *Le Peuple du désastre, 1939–1940* (Paris, 1976), p. 132.

81. Luguet, French air attaché in Moscow, to Guy La Chambre, air minister, no. 463, secret, Aug. 29, 1939, SHAT 7N 3186.

82. Sherwood, *Mandel*, p. 226; and William Strang, *Home and Abroad* (London, 1956), p. 159.

Chapter 7. "A Situation of Delicacy and Danger"

1. See Shirer's contemporary impressions in *Berlin Diary: The Journal of a Foreign Correspondent, 1934–1941* (New York, 1941), pp. 180–183.

2. Amouroux, *Peuple du désastre*, pp. 121–154; A.J.P. Taylor, *English History, 1914–1945* (New York, 1965), p. 450.

3. Alistair Horne, *To Lose a Battle: France 1940* (London, 1990), pp. 138–142.

4. Jean-Paul Sartre, *Carnets de la drôle de guerre, septembre 1939–mars 1940* (Paris, 1995), p. 202; and Horne, *France 1940*, p. 142.

5. Martin Gilbert, *Finest Hour: Winston S. Churchill, 1939–1941* (London, 1989), pp. 90–91.

6. Shirer, *Diary*, p. 203; and Horne, *France 1940*, p. 146.

7. Excerpt from Maiskii's journal, secret, Sept. 7, 1939, *DVP*, XXII, bk. 2, 44–45; Alexander, *Gamelin*, pp. 317, 346–347; and Elisabeth du Réau, "Édouard

Daladier: la conduite de la guerre et les prémices de la défaite," *Historical Reflections,* vol. 22, no. 1 (Winter 1996), 97.

8. "I received your communication . . . ," Molotov, Sept. 8, 1939, *DVP,* XXII, bk. 2, 602.

9. Geoffrey Roberts, "Soviet Policy and the Baltic States, 1939–1940: A Reappraisal," *Diplomacy & Statecraft,* vol. 6, no. 3 (November 1995), 672–700.

10. "Sir A. Cadogan," Gladwyn Jebb, Sept. 18, 1939, reporting a meeting with the French chargé d'affaires, Roger Cambon, C14998/13953/18, PRO FO 371 23103; and Seeds, no. 270, Sept. 29, 1939, C15399/13953/19, *ibid.*

11. For earlier works that touch upon Anglo-Soviet relations in this period, see *inter alia* Gabriel Gorodetsky, *Stafford Cripps' Mission to Moscow, 1940–42* (London, 1984); Martin Kitchen, *British Policy Towards the Soviet Union During the Second World War* (London, 1986); Steven Merritt Miner, *Between Churchill and Stalin: The Soviet Union, Great Britain, and the Origins of the Grand Alliance* (Chapel Hill, 1988); Roberts, *Unholy Alliance;* and Lloyd C. Gardner, *Spheres of Influence: The Great Powers Partition Europe, from Munich to Yalta* (Chicago, 1993). See also Geoffrey Roberts, "Churchill and Stalin on the Eve of War: Episodes in Anglo-Soviet Relations, September 1939–June 1941," unpublished manuscript.

12. Sargent's minute, Aug. 24, 1939, C12678/15/18, PRO FO 371 22980.

13. Kennard, no. 105 saving, Aug. 24, 1939, C11985/15/18, PRO FO 371 22977.

14. D. W. Lascelles's minute, Oct. 22, 1939, N5544/92/38, PRO FO 371 23683.

15. Carley, "Fearful Concatenation," *passim.*

16. Excerpts from Maiskii's journal, secret, Aug. 5, 24, 26, 1939, *DVP,* XXII, bk. 1, 582–583, 647, 659.

17. Pierre Broué, *Histoire de l'Internationale communiste, 1919–1943* (Paris, 1997), pp. 734–742.

18. Kirkpatrick's untitled note and minutes, Sept. 27, 1939, C16202/3356/18. PRO FO 371 23074.

19. "Conversation between Lord Strabolgi [Joseph Montague Kenworthy] and Mr. Maisky . . . 20th September 1939," private and confidential, C14877/13953/18, PRO FO 371 23103.

20. "Sir L. Oliphant," Collier, Sept. 21, 1939, C14296/13953/18, PRO FO 371 23103; and Roberts's minute, Sept. 27, 1939, C14877/13953/18, *ibid.*

21. Halifax to Seeds, no. 686, Sept. 23, 1939, N4736/1459/38, PRO FO 371 23697; and Maiskii to Molotov, highest priority, very secret, Sept. 23, 1939, *DVP,* XXII, bk. 2, 124–125.

22. Molotov to Maiskii, very secret, Sept. 26, 1939, *DVP,* XXII, bk. 2, 130.

23. Halifax to Seeds, no. 710, Sept. 27, 1939, N4803/1459/38, PRO FO 371 23697; and Maiskii to Molotov, highest priority, very secret, Sept. 27, 1939, *DVP,* XXII, bk. 2, 131–132.

24. Seeds, no. 349, immediate, confidential, Sept. 30, 1939, C15320/13953/18, PRO FO 371 23103.

25. "S of S," Cadogan, Sept. 23, 1939, N4571/57/38, PRO FO 371 23678; and "Secretary of State," Vansittart, Sept. 26, 1939, N4807/57/38, *ibid.*

26. Surits to Narkomindel, very secret, Sept. 10, 1939, *DVP,* XXII, bk. 2, 59–61; Surits to Narkomindel, highest priority, very secret, Sept. 14, 1939, *ibid.,* 79–80; and Surits to Narkomindel, immediate, very secret, Sept. 16, 1939, *ibid.,* 90–91.

27. Surits to Narkomindel, highest priority, very secret, Sept. 18, 1939, *DVP,* XXII, bk. 2, 98–99; J.-B. Duroselle, *Politique étrangère de la France. L'Abîme, 1939–1944* (Paris, 1986), p. 50; and Jeanneney, *Journal politique,* p. 12.

28. Surits to Narkomindel, immediate, extremely secret, Sept. 20, 1939, *DVP,*

XXII, bk. 2, 108–109; Surits to Narkomindel, immediate, very secret, Sept. 23, 1939, *ibid.*, 122–123; Molotov to Surits, very secret, Sept. 27, 1939, *ibid.*, 130–131.

29. "Sir A. Cadogan," Oliphant, Sept. 25, 1939, N4862/57/38, PRO FO 371 23678.

30. Churchill, *Gathering Storm*, p. 449.

31. War Cabinet Conclusions, no. 38 (39), Oct. 5, 1939, N5057/92/38, PRO FO 371 23682; and War Cabinet Conclusions, no. 43 (39), Oct. 10, 1939, N5169/92/38, *ibid.*

32. Maiskii to Narkomindel, highest priority, very secret, Oct. 7, 1939, *DVP*, XXII, bk. 2, 167–169.

33. Maiskii to Narkomindel, immediate, very secret, Oct. 8, 1939, *DVP*, XXII, bk. 2, 170–171.

34. Maiskii to Narkomindel, highest priority, very secret, Oct. 13, 1939, *DVP*, XXII, bk. 2, 183–184.

35. Eden to Halifax, personal and confidential, Oct. 13, 1939, N5426/92/38, PRO FO 371 23682.

36. Halifax to Stanley, Oct. 14, 1939, N5296/92/38, PRO FO 371 23682.

37. Maiskii to Narkomindel, highest priority, very secret, Oct. 16, 1939, *DVP*, XXII, bk. 2, 190–191.

38. Halifax to Seeds, no. 736, Oct. 16, 1939, N5342/92/38, PRO FO 371 23682.

39. Maiskii to Narkomindel, Oct. 16, 1939, *DVP*, XXII, bk. 2, 190–191.

40. Maiskii to Narkomindel, highest priority, very secret, Oct. 17, 1939, *DVP*, XXII, bk. 2, 196–197.

41. "Sir A. Cadogan . . . ," Butler, Oct. 17, 1939, N5493/92/38, PRO FO 371 23682.

42. Antony Lentin, " 'A Conference *Now*': Lloyd George and Peacemaking, 1939: Sidelights from the Unpublished Letters of A.J. Sylvester," *Diplomacy & Statecraft*, vol. 7, no. 3 (November 1996), 563–588.

43. "Notes of a conversation of . . . Molotov with . . . Schulenberg," secret, Oct. 19, 1939, *DVP*, XXII, bk. 1, 200–201; and Molotov to Maiskii, very secret, Oct. 19, 1939, *ibid.*, 201–202.

44. "Declaration of the Soviet and Germany governments," signed by Molotov and Ribbentrop, published in *Izvestiia*, Sept. 29, 1939, *DVP*, XXII, bk. 2, 136–137.

45. Maiskii to Molotov, highest priority, very secret, Oct. 20, 1939, *DVP*, XXII, bk. 2, 204–205.

46. "Notes of a conversation of . . . Molotov with . . . Schulenberg," secret, Nov. 13, 1939, *DVP*, XXII, bk. 2, 285–287.

47. Maiskii to Narkomindel, immediate, very secret, Oct. 27, 1939, *DVP*, XXII, bk. 2, 234–235 (concerning a breakfast meeting with Horace Wilson); and the excerpt from Maiskii's journal, secret, Oct. 30, 1939, *ibid.*, 247–248 (concerning a dinner meeting with Elliot).

48. I.M. Maiskii, *Memoirs of a Soviet Ambassador: The War, 1939–43* (New York, 1968), pp. 14–15.

49. Excerpt from Maiskii's journal, secret, Oct. 24, 1939, *DVP*, XXII, bk. 2, 213–215.

50. Untitled Foreign Office memorandum, secret, not signed, Oct. 19, 1939, C16324/15/18, PRO FO 371 22985; and "First Month of the War," Leeper, Oct. 4, 1939, C16151/15/18, *ibid.*

51. Sargent's minute, Oct. 11, 1939, C16404/15/18, PRO FO 371 22985; Halifax's minute, Oct. 11, 1939, *ibid.*; and John Colville, *Fringes of Power: Downing*

Street Diaries, 1939–1955 (London, 1985), entry of Oct. 13, 1939, p. 40; and *Channon Diaries*, entries of Sept. 3, 19, 1939, pp. 215, 220–221.

52. Excerpt from Maiskii's journal, Oct. 30, 1939, *DVP*, XXII, bk. 2, 247–248; excerpt from Maiskii's journal reporting on discussions over lunch on the previous day with Leslie Burgin, minister of supply, and Sir F. Leith Ross, ministry of economic warfare, secret, Oct. 21, 1939, *DVP*, XXII, bk. 2, 208; and "Russia," ns [but probably by Leith Ross], Oct. 20, 1939, N5647/92/38, PRO FO 371 23683.

53. Maiskii to Narkomindel, very secret, Oct. 25, 1939, *DVP*, XXII, bk. 2, 219.

54. Halifax to Seeds, no. 762, Oct. 25, 1939, N5634/92/38, PRO FO 371 23683.

55. Untitled memorandum, secret, Stanley, Oct. 25, 1939, N5678/92/38, PRO FO 371 23683; Maiskii to Narkomindel and Narkomvneshtorg, highest priority, very secret, Oct. 26, 1939, *DVP*, XXII, bk. 2, 223–224; and War Cabinet conclusions, no. 62 (39), Oct. 27, 1939, N5783/92/38, PRO FO 371 23683.

56. Molotov to Maiskii, very secret, Nov. 11, 1939, *DVP*, XXII, bk. 2, 278.

57. Maiskii to Narkomindel, immediate, very secret, Nov. 12, 1939, *DVP*, XXII, bk. 2, 280–281.

58. Maiskii to Narkomindel, highest priority, very secret, Nov. 13, 1939, *DVP*, XXII, bk. 2, 289–291.

59. Extract from War Cabinet conclusions, no. 85 (39), Nov. 16, 1939, N6384/92/38, PRO FO 371 23683; and War Cabinet conclusions, no. 67, Nov. 1, 1939, N5909/92/38, *ibid.*

60. Maiskii to Molotov, very secret, Nov. 20, 1939, *DVP*, XXII, bk. 2, 320–321; and untitled memorandum, Elliot, Nov. 20, 1939, N6574/57/38, PRO FO 371 23678.

61. Surits to Narkomindel, immediate, extremely secret, Oct. 4, 1939, *DVP*, XXII, bk. 2, 159–160; Surits to Narkomindel, immediate, very secret, Oct. 19, 1939, *ibid.*, 202–203; Surits to Narkomindel, immediate, very secret, Oct. 21, 1939, *ibid.*, 207–208; Surits to Narkomindel, very secret, Nov. 21, 1939, *ibid.*, 324; and Surits to Narkomindel, Nov. 18, 1939, *ibid.*, 633–634.

62. War Cabinet conclusions, no. 91 (39), Nov. 23, 1939, N6602/92/38, PRO FO 371 23683; and Maiskii to Narkomindel, very secret, Nov. 24, 1939, *DVP*, XXII, bk. 2, 335–336.

63. Maiskii to Molotov, highest priority, very secret, Nov. 27, 1939, *DVP*, XXII, bk. 2, 340–342; and Halifax to Seeds, no. 836, Nov. 27, 1939, N6717/991/38, PRO FO 371 23693.

64. Minute by W. Ridsdale, News department, quoting Tass correspondent Andrei Rothstein, Nov. 18, 1939, N6423/57/38, PRO FO 371 23678.

65. Thomas Snow, no. 163, Oct. 24, 1939, N5595/991/38, PRO FO 371 23692; and Kirkpatrick's minute, Oct. 17, 1939, N5263/991/38, *ibid.* See also Roberts, *Soviet Union*, pp. 112–113; Cairns, "Reflections on the Winter War," *passim*; and O. A. Rzheshevskii and O. Vekhviliainen, eds., *Zimniaia voina, 1939–1940*, 2 vols. (Moscow, 1998).

66. "Sir L. Oliphant," Collier, Sept. 21, 1939, N4712/194/38; and Collier to War Office, Sept. 25, 1939, *ibid.*, PRO FO 371 23643.

67. V. K. Derevianskii, Soviet ambassador in Helsinki, to Narkomindel, very secret, Oct. 9, 1939, *DVP*, XXII, bk. 2, 171–172; and M. G. Iudanov, Soviet chargé d'affaires in Helsinki, to Narkomindel, very secret, Oct. 13, Nov. 4, 1939, *ibid.*, 184, 257–258.

68. Halifax to Seeds, no. 762, Oct. 25, 1939, N5634/92/38, PRO FO 371

23683; and Maiskii to Narkomindel, very secret, Oct. 25, 1939, *DVP,* XXII, bk. 2, 289–291.

69. Maiskii to Narkomindel, Nov. 13, 1939, *DVP,* XXII, bk. 2, 289–291.

70. Extract from War Cabinet conclusions, no. 85 (39), Nov. 16, 1939, N6384/92/38, PRO FO 371 23683; "Sir O. Sargent," Collier, Nov. 20, 1939, *ibid.;* and Halifax to Churchill, Nov. 25, 1939, *ibid.*

71. Collier to H. Knatchbull-Hugessen, British ambassador in Turkey, most secret, Nov. 10, 1939, N6125/57/38, PRO FO 371 23678; Knatchbull-Hugessen to Collier, most secret, Nov. 18, 1939, N6585/57/38, PRO FO 371 23678; and Collier to Knatchbull-Hugessen, secret, Dec. 1, 1939, *ibid.*

72. Burgin, ministry of supply, to Halifax, most secret, Oct. 31, 1939, N5894/1290/38, PRO FO 371 23697; Halifax to Burgin, secret, Nov. 8, 1939, *ibid.;* Burgin to Halifax, secret, Nov. 4, 1939, N6037/1290/38, *ibid.;* Halifax to Burgin, secret, Nov. 16, 1939, *ibid.;* and "Russia: Vulnerability of Oil Supplies," Chiefs of Staff Committee, no. (39) 142, Dec. 2, 1939, N7104/1290/38, *ibid.*

73. Terent'ev to Narkomindel, highest priority, very secret, Oct. 27, 1939, *DVP,* XXII, bk. 2, 235–238; Terent'ev to Molotov, very secret, Nov. 6, 1939, *ibid.,* 263–270; and Terent'ev to Stalin, Molotov, and Voroshilov, very secret, Dec. 7, 1939, *ibid.,* 373–380.

74. Maiskii to Narkomindel, immediate, very secret, Nov. 29, 1939, *DVP,* XXII, bk. 2, 347–349.

75. Maiskii to Narkomindel, secret, Dec. 11, 1939, *DVP,* XXII, bk. 2, 391–396.

76. Excerpt from Maiskii's journal, secret, Nov. 29, 1939, *DVP,* XXII, bk. 2, 350.

77. Seeds, no. 503, Dec. 6, 1939, and various minutes by Foreign Office officials, Dec. 8, 1939, N7134/57/38, PRO FO 371 23678, and Snow to FO, Nov. 6, 1939, and FO to Snow, Nov. 24, 1939, N6667/991/38, PRO FO 371 23693.

78. Cairns, "Reflections on the Winter War," p. 212; and Horne, *France 1940,* pp. 179–180.

79. Excerpt from Maiskii's journal, Dec. 12, 1939, *DVP,* XXII, bk. 2, 400–401.

80. Cadogan's minute, Dec. 1, 1939, N7143/57/38, PRO FO 371 23678.

81. Minutes by Sargent and Halifax, Dec. 2, 1939, C19731/3356/18, PRO FO 371 23074.

82. Surits to Narkomindel, very secret, Dec. 23, 1939, *DVP,* XXII, bk. 2, 439–440.

83. Duroselle, *L'Abîme,* pp. 111–114; Bullitt to Hull, strictly confidential, Jan. 15, 1940, *For the President,* pp. 400–402; Amouroux, *Peuple du désastre,* pp. 217–225; and Michael J. Carley, *Revolution and Intervention: The French Government and the Russian Civil War, 1917–1919* (Montreal, 1983), pp. 105–115.

84. E.g., "Record of conversation of . . . Molotov with the ambassador of Turkey in the USSR A. Kh. Aktai," secret, Dec. 28, 1939, *DVP,* XXII, bk. 2, 452–454.

85. Maiskii to Narkomindel, immediate, very secret, Dec. 23, 1939, *DVP,* XXII, bk. 2, 441–442.

86. Molotov to Maiskii, very secret, Dec. 25, 1939, *DVP,* XXII, bk. 2, 446 (Karl Gustav Mannerheim was a former tsarist officer and commander-in-chief of Finnish armed forces; Väianö Tanner was foreign minister in the Finnish government).

87. Maiskii to Narkomindel, immediate, very secret, Dec. 25, 1939, *DVP*, XXII, bk. 2, 448–449.

88. Harvey, *Diplomatic Diaries,* entry of Dec. 24, 1939, p. 332.

Chapter 8. Epilogue: Anglo-Soviet Relations Are Like a Taut String

1. Jeanneney, *Journal politique,* entries of Dec. 9, 20, 1939, pp. 24–25.

2. Brock Millman, *The Ill-Made Alliance: Anglo-Turkish Relations, 1934–1940* (Montreal, 1998), pp. 351–356; and Sargent's minute, Jan. 19, 1940, N1147/283/38, PRO FO 371 24851.

3. Vansittart's untitled memorandum, Mar. 29, 1940, N3210/40/38, PRO FO 371 24846.

4. Cadogan's minutes, Jan. 19, 1940, N1147/283/38, PRO FO 371 24851; and Mar. 25, 1940, N3698/40/38, PRO FO 371 24846.

5. R. Campbell, British ambassador in Paris, no. 36 saving, Jan. 12, 1940, N546/341/38, PRO FO 371 24853; *Zimniaia voina,* I, 338–339, 351–354; and Harvey, *Diplomatic Diaries,* entry of Feb. 29, 1940, p. 338.

6. Horne, *France 1940,* p. 183; and Cadogan's minute, Mar. 25, 1940, N3698/40/38, PRO FO 371 24846.

7. Taylor, *English History,* p. 469, n. 1.

8. For example, see "Record[s] of conversation of . . . Molotov with . . . Schulenberg," secret, Oct. 17, 26; Nov. 2; Dec. 4, 9, 17, 22, 1939, *DVP*, XXII, bk. 2, 193–194, 222–223, 252–253, 365–367, 386–387, 418–420, 436–437; "From notes of a conversation of the deputy commissar for foreign affairs V. P. Potemkin with the ambassador of Germany in the USSR von der Schulenberg," secret, Oct. 11, 1939, *ibid.,* 176–177; "Record[s] of conversation of the people's commissar for foreign affairs V.M. Molotov with the ambassador of Germany in the USSR von der Schulenberg," secret, Jan. 7, 25; Mar. 5, 26, 1940, *DVP*, XXIII, bk. 1, 23–26, 49–53, 128–129, 184–187; and "Conversation in the Kremlin of the general secretary TsK VKP(b) I.V. Stalin with the special representative . . . of Germany K. Ritter," special file, Jan. 29, 1940, *ibid.,* 57–61.

9. Cf. Taylor, *Origins,* p. 318.

10. *Molotov Remembers,* pp. 11, 21–32.

11. Maiskii to Molotov, Jan. 26, 1940, *DVP*, XXIII, bk. 1, 53–56.

12. Halifax to J.H. Le Rougetel, British chargé d'affaires in Moscow, no. 52, confidential, Feb. 8, 1940, N1390/30/38, PRO FO 371 24843.

13. "Conversation . . . with . . . Butler," Maiskii, Jan. 30, 1940, *DVP*, XXIII, bk. 1, 61–63; and Fitzroy Maclean's minute, Feb. 7, 1940, N1390/30/38, PRO FO 371 24843.

14. "Conversation . . . with . . . Butler," Maiskii, Feb. 16, 1940, *DVP*, XXIII, bk. 1, 88–90.

15. Molotov to Maiskii, Feb. 21–22, 1940, *DVP*, XXIII, bk. 1, 101–102.

16. "Conversation . . . with . . . Butler," Maiskii, Feb. 22, 1940, *DVP*, XXIII, bk. 1, 102–105.

17. "Conversation of the *Narkom* for foreign affairs of the USSR V.M. Molotov with the member of the House of Commons of Great Britain Sir Stafford Cripps," Feb. 16, 1940 (this record of conversation was circulated to Stalin and other members of the Soviet Politburo), *DVP*, XXIII, bk. 1, 91–94; and Sir A. Clark Kerr, British ambassador in Chungking, from Cripps, no. 87 Tour Series (this cable was circulated to the War Cabinet), Mar 4, 1940, N2779/40/38, PRO FO 371 24846.

18. "Conversation . . . with . . . Butler," Maiskii, Feb. 24, 1940, *DVP*, XXIII, bk. 1, 107–108; *Cadogan Diaries*, entries of Feb. 23–24, 1940, pp. 255–256; Maclean's minute, Mar. 8, 1940, N2779/40/38, PRO FO 371 24846; and Collier's minute, Mar. 25, 1940, N3485/40/38, *ibid.*

19. "Sir O. Sargent," Cadogan, Mar. 18, 1939, N3623/283/38, PRO FO 371 24852; Sargent's minute, Mar. 18, 1939, *ibid.*; Campbell (Paris) to Cadogan, Mar. 24, 1940, N3608/341/38, PRO FO 371 24853; and French embassy to Foreign Office, Apr. 5, 1940, N4007/40/38, PRO FO 371 24846.

20. Parker, *Chamberlain*, pp. 226, 230; John Costello, *Ten Days to Destiny: The Secret Story of the Hess Peace Initiative and British Efforts to Strike a Deal with Hitler* (New York, 1991), p. 54; Clive Ponting, *1940: Myth and Reality* (Chicago, 1993), *passim*; and Gilbert, *Finest Hour*, p. 190.

21. Butler's minutes, Mar. 18, 1940, N3485/40/38, PRO FO 371 24846; Mar. 29, 1940, *ibid.*; "Attitude to Russia," Butler, Apr. 5, 1940, N3867/40/38, *ibid.*; and "Conversation . . . with . . . Butler," Maiskii, Mar. 18, 1940, *DVP*, XXIII, bk. 1, 156–159.

22. Minutes by Maclean, Collier, and Sargent, Mar. 21–26, 1940, N3485/40/38, PRO FO 371 24846.

23. Halifax's minute, Mar. 22, 1940, N3623/283/38, PRO FO 371 24852; and Chatfield to Halifax, Mar. 27, 1940, N3715/40/38, PRO FO 371 24846.

24. "Conversation of the plenipotentiary representative of the USSR in Great Britain I.M. Maiskii with the minister for foreign affairs . . . Halifax," Mar. 27, 1940, *DVP*, XXIII, bk. 1, 188–191; Halifax to Le Rougetel, no. 146, confidential, Mar. 28, 1940, N3706/5/38, PRO FO 371 24839.

25. "Extract from War Cabinet Conclusions," no. 77 (40), Mar. 29, 1940, N3738/40/38, PRO FO 371 24846; and "Conversation[s] of the *Narkom* for foreign affairs V.M. Molotov with the ambassador of Germany von der Schulenberg," Mar. 26, Apr. 5, 1940, *DVP*, XXIII, bk. 1, 184–187, 207–209.

26. Maclean's untitled note, Apr. 1, 1940, and Sargent's minute, May 18, 1940, N4091/40/38, PRO FO 371 24846.

27. Alexander, *Gamelin*, pp. 291–298.

28. Gorodetsky, *Cripps*, pp. 177ff; and *Cadogan Diary*, entry of Dec. 4, 1940, p. 338.

29. Carley and Debo, "Always in Need of Credit," *passim*.

30. "Note: Attitude l'URSS-Représentation diplomatique française à Moscou," Direction politique, ns, May 26, 1940, MAE Papiers 1940, Papiers Henri Hoppenot/5; "Note: Instructions pour M. Labonne," Hoppenot, June 5, 1940, *ibid.*; and "Conversation of . . . Molotov with . . . Payart," June 4, 1940, *DVP*, XXIII, bk. 1, 315–316.

31. "Conversation of . . . Molotov with . . . Labonne," June 14, 1940, *DVP*, XXIII, bk. 1, 342–345; and Labonne to Corbin, nos. 1–5, June 15, 1940, N5808/30/38, PRO FO 371 24844.

32. Carley, "Five Kopecks for Five Kopecks," pp. 46–47.

33. "Conversation of . . . Maiskii with . . . Butler," June 10, 1940, *DVP*, XXIII, bk. 1, 327–328.

34. "Conversation in the Kremlin of the general secretary of the TsK VKP(b) I. V. Stalin with the ambassador of Great Britain in the USSR Sir S. Cripps," very secret, July 1, 1940, *DVP*, XXIII, bk. 1, 394–400; Cripps to Collier, July 16, 1940, N6526/30/38, PRO FO 371 24845; and "Comments on the Recent Conversation between His Majesty's Ambassador at Moscow and M. Stalin," W.P. (40) 254, July 9, 1940, R6763/316/44, PRO FO 371 25016.

35. Maiskii to Narkomindel, immediate, June 22, 1940, *DVP,* XXIII, bk. 1, 361–363.

36. Maiskii to Narkomindel, highest priority, July 3–4, 1940, *DVP,* XXIII, bk. 1, 408–409 (cf. Churchill's brief minute on the meeting, July 9, 1940, N5973/5496/38, PRO FO 371 24856); and Gilbert, *Finest Hour,* pp. 478, 503.

37. "Conversation of the *Narkom* for foreign affairs of the USSR V.M. Molotov with the ambassador of Great Britain in the USSR Sir S. Cripps," Aug. 7, 1940, *DVP,* XXIII, bk. 1, 485–488.

38. Cripps, nos. 591–592, Aug. 8, 1940, N6105/40/38, PRO FO 371 24847.

39. "Secretary of State," Vansittart, Aug. 9, 1940, N6105/40/38, PRO FO 371 24847.

40. "Secretary of State, Sir Orme Sargent," Butler, Oct. 3, 1940, N6783/30/38, PRO FO 371 24845; and "Conversation . . . with . . . Butler," Maiskii, Oct. 3, 1940, *DVP,* XXIII, bk. 1, 647–651.

41. Cripps, no. 865, immediate, Oct. 15, 1940, N6875/30/38, PRO FO 371 24845; and "Secretary of State," Vansittart, Oct. 16, 1940, *ibid.*

42. Notes from the commissariat for defense of the USSR (for Stalin and Molotov), no. 103202/06, Sept. 18, 1940, *Organy gosudarstvennoi bezopasnosti SSSR v Velikoi Otechestvennoi voine* (Moscow, 1995), I, bk. 1, 253–258; and Shirer, *Diary,* pp. 550, 558.

43. Jonathan Haslam, "Soviet-German Relations and the Origins of the Second World War: The Jury Is Still Out," *Journal of Modern History,* vol. 69, no. 4 (December 1997), 788.

44. From Eden's speech after the signature of the Anglo-Soviet treaty of mutual assistance, in Oleg A. Rzheshevsky, ed., *War and Diplomacy: The Making of the Grand Alliance* (Amsterdam, 1996), p. 159; and Maiskii, *Memoirs,* p. 33.

45. Cf. Parker, *Chamberlain,* p. 240.

Selected Bibliography

UNPUBLISHED DOCUMENTS

France:
Archives nationales, Paris
Ministère des Affaires étrangères, Paris
Service historique de l'Armée de terre, Château de Vincennes

Great Britain:
Public Record Office, Kew
University of Birmingham

OFFICIAL PUBLISHED DOCUMENTS

Documents diplomatiques français, 1re série, 13 vols. Paris, 1964–1984; 2e série, 18 vols. Paris, 1963– .

Documents on British Foreign Policy, 2nd series, 19 vols. London, 1947–1984; 3rd series, 9 vols. London, 1949–1957.

Documents on German Foreign Policy, series D, 7 vols. London, Paris, and Washington, D.C., 1949–1956.

Dokumenty i materialy po istorii sovetsko-chekhoslovatskikh otnoshenii, vol. 3, *iiun' 1934g.–mart 1939g.* Moscow, 1978.

Dokumenty i materialy po istorii sovetsko-pol'skikh otnoshenii, vols. 6–7, *1933–1943gg.* Moscow, 1969–1973.

Dokumenty po istorii miunkhenskogo sgovora, 1937–1939. Moscow, 1979.

Dokumenty vneshnei politiki SSSR, 23 vols. Moscow, 1958– .

God krizisa: dokumenty i materialy, 2 vols. Moscow, 1990.

Komintern i vtoraia mirovaia voina, 1939–1941gg. Moscow, 1994.

Organy gosudarstvennoi bezopasnosti SSSR v Velikoi Otechestvennoi voine, vol. 1 (books 1 and 2). Moscow, 1995.

Soviet Peace Efforts on the Eve of World War II (September 1938–August 1939), 2 vols. Moscow, 1973.

BOOKS AND ARTICLES

Adamthwaite, Anthony, *France and the Coming of the Second World War, 1936–1939*. London, 1977.

———, "French Military Intelligence and the Coming of War, 1935–1939," in Christopher Andrews and Jeremy Noakes, eds., *Intelligence and International Relations, 1900–1945*. Exeter, 1987, pp. 191–208.

———, *Grandeur and Misery: France's Bid for Power in Europe, 1914–1940*. London, 1995.

Alexander, Martin S., "The Fall of France, 1940," in John Gooch, ed., *Decisive Campaigns of the Second World War*. London, 1990, pp. 10–43.

———, "Did the Deuxième Bureau Work? The Role of Intelligence in French Defence Policy and Strategy, 1919–39," *Intelligence and National Security*, vol. 6, no. 2 (April 1991), 293–333.

———, *The Republic in Danger: General Maurice Gamelin and the Politics of French Defence, 1933–1940*. Cambridge, England, 1992.

Alphand, Hervé, *L'Étonnement d'être*. Paris, 1977.

Amouroux, Henri, *Le Peuple du désastre, 1939–1940*. Paris, 1976.

Andrew, Christopher, *Secret Service: The Making of the British Intelligence Community*. London, 1987.

Aster, Sidney, "Ivan Maisky and Parliamentary Anti-Appeasement, 1938–1939," in A. J. P. Taylor, ed., *Lloyd George: Twelve Essays* (London, 1971), pp. 317–357.

———, *1939: The Making of the Second World War*. London, 1973.

Beaufre, André, *1940: The Fall of France*. London, 1967.

Bell, P. M. H., *France and Britain, 1900–1940: Entente and Estrangement*. London, 1996.

Berstein, Serge, and Jean-Jacques Becker, *Histoire de l'anti-communisme, 1917–1940*. Paris, 1987.

Bezymenskii, L. A., "Sovetsko-Germanskie dogovory 1939g.; novye dokumenty i starye problemy," *Novaia i Noveishaia Istoriia*, no. 3 (1998), pp. 3–26.

Earl of Birkenhead, *Halifax*. London, 1965.

Blatt, Joel, ed., *The French Defeat of 1940: Reassessments*. Providence, R.I., 1998.

Bloch, Marc, *Strange Defeat: A Statement of Evidence Written in 1940*. New York, 1968.

Bonnet, Georges, *Défense de la paix: de Washington au Quai d'Orsay*. Geneva, 1946.

———, *Défense de la paix: fin d'une Europe*. Geneva, 1948.

Brogan, D. W., *The Development of Modern France, 1870–1939*, 2 vols. Gloucester, Mass, 1970.

Broué, Pierre, *Histoire de l'Internationale communiste, 1919–1943*. Paris, 1997.

Brower, Daniel R., *The New Jacobins: The French Communist Party and the Popular Front*. Ithaca, N.Y., 1968.

Bullitt, Orville H., ed., *For the President, Personal and Secret: Correspondence between Franklin D. Roosevelt and William C. Bullitt*. Boston, 1972.

Cairns, John C., "March 7, 1936, Again: The View from Paris," in Hans W. Gatzke, ed., *European Diplomacy Between Two Wars, 1919–1939*. Chicago, 1972, pp. 172–189.

———, "Reflections on France, Britain and the Winter War Prodrome, 1939–1940," *Historical Reflections*, vol. 22, no. 1 (Winter 1996), 211–234.

Carley, Michael Jabara, *Revolution and Intervention: The French Government and the Russian Civil War, 1917–1919*. Montreal, 1983.

———, "Five Kopecks for Five Kopecks: Franco-Soviet Trade Relations, 1928–1939," *Cahiers du monde russe et soviétique*, vol. 33, no. 1 (January–March 1992), 23–58.

———, "End of the 'Low, Dishonest Decade': Failure of the Anglo-Franco-Soviet Alliance in 1939," *Europe-Asia Studies*, vol. 45, no. 2 (1993), 303–341.

———, "Down a Blind-Alley: Anglo-Franco-Soviet Relations, 1920–1939," *Canadian Journal of History*, vol. 29, no. 1 (April 1994), 147–172.

———, "Generals, Diplomats, and International Politics in Europe, 1898–1945," *Canadian Journal of History*, vol. 30, no. 2 (August 1995), 289–321.

———, "Fearful Concatenation of Circumstances: The Anglo-Soviet Rapprochement, 1934–1936," *Contemporary European History*, vol. 5, no. 1 (March 1996), 29–69.

———, "Prelude to Defeat: Franco-Soviet Relations, 1919–1939," *Historical Reflections*, vol. 22, no. 1 (Winter 1996), 159–188.

———, "The Early Cold War, 1917–1939," *Relevance*, vol. 5, no. 4 (Fall 1996), 6–11.

Carley, Michael Jabara, and Richard K. Debo, "Always in Need of Credit: The USSR and Franco-German Economic Cooperation, 1926–1929," *French Historical Studies*, vol. 20, no. 3 (Summer 1997), 315–356.

Carswell, John, *The Exile: A Life of Ivy Litvinov*. London, 1983.

Charmley, John, *Chamberlain and the Lost Peace*. London, 1989.

———, *Churchill: The End of Glory*. Toronto, 1993.

Chauvel, Jean, *Commentaire, de Vienne à Alger (1938–1944)*. Paris, 1971.

Chubar'ian, A. O., ed., *Evropa mezhdu mirom i voinoi, 1918–1939*. Moscow, 1992.

Churchill, Winston S., *The Gathering Storm*. Boston, 1948.

Colton, Joel, *Léon Blum: Humanist in Politics*. New York, 1966.

Colville, John, *Fringes of Power: Downing Street Diaries, 1939–1955.* London, 1985.

Colvin, Ian, *Vansittart in Office.* London, 1965.

———, *The Chamberlain Cabinet.* London, 1971.

Costello, John, *Ten Days to Destiny: The Secret Story of the Hess Peace Initiative and British Efforts to Strike a Deal with Hitler.* New York, 1991.

Coulondre, Robert, *De Staline à Hitler, souvenirs de deux ambassades, 1936–1939.* Paris, 1950.

Cowling, Maurice, *The Impact of Hitler: British Politics and British Policy, 1933–1940.* London, 1975.

Craig, Gordon A., and Felix Gilbert, eds., *The Diplomats,* 2 vols. New York, 1965.

Dalton, Hugh, *The Fateful Years: Memoirs 1931–1945.* London, 1957.

Dilks, David, ed., *The Diaries of Sir Alexander Cadogan, 1938–1945.* London, 1971.

Dockrill, Michael, and Brian McKercher, eds., *Diplomacy and World Power: Studies in British Foreign Policy, 1890–1950.* Cambridge, England, 1996.

Dullin, Sabine, "Les Diplomates soviétiques à la Société des Nations," *Relations internationales,* no. 75 (Autumn 1993), pp. 329–343.

———, "Le Rôle de Maxime Litvinov dans les années trente," *Communisme,* no. 42/43/44 (1995), pp. 75–93.

Duroselle, Jean-Baptiste, "L'Influence de la politique intérieure sur la politique extérieure de la France, l'exemple de 1938 et 1939," *Les Relations franco-britanniques de 1935 à 1939.* Paris, 1975, pp. 225–241.

———, *La Décadence, 1932–1939.* Paris, 1985.

———, *Politique étrangère de la France. L'Abîme, 1939–1944.* Paris, 1986.

Eden, Anthony, *Facing the Dictators.* Boston, 1962.

Feiling, Keith, *The Life of Neville Chamberlain.* London, 1947.

Finkel, Alvin, and Clement Leibovitz, *The Chamberlain-Hitler Collusion.* Redlesham, England, 1997.

Fleischhauer, Ingeborg, *Pakt. Gitler, Stalin i initsiativa Germanskoi diplomatii, 1938–1939.* Moscow, 1991.

Frankenstein, Robert, *Le Prix du réarmement français (1935–1939).* Paris, 1982.

Gamelin, Maurice, *Servir.* 3 vols. Paris, 1946.

Gardner, Lloyd C., *Spheres of Influence: The Great Powers Partition Europe, from Munich to Yalta.* Chicago, 1993.

George, Margaret, *Warped Vision: British Foreign Policy, 1933–1939.* Pittsburgh, 1965.

Gilbert, Martin, *Finest Hour: Winston S. Churchill, 1939–1941.* London, 1989.

————, *Prophet of Truth, Winston S. Churchill, 1922–1939*. London, 1990.

Gilbert, Martin, and Richard Gott, *The Appeasers*. London, 1963.

Girault, René, and Robert Frank, eds., *La Puissance en Europe, 1938–1940*. Paris, 1984.

Gorodetsky, Gabriel, *Stafford Cripps' Mission to Moscow, 1940–42*. London, 1984.

————, "The Impact of the Ribbentrop-Molotov Pact on the Course of Soviet Foreign Policy," *Cahiers du monde russe et soviétique*, vol. 31, no. 1 (January–March 1990), 27–28.

Harvey, John, ed., *The Diplomatic Diaries of Oliver Harvey, 1937–1940*. London, 1970.

Haslam, Jonathan, *The Soviet Union and the Struggle for Collective Security in Europe, 1933–39*. New York, 1984.

————, *The Soviet Union and the Threat from the East: Moscow, Tokyo and the Prelude to the Pacific War*. Pittsburgh, 1992.

————, "Soviet-German Relations and the Origins of the Second World War: The Jury Is Still Out," *Journal of Modern History*, vol. 69, no. 4 (December 1997), 785–797.

Herriot, Édouard, *Jadis: D'une guerre à l'autre, 1914–1936*. Paris, 1952.

Horne, Alistair, *To Lose a Battle: France 1940*. London, 1990.

Irvine, William D., *French Conservatism in Crisis: The Republican Federation of France in the 1930s*. Baton Rouge, 1979.

————, "Domestic Politics and the Fall of France in 1940," *Historical Reflections*, vol. 22, no. 1 (Winter 1996), 77–90.

Jackson, Peter, "French Military Intelligence and Czechoslovakia, 1938," *Diplomacy & Statecraft*, vol. 5, no. 1 (March 1994), 81–106.

————, "France and the Guarantee to Romania, April 1939," *Intelligence and National Security*, vol. 10, no. 2 (April 1995), 242–272.

————, "Recent Journeys Along the Road Back to France, 1940," *The Historical Journal*, vol. 39, no. 2 (1996), 497–510.

James, Robert Rhodes, ed., *Chips: The Diaries of Sir Henry Channon*. London, 1967.

Jeanneney, Jules E. (Jean-Noël Jeanneney, ed.), *Journal politique, septembre 1939–juillet 1942*. Paris, 1972.

Jędrzejewicz, Wacław, ed., *Diplomat in Berlin, 1933–1939: Papers and Memoirs of Jozef Lipski*. New York, 1968.

————, ed., *Diplomat in Paris, 1936–1939: Papers and Memoirs of Juliusz Łukasiewicz*. New York, 1970.

Jones, Thomas, *A Diary with Letters, 1931–1950*. London, 1954.

Jukes, G., "The Red Army and the Munich Crisis," *Journal of Contemporary History*, vol. 26 (1991), 195–214.

Kennedy, Paul, "Appeasement," in Gordon Martel, ed., *The Origins of the Second World War Reconsidered*. Boston, 1986, pp. 140–161.

Kitchen, Martin, *British Policy Towards the Soviet Union During the Second World War*. London, 1986.

Kobliakov, I. K., *USSR: For Peace Against Aggression, 1933–1941*. Moscow, 1976.

Laloy, Jean, "Remarques sur les négociations anglo-franco-soviétiques de 1939," *Les Relations franco-britanniques de 1935 à 1939*. Paris, 1975, pp. 403–413.

Lamb, Richard, *The Drift to War, 1922–1939*. London, 1991.

Lentin, Anthony, " 'A Conference Now': Lloyd George and Peacemaking, 1939: Sidelights from the Unpublished Letters of A. J. Sylvester," *Diplomacy & Statecraft*, vol. 7, no. 3 (November 1996), 563–588.

Lukes, Igor, *Czechoslovakia Between Stalin and Hitler: The Diplomacy of Edvard Beneš in the 1930s*. New York, 1996.

Lungo, Dov B., *Romania and the Great Powers, 1933–1940*. Durham, N.C., 1989.

Maiskii, Ivan M., *Memoirs of a Soviet Ambassador: The War, 1939–43*. New York, 1968.

———, *Vospominaniia sovetskogo diplomata, 1925–1945gg*. Moscow, 1971.

Malkov, Viktor L., et al., "<<Kruglyi stol>>: vtoraia mirovaia voina—istoki i prichiny," *Voprosy istorii*, no. 6 (June 1989), pp. 3–33.

Manchester, William, *The Caged Lion: Winston Spencer Churchill, 1932–1940*. London, 1989.

Manne, Robert, "The Foreign Office and the Failure of Anglo-Soviet Rapprochement," *Journal of Contemporary History*, vol. 16, no. 4 (1981), 725–755.

McDermott, Kevin, and Jeremy Agnew, *The Comintern: A History of International Communism from Lenin to Stalin*. New York, 1997.

McKercher, B. J. C., Charles Morrisey and M. A. Ramsay, M. L. Roi, Simon Bourette-Knowles, and John R. Ferris, *Diplomacy & Statecraft*, vol. 6, no. 1 (March 1995), special issue on Robert Vansittart, 1–175.

Medvedev, Roy, *Let History Judge: The Origins and Consequences of Stalinism*. New York, 1989.

Micaud, Charles, *The French Right and Nazi Germany, 1933–1939*. New York, 1964 (reprint).

Michel, Henri, "France, Grande Bretagne et Pologne (mars–août 1939)," *Les Relations franco-britanniques de 1935 à 1939*. Paris, 1975, pp. 383–401.

Middlemas, Keith, *Diplomacy of Illusion: The British Government and Germany, 1937–1939*. London, 1972.

Millman, Brock, *The Ill-Made Alliance: Anglo-Turkish Relations, 1934–1940*. Montreal, 1998.

Miner, Steven Merritt, *Between Churchill and Stalin: The Soviet Union, Great Britain, and the Origins of the Grand Alliance*. Chapel Hill, 1988.

————, "His Master's Voice: Viacheslav Mikhailovich Molotov as Stalin's Foreign Commissar," in G. A. Craig and F. L. Loewenheim, eds., *The Diplomats, 1939–1979*. Princeton, 1994, pp. 65–100.

Namier, Lewis B., *Diplomatic Prelude, 1938–1939*. London, 1948.

Neilson, Keith, "Pursued by a Bear: British Estimates of Soviet Military Strength and Anglo-Soviet Relations, 1922–1939," *Canadian Journal of History*, vol. 28, no. 2 (August 1993), 189–221.

Nekrich, Aleksandr M., *Pariahs, Partners, Predators: German-Soviet Relations, 1922–1941*. New York, 1997.

Nevezhin, V. A., *Sindrom nastupatel'noi voiny: Sovetskaia propaganda v preddverii "sviashchennykh boev," 1939–1941gg*. Moscow, 1997.

Nezhinskii, L. N., ed., *Sovetzkaia vneshniaia politika, 1917–1945gg.: Poiski novykh podkhodov*. Moscow, 1992.

Nicolson, Harold, *Diaries and Letters, 1930–1939*. New York, 1966.

Noël, Léon, *L'Agression allemande contre la Pologne*. Paris, 1946.

Parker, R. A. C., *Chamberlain and Appeasement: British Policy and the Coming of the Second World War*. London, 1993.

Paul-Boncour, Joseph, *Entre deux guerres: souvenirs sur la IIIe Républic*, 3 vols. Paris, 1946.

Peden, G. C., *British Rearmament and the Treasury, 1932–1939*. Edinburgh, 1979.

Pertinax (André Géraud), *Les Fossoyeurs*, 2 vols. New York, 1943.

Phillips, Hugh D., *Between the Revolution and the West: A Political Biography of Maxim M. Litvinov*. Boulder, Colo., 1992.

Ponting, Clive, *1940: Myth and Reality*. Chicago, 1993.

Porch, Douglas, *The French Secret Services: From the Dreyfus Affair to the Gulf War*. New York, 1995.

Post, Gaines, Jr., *Dilemmas of Appeasement: British Deterrence and Defense, 1934–1937*. Ithaca, N.Y., 1993.

Prażmowska, Anita, *Britain, Poland, and the Eastern Front, 1939*. Cambridge, England, 1987.

————, *Britain and Poland, 1939–1943: The Betrayed Ally*. Cambridge, England, 1995.

Ragsdale, Hugh, "The Munich Crisis and the Issue of Red Army Transit Across Romania," *Russian Review*, vol. 47, no. 4 (October 1998), 614–617.

————, "Soviet Military Preparations and Policy in the Munich Crisis: New Evidence," *Jahrbücher für Geschichte Osteuropas*, forthcoming, 1999.

Read, Anthony, and David Fisher, *The Deadly Embrace: Hitler, Stalin, and the Nazi-Soviet Pact, 1939–1941*. New York, 1988.

du Réau, Elisabeth, "Édouard Daladier: la conduite de la guerre et les prémices de la défaite," *Historical Reflections,* vol. 22, no. 1 (Winter 1996), 91–114.

———, *Édouard Daladier, 1884–1970.* Paris, 1993.

Resis, Albert, ed., *Molotov Remembers: Inside Kremlin Politics, Conversations with Felix Chuev.* Chicago, 1993.

Roberts, Geoffrey, *The Unholy Alliance: Stalin's Pact with Hitler.* Bloomington, Ind., 1989.

———, "The Soviet Decision for a Pact with Nazi Germany," *Soviet Studies,* vol. 44, no. 1 (1992), 57–78.

———, "The Fall of Litvinov: A Revisionist View," *Journal of Contemporary History,* vol. 27, no. 4 (October 1992), 639–657.

———, "Infamous Encounter?: The Merekalov-Weizsäcker Meeting of 17 April 1939," *Historical Journal,* vol. 35, no. 4 (1992), 921–926.

———, *The Soviet Union and the Origins of the Second World War: Russo-German Relations and the Road to War, 1933–1941.* London, 1995.

———, "Soviet Policy and the Baltic States, 1939–1940: A Reappraisal," *Diplomacy & Statecraft,* vol. 6, no. 3 (November 1995), 672–700.

———, "The Alliance That Failed: Moscow and Triple Alliance Negotiations, 1939," *European History Quarterly,* vol. 26, no. 3 (1996), 383–414.

Rose, Norman, *Vansittart: Study of a Diplomat.* London, 1978.

Rowse, A. L., *Appeasement: A Study in Political Decline, 1933–1939.* New York, 1963.

Rzheshevskii, O. A., ed., *1939 god: uroki istorii.* Moscow, 1990.

———, ed., *War and Diplomacy: The Making of the Grand Alliance.* Amsterdam, 1996.

Rzheshevskii, O.A., and O. Vekhviliainen, eds., *Zimniaia voina, 1939–1940,* 2 vols. Moscow, 1998.

Sartre, Jean-Paul, *Carnets de la drôle de guerre, septembre 1939–mars 1940.* Paris, 1995.

Schuker, Stephen A., "France and the Remilitarization of the Rhineland, 1936," *French Historical Studies,* vol. 14, no. 3 (Spring 1986), 299–338.

———, "Two Cheers for Appeasement," unpublished paper, Society for French Historical Studies conference, Boston, March 1996.

Scott, William Evans, *Alliance Against Hitler: The Origins of the Franco-Soviet Pact.* Durham, N.C., 1962.

Sheinis, Zinovy, *Maxim Litvinov.* Moscow, 1990.

Sheviakov, A. A., *Sovetsko-Rumynskie otnosheniia i problema evropeiskoi bezopasnosti, 1932–1939.* Moscow, 1977.

Sherwood, John Michael, *Georges Mandel and the Third Republic.* Stanford, 1970.

Shirer, William L., *Berlin Diary: The Journal of a Foreign Correspondent, 1934–1941*. New York, 1941.

———, *The Collapse of the Third Republic: An Inquiry into the Fall of France in 1940*. New York, 1969.

Sipols, V. Ia., *Vneshniaia politika Sovetskogo Soiuza, 1933–1935gg.* Moscow, 1980.

———, *Diplomaticheskaia borba nakanune vtoroi mirovoi voiny.* Moscow, 1989.

———, "A Few Months Before August 23, 1939," *International Affairs* (June 1989), 124–136.

Smith, Bradley F., *Sharing Secrets with Stalin: How the Allies Traded Intelligence, 1941–1945*. Lawrence, Kans., 1996.

Strang, Bruce, "Two Unequal Tempers: Sir George Ogilvie-Forbes, Sir Nevile Henderson and British Foreign Policy, 1938–39," *Diplomacy & Statecraft*, vol. 5, no. 1 (March 1994), 107–137.

Strang, William, *Home and Abroad*. London, 1956.

Szembek, Jean, *Journal, 1933–1939*. Paris, 1952.

Tabouis, Geneviève, *They Called Me Cassandra*. New York, 1942.

Taylor, A. J. P., *Origins of the Second World War*. Middlesex, 1964.

———, *English History, 1914–1945*. New York, 1965.

Taylor, Telford, *Munich: The Price of Peace*. New York, 1979.

Thompson, Neville, *The Anti-Appeasers: Conservative Opposition to Appeasement in the 1930s*. Oxford, 1971.

Torrès, Henry, *Pierre Laval*. New York, 1941.

Ulam, Adam, *Expansion and Coexistence: The History of Soviet Foreign Policy, 1917–1967*. New York, 1968.

Uldricks, T. J., "A. J. P. Taylor and the Russians," in Gordon Martel, ed., *The Origins of the Second World War Reconsidered*. Boston, 1986.

Vaïsse, Maurice, "Les Militaires français et l'alliance franco-soviétique au cours des années 1930," *Forces armées et systèmes d'alliances: Colloque international d'histoire militaire et d'études de défense nationale*. 3 vols. Montpellier, 1981, II, 689–704.

Vansittart, Robert G., *The Mist Procession: The Autobiography of Lord Vansittart*. London, 1958.

Villelume, Paul de, *Journal d'une défaite, août 1939–juin 1940*. Paris, 1976.

Volkogonov, Dimitri, *Staline*. Paris, 1991.

Volkov, V. K., *Miunkhenskii sgovor i Balkanskie strany*. Moscow, 1978.

Wark, Wesley K., "Something Very Stern: British Political Intelligence, Moralism and Grand Strategy in 1939," *Intelligence and National Security*, vol. 5, no. 1 (January 1990), 150–170.

———, "Appeasement Revisited," *International History Review*, vol. 17, no. 3 (August 1995), 545–562.

Watt, D. Cameron, "British Domestic Politics and the Onset of War," *Les Relations franco-britanniques de 1935 à 1939*. Paris, 1975, pp. 243–261.

——, "An Intelligence Surprise: The Failure of the Foreign Office to Anticipate the Nazi-Soviet Pact," *Intelligence and National Security*, vol. 4, no. 3 (July 1989), 512–534.

——, *How War Came: The Immediate Origins of the Second World War, 1938–1939*. London, 1990.

Weber, Eugen, *Action Française: Royalism and Reaction in Twentieth-Century France*. Stanford, 1962.

——, *The Hollow Years: France in the 1930s*. New York, 1994.

Wegner, Bernd, ed., *From Peace to War: Germany, Soviet Russia and the World, 1939–1941*. Providence, R.I., 1997.

Weinberg, Gerhard, *The Foreign Policy of Hitler's Germany: Starting World War II, 1937–1939*. Chicago, 1980.

Wheatley, Robert, "Britain and the Anglo-Franco-Russian Negotiations in 1939," *Les Relations franco-britanniques de 1935 à 1939*. Paris, 1975, pp. 201–221.

Wheeler-Bennett, John W., *Munich: Prologue to Tragedy*. London, 1948.

Young, Robert J., *In Command of France: French Foreign Policy and Military Planning, 1933–1940*. Cambridge, Mass., 1978.

——, "French Military Intelligence," in Ernest R. May, ed., *Knowing One's Enemies: Intelligence Assessment Before the Two World Wars* (Princeton, 1986), pp. 271–309.

——, "A. J. P. Taylor and the Problem with France," in Gordon Martel, ed., *The Origins of the Second World War Reconsidered*. Boston, 1986, pp. 97–118.

——, *France and the Origins of the Second World War*. New York, 1996.

Index

A NOTE ON THE AUTHOR

Michael Jabara Carley is an historian of relations between the West and the Soviet Union. "I am what the French call a *rat des archives*," he writes, "having spent a lot of time in archives in Paris, London, Moscow, and Washington, D.C." Mr. Carley was born in Brooklyn, New York, and studied at George Washington University and at Queen's University in Kingston, Ontario. In addition to a great many articles for historical journals, he has also written *Revolution and Intervention: The French Government and the Russian Civil War, 1917–1919*. He is the former director of the Aid to Scholarly Publications Programme in Canada and now lives in Vanier, a French-speaking suburb of Ottawa.